Portugal

WORLD BIBLIOGRAPHICAL SERIES
General Editors:
Robert G. Neville (Executive Editor)
John J. Horton
Robert A. Myers   Hans H. Wellisch
Ian Wallace   Ralph Lee Woodward, Jr.

John J. Horton is Deputy Librarian of the University of Bradford and was formerly Chairman of its Academic Board of Studies in Social Sciences. He has maintained a longstanding interest in the discipline of area studies and its associated bibliographical problems, with special reference to European Studies. In particular he has published in the field of Icelandic and of Yugoslav studies, including the two relevant volumes in the World Bibliographical Series.

Robert A. Myers is Associate Professor of Anthropology in the Division of Social Sciences and Director of Study Abroad Programs at Alfred University, Alfred, New York. He has studied post-colonial island nations of the Caribbean and has spent two years in Nigeria on a Fulbright Lectureship. His interests include international public health, historical anthropology and developing societies. In addition to *Amerindians of the Lesser Antilles: a bibliography* (1981), *A Resource Guide to Dominica, 1493-1986* (1987) and numerous articles, he has compiled the World Bibliographical Series volumes on *Dominica* (1987), *Nigeria* (1989) and *Ghana* (1991).

Ian Wallace is Professor of German at the University of Bath. A graduate of Oxford in French and German, he also studied in Tübingen, Heidelberg and Lausanne before taking teaching posts at universities in the USA, Scotland and England. He specializes in contemporary German affairs, especially literature and culture, on which he has published numerous articles and books. In 1979 he founded the journal *GDR Monitor*, which he continues to edit under its new title *German Monitor*.

Hans H. Wellisch is Professor emeritus at the College of Library and Information Services, University of Maryland. He was President of the American Society of Indexers and was a member of the International Federation for Documentation. He is the author of numerous articles and several books on indexing and abstracting, and has published *The Conversion of Scripts and Indexing and Abstracting: an International Bibliography*, and *Indexing from A to Z*. He also contributes frequently to *Journal of the American Society for Information Science*, *The Indexer* and other professional journals.

Ralph Lee Woodward, Jr. is Director of Graduate Studies at Tulane University, New Orleans. He is the author of *Central America, a Nation Divided*, 2nd ed. (1985), as well as several monographs and more than seventy scholarly articles on modern Latin America. He has also compiled volumes in the World Bibliographical Series on *Belize* (1980), *El Salvador* (1988), *Guatemala* (Rev. Ed.) (1992) and *Nicaragua* (Rev. Ed.) (1994). Dr. Woodward edited the Central American section of the *Research Guide to Central America and the Caribbean* (1985) and is currently associate editor of Scribner's *Encyclopedia of Latin American History*.

VOLUME 71

Portugal

Revised Edition

John Laidlar
Compiler

CLIO PRESS
OXFORD, ENGLAND · SANTA BARBARA, CALIFORNIA
DENVER, COLORADO

REF.
DP
517
.L3
2000

© Copyright 2000 by ABC-CLIO Ltd

All rights reserved. No part of this publication may be reproduced, stored in any retrieval system, or transmitted in any form or by any means, electronic, mechanical, photocopying or otherwise, without the prior permission in writing of the publishers.

British Library Cataloguing in Publication Data

Laidlar, John
Portugal. – Rev. ed. – (World bibliographical series; v. 71)
1. Portugal – Bibliography
I. Title
016.9´469

ISBN 1–85109–331–1

ABC-CLIO Ltd,
Old Clarendon Ironworks,
35A Great Clarendon Street,
Oxford OX2 6AT, England.

ABC-CLIO Inc.,
130 Cremona Drive,
Santa Barbara,
CA 93117, USA

Designed by Bernard Crossland.
Typeset by ABC-CLIO Ltd, Oxford, England.
Printed and bound in Great Britain by print in black, Midsomer Norton.

THE WORLD BIBLIOGRAPHICAL SERIES

This series, which is principally designed for the English speaker, will eventually cover every country (and some of the world's principal regions and cities), each in a separate volume comprising annotated entries on works dealing with its history, geography, economy and politics; and with its people, their culture, customs, religion and social organization. Attention will also be paid to current living conditions – housing, education, newspapers, clothing, etc. – that are all too often ignored in standard bibliographies; and to those particular aspects relevant to individual countries. Each volume seeks to achieve, by use of careful selectivity and critical assessment of the literature, an expression of the country and an appreciation of its nature and national aspirations, to guide the reader towards an understanding of its importance. The keynote of the series is to provide, in a uniform format, an interpretation of each country that will express its culture, its place in the world, and the qualities and background that make it unique. The views expressed in individual volumes, however, are not necessarily those of the publisher.

VOLUMES IN THE SERIES

1 *Yugoslavia*, Rev. Ed., John J. Horton
2 *Lebanon*, Rev. Ed., C. H. Bleaney
3 *Lesotho*, Rev. Ed., Deborah Johnston
4 *Zimbabwe*, Rev. Ed., Deborah Potts
5 *Saudi Arabia*, Rev. Ed., Frank A. Clements
6 *Russia/USSR*, Second Ed., Lesley Pitman
7 *South Africa*, Rev. Ed., Geoffrey V. Davis
8 *Malawi*, Rev. Ed., Samuel Decalo
9 *Guatemala*, Rev. Ed., Ralph Lee Woodward, Jr.
10 *Pakistan*, David Taylor
11 *Uganda*, Rev. Ed., Balam Nyeko
12 *Malaysia*, Rev. Ed., Ooi Keat Gin
13 *France*, Rev. Ed., Frances Chambers
14 *Panama*, Rev. Ed., Eleanor DeSelms Langstaff
15 *Hungary*, Thomas Kabdebo
16 *USA*, Sheila R. Herstein and Naomi Robbins
17 *Greece*, Rev. Ed., Thanos Veremis and Mark Dragoumis
18 *New Zealand*, Rev. Ed., Brad Patterson and Kathryn Patterson
19 *Algeria*, Rev. Ed., Richard I. Lawless
20 *Sri Lanka*, Vijaya Samaraweera
21 *Belize*, Second Ed., Peggy Wright and Brian E. Coutts
22 *Luxembourg*, Rev. Ed., Jul Christophory and Emile Thoma
24 *Swaziland*, Rev. Ed., Balam Nyeko
25 *Kenya*, Rev. Ed., Dalvan Coger
26 *India*, Rev. Ed., Ian Derbyshire
27 *Turkey*, Rev. Ed., Çigdem Balım-Harding
28 *Cyprus*, Rev. Ed., P. M. Kitromilides and M. L. Evriviades
29 *Oman*, Rev. Ed., Frank A. Clements
30 *Italy*, Lucio Sponza and Diego Zancani
31 *Finland*, Rev. Ed., J. E. O. Screen
32 *Poland*, Rev. Ed., George Sanford and Adriana Gozdecka-Sanford
33 *Tunisia*, Allan M. Findlay, Anne M. Findlay and Richard I. Lawless
34 *Scotland*, Rev. Ed., Dennis Smith
35 *China*, New Ed., Charles W. Hayford
36 *Qatar*, P. T. H. Unwin
37 *Iceland*, Rev. Ed., Francis R. McBride
38 *Nepal*, John Whelpton
39 *Haiti*, Rev. Ed., Frances Chambers

40 *Sudan*, Rev. Ed., M. W. Daly
41 *Vatican City State*, Michael J. Walsh
42 *Iraq*, Second Ed., C. H. Bleaney
43 *United Arab Emirates*, Rev. Ed., Frank A. Clements
44 *Nicaragua*, Rev. Ed., Ralph Lee Woodward, Jr.
45 *Jamaica*, Rev. Ed., K. E. Ingram
46 *Australia*, Second Ed., I. Kepars
47 *Morocco*, Rev. Ed., Anne M. Findlay
48 *Mexico*, Rev. Ed., George Philip
49 *Bahrain*, P. T. H. Unwin
50 *Yemen*, Rev. Ed., Paul Auchterlonie
51 *Zambia*, Anne M. Bliss and J. A. Rigg
52 *Puerto Rico*, Elena E. Cevallos
53 *Namibia*, Rev. Ed., Stanley Schoeman and Elna Schoeman
54 *Tanzania*, Rev. Ed., Colin Darch
55 *Jordan*, Rev. Ed., Vartan M. Amadouny
56 *Kuwait*, Rev. Ed., Frank A. Clements
57 *Brazil*, Rev. Ed., John Dickenson
58 *Israel*, Second Ed., C. H. Bleaney
59 *Romania*, Rev. Ed., Peter Siani-Davies and Mary Siani-Davies
60 *Spain*, Second Ed., Graham Shields
61 *Atlantic Ocean*, H. G. R. King
62 *Canada*, Ernest Ingles
63 *Cameroon*, Rev. Ed., Mark W. DeLancey and Mark D. DeLancey
64 *Malta*, Rev. Ed., David M. Boswell and Brian W. Beeley
65 *Thailand*, Rev. Ed., David Smyth
66 *Austria*, Rev. Ed., Michael Mitchell
67 *Norway*, Leland B. Sather
68 *Czechoslovakia*, David Short
69 *Irish Republic*, Michael Owen Shannon
70 *Pacific Basin and Oceania*, Gerald W. Fry and Rufino Mauricio
71 *Portugal*, Rev. Ed., John Laidlar
72 *West Germany*, Donald S. Detwiler and Ilse E. Detwiler
73 *Syria*, Rev. Ed., Neil Quilliam
74 *Trinidad and Tobago*, Frances Chambers
75 *Cuba*, Jean Stubbs, Lila Haines and Meic F. Haines
76 *Barbados*, Robert B. Potter and Graham M. S. Dann
77 *East Germany*, Ian Wallace
78 *Mozambique*, Colin Darch
79 *Libya*, Richard I. Lawless
80 *Sweden*, Leland B. Sather and Alan Swanson
81 *Iran*, Reza Navabpour
82 *Dominica*, Robert A. Myers
83 *Denmark*, Rev. Ed., LeeAnn Iovanni
84 *Paraguay*, Rev. Ed., R. Andrew Nickson
85 *Indian Ocean*, Julia J. Gotthold with the assistance of Donald W. Gotthold
86 *Egypt*, Ragai N. Makar
87 *Gibraltar*, Graham J. Shields
88 *The Netherlands*, Peter King and Michael Wintle
89 *Bolivia*, Gertrude M. Yeager
90 *Papua New Guinea*, Frasier McConnell
91 *The Gambia*, David P. Gamble
92 *Somalia*, Mark W. DeLancey, Sheila L. Elliott, December Green, Kenneth J. Menkhaus, Mohammad Haji Moqtar, Peter J. Schraeder
93 *Brunei*, Sylvia C. Engelen Krausse and Gerald H. Krausse
94 *Albania*, Rev. Ed., Antonia Young
95 *Singapore*, Stella R. Quah and Jon S. T. Quah
96 *Guyana*, Frances Chambers
97 *Chile*, Harold Blakemore
98 *El Salvador*, Ralph Lee Woodward, Jr.
99 *The Arctic*, H. G. R. King
100 *Nigeria*, Rev. Ed., Ruby Bell-Gam and David Uru Iyam
101 *Ecuador*, David Corkhill
102 *Uruguay*, Henry Finch with the assistance of Alicia Casas de Barrán
103 *Japan*, Frank Joseph Shulman
104 *Belgium*, R. C. Riley
105 *Macau*, Richard Louis Edmonds
106 *Philippines*, Jim Richardson
107 *Bulgaria*, Richard J. Crampton
108 *The Bahamas*, Paul G. Boultbee
109 *Peru*, John Robert Fisher
110 *Venezuela*, D. A. G. Waddell
111 *Dominican Republic*, Kai Schoenhals
112 *Columbia*, Robert H. Davies
113 *Taiwan*, Wei-chin Lee
114 *Switzerland*, Heinz K. Meier and Regula A. Meier

115 *Hong Kong*, Ian Scott
116 *Bhutan*, Ramesh C. Dogra
117 *Suriname*, Rosemarijn Hoefte
118 *Djibouti*, Peter J. Schraeder
119 *Grenada*, Kai Schoenhals
120 *Monaco*, Grace L. Hudson
121 *Guinea-Bissau*, Rosemary Galli
122 *Wales*, Gwilym Huws and D. Hywel E. Roberts
123 *Cape Verde*, Caroline S. Shaw
124 *Ghana*, Robert A. Myers
125 *Greenland*, Kenneth E. Miller
126 *Costa Rica*, Charles L. Stansifer
127 *Siberia*, David N. Collins
128 *Tibet*, John Pinfold
129 *Northern Ireland*, Michael Owen Shannon
130 *Argentina*, Alan Biggins
131 *Côte d'Ivoire*, Morna Daniels
132 *Burma*, Patricia M. Herbert
133 *Laos*, Helen Cordell
134 *Montserrat*, Riva Berleant-Schiller
135 *Afghanistan*, Schuyler Jones
136 *Equatorial Guinea*, Randall Fegley
137 *Turks and Caicos Islands*, Paul G. Boultbee
138 *Virgin Islands*, Verna Penn Moll
139 *Honduras*, Pamela F. Howard-Reguindin
140 *Mauritius*, Pramila Ramgulam Bennett
141 *Mauritania*, Simonetta Calderini, Delia Cortese, James L. A. Webb, Jr.
142 *Timor*, Ian Rowland
143 *St. Vincent and the Grenadines*, Robert B. Potter
144 *Texas*, James Marten
145 *Burundi*, Morna Daniels
146 *Hawai'i*, Nancy J. Morris and Love Dean
147 *Vietnam*, David Marr and Kristine Alilunas-Rodgers
148 *Sierra Leone*, Margaret Binns and Tony Binns
149 *Gabon*, David Gardinier
150 *Botswana*, John A. Wiseman
151 *Angola*, Richard Black
152 *Central African Republic*, Pierre Kalck
153 *Seychelles*, George Bennett, with the collaboration of Pramila Ramgulam Bennett
154 *Rwanda*, Randall Fegley
155 *Berlin*, Ian Wallace
156 *Mongolia*, Judith Nordby
157 *Liberia*, D. Elwood Dunn
158 *Maldives*, Christopher H. B. Reynolds
159 *Liechtenstein*, Regula A. Meier
160 *England*, Alan Day
161 *The Baltic States*, Inese A. Smith and Marita V. Grunts
162 *Congo*, Randall Fegley
163 *Armenia*, Vrej Nersessian
164 *Niger*, Lynda F. Zamponi
165 *Madagascar*, Hilary Bradt
166 *Senegal*, Roy Dilley and Jerry Eades
167 *Andorra*, Barry Taylor
168 *Netherlands Antilles and Aruba*, Kai Schoenhals
169 *Burkina Faso*, Samuel Decalo
170 *Indonesia*, Sylvia C. Engelen Krausse and Gerald H. Krausse
171 *The Antarctic*, Janice Meadows, William Mills, H. G. R. King
172 *São Tomé and Príncipe*, Caroline S. Shaw
173 *Fiji*, G. E. Gorman and J. J. Mills
174 *St. Kitts-Nevis*, Verna Penn Moll
175 *Martinique*, Janet Crane
176 *Zaire*, Dawn Bastian Williams, Robert W. Lesh and Andrea L. Stamm
177 *Chad*, George Joffé and Valérie Day-Viaud
178 *Togo*, Samuel Decalo
179 *Ethiopia*, Stuart Munro-Hay and Richard Pankhurst
180 *Punjab*, Darshan Singh Tatla and Ian Talbot
181 *Eritrea*, Randall Fegley
182 *Antigua and Barbuda*, Riva Berleant-Schiller and Susan Lowes with Milton Benjamin
183 *Alaska*, Marvin W. Falk
184 *The Falkland Islands*, Alan Day
185 *St Lucia*, Janet Henshall Momsen
186 *Slovenia*, Cathie Carmichael
187 *Cayman Islands*, Paul G. Boultbee
188 *San Marino*, Adrian Edwards and Chris Michaelides
189 *London*, Heather Creaton

190 *Western Sahara*, Anthony G. Pazzanita
191 *Guinea*, Margaret Binns
192 *Benin*, J. S. Eades and Chris Allen
193 *Madrid*, Graham Shields
194 *Tasmania*, I. Kepars
195 *Prague*, Susie Lunt
196 *Samoa*, H. G. A. Hughes
197 *St. Helena, Ascension and Tristan da Cunha*, Alan Day
198 *Budapest*, Mátyás Sárközi
199 *Lisbon*, John Laidlar
200 *Cambodia*, Helen Jarvis
201 *Vienna*, C. M. Peniston-Bird
202 *Corsica*, Grace L. Hudson
203 *Amsterdam*, André van Os
204 *Korea*, J. E. Hoare
205 *Bermuda*, Paul G. Boultbee and David F. Raine
206 *Paris*, Frances Chambers
207 *Mali*, Andrea Stamm, Dawn Bastian and Robert Myers
208 *The Maghreb*, Anthony G. Pazzanita
209 *The Channel Islands*, Vince Gardiner
210 *French Guiana*, Janet Crane
211 *Québec*, Alain-G. Gagnon
212 *The Basque Region*, Geoffrey West
213 *Sicily*, Valentina Olivastri
214 *Tokyo*, J. S. Eades
215 *Crete*, Adrian Edwards
216 *Croatia*, Cathie Carmichael
217 *Tonga*, Martin Daly
218 *Uzbekistan*, Reuel Hanks
219 *Czech Republic*, Vladka Edmondson with David Short
220 *Micronesia*, Monique Carriveau Storie and William L. Wuerch
221 *Azores*, Miguel Moniz
222 *Rome*, Chris Michaelides
223 *Sydney*, I. Kepars
224 *Guadeloupe*, Marian Goslinga

*To my wife,
daughter and father*

Contents

PREFACE	xvii
INTRODUCTION	xix
RULERS OF PORTUGAL	liii
THE COUNTRY AND ITS PEOPLE	1

General   1
Books of photographs   3

GEOGRAPHY	9

General   9
Maps and atlases   10
Geology and earthquakes   15

TOURISM AND TRAVEL GUIDEBOOKS	17

General   17
Accommodation guides   29
Walks and walking guides   32

TRAVELLERS' ACCOUNTS	34

Pre-20th century   34
20th century   39

FLORA AND FAUNA	43
PREHISTORY AND ARCHAEOLOGY	48
HISTORY	52

General   52
Muslim occupation (711-1147)   55

Contents

    Mediaeval and Renaissance period (1147-1639)   55
    Independence and consolidation (1640-1799)   57
    Early 19th century   58
    Mid- and late 19th century   60
    Early 20th century (1900-26)   61
    Estado Novo (1926-74)   62
    1974 Revolution   63
    Contemporary era (1974 to date)   63
    Overseas territories   65
        General   65
        Africa   66
        Asia   69
        Brazil and the Americas   74

BIOGRAPHIES AND AUTOBIOGRAPHIES 76

EMIGRANTS FROM PORTUGAL 82

IMMIGRANTS IN PORTUGAL 85

RACE RELATIONS 88

LANGUAGE 89
    General   89
    Language courses   93
    Dictionaries   99
    Phrasebooks   102

RELIGION AND RELIGIOUS BUILDINGS 105

SOCIETY 113
    General   113
    Social anthropology   115

STATISTICS 116

GENDER AND WOMEN'S STUDIES 117

POLITICS 119

FOREIGN RELATIONS 124
    General   124
    Anglo-Portuguese alliance   126

CONSTITUTION AND LAW 127

Contents

ADMINISTRATION AND LOCAL GOVERNMENT 129

ECONOMY 130

FINANCE AND BANKING 135

TRADE, COMMERCE AND BUSINESS 137

INDUSTRY 141

AGRICULTURE AND FISHING 143

COMMUNICATIONS 148

TRANSPORT 150
   Aerial   150
   Maritime   151
   Terrestrial   152

LABOUR AND EMPLOYMENT 155

ARCHITECTURE AND PLANNING 158

HOUSING 164

EDUCATION AND TRAINING 165

SCIENCE AND TECHNOLOGY 169

LITERATURE 171
   Literary history and criticism   171
   Major authors   175
      Eugénio de Andrade   175
      António Lobo Antunes   175
      Luís Vaz de Camões   176
      Fernando Pessoa   177
         General   177
         Critical works   179
      José Maria Eça de Queiroz   180
      Mário de Sá-Carneiro   182
      José Saramago   183
      Gil Vicente   185
         General   185
         Critical works   185

Contents

    Other authors   186
        Maria Isabel Barreno   186
        Al Berto   187
        Sophia de Mello Breyner   187
        Mário de Carvalho   187
        Camilo Castelo-Branco   188
        António Ferreira   188
        Herberto Helder   188
        David Mourão-Ferreira   189
        Fernando Gonçalves Namora   189
        André de Resende   189
        Jorge de Sena   190
        Miguel Torga   190
    Anthologies   191
    Literary works relating to Portugal published in English   194
    Festschriften   198

ARTS 199
    Visual arts   199
        General   199
        Paula Rego   201
            General   201
            Critical works   202
        Other artists   204
    Decorative arts   204
    Ceramics   205
    Plastic arts   206
    Music   207
    Film and theatre   208

DANCE AND COSTUME 210

CUSTOMS AND FAIRYTALES 212

FOOD AND DRINK 214

SPORT 220

RECREATION 223

LIBRARIES AND ARCHIVES 225

MUSEUMS 227

Contents

PUBLISHING	229
CHILDREN'S PUBLICATIONS	230
NEWSPAPERS	232
Newspaper directories 232	
Individual newspapers 232	
PERIODICALS	236
ENCYCLOPAEDIAS AND GENERAL DIRECTORIES	241
BIBLIOGRAPHIES AND CATALOGUES	243
INDEX OF AUTHORS	249
INDEX OF TITLES	263
INDEX OF SUBJECTS	279
MAP OF PORTUGAL	295

Preface

The scope of this volume

The contents of this volume have been determined by the following factors. Firstly, the policy of the World Bibliographical Series (WBS) is to include works published in English, which will generally be monographs, available in or through reference or research libraries, and which relate to the geographical area in question. Exceptionally, foreign-language works have been included but these are chiefly highly-illustrated volumes.

Secondly, Portugal established and oversaw an extensive colonial empire for some 500 years. As other WBS titles cover Angola (volume 121), Guinea-Bissau (volume 151), Mozambique (volume 78), India (volume 26) and the Azores (volume 221), this volume only includes a small selection of titles covering those territories.

Thirdly, the desire to avoid repetition of the entries included in the first edition of *Portugal* (WBS, volume 71, 1987), by P. T. H. Unwin, and in *Lisbon* (WBS, volume 199, 1997), by the same author as this volume, means that the works listed here are predominantly ones published in the last fifteen years, although there are also a number of earlier titles not included in Unwin's work. It follows, therefore, that this edition of Portugal should be used in conjunction with the first edition, and with the *Lisbon* volume. A very small number of entries in this volume are also included in the earlier volumes but in these cases, their inclusion is justified by the appearance of a significant new edition or by their relevance to Portugal as a whole rather than Lisbon only.

Compilation and acknowledgements

This volume has been compiled by a mixture of visits to libraries and to bookshops, accompanied by extensive use of electronic databases to identify suitable material. In addition to the catalogues of the John Rylands

Preface

University Library of Manchester, particularly useful were the British Library, the Library of Congress, the COPAC and PORBASE on-line catalogues, as well as the Bookfind and Books in Print databases. I am particularly grateful to my colleagues in the Document Supply Unit of the John Rylands University Library of Manchester who obtained numerous items for me through the inter-library loan system. For their help, I am also obliged to the staff of the Manchester Metropolitan Library, Manchester Business School Library, UMIST Library, Salford University Library, Manchester Public Libraries, The British Library of Political and Economic Sciences and The British Library, both at its St Pancras site and at the Document Supply Centre at Boston Spa.

I should also like to thank my wife, Dana, for proofreading the entries, although I must stress that any remaining errors are entirely my responsibility. I am also grateful to my daughter, Katherine, who with my wife not only endured the necessarily anti-social activity of compilation but also assisted me in scouring the shelves of numerous bookshops.

March 2000

John Laidlar
John Rylands University Library of Manchester
Oxford Road
Manchester M13 9PP
England
(Email address: john.laidlar@man.ac.uk)

Introduction

Portugal: the Country

The Portuguese Republic comprises both Continental Portugal on the European mainland and the autonomous regions of the Azores and Madeira in the Atlantic Ocean. Continental Portugal, lying between latitudes of 42°9'8"N and 36°58'23"N and longitudes of 6°11'48"W and 9°29'45"W, is one of mainland Europe's most southerly nations as well as being its most westerly. The Azores (2,335 sq.km) and Madeira (796 sq.km) are located respectively 1400km west and 924km south-west of Lisbon. Continental Portugal is broadly rectangular in shape, 550km long from north to south, but on average only 150km in breadth. Including the autonomous regions, Portugal occupies 91,905 sq.km of which Continental Portugal comprises 88,796 sq.km, an area approximately equivalent to thirty-five per cent of the United Kingdom.

The country's position on the south-western edge of Europe, combined with its long coastline (845km), has meant that maritime exploration has been a vitally important feature of Portugal's history. It is Europe's closest territory to west Africa and to south and central America and, indeed, until 1974 Portugal possessed substantial overseas territories (the *Ultramar*), which included Angola, Mozambique, Guinea-Bissau, the islands of Cape Verde and São Tomé e Príncipe, Portuguese India, East Timor and the Chinese enclave of Macao. This empire allowed Portugal to claim a total land area in the region of 2,200,000 sq.km – or an area greater than any single country in Europe except the then Soviet Union. Today, however, Portugal's territorial rights reach a mere 12 nautical miles, although its maritime claims extend to 200 nautical miles as regards exclusive fishing rights. The location of its capital city, Lisbon (pop. c.800,000), also owes much to its position, being a large natural harbour on the estuary of the River Tagus (Rio Tejo) which is ideal both for transatlantic trade and for the servicing of ships plying routes to the Mediterranean and Africa.

Introduction

Continental Portugal is bounded to the north and east by Spain, whilst its western and southern borders are defined by the Atlantic Ocean. Its 1215km of land frontiers are entirely with Spain and, as they date from the 13th century, are amongst the oldest extant national borders in Europe. They do not follow natural boundaries for much of their length but their line was determined in many places by the vagaries of reconquest from the Moors and by other historical factors.

Geology

Crudely, Portugal is divided by the River Tagus, with more mountainous country to the north, whilst the south is mainly plains. The country has a narrow coastal plain, mostly under 600m, where the majority of the population resides. The central zone of Portugal comprises a plateau (Estremadura) intersected by ridges and hills but the main mountain ranges lie in the north-east of the country, where the Serra do Gerês reaches 1538m. In the north-easterly province of Trás-os-Montes fast-flowing rivers drain generally southwards into the westerly-flowing Douro. To the south of this, in the Beira Alta region, is the granite Serra da Estrela range where Portugal's highest point (1991m) is reached at Malhão da Estrela. South of the Tagus the maximum height reached is only 1025m in the Serra de S. Mamede. Overall some twenty-eight per cent of the country is higher than 400m above sea-level, twelve per cent is higher than 700m but a mere 0.57 per cent is above 1200m.

Portugal's major rivers for the most part run in a north-east to south-west orientation which allows Atlantic climatic influences to penetrate the country. The only major river running south, as opposed to west, into the Atlantic is the Rio Guadiana on the southern Portuguese border with Spain. Most of the longer rivers rise in Spain and the longest of these is the Rio Douro, which originates in the Sierra de Urbión and enters the Atlantic at São João da Foz, near Oporto, 330km after crossing the Portuguese border. However, the most important waterway from the point of view of commerce is the Tagus, which runs through Spain from the Sierra de Albarracín, via Toledo to Lisbon, with 273km of its length being within Portugal. Indeed, thirty-nine per cent of Portugal is irrigated by the Tagus basin system and between Lisbon and the sea, the river's width varies between 1780m and 3220m. Its major tributary is the Zêzere, whose power has been harnessed by the Castelo de Bode hydroelectric plant near Tomar. The longest river lying entirely within Portugal is the 234km-long Rio Mondego, which reaches the Atlantic to the west of the university city of Coimbra in central Portugal. Also of note is the Rio Minho, which for 75km forms the northern border of Portugal with Spain. The coastline itself is generally straight with only four major indentations. From the north these are the lagoon of Aveiro,

Introduction

the Tagus estuary at Lisbon, the Sado estuary at Setúbal, and the creeks on the Algarve coast around Faro. Portugal has few islands, the most notable being the Berlengas, 10km off the coast at Peniche, north of Lisbon, but even the largest of these is only 1500m long.

Climate and Vegetation

The Portuguese climate is temperate, broadly of Atlantic type in the north and Mediterranean in the south, with the River Tagus as the rough climatic divide. However, there is also an east-west gradation between the coastal and interior regions, with the latter having a greater temperature range and lower rainfall. For example, typical annual rainfall in the city of Oporto on the northern coast is 875mm but, in contrast, only 380mm of annual precipitation is recorded typically at Praia da Rocha on the Algarve coast. Rainfall in the Serra da Estrela in the northern interior averages 2464mm, but only 756mm falls annually in Lisbon. Whereas the minimum temperature experienced in the northern interior at Bragança (Braganza) is typically 6ºC, it is as high as 12ºC at Praia da Rocha. The temperature range is at its greatest in the northern interior of the country, largely due to the influence of winds from Spain. The tourist trade in the Algarve enjoys a long summer period and a correspondingly short winter season and benefits from warm Saharan winds. Indeed, sea temperatures can be as high as 22ºC in the south of the country. The Costa do Estoril, to the west of Lisbon, enjoyed a vogue as a health resort in the 19th and early 20th centuries due to its moderate climate throughout the year. Average annual temperatures vary from almost 18ºC in Lagos on the western Algarve to a mere 10.5ºC at Guarda in the mountainous northern interior.

Vegetation in the north of the country is more lush due to the damper climate and the main arboreal species there are pine, eucalyptus and deciduous types such as oak, lime, maple and poplar. Oak is especially prevalent on the inland plateaux of the north, whilst chestnuts are abundant in the Trás-os-Montes and Beiras inland regions of the north and centre. Portugal is the world's largest producer of cork and cork trees abound in the Alentejo and southern part of the country. Olives are another prolific agricultural product of Portugal. Southern Portugal has a neo-Mediterranean climate with products which include almonds, carob and fig, whilst oleander and cistus form widespread undergrowth. Portuguese fauna include roe-deer, chamois, foxes, wolves, wild horses and golden eagles.

Population

At 31 December 1996, the population of Portugal, including the Azores and Madeira, was 9,934,110, living at a density of 108 per sq.km, a decline from

Introduction

the total of 10,007,050 in 1986. The population of Continental Portugal was 9,433,450, distributed at a density of 106 per sq.km. Of the total population, 4.78 million were men and 5.15 million were women; in Continental Portugal these totals were 4.54 million and 4.89 million respectively. The Atlantic island of Madeira is home to 257,000 people, whilst 241,000 people reside on the Azores archipelago. The national rate of infant mortality is 9.8 per 1000 live births (1993) whilst life expectancy (1996) is 74.9 years; 71.3 for men and 78.6 for women. A major element in the Portuguese economy, particularly in the 1960s and 1970s, was emigration, especially from the impoverished north, and from the rugged Trás-os-Montes province in particular. Today, some 4.5 million Portuguese still live outside the country, especially in France and Germany.

The Lisbon and Tagus valley area (11,931 sq.km) has a population of 3,313,450 (1996) at a density of 278 per sq.km. The north of Portugal, as defined by the *Anuário Estatístico de Portugal, 1997*, has a population of 3,544,780, residing at a density of 167 per sq.km, whilst the central area has 1,710,070 people living at a density of only 72 per sq.km. Less populous still are the Alentejo, with 519,040 inhabitants dispersed at 19 per sq.km and the Algarve, with 346,110 people residing at 69 per sq.km.

Roughly ninety-seven per cent of the Portuguese population is at least nominally Roman Catholic, the remainder being mostly Protestant. The labour force was 6,605,700 in 1993 with forty-five per cent of that total occupied in service industries, thirty-five per cent in industry and some twenty per cent in agriculture. About fifty-five per cent of Portuguese labour is organized in trade unions, with the Communist-led *CGTP-Intersindical Confederação Geral de Trabalhadores Portugueses* (General Confederation of Portuguese Workers) accounting for more than half of the unionized labour; its main rival is the socialist *UGT-União Geral de Trabalhadores* (General Union of Workers).

Language

Portuguese is a Romance language, albeit with other influences evident in its vocabulary, particularly Arabic elements which date from the country's Moorish occupation for over 400 years from the 8th century. Although it shares broadly similar orthography to Spanish, Portuguese pronunciation is less staccato and more nasal. Portuguese tends to be closer in orthography to Latin and also has a number of grammatical differences from Spanish. Portugal is, today, one of the few countries in Europe without a native linguistic minority though there are many recent immigrants in Portugal, notably from its former African territories. These include both native Africans and *retornados*, Portuguese who had emigrated to the colonies but returned on the fall of the *Estado Novo* and the resultant civil wars in those

Introduction

countries in the mid-1970s. There is also a significant Asian community, many of whom came to Portugal from the cities of Mozambique after 1974. As the Portuguese empire once extended to Africa, Asia and America, Portuguese remains an official language or lingua franca in Angola (10,300,000 inhabitants), Cape Verde (346,000), Guinea-Bissau (1,000,000), São Tomé e Príncipe (126,000) and Mozambique (15,300,000) in Africa; in Brazil (151,000,000); and also in Asia, with Macao (367,000). It also survives in pockets of India (Diu, Damão and Goa) as well as in East Timor. In all, over 185 million people speak Portuguese, making it the seventh language of the world and the third most spoken west European language after English and Spanish. However, within Portugal the rate of illiteracy, though falling, was as high as fifteen per cent in 1990 and is thus amongst the highest in Europe for those aged over fifteen, with a rate of eleven per cent for men and eighteen per cent for women.

National Features

Since the 1910 revolution, the Portuguese flag has been a rectangle in the proportion of 2:3, hoist to fly. The third of the flag nearer to the hoist is green, the remainder of the flag is red, which purports to represent Portuguese war dead. The country's anthem is *A Portuguesa* written by Alfredo Kiel. The *Dia de Portugal* (Portugal Day) holiday falls on 10 June, which is the anniversary of the death of the poet Luís de Camões (c.1525-80), author of the epic poem, *Os Lusíadas* (The Lusiads). Since 1912 the currency has been the escudo, which consists of 100 *centavos*, a unit which has effectively disappeared through inflation. Large sums, such as national debts or house prices are cited in *contos* (1,000 escudos units). Following the 1974 Revolution and the hasty nationalization of the banks and of other industries, as well as the strains placed on the economy by the influx of *retornados* (returnees) from the African territories, inflation exceeded thirty per cent p.a. However, following several years of political stability, inflation had fallen to 11.4 per cent by 1991 and declined in successive years to reach 2.3 per cent in 1997. In 1999 there were approximately 300 escudos to the pound sterling.

Administration

Continental Portugal has eighteen administrative districts which comprise Aveiro, Beja, Braga, Bragança (Braganza), Castelo Branco, Coimbra, Évora, Faro, Guarda, Leiria, Lisboa (Lisbon), Portalegre, Porto (Oporto), Santarém, Setúbal, Viana do Castelo, Viseu and Vila Real. These were formerly grouped into eleven provinces, namely: Minho (capital, Braga), Douro Litoral (Porto [Oporto]), Trás-os-Montes a Alto Douro (Bragança

Introduction

[Braganza]), Beira Alta (Viseu), Beira Baixa (Castelo Branco), Beira Litoral (Coimbra), Estremadura (Lisboa [Lisbon]), Ribatejo (Santarém), Alto Alentejo (Évora), Baixo Alentejo (Beja) and Algarve (Faro). In addition to the autonomous regions of the Azores and Madeira, Macao remained a dependency of Portugal until 20 December 1999.

The Early History of Portugal

In April 1999 a four-year-old child's skeleton was unearthed in the Lapedo valley, near Leiria north of Lisbon, which confirmed a mingling between Neanderthal man and the ancestors of so-called 'modern man' 25,000 years ago. As such it was the earliest evidence of 'modern man' in Iberia, although prior to this discovery, cave paintings had been found at Escoral, in south-central Portugal, which indicated the presence of Upper Palaeolithic man 15,000 years ago. Recent work on creation of a dam in the Coa valley, a tributary of the River Douro, has also revealed an extensive collection of wall paintings (petroglyphs) from the Ice Age. Amongst other significant archaeological finds are shell middens (*moitas*) at Muge, on the Tagus, from 5,000 BC and cave burials from 4,500 BC. At Vila Nova de São Pedro, near Santarém, artefacts have been unearthed confirming the activities of potters, weavers and farmers, using copper, horses and oxen in c.2,000 BC. After 1,000 BC contact has been surmised between the inhabitants of what is modern-day Portugal and the Phoenicians from the Near East, who traded metals including tin, silver and gold across the Mediterranean. Equally scant evidence has survived of contact with the Carthaginians who followed the Phoenicians to Iberia. Between 700 and 600 BC, the Celts introduced the fruits of the Iron Age to Iberia, from across the Pyrenees. They built *castros* (hilltop forts), of which a major surviving example is that at Citânia dos Briteiros (near Guimarães) in northern Portugal, which was inhabited between 300 BC and 300 AD.

The Romans arrived in Iberia in 218 BC and assigned names to the peoples whom they found. In what is today's Portugal, these included the *Gallaeci* (Galicians) in the north and the *Lusitani* and *Celtici* further south. Roman sites which are evident today as archaeological ruins include Conimbriga (Coimbra), Mirobriga (Santiago do Cacém) and Cetobriga (Setúbal). In around 137 BC Decimus Julius Brutus's Roman troops marched from Lisbon northwards via the inland town of Viseu to the Rivers Douro, Lima and Minho in the north of modern-day Portugal. Julius Caesar established a base in *Felicitas Iulia* (Lisbon) around 60 BC upon which the privilege of Roman Rights was bestowed. *Emerita Augusta* (Mérida, Spain) was capital of Lusitania Province, which had five 'colonies', including Beja and Santarém in Portugal. It also had four *municipia* at Lisbon, Évora, Mértola and Alcácer do Sal as well as thirty-six tribute-paying towns,

Introduction

making forty-five *populi* in all. Roman roads linked Mérida to Lisbon and these also linked Santarém, Alcácer, Évora and Setúbal, in addition to connecting Braga, Oporto, Coimbra and Lisbon to the southern town of Faro. Lusitania's main industries included mining, metalworking, fishing/preserving, cattle, weaving and esparto production.

Barbarians, comprising Alans, Vandals and Suevi, arrived in Portugal in the early 5th century and overran the Romans. The Suevi were mainly farmers whose stronghold was around Braga in the north. They themselves were usurped between 516 and 585 by the Visigoths who had been brought in by the Romans to control the Alans and the Vandals. The Visigoths remained as the dominant power in Portugal until the Moors invaded around 713. Visigoths coexisted alongside the Hispano-Romans, who remained Christians, whereas they themselves were Arian heretics who denied the divinity of Jesus Christ.

In 711 Taric led Berber forces into Iberia where they routed the Visigoths and occupied Córdoba and Toledo in Spain. Within two years the provinces of Lusitania and much of Gallaecia had also fallen to them. The Moors considered those who converted to Islam as equals with themselves but those who remained as Christians or Jews were required to pay taxes. Such Christians became known as *mozárabes*. The Arabs brought with them the exploitation of water-power and also encouraged smallholders, whereas the Romans had preferred to operate large estates for grain and wine production. The Christians' victory at the battle of Covadonga in Asturias in 718 helped to ensure that pockets of resistance remained, notably in Galicia and as far south as the Lima and Douro valleys, as well as in the mountainous interior of Beira Alta. By 868 the area known as *Portucale* (northern Portugal) was freed for the last time from Muslims. During the 9th and 10th century Vimara Peres and then Hermenegildo sought to organize the territory which is today northern Portugal. The Reconquest was a lengthy process; for example Coimbra was freed in 878, then recaptured and not finally liberated until 1064.

In 1065, Fernando I of Castile and Leon died and his kingdom was split between his three sons. The youngest, García, received Galicia, centred on Santiago de Compostela. However, his brother, Alfonso VI of Leon and Castile, imprisoned García and annexed Galicia. In addition, the Iberian territories were still prey to new waves of Moorish invaders from Africa, including the puritanical Almoravids (Berbers). Indeed, in 1094, Lisbon, which had been recaptured, was lost again to the Muslims. In 1095 Alfonso VI of Leon assigned Galicia, which included part of modern Portugal, to his daughter, Urraca, who married Raymond, son of the Count of Burgundy. Alfonso gave Portucale, south of Galicia and as far as the river Mondego, to Teresa, his illegitimate daughter. After her husband died, she married a Galician noble and ruled herself until her son Afonso Henriques rose up at

Introduction

the battle of São Mamede 1128 (near Guimarães), expelled his mother and styled himself as King.

The Christian Reconquest

In 1143 peace was reached between Portugal and Leon and Castile, allowing Afonso to concentrate on the reconquest of territory from the Arabs. In 1147, with help from English Crusaders, he seized both Santarém and Lisbon on the Tagus and Christian forces also captured Alenquer, Óbidos, Sintra and, south of the Tagus, Sesimbra and Palmela, with Alcácer do Sal falling in 1160. In the period between 1165 and 1169 Afonso also liberated, at least temporarily, the Alentejan plains and the Roman town of Évora. Afonso Henriques was recognized by the Pope as King of Portugal in 1179. The Moors, however, invited the fundamentalist Almoravids into Iberia and the even more fanatical Almohads arrived in the 1180s. They succeeded in driving the Christians back to the Tagus, taking captives as slaves to Africa.

On his death in 1185, Afonso was succeeded by his son Sancho I (1185-1211) and then by Afonso II (1211-23). Afonso profited from captured Muslim gold and set about consolidating Christian gains by codifying laws. However, the Leonese invaded Portuguese territory from the east and in 1220 Afonso also became embroiled in conflict with the Church in the north of his territory by laying claim to ecclesiastical lands. His son, eleven-year-old Sancho II (1223-48), succeeded but was eventually deposed by the Papacy in favour of his brother Afonso, who returned to Portugal from exile in 1246. Nevertheless, it was during Sancho's reign, from 1226, that lasting advances against the Moors were made south of the Tagus, after four decades of minimal progress. Although Afonso III (1248-79) owed his crown to the Church, he himself soon had poor relations with the ecclesiastical authorities. Militarily, however, he was successful for, by 1249, the southern port of Faro had been captured from the Arabs, effectively establishing Portugal as Europe's longest-lasting nation state. The Templars, Hospitalers and the Christian Orders of Calatrava and Santiago were instrumental in these gains and their rewards from the Crown included substantial tracts of land, particularly in the south. Here, relatively isolated towns formed a pattern of population markedly different from the more populous north of the country. Afonso's court was generally outside Lisbon at Coimbra or at Almeirim, on the Tagus and in 1254 all three Estates met at Leiria which constituted the first *Cortes* (parliament) to have representation from the commoners. The Crown increasingly sought revenue via the *Cortes* as its sources of captured Arab wealth dissipated.

In 1248 the Christians retook Seville which allowed merchants, especially Genoese, access to Lisbon from the Mediterranean. Afonso's reign also saw the granting to merchants of tax exemptions which further

Introduction

stimulated maritime trade. This commercial activity prompted the growth in Lisbon of shipbuilding and the related planting of pine forests in Leiria. Reinvigorated trade also prompted the emergence of a native merchant class. At this time, the main agricultural crops were wheat and, in the north, millet; rye was especially prevalent in the east, whilst barley was grown in the south of the country. Agricultural products, including cork and leather were major exports whilst English textiles were amongst the main imports.

Agriculture prospered under King Dinis (1279-1325), who was known as *O Lavrador* (The Farmer). He developed the Leiria pine forests and embarked on projects to reclaim marshes, whilst the magnificent cloisters of Alcobaça abbey, Estremoz castle and the keep at Beja were amongst the architectural monuments to his reign. He also patronized a court vogue for troubadour poetry and during his reign University faculties were set up in Lisbon (1288) which soon moved to Coimbra. However, by 1320-23 the nobles were embroiled in civil war and Dinis's heir-apparent, Afonso Sanches, sided with the rebels who seized Coimbra and Leiria. After the battle of Santarém in 1325 Afonso obliged Dinis to abdicate and assumed the throne himself as Afonso IV (1325-57). In 1348/49 the Black Death ravaged Portugal, leading to a labour shortage and Afonso was forced to devalue the currency and even to ban the charging of interest on loans. A faction in Castile opposed to their king, Pedro I, the Cruel, sought Afonso's son, Pedro, as their monarch since he was the grandson of Sancho IV of Castile. Prince Pedro's mistress was Inês de Castro, a lady-in-waiting at the court whom Afonso allowed to be murdered in January 1355. Pedro reacted by rising against his father in northern Portugal but in 1357 Afonso died. Pedro I then ruled from 1357 until his death in 1367, when his son Fernando I (1367-83) succeeded him.

Although peace was made with Spain at Alcoutim in 1371, Portugal soon became embroiled in Anglo-Spanish conflict. Fernando made an alliance against Castile with the Englishman, John of Gaunt who, through his marriage to Pedro's daughter, claimed the throne of that kingdom. Enrique II of Castile invaded Beira and Viseu and beseiged Lisbon in 1373, burning the Rua Nova and Judiaria. Fernando was forced to abandon John of Gaunt and to help Enrique against England but in 1381 Fernando revived his Anglo-Portuguese alliance and with the forces of the Earl of Cambridge, declared war on Castile. Once again he was obliged to accept peace terms which, this time, meant that Beatriz, his young daughter, would marry Juan I of Castile, an act which threatened the independence of Portugal.

The House of Aviz

On Fernando's death, João, *Mestre de Avis* (Master of the Order of Avis), with much support in Lisbon and from an element of the nobility, stabbed

Introduction

the favourite of the Spanish Queen of Portugal, Leonor Teles, whilst Álvaro Pais led a rising in Lisbon to install João as king. In 1384, the Castilians beseiged the city but pestilence struck the besieging army, forcing their retreat, and the following year João was finally proclaimed king as João I (1385-1433). The Castilians once more invaded but, on 14 August 1385, at the decisive battle of Aljubarrota, north of Lisbon, they were defeated by Nun'Álvares Pereira with the aid of English archers. To commemorate his victory, João ordered the construction of the imposing Batalha Abbey nearby, which is now a UNESCO world heritage site. In 1386 an Anglo-Portuguese alliance, the Treaty of Windsor, was signed and King João himself married Philippa of Lancaster, daughter of John of Gaunt. As many Portuguese nobles had been pro-Castile and therefore opposed to João's accession, the King created a new nobility under Nun'Álvares, whose son married the king's illegitimate daughter. Eventually, in 1411, peace was made with Castile.

The Portuguese Discoveries

Once his domestic supremacy was ensured, the king's attention was directed overseas, not least as a means of focusing the energies of the Portuguese nobility on a non-threatening enterprise, but also as a step towards economic recovery. João's forces took Ceuta in a day in 1415, whilst João Gonçalves Zarco and Tristão Vaz Teixeira reached the Atlantic islands of Madeira in 1418 and the Azores in 1427. One of the king's sons, Henrique (Prince Henry the Navigator), became the governor of Ceuta and the Algarve, as well as leading the military Order of Christ whose goal was to conquer Islam. From this position he orchestrated voyages of discovery from his base in the Algarve. Learning, including new navigational skills, flourished during his reign and João I himself even wrote a treatise on hunting.

His successor, Duarte (1433-38), also patronized culture and was the author of the *Leal Conselheiro* (The loyal counsellor), a philosophical tome. Inspired by the religious goal of conversion and by the quest for knowledge and commercial expansion, Portuguese maritime explorations continued with Gil Eanes's momentous passing of Cape Bojador on the north-west African coast in 1434. Further impetus came in 1442 when African gold was found. However, there were also reverses: in 1437 Henrique's forces failed to take Tangier and during the campaign his brother, Prince Fernando, was captured and left to die in captivity. Duarte's heir was Afonso V (1438-81) who was only six years old when he came to throne. Duarte's wife, Leonor of Aragon, acted as his regent but influential groups in Lisbon favoured Duarte's brother Pedro, Duque de Coimbra, as monarch. An accommodation was reached whereby Pedro would be regent from 1441 until 1448, whilst

Introduction

Afonso was in his minority. Pedro also married off his daughter, Isabel, to the king.

Overseas, an expedition to Africa seized Arguim in 1438/39 and a slave market was established at Lagos in the Algarve. In 1444 Cape Verde was reached and by 1445, there were 800 Portuguese based in Madeira and sugar cane was being cultivated in the Azores. The national hero, Nun'Álvares, entered a monastery but his son, the Conde de Barcelos, claimed the title of Constable on hereditary grounds. However, Afonso saw the title as being in his gift and awarded it to his own son, bestowing on the Conde de Barcelos the title of Duque de Bragança (Duke of Braganza) instead. Braganza curried favour with Afonso while at the same time stirring Pedro to rebel. His revolt was put down and Pedro was killed at the battle of Alfarrobeira in 1449, leaving the Braganzas as major powers in the land.

Papal Bulls ratified Portuguese claims to Africa and India. Sierra Leone and Cape Verde were reached before Henry the Navigator died in 1460. In 1453 the fall of the Byzantine empire encouraged the rise of Islam, whilst in 1463 the Portuguese failed once more to capture Tangier, although they finally succeeded in 1471. They also captured Arzila, giving rise to a string of African fortresses along the northern coast of that continent. Afonso also became embroiled in Castile but his forces were beaten at the battle of Toro (1476) and lost out in the peace of 1481. By the treaty of Alcaçovas (1479), the Portuguese Canary Islands were ceded to Spain while Portugal was to have the rights to lands discovered to the south of the islands and Spain to those lands to the north. The Canaries had been Portugal's first maritime discovery, prior to 1336.

João II (1481-95), Afonso's son, succeeded to the throne and soon asserted his authority. He had the Duke of Braganza beheaded at Évora in 1484 and even stabbed to death his own brother-in-law, the Duke of Viseu, in a quest to reduce the power of the nobles. João also had the Bishop of Évora and the Marquês de Távora executed. Ironically, despite these acts of violence, João II was known as *O Príncipe Perfeito*, the Perfect Prince.

By 1482 the Portuguese had constructed a fort at Mina on the African coast to police the gold trade and the navigator, Diogo Cão, had reached as far as the mouth of the Congo river before travelling on to a welcome from the natives of Angola. His second voyage (1485/86) almost reached the tropic of Capricorn. In 1487 Pero de Covilhã was sent, with Afonso de Paiva, to Alexandria, India, East Africa and Abyssinia, where the Portuguese sought the mythical Christian king, Prester John. The exploration to the east by Pero de Covilhã was followed by the southern discoveries of Bartolomeu Dias. He left Lisbon in July 1487 with three ships and a store vessel to round the Cape of Good Hope in February 1488, before returning to Lisbon in December of that year. Dias sailed via Mozambique

Introduction

to Calicut, India and returned with spices to Lisbon with two ships and only half of the original number of crew.

Christopher Columbus failed to persuade João II that a western route to the Indies was viable and discovered the Americas for Spain. However, his landfall was south of the demarcation line in the Treaty of Alcaçovas and therefore officially in Portuguese territory. The resultant dispute led to the momentous Treaty of Tordesillas (1494) which overturned the Treaty of Alcaçovas (1479) and changed the demarcation line between Spanish and Portuguese possessions from a north/south to an east/west axis. It has been argued that this was a reflection on Portugal's secret knowledge at the time of the existence of Brazil, which lay largely on their side of the agreed line, which ran 370 leagues west of the Cape Verde archipelago. Columbus was to die in penury, discredited by the Portuguese exploitation of the eastern spice trade.

As João's son had predeceased him, he was succeeded in 1495 by Duarte's grandson, Manuel I (1495-1521), who came unexpectedly to the throne having been the brother of João's wife and the family's ninth child. Manuel's three wives were all Spanish princesses and, consequently, he came under pressure to follow his Iberian neighbour's anti-Jewish policy. In 1492 many of the Jews expelled from Spain had fled to the more tolerant climate of Portugal but in December 1496 Portuguese Jews were pressed to convert to Catholicism. Not surprisingly, many opted to become *conversos*, superficial Christians.

More positively, in 1499, a fleet of thirteen vessels sailed for the Indies under Pedro Álvares Cabral and struck the coast of Brazil (1500) as they headed west to gain favourable winds. Cabral sent a ship back to report his discovery to Lisbon but his fleet continued to the Indies from whence it returned only half-intact but with a cargo of spices. Other major advances in Asia were made by the enterprising Afonso de Albuquerque (c.1462-1515) who journeyed to the Red Sea and Abyssinia and later captured Goa, Malacca and Ormuz. In 1508 the Portuguese also took Safim, in 1513 Azamor and 1514 Mazagão (today el-Jadida) but suffered a major reverse in 1515, when they lost 4,000 men and 200 ships at Mamora (near Casablanca). After 1541 the Portuguese abandoned their north African outposts except for Ceuta, Tangiers and Mazagão. Unlike the explorations of other European states, those of Portugal were state-directed, part of a national, planned undertaking, built upon an established impetus to drive the Moors out of Portugal itself, before pursuing them overseas.

King Manuel also took steps to reform his country's administration, establishing heraldic institutions, attempting to standardize weights and measures, and codifying the nation's laws (*ordenações*, 1512). On the negative side, Manuel kept 4,000 retainers and dispensed with the *Cortes* after 1502, largely because he did not need to raise additional taxes as a

Introduction

consequence of the wealth accruing from abroad. The spices obtained from the voyages to the East were used as preservatives, medicines, glues, dyes, varnishes and lacquers and were cheaper to acquire directly from Portugal than by caravans through Arabia and the Red Sea to Venice. By 1500 an annual Spring fleet was travelling round the Cape of Good Hope to India, albeit with a fifty per cent rate of mortality. In addition, local resistance, attacks by the Dutch, English and Muslim forces, as well as growing competition from the Italian city states, contributed to Portuguese difficulties and lay the seeds for a protracted economic decline and reliance on imports, which was exacerbated by an exodus from the land.

Overseas, Francisco de Almeida, Viceroy of India since 1505, was succeeded in 1509 by Afonso de Albuquerque who set about occupying ports on the trade routes to the East. By 1510 Ormuz and Goa were in Portuguese hands and in 1511 Malacca was taken, but attempts to seize Aden failed. In Goa the Portuguese mixed with the natives, catholicized them and developed trade, as well as creating a cultural and architectural legacy. By the mid-16th century Goa was effectively the second city of the Portuguese world, a Jesuit base and cultural *entrepôt* for Asia. The Portuguese were also active in the Far East, reaching the Pacific in 1511 and China in 1513. By the mid 1550s the Portuguese dominated trade between China and the West, and had established an enclave in Macao and a trading post at Nagasaki in Japan, a country which also attracted Portuguese Jesuits. Despite fierce Turkish opposition in the Red Sea, the Portuguese were also successful in taking Colombo (Ceylon), Pacém, Sumatra, Ternate (Moluccas), Maçaim, Diu and Damão in India.

The 16th century also witnessed a cultural flowering, including the emergence of Gil Vicente (c.1465-c.1536), who was both a major dramatist and goldsmith, and Fernão Mendes Pinto (1510-83) who wrote memorably of his exploits in the Orient. However, the greatest writer of the era was Luís Vaz de Camões (c.1524-80), whose national epic *Os Lusíadas* (The Lusiads, 1572) tells, in heroic form, the story of Vasco da Gama's voyage round the Cape. The more factual chronicles of João de Barros (1497-1562), Damião de Góis (1502-74), Diogo de Couto (1542-1616), Lopes de Castanheda (d. 1559) and Gaspar Correia provide a valuable record of Portuguese exploits. Another legacy of this era is Manueline architecture, a striking adaptation of the Gothic style, whose best examples may still be seen in the Lisbon suburb of Belém and in Setúbal and Tomar. This style used many nautical images, such as rope and the armillary sphere, a navigational implement and the personal emblem of Manuel I.

Manuel was succeeded by his son, João III (1521-57), who married the sister of the Emperor Charles V. João's accession in 1521 also marked the first circumnavigation of the world by the fleet of Fernão de Magalhães (Magellan) whose epoch-making endeavour was carried out under the flag

Introduction

of Spain, after his plans were rejected by Manuel. At home, João asked a reluctant Pope in 1531 for permission to set up an Inquisition, with the aim of appropriating the wealth of the Jews and eradicating their 'heresies'. The *Marranos* (crypto-Jews) included doctors, lawyers and teachers and were unpopular because of their financial acumen. Finally, in 1536, an Inquisition Bull was issued, leading to the first *auto-da-fé* in Portugal in 1541. By 1684 a total of 1,379 people had been burned alive by the Inquisition; thereafter the numbers declined until the mid-18th century. Run by the Dominican Order, the Inquisition also censored books but it was the Jesuit Order which, in 1537, was appointed by João to spread Christianity to the Orient and Brazil. Soon, too, the Jesuits were also to control Portuguese education. Meanwhile, the Portuguese economy was in decline and much of its shipping was being lost to the French and to corsairs. The cost of wars, including the defence of Brazil from the French (1539), maintaining outposts abroad, as well as the payment of dowry to Spain, were additional factors in this process.

When João III died his grandson, Sebastião (1557-78), only three years old, inherited the throne. His mother, Catarina, became Regent, but when Sebastião was fourteen the regency was assumed by Cardinal Henrique, his great uncle, who also headed the Inquisition and championed the Jesuits. Under Henrique's influence, Sebastião cut himself off from his mother and became a religious fanatic who even opened the royal tombs of Sintra to view the bones. Inspired by the Jesuits, Sebastião sought to defeat Islam in the Maghreb but on 4 August 1578 his crusading forces were annihilated at Alcácer-Quibir. Some 8,000 of his 17,000 men were killed and virtually all the remainder captured by an army of 40,000 Arabs. The King himself disappeared in the battle, presumed slaughtered by the forces of Sultan 'Abd al-Malek, but the lack of firm evidence spawned the phenomenon of *Sebastianismo* whose adherents expected the King's return. False Sebastiãos even emerged, including the celebrated 'pastry-cook of Madrigal' (Salamanca).

Union with Spain

The aged Cardinal Henrique (1578-80) succeeded his great-nephew to the throne. Henrique's heirs were the grandchildren of Manuel and included Philip II of Spain, António, *Prior de Crato* and Catherine of Braganza. Henrique convened a *Cortes* at Almeirim to determine the succession but died before it could be concluded. Philip II prepared to succeed Henrique but in June 1580 António, *Prior de Crato*, was crowned in Santarém and entered Lisbon. The Spaniards, led by the Duque de Alba, then invaded and defeated António at the battle of Alcântara. In 1580, shortly after the death of the poet Camões, Portugal lost its independence as Philip crossed the frontier in

Introduction

December to claim the throne. He remained in Portugal until February 1583 and at the Cortes of Tomar (1581) he was proclaimed King Filipe I. Lisbon was the starting point for the Spanish Armada (1588) which sailed for England with thirty-one large Portuguese vessels in its fleet. The following year Elizabeth I of England sent a force to Lisbon to support the claims of the Prior, but a motley force led by Norris and Drake failed in its goal. However, Filipe I (1580-98) did grant a number of privileges to Portugal; only the country's own *Cortes* could proclaim laws, the Portuguese currency remained in place and African and Indian trade remained in Portuguese hands. The absence of a Lisbon Court also reduced extravagant expenditure in Portugal. However, Filipe II (1598-1621) did not even visit Portugal until 1619 and by the time of Filipe III (1621-40), Portuguese coffers had been drained by Spain's wars in Europe. In 1623, Ormuz fell to England, whilst the Dutch held Rio de Janeiro for two years. Between 1623 and 1638 some 500 Portuguese vessels were seized by English, Dutch or French marauders.

Independence from Spain

In 1640 the Portuguese took advantage of a rising against Spain in Catalonia to reassert their own independence. Miguel de Vasconcelos, the Spaniards' Minister in Lisbon, was killed in the rising and after two weeks of hesitation João, Duke of Braganza agreed to accept the Portuguese throne as João IV (1640-56). Of the overseas possessions of Portugal, only Ceuta was not recovered from Spain after independence had been regained. However, it was not until 1668 that Spain and the Papacy recognized the renewed independence of Portugal, although as early as 1642 António de Sousa Macedo, the Portuguese ambassador in London, had secured English recognition of independence. That same year a new treaty was concluded with England which allowed its merchants freedom of religion in Portugal, as already enjoyed by the Dutch. However, Macedo sided with the Royalists in the English Civil War, thereby provoking animosity between the two countries. The 1642 treaty was nullified when Charles I of England was executed by Cromwell in 1649. During the Civil War, Princes Rupert and Maurice based a squadron of ships in the Tagus estuary, causing the Parliamentarians' Admiral Blake to confront them off Lisbon before the Royalists fled to the Mediterranean. As a reprisal, the 1654 treaty with the English Commonwealth secured merchants' rights in Portugal, and allowed English trade with the Portuguese colonies and freedom for British warships in Portugal. Skirmishes with Spain continued for a number of years, for example at Montijo on the border (1644). By 1654 Pernambuco in north-east Brazil had been recaptured from the Dutch and in 1656 a Franco-Spanish treaty was concluded. This reaffirmed Spanish sovereignty over Portugal, yet it did not inhibit the French Count of Schomberg and 500 officers from coming to Portugal to reorganize its army.

Introduction

João was succeeded by the semi-paralysed and mentally defective Afonso VI (1656-68) and the queen mother, Dona Luísa Gusmão, became regent until 1661. In 1657 a Dutch fleet sailed to Lisbon and declared war, but was halted in the Tagus by the Royal Navy and relations with Britain improved further in 1660 when King Charles II ascended the throne. In June 1661 a new treaty was agreed with England resulting in the marriage of Catherine of Braganza to the British monarch. She brought with her a huge dowry plus the territories of Tangiers and Bombay. 1661 also saw a peace with the Dutch, by which Portugal kept Brazil and its African possessions but ceded territories in the Orient. However, Spain was still troublesome and the southern town of Borba fell in 1662, with Évora following in 1663. Later that year, however, Schomberg's army won the battle of Ameixial and recovered Évora. His crowning victory over the Spaniards came in 1665 at Montes Claros and when Filipe III, (Spain's Felipe IV) died in 1666, his widow made peace with Portugal.

The influence of the Conde de Castelo-Melhor led Afonso to end the regency and the Count effectively ruled Portugal for five years until Afonso married Marie Françoise Isabelle de Savoie in 1666. She forced Castelo-Melhor to flee and join Catherine of Braganza in England in 1667. In November 1667 Marie left the king and entered a convent, but in 1668 a revolution resulted in Pedro, the king's brother, becoming regent. Marie then arranged a marriage annulment and married Pedro instead. Afonso was banished to the Azores and then Sintra, where he died in 1683, whilst Pedro ruled as regent until Afonso's death. Afonso was succeeded by Pedro II (1683-1706).

The Portuguese economy was now in poor condition despite the fact that in 1678 England had banned the import of French wine, and that from 1690 port and other Portuguese wines had entered England more freely. Attempts were made to reform industry, notably by the establishment of wool processing at Covilhã and Estremoz. Import restrictions were also applied and tanneries, glassworks and silk spinning mills were established. On the agricultural front maize was planted and the Douro vineyards were extended. In 1702 the Grand Alliance of England, Holland and Austria, united against France, forced Portugal to tow the line by means of the first Methuen Treaty of 1703. Portugal became embroiled in the War of the Spanish Succession and her troops even entered Madrid in 1706. The Methuen Treaty allowed English worsted goods into Portugal and facilitated the export of wine in reverse. But the French seized Serpa and Moura and won the battle of Valencia before peace was made. By the 1713 Peace of Utrecht Portugal gained safeguards against French claims in Brazil and Spain abandoned its claim to Sacramento in South America. The discovery of gold in Mato Grosso, Brazil in 1692 and a bigger find in Minas Gerais gave the economy a boost with the first 500kg cargo of gold reaching Lisbon

Introduction

in 1699. In 1728 diamonds were also discovered in Brazil near Ouro Preto and two million carats were produced by 1800.

18th Century

João V reigned from 1706-50 and was married to the sister of the Austrian Habsburg emperor. With the income from gold and diamonds João was able to rule as an absolutist, with little need of the *Cortes* for taxes. He spent vast sums on constructing a huge palace at Mafra, and on acquiring the Pope's agreement to creation of a patriarchy of Lisbon. His reign also saw the erection of magnificent buildings at Coimbra University and the Águas Livres aqueduct in Lisbon. Brazilian income, however, led to more English imports as home industries stagnated, although some, such as paper-making, were created at Lousã in 1717. Leather processing was also encouraged but a glass industry on the Tagus failed, only to be reopened more successfully at Marinha Grande in 1748. The longer-established silk industry, however, made losses.

However, the new monarch, José I (1750-77) was an idler who disregarded national problems, preferring to spend his time and money on opera and concerts. Government was left to the Marquis of Pombal who had entered government as Sebastião José de Carvalho e Melo in 1750. In politics, Pombal sought to diminish the power of the Jesuits and to promote the upper middle classes, a trend he had witnessed as a diplomat in London. His diplomatic experiences in Vienna brought new ideas of enlightened absolutism to Portugal whilst his reforms encouraged the promotion of Portuguese industries. He also sought to impose a levy on Brazilian gold imports, a trade which was, however, now declining and in 1750 he set about reforming the Upper Douro wine industry. His finest hour was after the Lisbon earthquake of 1 November 1755, in which more than 20,000 were killed and the centre of the Portuguese capital was destroyed by tremors and tidal waves. His methodical rebuilding of the *Baixa* area of Lisbon, using modular designs and anti-earthquake features, was testimony to his prowess as national leader. The consistency of building design underlined his desire to replace the ostentatious architecture of the Portuguese nobility with functional buildings for traders and merchants. In contrast to Pombal's calm authority, the king refused to sleep in a stone building for many years after the earthquake.

There was, nevertheless, a ruthless streak in Pombal and this was clearly seen after an assassination attempt on José I in 1758. The conspirators were rounded up and the Marquis of Távora, the Duke of Aveiro, his son the Marquis of Gouveia and others were savagely executed. Pombal outlawed the Jesuits and had one of its leaders, Gabriel Malagrida, executed. Censorship was imposed in 1768 and in 1772 university reforms were

Introduction

applied. Yet despite Pombal's actions, Portuguese trade remained in overall decline and when José I died, Pombal was swept from office. He lived out his remaining years in his palace at Oeiras, outside Lisbon.

The new ruler was Maria I (1777-1816) who married her uncle, who thus became Pedro III. She moved the royal court to the recently-built rococo palace of Queluz, to the north-west of the capital. Indeed, Maria presided over a period of palace-building in Lisbon, funded from Brazilian imports. In 1781 Pombal was arraigned before a court but escaped serious punishment, although he was required to keep twenty leagues away from the Royal Court. In his absence the country's economy stagnated as money was squandered by the Crown and nobility. Workers at the Lisbon Arsenal were sacked and popular pursuits such as bullfighting were banned. Ominously, trade with Brazil was opened up to other countries.

Peninsular War and Royal Exile

On the international front, in 1797 a Portuguese squadron assisted Nelson in the prelude to the Battle of the Nile, but in 1801, the Spanish leader, Godoy, initiated an invasion of Portugal. The Franco-Spanish Treaty of 1801 required Portugal to close her ports to Britain, which she was reluctant to do. Spain annexed several villages east of the River Guadiana in southern Portugal and although this territory should have been returned to Portugal by the 1814 Treaty of Paris, it never was. Portugal tried strenuously to retain its neutrality in the climate of Franco-British hostility but in 1802 the French general, Lannes, came to Lisbon to demand the expulsion of French royalist exiles from the country. Three years later, in 1805, General Junot required the Portuguese to side with France against the British, to close its ports to the Royal Navy and to arrest the members of the British *feitoria* (factory) in Lisbon. As the French forces closed in on Lisbon in 1807, the Portuguese royal family and an entourage of some 10,000 people fled by sea to Brazil, where the Portuguese Court was to remain until 1821 as the Peninsular War raged on.

In 1808 Spain rose against its French occupiers and with the help of Arthur Wellesley, later the Duke of Wellington, the French were driven out of Portugal following the battles of Roliça (Óbidos) and Vimeiro (1808). By the Convention of Sintra in 1808, the French were controversially allowed to leave Portugal with booty plundered from the country, on board British ships. In 1809 the British sent Beresford to reform the Portuguese army but that same year the French, under General Soult, invaded the Minho area of northern Portugal, taking Braga and Oporto before the forces of Wellesley drove him out. French progress towards Lisbon was stopped following Wellington's masterly creation of the defensive Lines of Torres Vedras, before which a scorched-earth policy was adopted to deprive the French of supplies.

Introduction

The establishment of the Royal Court in Brazil favoured that country's economy to the detriment of Portugal and in 1815 Brazil and Portugal were declared a united kingdom. Portugal was in a terrible state after the Peninsular War; 100,000 lives had been lost and much land had been despoiled. Brazil had seized much of Portugal's trade and seventy-five per cent of Portuguese national revenue was being expended on the army. In 1817 a Liberal uprising was put down and the leaders, including General Gomes Freire, executed. Nevertheless, a new middle class of army officers, lawyers and merchants was emerging as João VI (1816-26) returned from Brazil in 1821. He accepted a new liberal constitution, but his son, Pedro, remained in Brazil and led her to independence in 1822. Carlota Joaquina, João's queen, would not accept the constitution and was exiled to Ramalhão, outside Lisbon.

Liberal Revolution and Civil Wars

Following a rising in Oporto (1818) which spread to Lisbon, a *junta* took power in 1820 and set up a constituent parliament (*Cortes*) to subject the monarchy to its will. However, in 1823 the Count of Amarante and the north of the country declared itself against the liberal Constitution and on 24 June his 3,000 men entered Lisbon to a welcome by both King João and his third son, Dom Miguel. The king bestowed upon Amarante the title of Marquês de Chaves and Miguel marched on Santarém to reassert the monarchy' s 'inalienable rights' (1823). João repudiated the liberal Constitution and with the Miguelist absolutists in the ascendant, Queen Carlota Joaquina, had her rights restored. Indeed, by the end of April 1824, Miguel was strong enough to threaten his father's throne to such a degree that the monarch took refuge on HMS *Windsor Castle*, a Royal Navy ship, from which he dismissed Miguel as commander-in-chief of the army and exiled him to Vienna.

On 29 August 1825 Portugal recognized the independence of Brazil. On João's death in 1826 his successor Pedro IV was still in Brazil, so in Portugal a period of regency ensued under Princess Isabel Maria. On 2 May 1826 Pedro abdicated from the Portuguese throne in favour of his daughter Maria da Glória, aged seven. From Brazil, Pedro sent to Portugal his own *Carta Constitucional* (Constitutional Charter) through Sir Charles Stuart (1826). This document required his brother, Miguel, to marry Pedro's infant daughter and Miguel's own niece, Maria da Glória. In these circumstances, Pedro would abdicate the Portuguese throne and Miguel would become regent until Maria reached her maturity in 1837. Pedro's *Carta*, like the Brazilian constitution, was based on the 1814 French Constitution and accorded the sovereign the right to dissolve parliament and veto its decisions. It was a constitution granted by the monarch, rather than one imposed upon him. After some hesitation Isabel Maria, the regent, accepted

xxxvii

Introduction

the *Carta* on 24 July 1826, following threats of enforcement from the power-broker, Saldanha. The exiled Miguel also swore allegiance to the *Carta* on 4 October in Vienna and George Canning, was sent to Lisbon by Britain with a division, under General Clinton, to enforce the *Carta*.

It was the Marquis of Saldanha, grandson of Pombal, who effectively imposed the *Carta* which posited two chambers. As early as 4 October 1826 Miguel had been proclaimed king in the northern town of Vila Real by the Marquis of Chaves but the usurper did not return to Lisbon from Austria till 22 February 1828. He promptly dissolved the *Cortes* and had himself proclaimed King on 25 April. A liberal uprising in the north, in the Algarve, and in Terceira in 1828 was put down and many liberals fled to Bruges and to England, particularly, to Plymouth where 3,000 exiles gathered. On hearing of Miguel's usurpation, Pedro had Maria's ship diverted to England and renounced the marriage proposal to Miguel. From 1828 to 1830 Liberals controlled the Azores but Miguel's position in Portugal was strengthened in October 1829 when Spain recognized him as monarch. Pedro abdicated as Emperor in Brazil in 1831, in favour of his son, who became Emperor Pedro II. The ex-Emperor meanwhile headed for England, arriving on 26 January 1831 to a welcome from Lord Palmerston. Based in London's Clarendon Hotel, Pedro sought to raise funds and support to install Maria da Glória as Queen of Portugal. Liberal forces sailed from the Azores and with a force of 7,000 men they landed at Mindelo in 1832 and took Oporto. Miguel's 13,000-strong force besieged them there but eventually was obliged to withdraw, as the British flotilla lurked at nearby Foz. The ideological leaders of the Liberal movement included Alexandre Herculano, later to become his country's major historian, and Mousinho da Silveira. Further Liberal forces landed in the Algarve in 1833, led by the Duke of Terceira, and took Lisbon in July of that year. Miguel's surrender was formalised by the Treaty of Évora-Monte in March 1834, and he was once more exiled.

Although peace had been restored, the country's economy was in ruins. The State confiscated Church and nobles' property alike and in May 1834 Pedro even abolished all religious orders. The *Carta* had been implemented but Pedro died, aged thirty-six, in the royal palace at Sintra on 24 September 1834 whilst still acting as regent for Maria. His daughter, Maria II (1834-53), inherited serious political infighting, with the radical liberal *Setembristas* ascendant. Their aim was to restore the first *Carta* and, led by Passos Manuel, they rose up in 1836 against the more moderate *Cartistas*. A new 1838 Constitution sought to balance the more radical 1822 Constitution with the more sober Constitutional Charter of 1826. The 1838 Constitution reinforced the sovereign's power, allowing her to dissolve the chamber of deputies and by 1844 there were growing demands for a return to the monarchist charter of 1826.

Introduction

Maria's first husband, August von Leuchtenberg, died only a week after reaching Portugal in March 1835, so she married again in April 1836, this time to Ferdinand of Saxe-Coburg, cousin of Prince Albert, consort of Queen Victoria.

In September 1836, the *Setembristas* overcame their conservative rivals, the *Cartistas*, with Passos Manuel ruling as a virtual dictator. A new Constitution was in place from 1838 but, in 1844 Costa Cabral, the Minister of Justice, redeclared the 1826 *Carta*. His dynamism brought about administrative and educational reform and the establishment of such bodies as a national press and national theatre. However, Cabral created enemies and was overthrown in 1846; the country soon descended into civil war between the *Cartistas*, led by Saldanha, and the *Setembristas*. Although peace was reached in 1847, the country remained unstable. The *Cartistas* split into factions of Regenerators and Historicals, the latter group being led by the Duque de Loulé. On his death in 1875 a new Progressive Party was formed which was alternately to share power with the Regenerators from 1879 to 1906.

Mid- to late 19th Century

In November 1853, Maria died during the birth of her eleventh child, aged only thirty-four, and her husband Fernando acted as Regent as the crown prince, Pedro, was only sixteen. Pedro V (1853-61) took over from his father's regency in 1855, with a government led by Saldanha. Between 1834 and 1859 there were twenty-five governments and there were signs that Pedro's attitude to his duties would eventually make him a strong leader.

Apart from Lisbon and Oporto, the rest of Portugal was undeveloped. 1848 had seen the arrival of gaslights to Lisbon's streets and 1854 witnessed the establishment of Portugal's first telegraph station. The country's first railway line, 36km from Lisbon to Carregado, towards Santarém, opened on the King's birthday, 29 October 1856. Despite the natural disaster of floods in the Lisbon and Ribatejo area in 1856, the country proudly participated that year in the Grande Exposition de Paris, where its awards ranked it seventh of all the participants. However, a worse disaster was the Yellow Fever outbreak which hit Lisbon in 1851 and killed 18,000. In 1858 Pedro married the Princess Estefânia of Hohenzollern Signarigen who, after only fourteen months in Portugal, contracted diphtheria and died on 17 July 1859, just two years before Pedro himself succumbed to typhus on 11 November 1861. Two of his brothers also died of the disease but another, Luís I (1861-89), ascended the throne. He was in London when his brother died and a three-day regency, under the former consort Fernando, ensued, before Luís reached Lisbon. In 1862 he married the Italian princess, Maria Pia de Sabóia. Unlike his brother, Luís was more interested in the arts and literature

Introduction

than in affairs of State and he allowed politicians to augment their power in the land. By 1868 the Historicals, under Sá da Bandeira, were in power and took long overdue steps to cut the overblown civil service and civil list. Between 1871 and 1876 Fontes Pereira de Melo and the Regenerators embarked on a policy of economic expansion, but in 1876 there was a financial crash and three Lisbon banks folded. A measure of stability was afforded by the agreed rotation of power between Progressives and Regenerators from 1879.

Regicide and Revolution

Luís died on 19 October 1889. The 1880s had seen political rivalry between the Regenerators and the Progressives, with the Regenerators' leader, Fontes Pereira de Melo, holding power for twelve years of Luís's reign. The new king was twenty-six-year-old Carlos I (1889-1908) who was almost immediately confronted by a British Ultimatum (11 January 1890). This forced a withdrawal of the Portuguese from Mashonaland (Rhodesia, now Zimbabwe), a presence which Britain had seen as a threat to its own imperial plans. Widespread feelings of national humiliation at the hands of Britain did not enhance Carlos's appeal to his subjects. Indeed, Portuguese troops rose up in Oporto but were soon suppressed by loyal forces. British influence consequently waned and there was revived interest in French Republicanism, the origins of which can be traced back in Portugal to well before the Ultimatum. As early as 1871 the so-called *Conferências do Casino* (Lisbon Casino lectures) were organized by leading left-wing intellectuals, including the poet Antero de Quental, the novelist Eça de Queirós and the historian, Oliveira Martins. Many such figures felt that progress would best be achieved by a joining of the workers with the lower middle class. Republican fires had also been stoked by the 1880 celebrations to mark the tercentenary of the death of Camões, author of the national epic *Os Lusíadas* (The Lusiads). The celebrations became a focus for a re-examination of Portugal's history and contemporary decline.

However, even by 1900, the Republicans were still politically ineffectual and the Boer War (1899-1902) had led to an Anglo-Portuguese *rapprochement* and a new Treaty of Windsor. Reciprocal Anglo-Portuguese royal visits took place between London and Lisbon in 1902, 1903 and 1904. Indeed, between 1903 and 1907 there were also visits to Portugal from the monarchs of Spain, Germany, Denmark and Saxony, as well as from the French President. Such *bonhomie* could not conceal growing anti-monarchist feelings which were exacerbated by the poor state of the economy. By 1900 Portugal was £177 million in debt and its *per capita* debt of £35 was reputed to be the highest in Europe.

Introduction

In 1901 the Regenerative Party split into two factions and a schism within the Progressives resulted in four major parties, plus the newly formed Socialists, all vying for power. April 1906 saw a revolt on the cruiser *D. Carlos*, which was put down, and by May 1906 the king had installed the authoritarian João Franco to head his government. Following controversy regarding the financing of the monarchy, the *Cortes* were dissolved in 1907 and political bombings occurred in Lisbon. On 28 January 1908 the Republican leaders, Afonso Costa and Egas Moniz, were arrested along with 120 others in Lisbon and three days later the king signed a decree facilitating their transportation to Africa or Timor. At 5.30pm on 1 February 1908, the king and his family were attacked as their carriage turned out of Lisbon's Praça do Comércio into the Rua do Arsenal en route from their palace at Vila Viçosa. The forty-four-year-old king and the crown prince, Luís Filipe, were shot dead by Manuel da Silva Buíça and Alfredo Luís da Costa, but Prince Manuel and Queen Amélia escaped alive. In the aftermath, João Franco was sacked.

Manuel II (1908-10), King Carlos's second son, was thus catapulted to the throne in violent circumstances and amidst political turmoil. Unrest continued, despite Manuel's attempts to introduce social reforms, and the thirty months of his reign witnessed seven governments. Nevertheless, Manuel felt able to undertake a royal visit to Spain and Great Britain in November 1909 but in the August 1910 elections the Republicans won eleven seats, seven of them in Lisbon. On 4 October 1910 the Necessidades royal palace, in western Lisbon, was bombarded and Manuel fled, via Mafra and the fishing port of Ericeira to a life of exile at Fulwell Park, Twickenham in the London suburbs. A double irony of the Revolution was that on 3 October one of the foremost Republicans, Dr Miguel Bombarda, was murdered by a mental patient in his office at the Rilhafoles mental hospital in Lisbon and in the morning of 4 October, Admiral Cândido dos Reis, a leader of the rising, believing the revolt to have failed, committed suicide. Thirty hours after his body had been found the Republic was proclaimed by José Relvas from the balcony of Lisbon's Town Hall.

The Republic, 1910-26

Between 5 October 1910 and 31 May 1926 there were nine presidencies and forty-five governments as well as a number of political assassinations, including those of two prime ministers, Sidónio Pais (1918) and António Granjo (1921). Although some significant cultural progress was made, such as the founding of Lisbon and Oporto universities in April 1911, there were also widespread strikes by 1912. In July 1912 Captain Henrique de Paiva Couceiro, who had commanded machine guns against the 1910 revolutionaries in Lisbon, led a royalist invasion of northern Portugal from

Introduction

Spain. Despite the town of Vila Real re-proclaiming the monarchy, Couceiro was soon forced to withdraw. A second uprising by Paiva Couceiro, with 1,000 men, also failed when 120 of them were killed in only two hours near Chaves in northern Portugal. As well as from the Right, the Republicans also faced opposition by 1913 from the Socialists, although a uprising against Afonso Costa was put down in April of that year. In 1914 such was the chaos that President Arriaga was forced to call on the military for assistance and General Pimenta de Castro was drafted in to lead the executive. Nevertheless, June 1916 saw symbolic changes as the new Portuguese flag of red and green was adopted, replacing the blue and white of the monarchy, and Alfredo Kiel's *A Portuguesa* became the new national anthem. In addition, the currency unit was changed from the *real* to the escudo.

But, as the First World War raged in northern Europe, Costa's attempts to protect Portugal's colonies by joining the Allies were initially rebuffed by Britain which possibly saw those territories falling into its hands if Portugal remained on the sidelines. However, in March 1916 at Britain's behest, Portugal seized seventy German ships moored in Portuguese harbours, prompting the Germans to declare war on Portugal. As the war progressed, with Portuguese troops notably involved in the Battle of Lys, there was continued unrest in Lisbon. In May 1917, thirty people were killed in Lisbon during a period of civil commotion and looting. The country was reduced to a state of near famine and on 5 December 1917, General Sidónio Pais staged a coup, but he himself faced naval bombardment of the Castelo de São Jorge in Lisbon by January 1918. Even though subsequent elections confirmed him as President, with support of Catholics, monarchists, the lower middle classes and those opposed to the Great War, Pais felt that parliamentary democracy had failed and that a more presidential style was required. However, shortly before midnight on 14 December 1918, he was assassinated at Rossio railway station in Lisbon.

In Oporto in January 1919 Paiva Couceiro again proclaimed the monarchy and support rallied to him in the northern towns of Braga, Guimarães, Viana do Castelo, Vila Real, Braganza, Viseu and Lamego before the 'monarchy in the north' movement was put down on 13 February 1919. A national strike took place in June 1919 and in an eight-month period of 1921 there were four governments. Indeed, over 200 major strikes occurred between 1917 and 1923 and the cost of living rose by 200 per cent. Instability grew as a maverick military band rounded up leading politicians including the prime minister, Granjo, and executed him and others at Lisbon's Arsenal on 19 October 1921. The Portuguese Navy stationed warships in the Tagus, off Lisbon and in these volatile political circumstances, compounded by deep economic depression, it is not surprising that a military dictatorship soon ensued. Following a *coup d'état* by General Gomes da Costa on 28 May 1926, he and General Cabeçadas

Introduction

successively assumed the presidency but, after their brief tenures, it was General António Óscar de Fragoso Carmona who brought stability with a presidency that ran from his election in April 1928 until his death in 1951.

Estado Novo (1926-74)

The dictatorship began with the deportation in 1926-27 of some 600 politicians to the Azores, Cape Verde islands and Angola. The volatile atmosphere can be gauged from the fact that all of the governments between 1926 and 1933 were led by a General. However, in April 1928, António de Oliveira Salazar, was plucked from academic life at Coimbra University and installed by Carmona as Finance Minister. Although Salazar brought fiscal probity to government, the country was rocked by the 'Portuguese Banknote Case', a *cause célèbre* which ended in 1930 with Artur Virgilio Alves dos Reis being found guilty of obtaining 200,000 five-hundred escudo banknotes illicitly from British printers, Waterlows. Nevertheless, Salazar's budgetary success was such that in 1932 he was invited to become prime minister and form a government. In March 1933 a plebiscite approved Salazar's constitution; the *Estado Novo* (New State) was thereby established. The *Estado Novo* was anti-parliamentary, anti-communist and nationalistic. It openly placed individual rights in a subsidiary position to the interests of the State. Under this regime, the President answered to the people and was elected by direct universal suffrage and the government answered to him, rather than to the parliament. Parliamentary candidates were chosen by the *União Nacional* (National Union), the only authorised political organization. Within the Corporative Assembly, each trade guild had a number of allotted seats and its members handled Portugal's socio-economic affairs. Their views were passed to the legislature, the National Assembly, whose members were elected by heads of families for a four-year period. Whilst the President could veto the National Assembly's legislation, this could be resubmitted and, if passed by a two-thirds majority, would become law. Whilst the Corporative Assembly met in public, the National Assembly did not. The 1932 Constitution was modelled on various antecedents, including that of the Weimar Republic, but also took heed of Roman Catholic social policy and the home-grown philosophy of *Integralismo Lusitano*. It replaced the Revolutionary Constitution of 1911 which had been overturned in May 1926 when the military took power. Ironically, 1932 was also the year in which the last Portuguese king, Manuel II, died in Twickenham where he had spent his exile amassing a collection of rare books.

Perhaps the most overtly fascist aspect of the *Estado Novo* was the *Legião Portuguesa* (Portuguese Legion), established in September 1936 as an unarmed body to counter the threat of communism. *Legião* members were

Introduction

aged seven to eighteen years and would normally move onto their military service obligations. Across the border in Spain, the Communist Party was embroiled in the Spanish Civil War (1936-39) and on 8 September 1936 government forces in Lisbon were obliged to open fire on two of their own Navy's ships as they prepared to sail and join the Spanish Republicans. In Portugal, resistance to the *Estado Novo* continued, with a bomb attack on Salazar himself as he went to mass in Lisbon in July 1937. Salazar declared neutrality during the Second World War.

The only dissent officially permitted in the *Estado Novo* was before presidential elections when opposition candidates were sanctioned. These, nevertheless, were normally military figures themselves, such as General Norton de Matos who stood, unsuccessfully, against Carmona in 1949. However, in 1951 Carmona died and General Francisco Craveiro Lopes was elected to succeed him. His brief term ended in 1958 when he was replaced by Admiral Américo Rodrigues Tomás whose opponent in the presidential elections of 1958 was Brigadier Humberto Delgado. Tomás triumphed, the official voting figures giving him 77.5 per cent of the votes against Delgado's 22.5 per cent. Delgado continued to be a thorn in the side of Salazar and was exiled and subsequently murdered in Spain. International attention was called to the oppressive nature of the *Estado Novo* by the daring hijack on the high seas of the liner *Santa Maria*, off Venezuela in 1961. The leading figure in this dramatic gesture was Henrique Galvão, a former military commander in Portuguese Africa.

The *Estado Novo* bolstered its standing amongst its citizens by propaganda. Street posters told the Portuguese that 'Portugal is not a small country' and showed a map of western Europe onto which were superimposed the outlines of its substantial colonial territories. In the early 1960s the first moves for independence arose in Angola and, in 1961, taking advantage of these, the Indian government asserted its geographically strong but historically weak claim to the enclaves of Goa, Diu and Damão, which had been in Portuguese hands for over four centuries. Portugal's alliance with Britain served for nothing as the Macmillan government allowed the Indian Army's seizure to be consolidated. At home that year there was also an abortive uprising in the Alentejan town of Beja. Although many Africans, especially Cape Verdeans, arrived in Portugal to work predominantly as labourers in Lisbon, unrest continued to grow in these territories during the 1960s, despite Portuguese claims of racial harmony. By 1964, about forty per cent of the national budget was being expended on sending troops to the African territories where, by the late 1960s, civil wars were being fought in Angola, Mozambique and Portuguese Guinea. Although the *Estado Novo* period witnessed urban and industrial growth, as well as public works, such as roads, bridges, airports, courts, hospitals, museums, barracks and post offices, economic progress lagged behind that of western Europe, wages remained low, censorship operated and protest marches were banned. Nevertheless, the *Estado Novo* did introduce five-year economic plans. The first two of these plans (1953 and 1959) concentrated on the country's infrastructure, with the construction of hydroelectric dams and improvements being made to communications in the 1950s and 1960s. Six dams were built on the River Cávado, north of Oporto, whilst others were erected at Castelo do Bode on the Zêzere river from 1952, as well as on the Rivers Ave and Douro at Miranda and Picote, near the Spanish border. Benefiting from such improvements and from protectionism, large companies grew up, notably the nationalized conglomerate, CUF (Companhia União Fabril), founded in 1865. CUF came to dominate in fields as diverse as chemicals, textiles and cigarettes by the 1970s, whilst SACOR held a virtual monopoly in the petroleum industry.

1974 Revolution

In 1968, Salazar fell from a deckchair and was obliged by resultant incapacity to give way as prime minister to Marcello Caetano. Despite some attempts at liberalization, the toll of the African wars continued. By early 1974 dissent had spread to the armed forces and was epitomized by the publication of General António de Spínola's *Portugal e o futuro* (Portugal and the future) which proposed greater autonomy for Portugal's colonies. The end for the *Estado Novo* came on 25 April 1974 when a military uprising overthrew the regime. Only four people were killed, in a skirmish at the Lisbon HQ of the security police, the DGS.

The first President of the new Republic was General António de Spínola (1910-) but within months he had been replaced by the more left-wing General Francisco da Costa Gomes (1914-) who presided over a period of political turmoil, as the far Left sought to gain power. The country lurched to the Left, with Communist and other Marxist-Leninist factions much in evidence. A form of counter-coup occurred in September 1975, following which the Constitution of 25 April 1976 brought about the establishment of a western-style capitalist democracy. The Constitution has since been amended in October 1982, June 1989, November 1992 and September 1997. Portugal's legislature is a unicameral assembly of 230 members who are elected for four-year periods and its civil law system is overseen by a Supreme Tribunal of Justice.

In 1976 a relatively young General, António Ramalho Eanes (1935-), was elected as President and subsequently re-elected in 1981, only leaving office in March 1986 when the country's first post-revolution civilian president, the former Socialist Party leader Mário Soares (1924-), was elected. Eanes's legacy was political stability and economic progress. In 1986 Portugal was admitted to the EC and the country is also a member of

Introduction

the FAO, GATT, IEA, ILO, IMF, NATO, OECD, UN, WHO and UNESCO. Soares remained in power until 1996 when the former Socialist mayor of Lisbon, Jorge Sampaio, won the presidency for a five-year term. The centre-right's Aníbal Cavaco e Silva was prime minister from 1987 and was re-elected in 1991 when his social-democratic PSD party won fifty per cent of the vote compared to the Socialists' 29.3 per cent share. However, the Socialists regained power in the 1995 elections and their prime minister, António Guterres, retained it, albeit without an absolute majority, in the polls of 10 October 1999.

Economy and EU Aid

Since the 1974 Revolution a free-market capitalist economy has been established. But despite growth in manufacturing, wages and productivity have remained low and much energy is still imported. Inherited deficiencies in infrastructure have been addressed since 1974, particularly in the fields of power supply, water, telecommunications and roads. The health and education systems have been modernized and, perhaps most importantly, the country has received large amounts of inward investment from the European Union. Indeed, in 1996, ten years after joining the European Union, Portugal received 505 billion escudos (£1.84 billion) which made it one of largest *per capita* recipients of EU funds. EU-funded projects in the Lisbon area alone included the Vasco da Gama bridge construction, renovation of the docks, expansion of the Metro system and upgrading of railway lines. But the country has also transformed itself; in 1998, the IMF cited Portugal as the only country in the EU which had cut its public deficit whilst increasing public expenditure.

The Portuguese economy today is dominated by service industries, which account for fifty-eight per cent of the Gross Domestic Product (GDP), whilst the industrial sector provides thirty-six per cent of the GDP and thirty-two per cent of employment. The national GDP rose annually by an average of 4.4 per cent between 1951 and 1960, prior to the African wars, and by 4.7 per cent per annum from 1985 to 1991. Although this rate declined to 2.8 per cent between 1991 and 1995, it rose again to 3.8 per cent by 1998, against an EU average of 1.5 per cent (1991-95). Latterly this has been because of high inward investment, strong exports and greater internal demand. On 1 January 1993 Portugal fully liberalized its capital markets and most trade markets. Portuguese GDP in 1996 was $US107 billion. The *per capita* GDP in 1996 was $US10,270. In 1998 the Portuguese budget deficit was 2.4 per cent (compared with the Maastricht guideline of three per cent); the country's public debt was sixty-two per cent (guideline sixty per cent) and inflation was running at 2.2 per cent per annum (guideline two per cent).

Introduction

The reasons for recent growth in the Portuguese economy are many. They include: the removal of trade barriers; the receipt of EU grants which has helped to fund a vast construction boom and improvements to the nation's infrastructure; increased foreign investment, as in the motor construction industry; privatization; and improved competitiveness. In both economic and employment terms, the traditional spheres of agriculture and fishing have been in decline, with rural drift to the cities increasing. By 1995 this sector accounted for only twelve per cent of all employment and six per cent of GDP. Portugal still has many small, inefficient farms and has to import more than half of its food requirements. Today, wheat, rye, barley, oats and maize are the main crops, but in the Algarve crops of fruit and nuts are also significant, whilst grapes are widely grown in northern Portugal, often on large estates of stepped terraces in the Douro and neighbouring valleys. Despite the advent of the plastic wine-bottle closure, Portugal remains the world leader in cork production, with sixty per cent of the world market, the major output being from the Alentejo region, south-east of Lisbon. Portuguese fishing products include canned sardines, cod and tunny but the Portuguese White Fleet, which sought cod off the Newfoundland coast, has become a casualty of tightening regulation.

Trade

Eighty per cent of Portugal's trade is with member states of the European Union, with other major trading partners being the United States, Japan and the EFTA countries. Imports exceeded exports in the 1990-96 period and its chief trading partners were Germany, Spain, France, the United Kingdom, Italy and the Netherlands. Portugal was a founder member of EFTA and in recent years has been building up trade with its former African territories, although only 2.6 per cent of its exports and 1.3 per cent of imports are with those countries. This compares with trade with the United States which accounts for 4.6 per cent of Portuguese exports and 3.2 per cent of its imports. However, Portugal remains the most dependent country in western Europe on petroleum imports and other major imports include machinery and consumer durables.

Industry

Portuguese industrial output rose three per cent in 1996 against the EU average of 1.6 per cent. The traditional industrial manufacturing centres remain in the Lisbon and Oporto areas, with products which include shoes, cork, china, glass, paper, textiles, and the processing of olive oil and sugar. Recently, Portugal has seen the expansion of the electrical goods and motor construction industries, aided by its low labour costs. Indeed, the country is

Introduction

now Europe's leading exporter of minivans following three billion dollars of investment by Ford and Volkswagen. Although exports of textiles and clothing as well as of wood, cork, paper and pulp, exceed imports of those products, overall the country imports more agricultural products, chemicals and food than it exports. Of the more traditional Portuguese industries, textile manufacture has been modernized and is still the most significant of the longstanding commercial activities, with cotton mills particularly active in the northern areas of Oporto, Braga and Guimarães. Ceramic tile manufacture, exemplified by Vista Alegre at Aveiro, and other factories at Sacavém, also retains an important position, as does the wool industry in the Beiras Alta and Baixa. The timber industry produces pine for building and resin for pitch and turpentine, of which substance Portugal is a leading world producer. Eucalyptus is widely grown for both paper production and cellulose. The Margueira shipyard installation, built across the river from Lisbon by Lisnave using Swedish and Dutch capital, is still an important repair facility on the Atlantic shipping routes.

Natural Resources

Portugal's natural resources are varied but not prodigious in quantity. Tungsten, zinc, copper and marble are important, but there are also other significant national metallic ore deposits, albeit fairly poor in quality and now largely exhausted. However, tin and tungsten are to be found at Fundão and Panasqueira in central Portugal and there are reserves of iron ore at Torre de Moncorvo which are not currently exploited. Aljustrel and S. Domingos have copper pyrites and iron, and at Urgeiriça (central Portugal) there is a significant uranium deposit. The country's main coal beds are at Cabo Mondego, S. Pedro da Cova (near Oporto) and Pejão. Limestone, china clay and granite mining are also active industries, but mining in general is in decline. Exploration for terrestrial natural gas has also enjoyed some success. Portugal has abundant sources of mineral waters in the Gerês area and at Pedras Salgadas (bicarbonates) whilst sulphurous waters are found at Vizela and Caldas da Rainha, and saline waters are exploited at Luso and Sertã.

By 1998, arable land comprised thirty-four per cent of the country, with permanent crops utilizing a further six per cent and another six per cent occupied by meadow or pasture lands. Afforested land and woodland accounted for thirty-nine per cent of the countryside, leaving fifteen per cent in use for building and other purposes.

Infrastructure

Portugal's major ports are all on estuaries and in descending order of importance are Lisbon (on the River Tagus), Leixões (on the River Leça),

Introduction

Setúbal (River Sado) and Sines. Leixões is an artificial harbour created in 1886-92, four miles from Oporto. In terms of total tonnage, Sines is the major port, not least due to its extensive connections to refinery pipelines. The Portuguese merchant fleet comprised fifty-one ships of 1,000GRT or more in 1993. Portugal has 820km of navigable inland waterways (1993) accessible to vessels of shallow draft or 300 metric ton cargo capacity.

Railways came relatively late to Portugal, with the first line being built between Lisbon and Carregado in 1856. By 1932 there were 3,450km of track, which had risen to 3,625km in 1993, of which 2,858km were 1.665m gauge, 755km were metre-gauge and 12km was 1.435m gauge; 434km of line were electrified and 426km were double track. A number of closures have taken place in the post-1974 era, notably of the valley lines in the northern interior, but new lines have been created, most notably that across the Tagus at Lisbon which opened in 1999. Although heavily used, public transport usage is in decline from 208 million journeys in 1993 to 177 million in 1996.

National road length was 73,661km in 1996, of which 61,599km were surfaced by bitumen, gravel or crushed stone. 710km of this total was motorway, an increase of 131km since 1993. However, carnage on Portuguese roads is horrendous; 2,100 people were killed and 66,627 injured in mainland Portugal in 1996, even though the speed limit is 120kph (74mph).

TAP-Air Portugal was founded in 1944 and is one of the world's safest airlines, having experienced only one major accident. TAP provides services, with a fleet of mostly Airbuses, to the United States and Britain, as well as throughout western Europe and to the Portuguese-speaking countries of Africa and Brazil. Domestic services are operated by TAP, Portugália and Aero Condor. The country has sixty-four airports of which thirty-six have permanent runways, but only two have runways of more than 3,659 metres. Lisbon airport, Portela de Sacavém, was built between 1938 and 1942, to replace the former Granja do Marquês airport, near Sintra. Today it handles 7,998,500 passengers and 99,514 aircraft movements (1998) but despite recent extensions and refurbishment, its future is threatened by its proximity to the city centre (7km) and plans for a new airport at Ota, some 50km away, have been proposed. The other major Portuguese civil airport facilities are at Oporto, which handled 14,547 arrivals and 972,000 passengers in 1996 and at Faro in the Algarve. Domestic airports include Bragança (Braganza) and Vila Real in the north of the country.

Society

Unemployment, which stood at 10.4 per cent in 1983, dropped to 4.7 per cent by 1993 but these figures concealed a lot of underemployment and low

Introduction

wages. The implementation of the Euro monetary unit may make local workers realize how badly paid they are, though in general the workforce is unskilled and has low productivity. Portugal has a significant racial mixture, with 200,000 ethnic Africans in Lisbon alone and even a national Africa Culture Day on 16 May each year. In addition, following the 1974 Revolution, large numbers of *retornados* (European Portuguese) returned to Portugal from Africa, fleeing the civil wars. These were joined by many Asians who had settled in Mozambique. There are also some 20,000 Brazilians resident in Lisbon. Portugal shares many of Europe's social problems, not least drugs which enter the country from Africa and Spain especially. The homeless are also in evidence and a magazine, *Cais*, is the equivalent of Britain's *Big Issue*.

Culture

In 1994 Lisbon was appointed the European Capital of Culture and Oporto will have the same honour in 2001. In 1998, to mark the 500th anniversary of Vasco da Gama's rounding of the Cape of Good Hope, an international exhibition, Expo '98, was held on reclaimed dock and industrial land in north-eastern Lisbon outskirts and was a great success. Four of the pavilions remain in use, including Europe's largest oceanarium and the *Feira Internacional de Lisboa*, (a commercial exhibition centre). Also on the site is a major shopping centre and a new international railway station, the *Estação do Oriente* (Eastern Station), whose striking design by the architect Santiago Calatrava makes it a landmark as well as an important transport hub. Portugal's previous attempt at such an event, the 1940 Expo at Belém was blighted by the Second World War.

Arts

José Saramago (1922-) became Portugal's first Nobel Prize-winner for Literature in 1998 and Paula Rego, though resident in London, has put Portuguese modern art on the map. The Portuguese architect Álvaro Siza has also achieved international fame. 'Fátima, Football and *Fado*' (folk music) were often said to be Salazar's stratagems for diverting popular unrest. In recent years these diversions have enjoyed mixed fortunes. The once-mighty Benfica football club, for example, is racked by financial scandal and falling crowds. Nevertheless, in terms of membership of sports clubs or societies, football still leads the way, followed by basketball, handball, gymnastics and, surprisingly, pigeon-fancying. *Fado* has as its chief theme *saudade* (longing, nostalgia) and often has maritime associations. Its origins are still uncertain, with claims made for both African or Brazilian antecedents. *Fado* employs the *guitarra* and *viola* (Spanish acoustic guitar) and has two

Introduction

schools. In Coimbra *fado* is the preserve of university students who ply sentimental themes, whereas the Lisbon variant is a more popular genre with violence, betrayals and murders as common themes. *Fado*'s great exponents included Maria Severa, a gipsy who died at the age of twenty-six in 1846, and in recent times, Amália Rodrigues (1920-). Other contemporary exponents include Nuno da Câmara Pereira, João Braga and Carlos do Carmo, whilst in Coimbra a leading light is Dr Fernando Machado Soares. Popular culture now includes *telenovelas* (soap operas), a genre introduced from Brazil, and pop music, which has prompted a rash of nightclubs, not least in the abandoned areas of Lisbon's dockland. Portugal now has four television channels (RTP1, and 2 and the independent SIC and RT-I). Including its autonomous regions, Portugal has twenty-four daily morning newspapers but only three daily evening papers. Overall newspaper readership is 360,199,854 (1996), whilst Portuguese libraries boast 31,227,863 documents.

Tourism has brought prosperity and development especially to the Algarve. However, even the religious basilica of Fátima continues to attract five million pilgrims a year (1998/99). Overall there were 23,252,000 tourist arrivals in 1996, an increase on 20,742,000 in 1992, and the Expo '98 attractions brought even more people to Portugal.

Today and the Future

Although it avoided direct involvement in the Second World War, Portugal endured two revolutions, protracted colonial wars and fifty years of dictatorship during the 20th century. Despite the traumatic loss in 1974/75 of overseas territories held for almost 500 years and the economic and social chaos following the 1974 Revolution, Portugal's accession to the European Communities has transformed the country economically and socially. Political stability has been achieved with democratically elected governments now providing citizens with unprecedented standards of living. Despite these momentous and rapid advances, Portugal has largely come to terms with the sudden loss of its empire and is justifiably proud of its transcontinental heritage and historical achievements. Recent events, such as the successful Expo '98 trade fair, the award to José Saramago of the Nobel Prize for Literature and the designation of both Lisbon and Oporto as European Cultural Capitals, in 1994 and 2001 respectively, underline Portugal's emergence as a vibrant and active participant in the regeneration of Europe.

Rulers of Portugal

Kings

House of Burgundy
1139-85	Afonso (Henriques) I
1185-1211	Sancho I
1211-23	Afonso II
1223-48	Sancho II
1248-79	Afonso III
1279-1325	Dinis
1325-57	Afonso IV
1357-67	Pedro I
1367-83	Fernando I
1383-85	*Interregnum*

House of Aviz
1385-1433	João I
1433-38	Duarte
1438-81	Afonso V
1481-95	João II
1495-1521	Manuel I
1521-57	João III
1557-78	Sebastião
1578-80	Henrique

Union of Crowns with Spain
1580-98	Filipe I (Felipe II of Spain)
1598-1621	Filipe II (Felipe III of Spain)

Rulers of Portugal

1621-40	Filipe III (Felipe IV of Spain)

House of Braganza

1640-56	João IV
1656-67	Afonso VI
1667-1706	Pedro II
1706-50	João V
1750-77	José I
1777-86	Maria I and Pedro III
1786-1816	Maria I
1816-26	João VI
1826	Pedro IV
1826-28	Maria II (deposed)
1828-34	Miguel I
1834-53	Maria II (restored)
1853-61	Pedro V
1861-89	Luís I
1889-1908	Carlos I
1908-10	Manuel II

Presidents

First Republic

1910-11	Teófilo Braga
1911-15	Manuel de Arriaga
1915	Teófilo Braga
1915-17	Bernardino Machado
1918	Sidónio Pais
1918-19	Admiral João do Canto e Castro
1919-23	António José de Almeida
1923-25	Manuel Teixeira Gomes
1925-26	Bernardino Machado
1926	Commander José Mendes Cabeçadas
1926	General Manuel Gomes da Costa
1926-51	General António Óscar de Fragoso Carmona (António de Oliveira Salazar, prime minister 1932-68)
1951-58	General Francisco Craveiro Lopes
1958-74	Admiral Américo Tomás (Marcelo Caetano, prime minister 1968-74)

Rulers of Portugal

Second Republic
1974	General António de Spínola
1974-76	General Francisco da Costa Gomes
1976-86	General António Ramalho Eanes
1986-96	Mário Soares
1996-	Jorge Sampaio

The Country and Its People

General

1 Portugal: gateway to greatness.
W. J. Barnes.   London: Edward Stanford Limited, 1950. 188p. 11 maps.

A photographically illustrated introduction to the history and the contemporary way of life of the Portuguese people in an era before the impact of mass tourism and economic development had affected the country. The text combines effectively a wealth of factual information on Portugal with a more subjective interpretation of its daily life. An appendix provides a useful reference list of the dynastic houses and rulers of the country.

2 Lisboa: Lisbon, past and present; Lisboa, historia y presente; Lissabon, Gestern und Heute.
Marina Tavares Dias, translated by Dionísio Martínez Soler, Klemens Detering.   Lisbon: Quimera, 1998. 122p.

After brief, successive introductions in English, Spanish and German, the remainder of this colourful introduction to the Portuguese capital has parallel texts in the same three languages. The book imparts a wealth of socio-historical information on the city and is illustrated by many old postcards, drawings and photographs as well as contemporary views. As such it is an ideal volume for the visitor who wishes to go beyond the normal tourist guide to discover more about the city of Lisbon.

3 Progressive Portugal.
Ethel C. Hargrove.   London: T. Werner Laurie Ltd, c.1914. 276p. map. bibliog.

A Fellow of the Royal Geographical Society, Ethel Hargrove visited Portugal in 1913 as one of a party of British journalists invited by the Sociedade Propaganda de Portugal. Although marred by editorial carelessness in the transcription of Portuguese names (e.g. 'Sumthal' instead of 'Quental'), the book's thirty-three chapters and detailed appendices

The Country and Its People. General

provide an excellent introduction to Republican Portugal. Particular strengths are the reviews of the artistic, literary and journalistic situation of the country in the early years of the Portuguese Republic, which are enhanced by Hargrove's meetings with such leading artists as Columbano Bordalo Pinheiro and Alberto Sousa. Her travels took her through much of the country and are illustrated by seventeen pages of photographs of people and places.

4   Iberian identity: essays on the nature of identity in Portugal and Spain.
Edited by Richard Herr, John H. R. Polt.   Berkeley, California: Institute of International Studies, 1989. 243p. bibliog. (Research Series, no. 75).

The papers in this volume derive from a Conference on Iberian Identity, held at Berkeley in 1987 and attended by academics from both Iberia and the United States. Amongst the topics covered are regional identity in Portugal by João de Pina-Cabral, 'State, nation and regional diversity in Portugal' by Rui Graça Feijó and 'Portugal: European, Hispanic or *sui generis?*' by Francis M. Rogers. Most of the papers have bibliographies appended to them.

5   The Portuguese: the land and its people.
Marion Kaplan.   Harmondsworth, England: Penguin Books, 1998. rev. ed. 391p. maps. bibliog.

A pot-pourri of information on Portugal for the inquisitive English-speaking reader is provided here as Marion Kaplan sets out to bring together a wealth of factual information which she rightly judged was hitherto unavailable in a single volume. The book's twelve chapters are thus a valuable introduction to the country, its people, their history and culture. The book is illustrated by monochrome photographs and excellent bibliographies, which reflect Kaplan's wide reading, accompany each of the chapters. A useful list of Portuguese monarchs and presidents is also provided.

6   We, the future.
Eduardo Lourenço, photographs by Jorge Molder.   Lisbon: Portuguese Pavilion Expo 98/ Assírio & Alvim, 1997. 31p. + photographs. (Notebooks on the Portuguese Pavilion).

An essay in which the celebrated Portuguese philosopher and literary theoretician Eduardo Lourenço concludes that to get to its future, Portugal 'will have to relive her past as an active, ever revisited and even reinvented, memory'. A bizarre sequence of photographs, ending with a pair of bare feet, completes the volume. This is one of a series of tomes produced to commemorate the Expo '98 event in Lisbon but it also serves to bring the somewhat esoteric writing of Lourenço to an English-speaking audience.

The Country and Its People. Books of photographs

7 Portugal, institutions and facts.
Guilherme d'Oliveira Martins, translated by Maria Teresa Pereira Martins. Lisbon: Comissariado para a Européalia 91 Portugal/ Imprensa Nacional-Casa da Moeda, 1991. 185p. bibliog. (Synthesis of Portuguese Culture).

A most accessible description of contemporary Portuguese institutions is provided in this handy volume. Written in 200 numbered paragraphs, the topics covered include the Portuguese Constitution, the country's administrative, electoral, fiscal, educational and social security systems, as well as its economic organization and its cultural policies. In contrast, an appraisal of the final years of the *Estado Novo* is to be found in *Introducing Portugal* (Lisbon: Office of the Secretary of State for Tourism, General Direction for Information, 1972. 117p.), which is an uncritical but nevertheless very useful overview of Portugal and her overseas territories. Copious black-and-white photographs illustrate the twelve chapters which cover Situation, Territory and Population, History, Religion, Political Organization, Education, The Economy, Communications, Social Policy, Health and Assistance, Culture, Tourism and Folk Festivals. The book is also a good source of official statistics of population, trade and industrial output.

8 Portugal and the sea: a world embraced.
A. J. R. Russell-Wood, photographs by Michael Teague.   Lisbon: Portuguese Pavilion Expo '98/ Assírio & Alvim, 1997. 95p. bibliog. (Notebooks on the Portuguese Pavilion).

In this companion volume to item no. 6, the historian A. J. R. Russell-Wood sets out to survey concisely Portugal's remarkable relationship with the sea, starting from the fact that no Portuguese citizen lives more than 218km from the Atlantic and that the 832km of the 2,047km of the country's borders are coastline. He reviews the early voyages of discovery and the subsequent maintenance of Portugal's empire across the oceans over a period of 500 years. Monochrome photographs depict Portuguese possessions in Africa, Asia and the mid-Atlantic.

9 Cultures of the world: Portugal.
Time Editions.   Singapore: Times Editions, 1997. 128p. maps.

This volume is one in the Time Editions series, with a text by Jay Heale. It is heavily illustrated in both colour and black-and-white and provides an attractive, if not particularly innovative, overview of Portuguese culture.

Books of photographs

10 Lisboa e os seus arredores. (Lisbon and its hinterland.)
Pilar Alonso, Albert Gil, translated by Artur Lopes Cardoso.   Rio de Mouro, Portugal: Everest Editora, 1997. 80p. maps.

Based on an original Spanish edition, this is a high-quality photographic survey of Lisbon and its neighbouring tourist sights, which include Sintra, Queluz and Cascais. There is

The Country and Its People. Books of photographs

relatively little text and what exists is presented without chapter breaks. Clear and colourful folding card maps of the city are included in the front and back covers.

11 Cities of Europe: Oporto and Lisbon. Reprodução facsimilada do original bilingue, inglês e francês, com tradução em português.
(Facsimile reproduction of the original bilingual English and French edition, with a translation into Portuguese.)
Robert Batty. Lisbon: Instituto da Biblioteca Nacional e do Livro, Imprensa Nacional-Casa da Moeda, 1996. 119p.

Born in 1780, Batty studied medicine at Cambridge before fighting at the Battle of Waterloo. His subsequent publication of *Select views of some of the principal cities of Europe from original paintings by Lieut. Coll. Batty FRS, with illustrative notices* (London: Moon, Boys and Graves, 1832) included twelve watercolours by him of Lisbon and Oporto, which are here handsomely reproduced. Accompanying each coloured engraving is the artist's outline panorama of the same scene with a key denoting the geographical features which appear in the painting. In addition to a photographic reproduction of the English and French texts, a Portuguese version is also provided.

12 Portugal.
Alberto Bertolazzi, translated by Barbara Fisher. Twickenham, England: Tiger Books International, 1998. 128p.

A collection of attractive colour photographs, originally published as an Italian compilation entitled *Portogallo fra Europa e Atlantico* (Vercelli, Italy: Edizioni White Star, 1998). After a short introduction the photographs are presented, with captions, in three broad categories which effectively comprise: views of the rural and coastal landscape; images of the metropolises [*sic*], which include Lisbon, Oporto and Braga; and pictures of Portuguese people going about their lives.

13 O Porto em vários sentidos: Oporto's many sides.
Agustina Bessa-Luís, photographs by Nicolas Sapieha, translated by Richard Zimler. Lisbon: Quetzal, 1998. 155p.

A coffee-table book of colour photographs of Portugal's second city, the northern port of Oporto, which lies near the mouth of the River Douro. The accompanying text is by Portugal's leading female novelist of the pre-1974 Revolution, Agustina Bessa-Luís. The city's hilly nature and its spectacular setting, with its four striking bridges crossing the Douro, provide Sapieha with many opportunities for attractive photography.

14 Portugal contemporâneo. (Contemporary Portugal.)
Comissariado de Portugal para a Exposição Universal de Sevilha, 1992. Lisbon: Comissariado de Portugal para a Exposição Universal de Sevilha, 1992. unpaginated.

A collection of 319 colour photographs with a brief Portuguese introduction and even briefer list of captions. The collection captures the essence of modern Portugal, with images ranging from football and golf to historic buildings and landscapes throughout Portugal, but some further textual accompaniment would have been beneficial to the appreciation of those readers unfamiliar with the country.

The Country and Its People. Books of photographs

15 Portugal.
Hugues Demeude, photographs by Thierry Perrin. Cologne, Germany: Evergreen, 1999. 159p.

An English-language text introduces Portugal to a foreign audience in this volume which mostly comprises large-format colour photographs. The locations covered are, firstly, the Lisbon area, then the so-called 'heartland' of Portugal, followed by the Beiras, Oporto and the south of the country. A chapter of 'useful information' about the country completes the volume.

16 Lisboa desaparecida, vol. 6. (Disappeared Lisbon, vol. 6.)
Marina Tavares Dias. Lisbon: Quimera, 1998. 237p. maps. bibliog.

Details of the first five volumes of this title are to be found in the *Lisbon* volume of the World Bibliographical Series (vol. 199, 1997, item no. 11). This sixth tome has chapters on the period from the end of the Portuguese monarchy in 1910 to the start of the *Estado Novo* political regime in 1932, as well as sections on Lisbon dress-fashion, the Portas de Santo Antão and Rua do Ouro streets, and the Cais do Sodré district. Most importantly, this volume contains a bibliography pertinent to all six volumes in the set. As usual, the format is a mixture of plentiful black-and-white photographs from the earlier decades of the 20th century, together with a descriptive text.

17 Reflections by ten Portuguese photographers.
Selected, edited and translated by Amanda Hopkinson. London: Frontline/ Portugal 600, 1996. 116p.

The catalogue of an exhibition held at the Royal National Theatre in London in 1996, which included the work of leading exponents of Portuguese photography such as Pedro Baptista, Luísa Ferreira and Henrique Seruca. The examples date back to the 1950s and comprise only images of Portugal itself, taken by native photographers. These are almost entirely monochrome which, according to Jorge Calado's introductory essay, is appropriate for a country whose photographers produce 'images blacker than those found elsewhere'.

18 Nazaré.
Thomaz de Mello. Lisbon: Edições Ática, 1958. 80p.

A collection of drawings by a celebrated Portuguese artist of the picturesque fishing village of Nazaré, situated on the Atlantic coast to the north of Lisbon. The Portuguese introduction, by António Lopes Ribeiro, has a parallel English translation, and the work is completed by an essay in French by Suzanne Chantal.

19 Frederick William Flower: um pioneiro da fotografia portuguesa.
(Frederick William Flower: a pioneer of Portuguese photography.)
Museu do Chiado. Lisbon: Electa, 1994. 223p.

Although the four chapters of text which accompany this evocative collection of reproductions of 19th-century photographs are all in Portuguese, the photographs themselves provide a vivid record for all nationalities of the Oporto and Douro areas, for the most part, between 1853 and 1858. Flower, born in 1815 in Edinburgh, left the family home in Hull in 1834 to join the port shippers Smith, Woodhouse in Vila Nova de Gaia,

The Country and Its People. Books of photographs

the town which lies directly across the Douro from Oporto. After a brief return to Bristol, Flower returned to Oporto as a wine merchant.

20   **O bilhete postal ilustrado e a história urbana da Grande Lisboa. The illustrated postcard and the urban history of Lisbon metropolitan area.**
José Manuel da Silva Passos, translated by Maria do Carmo Gago da Silva.   Lisbon: Caminho, 1997. 215p. bibliog. (Memória da Cidade, no. 5).

A magnificent collection of 457 postcards depicting the seventeen municipalities which comprise, with Lisbon itself, the Lisbon metropolitan area. Companion volumes cover Lisbon itself (see the *Lisbon* volume in the World Bibliographical Series, vol. 199, 1997, item no. 51), and also the Algarve, Oporto and Braga areas. The postcards are reproduced, for the most part, in a slightly smaller than original format and include sepia tints as well as colour cards. Unfortunately, very few are dated even to a particular decade. There is an English introduction, but the Portuguese captions to each card are not translated; nevertheless, the postcards largely speak for themselves as a pictorial record of the area in question.

21   **Lisboa ao cair da tarde. Lisbon at day's end.**
João Paulo, poems translated by Richard Zenith.   Lisbon: João Paulo, 1997. 103p. map.

An attractive, large-format collection of colour photographs of Portugal's capital city which depict Lisbon at evening and night time. A number of these are long exposures which make use of car lights to create artistic effects. Interspersed amongst the evocative photographs are seventeen poems or quotations from poems about the city by Portuguese authors. Both these and the picture captions appear in both Portuguese and English. The subjects of the photographs are almost entirely the major sights and thoroughfares of the city centre area.

22   **Porto. (Oporto.)**
Werner Radasewsky, Günter Schneider.   Berlin: Nicolai, 1989. 119p.

An impressive collection of large-format colour photographs of Portugal's second city with an introductory text in English. A companion volume, *Lisbon* by Manfred Hamm, W. Radasewsky (Berlin: Nicolai, 1994. 236p.), is characterized by unusually-angled shots of the city's landmarks.

23   **Portugal and the sea.**
Rui Rasquilho, photographs by Jorge Barros, English version by George Dykes.   Lisbon: Distri Cultural/ Círculo de Leitores, 1983. 63p. 4 maps. bibliog.

Published simultaneously in English and in Portuguese, as *Portugal e o mar*, the text of this volume provides an introduction to the voyages of discovery, largely in the words of the Discoverers and of chroniclers. A chronology of the voyages is given, along with a brief bibliography. However, the bulk of the work comprises 156 unnumbered pages of colour photographs taken for this publication at locations throughout the world where the

The Country and Its People. Books of photographs

Portuguese landed. These illustrations are arranged into five sections, entitled Sea, Fortifications, Cities, Religious Architecture and People.

24 Costa do Estoril: blues and golds.
Text by Isabel Salema, photographs by Afonso Manuel Alves, Luís Leiria de Lima, translated by Joanna Howard. Lisbon: Publicações Dom Quixote, 1989. 89p.

This is a beautifully photographed compilation of images of the Estoril Coast, which embraces Cascais and Estoril, towns which lie just over half an hour from central Lisbon by the scenic Cascais Line railway. The towns lie on the Atlantic and although tourist centres, they have not suffered the worst excesses of high-rise development, as these pictures demonstrate. A companion volume by the same team, but translated by Joan Ennes, is *Algarve: southern lands* (Lisbon: Publicações Dom Quixote, 1989. 139p.).

25 Lisbon: the sparkling miracle on the western edge of Europe.
Text by Andrea Schäfler, editorial and historical details by Gabriela Wachter. Bournemouth, England: Parkstone Press, 1997. 96p.

A large-format collection of contemporary colour photographs of Lisbon outdoor scenes. Although the pictures and accompanying text are arranged into chapters, such as 'Praça da Figueira and Rossio' there is neither an overall list of contents nor an index. The book ends with a historical chronology of the city. Nevertheless, the book captures the spirit of the city through its mixture of coverage of both tourist sights and quieter corners.

26 Portuguese photography since 1854. Livro de viagens. (Book of travels.)
Edited by M. Teresa Siza, Peter Neiermair, texts by José Sarmento de Matos and others. Kilchberg, Zürich, Switzerland: Édition Stemmle, 1998. 236p. bibliog.

This book was produced to accompany an exhibition, entitled *Livro de viagens*, stimulated by the Frankfurt Book Fair of 1997, the theme of which was Portugal. As the title implies, the emphasis here is on depictions of the Portuguese as an itinerant people and consequently a number of the many plates do depict Portuguese-speaking territories in Africa, Asia and Brazil. The vast majority of the photographs show people rather than landscapes, whilst the final section of contemporary photographs comprises abstracts and depictions of individuals which convey little that is peculiarly Portuguese. Also of relevance is António Sena's *A history of photography* in the Synthesis of Portuguese Culture Series (Lisbon: Europália 91, 1991).

27 Portugal.
Neal Slavin, with an afterword by Mary McCarthy. New York: Lustrum Press, 1971. unpaginated.

A collection of monochrome photographs by Neal Slavin are here followed by a 'Letter from Portugal', an essay written by the celebrated American journalist, Mary McCarthy, in 1955 and culled from her book, *On the contrary: articles of belief, 1946-1961* (London: Weidenfeld & Nicolson, 1980. 312p.), for details of which see the *Lisbon* volume in the

The Country and Its People. Books of photographs

World Bibliographical Series (vol. 199, 1997, item no. 294). While the essay effectively captures the reality of life under the Salazar dictatorship, the pictures suffer from a complete lack of captioning.

Geography

General

28 Porto & north Portugal.
Brian Dicks. London: Hodder & Stoughton, 1999. 58p. maps. (Europe in Transition).

An illustrated study of the human geography of northern Portugal, aimed primarily at sixteen- to nineteen-year-olds in schools and universities, but also of more general interest. The Oporto area and the north Portuguese interior are presented as an 'illustration of a European region in the process of transition'. Subjects covered include river management in the Douro valley, agriculture, slum and shanty dwellings, tourism and the impact of economic change and tourism on a region of traditionally small-scale industry. The whole is attractively presented with many illustrations, charts and tables. The cover title is *Porto & northern Portugal*.

29 Portugal: a country study.
Edited by Eric Solsten for the Federal Research Division, Library of Congress. Washington, DC: Department of the Army, 1994. 2nd ed. 330p. 8 maps. bibliog. (Area Handbook Series DA Pam 550-181).

An updated edition of the 1977 edition of the same title, edited by Eugene K. Keefe and others (Washington, DC: Department of the Army, 1977. 456p. 18 maps. bibliog.). This new volume consists of research completed by January 1993. It is an area study of Portugal which provides an authoritative description and analysis of the political, economic and human geography of the country primarily for the benefit of United States government officials. It has five chapters entitled 'Historical setting', 'The society and its environment', 'The economy', 'Government and politics' and 'National security' which combine to provide an authoritative introduction to Portugal's place in the world in the 1990s. A thorough fifteen-page bibliography of mostly English-language material completes the work.

Geography. Maps and atlases

30 A geography of Spain and Portugal.
Ruth Way, assisted by Margaret Simmons.   London: Methuen, 1962.
362p. 52 maps. bibliog.

Though now somewhat dated, this remains a reliable geography of Portugal. The country is described region by region, from south to north, with an appendix addressing the country's colonies. A more modern and extensive work for the Portuguese-reader is *Geografia de Portugal* (Geography of Portugal) by Orlando Ribeiro and Hermann Lautensach, updated by Suzanne Daveau (Lisbon: Edições João Sá da Costa, 1987-91. 4 vols). With copious maps and diagrams, this covers the physical geography, climate, landscape, human geography and socio-economic geography of Portugal. Daveau's contribution is a section at the end of each chapter in which she comments upon and updates the preceding texts of Ribeiro and Lautensach.

Maps and atlases

31 Guide and plan of Lisbon.
Norberto de Araújo, António Soares, translated by Eva-Renate d'Esaguy.   Lisbon: Livraria Portugália, c.1950. 40p. maps.

A guide to Lisbon by one of its leading historians, Norberto de Araújo which is solely attributed to him on the title-page but only jointly so on the cover. It provides brief authoritative descriptions of the city's sights, divided into seven sections; Principal Monuments, Churches and Chapels, Museums and Libraries, Places and Public Buildings, Miradors and Picturesque Districts, Antiquities and Curiosities, and Squares, Gardens and Theatres. A large folding map (1:10,000) provides a detailed picture of the city, bounded by Campo Pequeno, Alto de S. João, the River Tagus and Ajuda. On its reverse are five excursion routes from Lisbon to Belém, Xabregas, Campo de Sant'Ana, Campolide and Benfica, along with maps of several of the main arterial routes outside the central area and a map of the greater Lisbon area. The back cover comprises a street map of the central Baixa area of the city.

32 AA Essential Spain and Portugal, scale 16 miles to 1 inch.
Automobile Association.   Basingstoke, England: Automobile Association, 1994. reprint. (Essential Road Map Series, no. 4).

A map which promotes itself on its clarity, it splits the Iberian peninsula in two with one half on each side of the sheet. Whilst it may achieve its stated aim of being easy to read, this is to some degree achieved by omitting the amount of topographical detail found on some other maps of this scale. The AA has also produced an *AA glovebox atlas, Spain & Portugal* (1998), which is explicitly aimed at the touring motorist rather than the general visitor, and a 1:75,000 *AA Baedeker Spain & Portugal* map.

Geography. Maps and atlases

33 Mapa das estradas, 1998/9. (Road map, 1998/9.)
Automóvel Clube de Portugal.   Lisbon: Automóvel Clube de Portugal, 1998. 91st ed.

An updated edition of an authoritative folding map of Portuguese roads, provided by the country's leading motoring organization. The large number of roads built in recent years, especially since accession to the European Community, means that up-to-date, locally produced maps such as this are a good investment for the visiting motorist once he or she arrives in Portugal.

34 Bartholomew road atlas, Spain and Portugal, including 21 town centre plans. 1:300,000.
Bartholomew.   Edinburgh: Bartholomew, 1993. 240p.

This approximately 5 miles to the inch atlas also includes twenty-one town maps at a more detailed 1:20,000 scale and also has an index of some 50,000 place-names. In addition, maps at 1:4,500,000 are provided for all of Europe to facilitate route-planning for those approaching Iberia by land. The same company produces *Bartholomew's European travel map: Spain & Portugal. 1:250,000* (Edinburgh, 1996). This is a folding map with a place-name index. Bartholomew also produces an *Algarve holiday map* and a *Madeira holiday map, including the island of Porto Santo and town plan of Funchal*. These have text in English, German, French and Portuguese and topographical detail that is strikingly clear.

35 Insight fleximap Lisbon. 1:15,500.
Mapping by Berndtson & Berndtson.   Singapore: APA Publications, 1998.

A weatherproof folding map which bears a striking resemblance to Berndtson & Berndtson's *City Streets* map of Lisbon (see the *Lisbon* volume in the World Bibliographical Series, vol. 199, 1997, item no. 105). Not only is the physical format of a two-sided plastic-laminated map common to the two publications but the actual mapping is virtually identical in all but scale. The publication includes a 1:15,500 map of the city together with a number of other smaller maps, including ones of the Estoril area (1:11,000), of the wider Tagus estuary area (1:340,000) and of the Lisbon Metro and tram systems. One significant difference from the *City Streets* map, however, is the increased amount of textual tourist information which accompanies the Insight maps, which are meant to complement the Insight series of tourist guides (see the *Lisbon* volume in the World Bibliographical Series, vol. 199, 1997, item nos. 177, 187, 191). In the same format is *Insight fleximap Algarve* (1:22,500).

36 Cartographia Spain, Portugal. 1:800,000.
Cartographia.   Bad Soden, Germany: Ravenstein Verlag, 1999. 63p. map.

A finely detailed map which is accompanied by a sixty-three-page index booklet of place-names. Ravenstein also publish a *Portugal Algarve* map at a scale of 1:176,000, as well as their own *Spain, Espagne, Portugal* map at a scale of 1:800,000, complete with index booklet.

11

Geography. Maps and atlases

37 Collins Spain & Portugal: all new mapping. 16 miles to 1 inch. 1:1,000,000.
Collins. Glasgow, Scotland: Collins, 1999.
This detailed map is, like that produced by Estate Publications (see item no. 38), based on mapping by the Swiss cartographers Hallwag. Earlier editions had the benefit of a substantial booklet-index attached to the map's cardboard cover, but the 1999 edition very much reduces the convenience of this important feature by placing the index on the reverse of the map itself. As well as the main map there are a number of smaller more detailed regional maps, one of which is of the Lisbon area. There is also a *Collins Madeira holiday map* which has text in English, German, French and Portuguese, giving details of hotels, currency, key phrases and other practical information.

38 Leisure map: Spain and Portugal: Canary Is, Madeira & Azores. 1:1,000,000.
Estate Publications. Tenterden, England: Estate Publications, 1995.
A highly detailed map of Iberia compiled by the Swiss cartographers Hallwag, with the cooperation of the Portuguese and Spanish ministries of tourism. As well as showing place-names, communication routes and topographical features, the map employs eighteen symbols to identify particular categories of leisure attraction, such as cathedrals, caves, zoos and tourist towns. These are supplemented by the English-language names of tourist sights next to major locations.

39 Globetrotter travel map Algarve.
Globetrotter. London: New Holland, c.1998. Scale 1:175,000.
This two-sided map of the Algarve provides excellent detail of Portugal's most southerly region and also incorporates several town and city plans, including ones of Évora, Portimão, Faro and its airport, and even the capital city of Lisbon. It is also available as a pack with the *Globetrotter travel guide* (see item no. 84). Another map of the Algarve is the two-sided *Portugal and the Algarve* (Brentford, England: Lascelles Red Cover Series, c.1998). One side depicts the Algarve region at 1:600,000 whilst the other portrays the whole country at 1:760,000.

40 City flash Lisboa, Lissabon. Tourist city guide, sightseeing, public transport, index, shopping.
Hallwag. Bern: Hallwag, [1998]. Scale 1:16,000.
A curious but innovative map in that it comprises nine panels, on shiny card, which only fold vertically and is therefore easily handled outdoors. Given its small size, both sides have to be used to cover the city; six panels on one side and four on the other cover the south and north of Lisbon respectively at a scale of 1:16,000. Details shown include the Metro and railway lines as well as car parks. There is also a 1:300,000 map of the Tagus estuary area and an innovative map of central Lisbon's Baixa and Rossio with all major shops named and colour-coded. Another map shows a 'Traffic plan' of Lisbon, by which is meant a diagram of the public transport network including bus, tram and ferry routes, and there is a separate map of Lisbon airport.

Geography. Maps and atlases

41 Distoguide Euro map, España, Spanien, Portugal.
Hallwag.   Bern: Hallwag, 1998. Scale 1:1,000,000.

A single-sided folding map of the Iberian peninsula, together with insets of the Azores, Madeira and the Canary Islands, which comes with a twenty-eight-page booklet index of place-names attached to the card cover. This publication has a number of distinctive features, notably the 'distoguide' on the back cover which is a map of Iberia perforated by holes denoting the major cities. By moving a card within the covers to set one's starting point, the distance in kilometres to any of the other towns can be read at a glance. Additionally, the map comes with information on such practicalities as Portuguese area telephone codes, customs allowances, speed limits and a list of Portuguese tourist information offices abroad.

42 Carta geológica de Portugal. 1:50,000. (Geological map of Portugal.)
Instituto Geológico e Mineiro de Portugal.   Lisbon: Instituto Geológico e Mineiro de Portugal, 1937- .

Still incomplete in 1999, after the production of 135 of its projected 175 sheets, this series of geological maps is accompanied by descriptive texts. More recently a 1:200,000 series of the same title has been appearing (Lisbon: IGMP, 1982-) and three of the projected eight sheets had appeared by 1999.

43 Carta de Portugal, M7810. 1:50,000. (Map of Portugal, M7810.)
Instituto Português de Cartografia e Cadastro.   Lisbon: Instituto Português de Cartografia e Cadastro, 1972-77.

A 175-sheet map of Portugal which has the authority of being produced by the country's national mapping agency, IPCC. It depicts the country in six colours and the terrain is shown by twenty-five-metre contour lines. National coverage was completed in 1977, although some sheets have been updated since then. IPCC also produce national maps at 1:100,000 in 53 sheets (no. M684, Lisbon: IPCC, 1938-) and 1:200,000 scale (no. M585, Lisbon: IPCC, 1969-).

44 Portugal: a Lonely Planet travel atlas. 1:400,000.
John King, Julia Wilkinson.   London: Lonely Planet, 1997. 76p.

Accompanied by a brief introduction to the country, illustrated by colour photographs and written in five languages, including English and Japanese, this is a book-format set of clear colour maps of Portugal at a scale of 1:400,000. Its handy book-format is more convenient to use than large sheet maps and its value is enhanced if used in conjunction with the Lonely Planet guide (see item no. 99).

45 Portugal, with places of interest. 1:500,000.
Kümmerly + Frey.   Bern: Kümmerly + Frey, c.1998.

A clear map of the entire country with more detailed inserts of the Lisbon and Oporto regions. The same publishers also produce an excellent 1:15,000 map of Lisbon, *City map Lissabon* (Bern, 1995), which is both more detailed and covers a wider area of the city than many of its rivals. In addition, it has a street index and suggestions for walks on its reverse.

13

Geography. Maps and atlases

46   **España, Portugal, Espagne. Carte routière et touristique. 1:1,000,000, 1cm:10km.** (Spain, Portugal. Road and tourist map.) Michelin.   Paris: Michelin, 1999. Scale 1:1,000,000 (1cm=10km). (Michelin 990).

Michelin have here produced a one-sided colour map depicting main roads in the Iberian peninsula. The map has particularly clear depiction of the terrain but lacks an index of place-names or any regional insets at smaller scale. More detail is to be found in the companion map, *Portugal, Madeira* (Michelin 940), a 1:400,000 map which has an index of place-names. A superbly detailed city map is the *Lisboa planta* (Michelin 39, Lisbon map), a 1:10,000 folding sheet map, with an accompanying booklet which contains a street index.

47   **Philips road map: Spain and Portugal. 1:1,000,000.**
Philips.   London: Philips, c.1998. new ed.

A single-sided sheet map of the Iberian peninsula with no supplementary textual details to accompany the cartography. The map shows major roads but is not as detailed as the Collins or Estates maps (q.v.) and is thus more suitable for the general tourist-driver rather than those wishing to go too far off the beaten track. The map's symbols are explained in four languages – English, French, German and Spanish.

48   **Portugal, with Madeira and the Azores. Euro-Road atlas. 1:300,000.**
RV Reise.   Berlin; Gütesloh, Germany; Leipzig, Germany; Munich; Potsdam-Werder, Germany; Stuttgart, Germany: RV Reise/GeoCenter International, 1993. 66p. + 16p. (Euro Atlas).

A large-scale book of clear and colourful Portuguese road maps which also show railways, rivers and topographical features in some detail. The glossary of map symbols is explained in eight languages, including English and Portuguese. The forty-seven-page main map section includes maps of the Portuguese islands of Madeira and the Azores. Street plans (1:20,000) of Coimbra, Évora, Lisbon, Oporto and Setúbal are also provided. There is a detailed index of place-names, followed by a final sixteen-page section comprising maps of the whole of Europe at 1:4,500,000 scale. The same publishers produce the *Euro-City map Lisbon* (1:15,000); the *Euro-Country maps* (see item no. 49); the *Euro-Regional map, Portugal, Galicia* (1:300,000), a two-sided map with city maps and a booklet index of place-names; the *Euro-Holiday map Lisbon and its coastal region* (1:250,000) and the *Euro-Holiday map Algarve* (1:200,000). The chief feature to distinguish the *Holiday* maps from others is to be found on the reverse of the folding sheet. Here are to be found suggestions for more than twenty excursions in the region, each of which is accompanied both by a description and a small colour photograph of the location in question.

49   **Spain, Portugal. 1:800,000.**
RV Reise.   Munich; Stuttgart, Germany: RV Reise/GeoCenter International, 1999. (Euro-Country Map).

A map which includes nine city plans, including Lisbon and Oporto, as well as providing a clear portrayal of the Iberian peninsula as a whole. From the same series is *Portugal, West Spain* (Euro-Country Map, 1:800,000), which incorporates city plans of Lisbon,

Oporto and Coimbra. For maps of Portugal in the Euro-Regional, Euro-Holiday and Euro-City Series, see item no. 48.

50 Cultural atlas of Spain and Portugal.
Mary Vincent, R. A. Stradling. Oxford: Andromeda; New York: Facts on File, 1994. 240p. 34 maps. bibliog.

A colourful atlas which graphically portrays Portugal at different stages of its history. Part one covers the physical background of Spain and Portugal, part two comprises a history of the peninsula and part three addresses the geographical regions, which here are taken to be the southern Mediterranean area, the Ebro region, the Atlantic coast and the Atlantic islands. Part two includes special features, such as articles on Batalha, the Portuguese navigators, the Marquis of Pombal and Lisbon, Portuguese tiles and port wine. As well as the colour maps of various historical periods, there are numerous colour illustrations which include paintings and reproductions of books. A full list of the monarchs of the various Iberian kingdoms is also provided.

European railway atlas.
See item no. 481.

Geology and earthquakes

51 Pre-Mesozoic geology of Iberia.
Edited by R. D. Dallmeyer, E. Martínez-García. Berlin; Heidelberg, Germany; London, Paris, Tokyo; Hong Kong; Barcelona, Spain: Springer-Verlag, 1990. 416p. maps. bibliog.

With 187 figures, this book surveys the evolution of the Iberian massif, more than 225 million years ago. The book's contents evolved from a conference organized by the International Geological Correlation Program (ICGP) held in Oviedo, Spain, in 1986. Iberia is studied in five geological zones which include the Southern Portuguese and the Central Iberian Zones. The latter includes the Lusitanian-Alcudian sector of modern Portugal.

52 Earthquake damage scenarios in Lisbon for disaster preparedness.
L. Mendes-Víctor, C. S. Oliveira, I. Pais, P. Teves-Costa. In: *Issues in urban earthquake risk.* Edited by Brian E. Tucker, Mustafa Erdik, Christina N. Hwang. Dordrecht, The Netherlands; Boston, Massachusetts; London: Kluwer Academic Publishers, 1994, p. 265-89. maps. bibliog. (NATO Advanced Science Institute Series).

This study identifies nine major earthquakes in Lisbon's history of which the 1755 earthquake was the most cataclysmic. The substantial English-language bibliography of that event is covered in the *Lisbon* volume in the World Bibliographical Series, vol. 199,

Geography. Geology and earthquakes

1997, item nos. 136-59. Illustrated by many maps and diagrams, the authors here describe Lisbon's topography and categorize its building stock against earthquake resistance criteria. Amongst the steps being taken to mitigate the effects of any future earthquake, the city council of Lisbon is investing in earthquake awareness programmes, particularly in schools.

Tourism and Travel Guidebooks

General

53 Landscapes of Algarve: a countryside guide.
Brian Anderson, Eileen Anderson. London: Sunflower Books, 1996. 2nd ed. 135p.

Formerly published in 1991 as *Landscapes of Portugal: Algarve*, this pocket-book is intended for the independent traveller who wishes to travel off the tourist track in the Algarve. With sections covering picnicking, touring and walking, there is something for everyone from the car-bound tourist to the serious walker. The twenty suggested walks and four car itineraries are carefully described and times and distances are provided. Colour pictures and contour maps as well as railway and bus timetable information should ensure that the inquisitive traveller will not get lost in his or her unfamiliar holiday environment. A companion volume, *Landscapes of Portugal: Sintra, Cascais, Estoril, a countryside guide* (1995. 65p. maps) covers the area to the north and west of Lisbon, whilst *Landscapes of Portugal: Costa Verde, Minho, Peneda-Gerês, a countryside guide*, by the same authors (1995. 66p. maps), with three tour itineraries and eight walks, covers the north of Portugal.

54 Northern Portugal.
Brian Anderson, Eileen Anderson. London: Black, 1996. 192p. 9 maps. (Black's Regional Guides to Portugal).

One of a series of three guides to Portugal's regions by the Andersons. The other two are *Algarve and southern Portugal* (1996. 195p. 12 maps), which includes the Alentejo region, and *Lisbon and central Portugal* (1997. 248p. maps). *Northern Portugal* includes the Oporto and Ponte da Barca areas, as well as the Gerês national park. All of the volumes follow the same format, comprising an introductory chapter followed by sections on history, touring, food and drink. These, in turn, are followed by descriptions of the individual areas which constitute the remit of the book. Colour photographs and maps complete what are well-informed guides for the tourist who has access to his or her own transport. The information given includes advice on where to stay and to eat, as well as details of Portugal's history, flora and fauna and environment.

Tourism and Travel Guidebooks. General

55 Portugal.
Edited by Pam Barrett, updated by Brian Anderson, Eileen Anderson. Singapore: ASA, 1999. 4th ed. 394p. maps. (Insight Guides).

The chief feature of this guide is the colour photographs, many of which are full-page. There are also useful fold-out card maps of Portugal as a whole and of Lisbon inside the front and back covers. The text includes narrative sections on Portuguese history and places as well as other information on the country described as 'features', 'insights on...' and 'information panels'. Earlier editions were edited by A. Friesinger Hill. Two smaller volumes, *Insight Compact Portugal* and *Insight Pocket Portugal*, provide briefer introductions.

56 This way Algarve.
Ken Bernstein. Lausanne, Switzerland: JPM, 1995. 63p. + 16p. maps.

A truly pocket-sized volume which incorporates a separate booklet, *The Portuguese way* (Lausanne, Switzerland: JPM, 1994. 16p.), which provides background information on Portuguese culture and practices. The main part of the book is divided regionally into quaintly named sections on 'The Landward Coast', 'The Leeward Coast' and 'Inland', illustrated by colour photographs. There are also suggestions for excursions.

57 Holiday tours in Spain, Portugal & Madeira.
The Booth Steamship Co. Liverpool, England. London: The Booth Steamship Co., 1913. 6th ed. 135p. 12 maps.

A volume which is redolent of a more genteel age, immediately before the First World War when ships conveyed the privileged few to Portugal. After a brief section on Galicia, the text describes Portugal (p. 39-123) and Madeira (p. 124-30) for the benefit of tourists. The book highlights some of the sights around Lisbon and Portugal which were accessible to those using one of the Booth Steamship Company's most popular routes. The guide is profusely illustrated and includes a number of colour portraits.

58 AA Thomas Cook travellers' Algarve and southern Portugal.
Susie Boulton, Joe Staines, Sarah Le Tellier, Martin Symington. Basingstoke, England: AA Publications, 1999. 192p. maps.

The combination of Britain's Automobile Association (AA), the renowned Thomas Cook company and a number of authors who have separately produced other excellent guides to Portugal lends an immediate authority to this guide which covers both the Algarve and the Alentejan plains to the north. Amongst its distinctive features are sections on geography and flora which are often lacking from tourist guides. Throughout, the book is illustrated by attractively presented colour photographs. The AA and its Dutch counterpart, ANWB, also publish *Where to stay in Spain, Portugal and Andorra 1994* (Basingstoke: AA/ANWB, 1994. 144p. maps [Where to Stay Series]), a guide for the motorist which covers more than a thousand hotels, all of which have been inspected prior to inclusion here. The amenities of each hotel are listed as are the accommodation tariffs. Maps are provided of major cities.

Tourism and Travel Guidebooks. General

59 Algarve.
Susie Boulton.   Singapore, APA Publications, 1998. 3rd rev. ed. 103p. maps. (Insight Pocket Guides).

The middle of the three sizes of Insight Guide produced by APA, a company which is now part of the German Langenscheidt language-publishing house. Although the text is informative, the format is probably the least satisfactory. This is because although the text is well-written and attractively illustrated by colour photographs, it is barely more lengthy than the tightly-packed and cheaper Insight Compact Guide series and the content is much thinner than the main Insight Guide. Nineteen full-day itineraries are provided for visitors to the Algarve, together with historical and practical information about visiting Portugal. The series' main benefit, in relation to the other formats of Insight Guide, is the large folding-map of the region, with several more detailed local inserts covering such places as Faro. Other Pocket Guides include *Portugal* and *Lisbon* (see the *Lisbon* volume in the World Bibliographical Series, vol. 199, 1997, item no. 191).

60 Lisbon.
Main contributor, Susie Boulton.   London; New York; Sydney; Moscow: Dorling Kindersley, 1997. 192p. maps. (Eyewitness Travel Guides).

An extremely attractive all-colour guide to Portugal's capital city. The series format includes cut-away drawings of major buildings, three-dimensional maps and innumerable colour photographs. The text is divided into sections on 'Introducing Lisbon', 'Lisbon area by area', 'Travellers' needs' and 'Survival guide'. The contributors include local English-speaking residents and is both authoritative and free of the spelling errors which afflict many guides to Portugal. The work ends with an eight-page colour map of the city, a street index, and a brief section of useful phrases and vocabulary.

61 The Algarve.
Callum Brines.   London: Diamond Books, 1995. 124p. maps.

A repackaged version of the *Collins Traveller Guide* of the same title. It is a pocket guide which consists of three colour-coded sections. The first covers ten 'Topics' which are an alphabetical mix of places (Albufeira, Faro, Lagos, Portimão) and facilities such as beaches, golf and tennis. The second section, a 'Cultural/ Historical Gazetteer', is a similar mixture of places and topics, whilst the book is completed by a 'Practical Information Gazetteer'. Colour photographs illustrate the area and clear, but basic maps even indicate hotel and restaurant locations in the major resorts.

62 AA essential Algarve.
Christopher Catling.   Basingstoke, England: Automobile Association, 1999. 126p. maps.

A colourful paperback guide to the Algarve in which the text is artfully broken up by copious colour photographs. The book comprises sections entitled 'Viewing the Algarve', 'Top ten', 'What to see' and 'Where to...'. These are followed by practical information for staying in and getting around the country. The book uses small pictograms to itemize the facilities of each place described. The 'Top Ten' sites described include Cape St Vincent and Estói.

Tourism and Travel Guidebooks. General

63 Goldenbook: Estoril coast and Sintra.
Edited by Henrique Cerqueira, text by Annegret Rangel.   Lisbon: Interpropo, 1997. 134p.

One of a series of regularly updated hardback books which also cover the Algarve, Lisbon, Madeira and Oporto. The book is replete with glossy colour photographs of the Estoril and Sintra areas, interspersed with descriptive text and advertising aimed at both the tourist and the business person. The volume comprises the following sections: the Estoril coast; Looking ahead; Origins and history; Ceramics; Art galleries and antiques; Shopping; Sports; Eating out; Night life; Sintra; Touring around; and Services.

64 Portugal guide: your passport to great travel.
Ron Charles.   New York: Open Road Publishing, 1997. 2nd ed. 550p. maps.

A comprehensive guide for the North American visitor to all areas of Portugal, not just the tourist sights. The volume is not illustrated but the compensation for this is the wealth of detail provided, including information on prices (in US dollars). Access to a car is assumed for those who wish to derive maximum benefit from this guide. Prior to a region-by-region description of the country, there are nine thematic chapters which include essays on the land and its people, planning trips, Portuguese food and drink, sports and recreations and suggested itineraries.

65 A.A. Baedeker Portugal.
Edited by Alec Court, text by Rosemarie Arnold and others.
Basingstoke, England: Automobile Association, 1999. 5th ed. 431p. maps.

This is the latest edition of what has become one of the standard guides to Portugal, particularly for the tourist with his or her own transport. A separate folded colour map of the country is included with the book, which has some 150 colour illustrations and very clear town plans. After an initial section covering the nature, culture and history of Portugal, the body of the text is an alphabetical gazetteer of places and sights. The final section of the work is another alphabetized section, conveying practical information about the country. Its cover title is *Baedeker's Portugal*. Companion volumes are Court's *A.A. Baedeker Lisbon* (1996. 2nd ed. 218p. maps) and *A.A. Baedeker Algarve* by Eva Missler (1997. 190p. maps).

66 Lisbon.
Gudrun Decker, Alexander Decker.   Singapore: APA, 1995. 96p. 5 maps. (Insight Compact Guides).

The smallest of the three grades of Insight Guides, this book is divided into sections on places, culture, leisure and practical information. Generally small colour photographs accompany the text which is informative and, despite a few spelling errors, usually accurate. For information on the main Insight Guide to Lisbon and the Insight Pocket Guide to the city, see the *Lisbon* volume in the World Bibliographical Series, vol. 199, 1997, item nos. 187 and 191 respectively.

Tourism and Travel Guidebooks. General

67 Welcome to Portugal.
R. A. N. Dixon. Glasgow, Scotland: Collins, 1984. 95p. maps. (A Collins Travel Guide).

An attractive pocket guide to Portugal, which contains many colour photographs of the country and its people. The core of the book is six sections on the regions of Portugal: Costa Verde, Costa de Prata, Lisbon and its coasts, the mountains, the plains, and the Algarve. These chapters are preceded by practical information on getting around, the language, cuisine and accommodation. A feature of the book's maps is the use of coloured contours to convey clearly the local terrain.

68 Portugal.
David J. J. Evans, updated by Alex Dixon. London: Cadogan Books, 1998. 468p. maps. bibliog. (Cadogan Guides).

A guide for the more discerning visitor who wishes to acquire some knowledge of Portugal's historical, artistic and cultural background as well as of its present-day appearance. The country is described in nine chapters arranged from the north to the south. The guide lacks any photographs, its only embellishments being monochrome drawings and maps, although the covers incorporate colour maps. A chronology of the country's rulers, notes on Portuguese history and language and an excellent bibliography complete the volume. In the same format is *Portugal: the Algarve* by Evans and K. Mohammadi (London: Cadogan Books, 1996. 182p. maps. bibliog.).

69 Time Out Lisbon.
Editorial director, Peter Fiennes, edited by Dave Rimmer. Harmondsworth, England: Penguin Books, 1998. 276p. maps.

Packed with information on Lisbon, in the customary Time Out format, this guide comprises six sections. The first, 'In context', provides historical information as well as a modern-day overview of the city. Other sections are self-explanatory: 'Sightseeing', 'Shopping and Sleeping', 'Arts and Entertainment', and 'Trips out of Town', whilst 'On the Town' covers restaurants, cafés and nightlife. Excellent colour maps complete the guide.

70 Let's go, Spain and Portugal, including Morocco, 1998.
Edited by Derek M. Glanz. London: Macmillan, 1997. 697p. maps.

The Let's Go Series prides itself on its up-to-date contents, with a new edition being produced each year, complete with revised prices for many of the facilities and accommodation described. It is primarily aimed at the budget end of the market but is nevertheless full of information of relevance to the general tourist. Portugal occupies approximately one hundred pages of the book, with coverage arranged into seven regional sections. The 1999 volume (1998. 752p.) exemplifies the changing nature of each year's issue as its editors are Elena Schneider, Ethan Thurow and Nicole Anne Barry.

Tourism and Travel Guidebooks. General

71 Lisbon.
Madeleine Gonçalves and others, translated by Michael Mayor, Ruth Blackburn. London: Everyman City Guide, 1998. 168p. maps. (Everyman City Guides).

An all-colour guide similar in layout and format to the Eyewitness Travel Guides (see item no. 60) but using photographs rather than a mixture of drawings and photos. There are also several small maps in the text and a larger, very clear colour map at the end. Translated from a French original, its coverage includes the Lisbon suburbs, such as Estoril and Cascais, as well as the city centre, and there is a substantial section on shopping in Lisbon. Photographs are numerous but generally very small.

72 Discover Portugal.
Martin Gostelow. Oxford: Berlitz, 1996. 351p. maps.

This glossy guidebook comprises seven sections on the different regions of Portugal. These are accompanied by chapters on history, geography, facts and figures, hotels and restaurants, as well as suggestions of 'What to do'. Some 150 illustrations and 30 maps and town plans accompany the text.

73 Lisbon: an unforgettable city.
José António Gurriarán. Mérida, Spain: Limite Visual, 1997. 422p. maps.

Very similar in format to the Eyewitness Travel Guides of Dorling Kindersley (see item no. 60), this superb full-colour guide is more comprehensive than its British counterpart. Packed with line drawings, three-dimensional illustrations, 1,500 colour photographs and numerous maps, it does merit its own description as 'the most thorough guide ever written on the city of Lisbon'. After an 'Introduction', the book has sections on 'The Natural Environment', 'History', 'Architecture and Town Planning', 'Traditions', 'Testimonies', 'Museums' and 'Itineraries', followed by a 'Practical Guide' and a particularly clear and detailed colour 'Map of Lisbon and Street Index'. The volume's one major defect is the absence of a detailed index to the places and sights it describes. The book is also available in Portuguese and Spanish versions.

74 Lisbon: the mini Rough Guide.
Matthew Hancock, with additional research by Amanda Tomlin. London: Rough Guides, 1998. 235p. maps.

A most useful pocket guide to the Portuguese capital, whose author resided there in the 1990s. The first section consists of ten chapters, seven of which deal with specified areas of the city, while the remainder are a brief introduction to Lisbon and essays on Expo '98 and 'Day trips from Lisbon'. The book's strength lies in the extensive listings which comprise the second section: these cover accommodation, places to eat and drink, places of entertainment, sport, shopping, festivals and events. Finally there is a brief history of Lisbon and notes on some books in English which relate to the city. The colour maps are attractive but somewhat lacking in detail both as regards street names and features such as Metro station names and routes. Rough Guides also produce *The music of Portugal*, which is available on CD or tape.

Tourism and Travel Guidebooks. General

75 AA Explorer Portugal.
Tim Jepson.   Basingstoke, England: Automobile Association, 1998. 264p. maps.

An informed guide which has five textual sections and is accompanied by a large, folding map in an attached pocket which also incorporates various town plans. The text comprises chapters on 'Portugal as it is' and 'Portugal as it was', as well as travel facts, hotel and restaurant information and a so-called A-Z section which is, in fact, a non-alphabetical guide to the regions of the country. Colour photographs enhance the descriptions and there are even a few monochrome photographs of historical events. Twenty-five key sights are categorized by a three-star marking system. The book's ten maps are clear regional road maps, rather than detailed city or town plans.

76 City Pack Lisbon.
Tim Jepson.   Basingstoke, England: Automobile Association, 1997. 96p. maps.

A concise tourist guide to the Portuguese capital which is divided into six main sections. These cover 'Life', 'How to organize your time', 'Top 25 sights', 'Best...', 'Where to...' and 'Travel facts'. The guide's brevity makes it most suitable for first-time visitors, who can follow any of its four suggested itineraries, rather than those seeking to go beyond the major tourist sights. It describes itself as the 'two-in-one' guide, a reference to its combination of a book and a separate folding map of the city.

77 Portugal.
Michael Khorian, photographs by Bruno Barnier, Nik Wheeler.
Ashbourne, England: Moorland Publishing Co., 1995. 269p. 10 maps. bibliog.

Alliterative titles such as 'Trundle on the trams' and 'Marvel at the Manueline' indicate the unpretentious approach of this book in its initial appraisal of the 'top spots' to visit in Portugal. Khorian also provides a brief history of the country as well as information on accommodation, restaurants and hints on shopping. The volume is packed with high-quality colour photographs of Portugal and its maps are also a strong point.

78 Fodor's Portugal.
Edited by Laura M. Kidder.   New York: Fodor, 1999. 4th ed. 317p. maps.

Nine chapters, arranged by region, provide detailed guidance for the North American visitor to Portugal. The volume is unusual in its lack of illustrations and its use of colour is virtually limited to typographical headings. Essential information such as arrival/departure procedures, currency and public holiday dates is provided, before each of the regions, including Madeira, is addressed. A vocabulary and a list of tourist highlights is provided and textual references to the maps makes locating places straightforward. Fodor also publish *Hotels of character and charm in Portugal* (see item no. 103).

Tourism and Travel Guidebooks. General

79   Algarve, with local tips.
Katja Krabielle, English edition by Cathy Muscat, Emma Kay. Derby, England: Marco Polo, 1997. 96p. maps.

As well as covering the popular parts of the Algarve, this pocket-sized colour guidebook also takes the reader off the beaten track into the interior of the region and even includes several pages on Lisbon, which lies well outside its proclaimed geographical remit. Attractive fold-out maps within the covers add to the volume's practicality for use whilst on the move. There is also a *Marco Polo España, Portugal* two-sided map (1:750,000), which includes city plans.

80   Lisbon for less.
Metropolis International.   London: Metropolis International Publications, 1999. 72p. maps.

A conveniently pocket-sized guide to Lisbon which uniquely includes discount vouchers for attractions in the city such as the Centro de Arte Moderna. These and the book's title underline the volume's stress on budget tourism. Another very practical innovation is the use of tiny colour maps of the immediate environs of all the sites described, which are located next to their entry in the text and which refer on to the larger folding map, inserted inside the front cover.

81   Lisbon in your pocket.
Michelin Tyre PLC.   Watford, England: Michelin Tyre PLC; Clermont-Ferrand, France: Manufacture Française des Pneumatiques Michelin, 1998. 128p. maps.

A handy and colourful guide to Lisbon, with four sections. The first supplies background information on the city and its history, whilst the second is called 'Exploring Lisbon' and suggests walks and excursions. In the third part, 'Enjoying your visit', there is advice on shopping, entertainment and accommodation. Finally, an 'A-Z Factfinder' gives brief information on such practicalities as using telephones, buying clothes and bank opening hours. The inside covers comprise folding maps. Throughout, the book is adorned by attractive and up-to-date colour photographs. A companion volume is *Southern Portugal, Algarve in your pocket* by Paul Murphy (1997. 128p. maps).

82   Portugal, Madeira, the Azores.
Michelin Tyre PLC.   Watford, England: Michelin Tyre PLC, 1998. rev. ed. 364p. maps. bibliog. (Tourist Guide, 04567).

This Michelin 'green guide' follows the series' well-established format of size and presentation, albeit modernized to the extent that colour photographs have now virtually supplanted the traditional line drawing illustrations. The indexed, colour maps and the clear floor-plans of major buildings remain a strong feature of this alphabetical guide to Portugal's tourist sights and towns. The introductory sections on Portuguese geography, history and culture are a model of clarity.

Tourism and Travel Guidebooks. General

83 Berlitz pocket guide Algarve.
Paul Murphy, edited by Sarah Hudson. Oxford; Princeton, New Jersey: Berlitz, 1998. 143p. maps. (Berlitz Pocket Guides).

A glossy, full-colour, pocket book which provides an admirable introduction to the Algarve for the tourist. The book includes a brief history of the area but is chiefly made up of sections on 'Where to go' and 'What to do', supplemented by brief lists of restaurants and accommodation. Its covers include three colour folding maps, two of which actually depict Lisbon and the Estoril coast which lie well outside the Algarve. These are justified by their inclusion as locations for excursions. The third map is of Faro. Murphy has also produced *Southern Portugal, Algarve in your pocket* (see item no. 81).

84 Algarve.
Jane O'Callaghan. London; Cape Town; Sydney; Singapore: New Holland, 1996. Reprinted, 1997. 128p. (Globetrotter Travel Guide).

A colourful guide which works outwards from most tourists' starting point of Faro, where the area's only international airport is sited. After describing the area around the town, there are sections on the central, western and eastern Algarve, as well as on the Alentejo region to the north of the Algarve. The book also includes a section of 'Travel Tips' which convey practical information for getting around the area. The guide is also available as a pack with the *Globetrotter travel map Algarve* (see item no. 39).

85 Berlitz pocket guide Portugal.
Timothy J. Page, edited by Chris Catling, Peter Duncan. Princeton, New Jersey; London: Berlitz, 1997. (2nd printing, 1998). 192p. maps. (Berlitz Pocket Guides).

A compact guide to Portugal, finely illustrated by colour photographs and maps throughout, this guide initially provides a brief background history of Portugal. It then moves on to describe tourist sites in sections entitled 'Where to go' and 'What to do', before dispensing advice on eating out, travelling around and finding suitable accommodation. In the same series is *Berlitz pocket guide Lisbon* by Martin Gostelow (1997. Reprinted, 1998. 144p.) and *Berlitz pocket guide Algarve* by Paul Murphy (see item no. 83) which also have colour folding maps on the covers, but no index.

86 Frommer's Portugal.
Darwin Porter, Danforth Price. New York: Macmillan USA, 1998. 15th ed. 401p. maps.

This popular North American guidebook is something of a curiosity in being entirely textual, with no illustrative material, other than maps. It is also conservative in its use of colour which is limited to red maps and headers; nevertheless, the volume is packed with reliable information for tourists. A shorter survey of Portugal is to be found in the companion volume *Frommer's Europe*, edited by Alice Fellows (New York: Macmillan USA, 1997. 1,006p. maps) where Portugal is covered on p. 749-91.

87 The magic of Al Gharb.
Colin Reid. Lewes, England: The Book Guild, 1992. 70p. map.

Al-Gharb is the transliterated Arabic name for the Algarve province of southern Portugal. Divided into twelve chapters, accompanied by black-and-white photographs and

Tourism and Travel Guidebooks. General

drawings, this work prides itself on being more than a mere travel guide. This claim is justified both by the diversity of subject matter which includes flora, fauna and folklore, and by the attention paid to locations off the tourist track. The area around Loulé is particularly well covered.

88 Portugal.
Heidrun Reinhard, translated by Paul Fletcher. Singapore: APA Publications (HK) Ltd, 1995. Reprinted, 1996. 103p. maps. (Insight Compact Guides).

The smallest of the three sizes of *Portugal* guides from APA. Liberally illustrated with colour photographs, mostly of a small size, this attractive volume provides the reader with a number of suggested routes which have clear but detailed maps. A grading system, using stars, identifies the major sites to visit. There are companion volumes in the same format for *Lisbon* (see item no. 66) and the *Algarve* (see item no. 91).

89 Portugal.
Ian Robertson. London: A. & C. Black; New York: W.W. Norton, 1996. 4th ed. 335p. 21 maps. (Blue Guide).

Some thirty-seven routes through Portugal are described by the author, most of which require the use of a private vehicle. Although the volume has colour maps inside the covers, the rest of the volume is devoid of colour and is ornamented only by a number of black-and-white illustrations. Nevertheless, the text is informative and the coverage is detailed with a smaller typeface being used for background information as in the Baedeker guides whose English editions were produced by the founders of the Blue Guides before the First World War.

90 Peeps at Portugal: a pocket guide to 'The Sun Coast' and Lisbon.
E. Rosenthal. Lisbon: The National Council of Turismo, c.1940. 225p. 7 maps. bibliog.

A detailed pocket book arranged into suggested itineraries for spending twelve days in the Lisbon, Cascais and Estoril area. In addition there is a guided 'Walk through the Alfama', the most historic sector of Lisbon. Seven appendices include a predominantly English-language bibliography, lists of Portugal's monarchs and presidents, hotel and theatre addresses and information on bus, tram and ship services. The volume conveys much of the genteel form of tourism which preceded the appearance of the cheap package holiday.

91 Algarve.
Beate Schümann, English version by David Ingram. Singapore: APA Publications, 1997. 78p. maps. (Insight Compact Guides).

A companion to the volumes on Lisbon and Portugal in the same series (see item no. 88), which derives from a German original. After an introductory essay there are sections on places, culture, leisure and the practicalities of staying and travelling in Portugal. Numerous, mainly small, colour photographs and attractive maps enhance the text.

Tourism and Travel Guidebooks. General

92 Exploring rural Portugal.
Joe Staines, Lia Duarte. London: Christopher Helm, A. & C. Black, 1992. 123p. maps. bibliog. (Exploring Rural Series).

After an introduction which covers the practical aspects of getting around Portugal, including driving, health matters and accommodation, this book comprises seven chapters on different regions of the country, namely Estremadura, Ribatejo, Alto Alentejo, Baixo Alentejo and Algarve, Trás-os-Montes, Entre-Minho e Douro and the Beiras. For each region excursions of mostly two or three days' duration are described, although some are as long as five days in length. These excursions have accompanying basic road maps and line drawings which make up a guide avowedly 'aimed at travellers with a sense of curiosity and adventure' and who have the use of a car. Many line drawings and black-and-white maps enhance the informative text which blends topographical and architectural description with background historical information. The bibliography comprises books in English about Portugal and translations of major Portuguese literary works.

93 Rick Steves' [sic] Spain and Portugal 1999.
Edited by Rick Steves. Santa Fe, New Mexico: John Muir Publications, 1999. 264p.

An enlarged development of *Rick Steves' [sic] Spain & Portugal in your pocket: a step-by-step guide and travel itinerary* (Plymouth, England: Northcote House, 1987. 127p. maps. [Pocket Travellers]), a volume which offered more than twenty itineraries and, like this 1999 version, included railway journeys and assumed the use of a car. Both titles are aimed at the independent traveller and, as a consequence, provide a wide range of practical information on planning journeys, where to eat and what to see in Portugal. The 1999 edition describes itself as an 'opinionated' guide and is characterized by hand-drawn maps. Portugal occupies p. 184-248 and is described in three sections covering the Lisbon, Algarve and central Portugal regions.

94 Portugal, with Madeira & the Azores.
Main consultant, Martin Symington. London: Dorling Kindersley, 1997. 480p. maps. (Eyewitness Travel Guides).

An alluring full-colour guide to Portugal, packed with photographs and distinctive aerial, line and cutaway drawings. After a section 'Introducing Portugal', the core of the book comprises sections on Lisbon, central, northern and southern Portugal, as well as 'Portugal's Islands'. The closing section, 'Travellers' Needs', includes practical information on public transport, banks, telephones, etc. The wealth of attractive illustrations dictates the use of art paper whose weight sadly makes the volume so heavy that it is more comfortable for the armchair tourist then for the pedestrian traveller in the field. For the companion volume on *Lisbon*, see item no. 60.

95 Off the beaten track: Portugal.
Nick Timmins. Ashbourne, England: Moorland Publishing/ The Globe Pequot Press, 1994. 2nd rev. ed. 298p. maps. (Off The Beaten Track).

Deliberately setting out to guide the reader to parts of Portugal which are not heavily frequented by tourists, the author arranges the text into ten discontinuous itineraries. These cover the Alto Minho, Costa Verde, Oporto, the Douro valley, Trás-os-Montes,

27

Tourism and Travel Guidebooks. General

Dão-Lafões, Évora, Alto Alentejo, south-west Alentejo and the eastern Algarve. The itineraries assume the availability of a car as the means of transport and, as the title implies, cover locations not described in other tourist guides. Colour and monochrome photographs reinforce the textual descriptions, in which renditions of Portuguese names are sometimes less than totally accurate.

96 The Algarve: a travel guide.
Mary Tisdall, Archie Tisdall. Brentford, England: Roger Lascelles, 1990. 197p. maps. bibliog.

In fourteen chapters the authors, experienced travel-writers, provide a mass of detailed information, including prices, on visiting the Algarve. They cover how to get there, where to stay, how to get around by car and public transport, food, drink, entertainment and a brief guide to the Portuguese language. There are also four chapters on the various regions within the Algarve. The book is illustrated by both colour and black-and-white photographs.

97 Berlitz travellers' guide to Portugal.
Edited by Alan Tucker. Oxford; New York: Berlitz, 1995. 4th ed. 560p. maps. bibliog.

A solid, slim-format guide to Portugal written by specialists on the country and developed from the *Penguin guide to Portugal* (see item no. 98). It is aimed at providing 'exceptional information for the experienced traveller'. Each chapter on the regions is thus written by one or more of these experts which necessarily leads to a slight inconsistency of approach but it is nevertheless more thorough and informative than most guides to Portugal. The book lacks colour illustrations but has a good number of monochrome maps, as well as a bibliography and historical chronology.

98 The Penguin guide to Portugal.
Edited by Alan Tucker. New York: Penguin Books, 1990. 440p. maps. bibliog. (The Penguin Travel Guides).

A reliable and readable illustrated guidebook arranged into twelve sections on the individual regions of the country, including the Azores and Madeira. It is the North American version of the *Berlitz travellers' guide to Portugal* (see item no. 97). The sections are written by a variety of travel writers, mostly North American or Portuguese. In the opening chapter there are overviews of the country, including its religion, customs and history, which are followed by a summary of 'useful facts' and a most useful annotated bibliography of English works about Portugal. Guidance is also given on Portuguese food and on finding accommodation.

99 Portugal.
Julia Wilkinson, John King. Hawthorn, Australia: Lonely Planet, 1999. 2nd ed. 544p. maps.

A compact and fact-filled guide to Portugal which, apart from the main sections on the diverse regions of the country, has nearly 100 'boxed asides' which break up the more formal text with cultural or historical information. There are several sections of small colour photographs and numerous black-and-white maps. The Lonely Planet newspaper *Planet Talk* and its website ensure that the content is updated by its readers' actual

Tourism and Travel Guidebooks. Accommodation guides

experiences and the series prides itself on its down-to-earth and up-to-date details of prices, opening hours and telephone numbers.

100 Portugal: visitor traffic to the U.K., a market summary. International passenger survey.
Compilation by Martin Withyman Associates and BTA/ETB Statistical Research, data supplied by Office for National Statistics. London: British Tourist Authority/ English Tourist Board, 1996. 15p.
A statistical analysis of the visits made to the United Kingdom by Portuguese nationals. For some of the data, the comparative statistics date in some cases back to 1978 while others, such as the visitors' purpose, age, sex and mode of travel, only date back to 1990.

Holiday Portuguese.
See item no. 348.

A travel guide to Jewish Europe.
See item no. 362.

A guide to the Douro amd port wine.
See item no. 666.

Accommodation guides

101 Pousadas of Portugal: unique lodgings in state-owned castles, palaces, mansions and hotels.
Sam Ballard, Jane Ballard.   Ashbourne, England: Moorland Publishing, 1986. 173p. maps.
A British edition of an American publication (Boston, Massachusetts: The Harvard Common Press, 1986) which guides the North American tourist to the luxury accommodation provided by Portugal's *pousadas* and related historical institutions. The book has five sections. The introduction covers practicalities such as making reservations, travel arrangements and cuisine. This is followed by the main section of 'Places to stay, eat and visit'. It is completed by twelve itineraries, a pronunciation guide and glossary, followed by indexes. Small black-and-white photographs illustrate many of the premises and thumbnail maps show their precise locations.

Tourism and Travel Guidebooks. Accommodation guides

102 International Tourism Reports, Portugal.
The Economist Intelligence Unit. London: The Economist Intelligence Unit, 1986- . irregular.

An authoritative review of the Portuguese tourist industry which was formerly published as *International Tourism Quarterly* and commenced publication in 1971. The reports are particularly useful as an objective assessment of the country's hotel industry.

103 Hotels of character and charm in Portugal.
Michelle Gastaut, Fabrice Camoin. New York: Fodor's Travel Publications, 1998. 2nd ed. 210p. maps. (Fodor's Rivages).

This is a much-expanded version of the 1996 edition of this title, which retains the same format whereby each hotel is illustrated in colour and details are given, even including meal times. The hotels are arranged according to ten regions of Portugal, together with a chapter on restaurants. As well as a general map there are smaller ones showing how to find the hotels.

104 Fielding's paradors, pousadas and charming villages of Spain & Portugal.
A. Hoyt Hobbs. Redondo Beach, California: Fielding, 1997. 697p. maps.

In this volume, aimed at the North American tourist making a visit to Iberia with a car at his or her disposal, the section on Portugal comprises some 200 pages (p. 453 *et seq.*). The author first provides background, historical and artistic information on the country. This is followed by descriptions of routes off the beaten track in the Lisbon area, the south and the north of Portugal, together with hotel and restaurant information. The book has monochrome maps, some of which are described, a little loosely, as '3D maps', and a small number of colour photographs complete the publication.

105 Alastair Sawday's special places to stay in Spain and Portugal.
Edited by Guy Hunter-Watts. Bristol, England: Alastair Sawday Publishing, 1999. 2nd ed. 346p. maps.

This volume is a compendium of up-market accommodation in the Iberian peninsula. The last 100 pages or so cover Portugal and are divided into sections for the north, south and centre of the country. Colour photographs are provided of each of the premises described and instructions are given on how to find them as well as details of their facilities, including ownership and price tariffs. This directory is aimed at those wishing to go beyond the package holiday to stay in premises with character or historical associations.

106 Aviz: uma história de Lisboa, a Lisbon story.
Jill Joliffe. Lisbon: Prolisipo, 1997. 187p. bibliog.

With text in both Portuguese and English, this is a sumptuous review of the history of Lisbon's Aviz Hotel which in its heyday was frequented by such names as Eva Perón, Queen Elizabeth II and Calouste Gulbenkian. The hotel, which was sited in the Avenida Fontes, is depicted in numerous black-and-white and colour photographs which capture the elegance of the guests and the style of the building and its decoration.

Tourism and Travel Guidebooks. Accommodation guides

107 An analysis of the hotel industry of Portugal.
Richard McElroy, Pauline Jackson, Gail Maguire, Paul Marshall, Heidi Miller, Victoria Morrell. Huddersfield, England: University of Huddersfield, 1992. 45p. + data section. map. bibliog.

One of a series of nine studies on European hotels, this volume concludes that the Portuguese hotel industry is relatively undeveloped, compared with its Iberian neighbour, Spain, and most of the rest of western Europe. Nearly eighty-eight per cent of the 296 hotels in mainland Portugal which were surveyed were found to be in private ownership. An extensive data section lists hotels, with their addresses, numbers of rooms and beds, and ownership category.

108 Hotéis, restaurantes, Portugal. (Hotels, restaurants, Portugal.)
Michelin Companhia Luso Pneu. Prior Velho, Portugal: Michelin Companhia Luso Pneu, 1998. 180p. maps.

After an introduction in various languages including English, this is an alphabetical gazetteer of hotels and restaurants in Portugal, illustrated by clear colour maps of the more important locations. Each entry is brief but the use of the usual Michelin symbols ensures that a great detail of factual information is conveyed about the facilities available. The volume ends with a short vocabulary and practical information on such matters as telephone dialling codes. For the wider Iberian peninsula, the Michelin red guide *Espagne, Portugal 1999* (Clermont-Ferrand, France, 1998. 795p.) uses a similar format.

109 Portugal's pousada route.
Stuart Ross. Lagoa, Portugal: Vista Ibérica Publicações, 1998. 4th ed. 152p. maps.

A guide to more than thirty Portuguese *pousadas* or state-owned buildings, usually of historical or architectural importance, which are nowadays used as luxury accommodation for tourists. Each entry is illustrated with colour photographs and a map indicating how to find the often remote locations of the premises.

110 Karen Brown's Portugal: charming inns and itineraries.
Cynthia Sauvage, Clare Brown, illustrated by Barbara Tripp. San Mateo, California: Karen Brown's Guides; New York: Fodor's Travel Publications, 1999. 5th ed. 260p. maps. (Karen Brown's Country Inn Series).

A guide for North American visitors to accommodation off the beaten track of international hotel chains. The text is divided into three sections which address general information on Portugal, seven suggested itineraries and information on where to stay. The illustrations are line drawings and the paper on which the book is printed is, surprisingly in a work aimed at the discerning traveller, somewhat less then top-quality. All the listed properties are included by invitation only, following personal visits from Karen Brown or one of her female relatives.

Tourism and Travel Guidebooks. Walks and walking guides

111 Bussaco Palace Hotel.
Jorge Tavares da Silva, Norma Stanway, Jacques Maréchal.
Brussels: Antonio Nardone Editeur, 1997. 131p. bibliog.

In parallel Portuguese, English and French texts, this volume tells the story of the luxurious Bussaco Palace Hotel, built over a long period before and after 1900 on the site of a former monastery near the Peninsular War battlefield of Buçaco (1810) in central Portugal. The building is a neo-Gothic fantasy, designed by the Italian architect, Luigi Manini. Such was its attraction to well-heeled visitors, it even had its own airfield, opened in 1923. With dozens of colour photographs, this book depicts the splendours of the hotel and catalogues the many famous film stars, politicians and nobility to have stayed there.

Walks and walking guides

112 Walking in Portugal.
Bethan Davies, Ben Cole. London: Footprint Guides, 1994. 208p. maps. (A Footprint Guide).

Portugal is undeveloped as a walking venue but Davies and Cole show that the country has a lot to offer the touring walker. After a general introduction to the country, the body of the book (p. 59-199) comprises six sections of walks, including the Lisbon and Oporto regions, national parks and other areas, particularly within northern and central Portugal. Helpful information on where to find maps, walking equipment and accommodation is also provided.

113 Walking in the Algarve.
June Parker. Milnthorpe, England: Cicerone, 1995. 160p. maps. (A Cicerone Guide).

Portugal's sunny Algarve region is not normally associated with energetic physical pursuits but here June Parker provides thirty-five varied walks through the southernmost province of the country. These are arranged by districts and are graded for difficulty. The walks are of up to five hours' duration and the descriptions are accompanied by maps and colour photographs.

114 Across the rivers of Portugal: a journey on foot from northern Spain to southern Portugal.
Bert Slader. Newcastle, Northern Ireland: Quest Books (NI), 1991. 116p.

In 1985 the author followed the pilgrim route across Spain to Santiago de Compostela. In 1987 he resumed his journey from Santiago, southwards through the length of Portugal, a journey recounted here. His journey ends on the Spanish border at Vila Real de Santo António in the Algarve. Apart from the narrative of his adventures, there is an 'Interlude in Lisbon' which describes his visit to the capital en route to Santiago and which includes a curious tram tour of Lisbon with fifty members of the Lisbon-based St Andrew's Society of mostly Scottish expatriates.

Tourism and Travel Guidebooks. Walks and walking guides

115 Mean feat: a 3,000 mile walk through Portugal, Spain, France, Switzerland and Italy.
John Waite. Yeovil, England: Oxford Illustrated Press, 1985. 288p.

The author recounts his walk from the south of Portugal (Lagos) to the north, via Oporto, in the early part of this volume, before his adventures take him east towards Italy.

Travellers' Accounts

Pre-20th century

116 Dias and his successors.
Edited by Eric Axelson, Charles Boxer, Graham Bell-Cross, Colin Martin.   Cape Town, South Africa: Saayman & Weber, 1988. 159p. maps. bibliog.

An attractively produced homage to the Portuguese explorer, Bartolomeu Dias, published in the 500th anniversary year of his rounding the Cape of Good Hope in search of the Indies. The volume includes translations of extracts from four contemporary accounts of the African maritime exploits of Dias and his fellow 'Discoverers' Vasco da Gama, João de Lisboa and Mesquita Perestrelo. Three essays follow, on the voyages to India, on Portuguese shipwrecks and on Portuguese maritime cartography of southern Africa. Thirty-two early maps of the area, some in colour, are reproduced and elucidated in this large-format book.

117 The grand peregrination; being the life and adventures of Fernão Mendes Pinto.
Maurice Collis.   Manchester, England: Carcanet in association with the Calouste Gulbenkian Foundation, 1990. 313p. bibliog. (Aspects of Portugal, no. 3).

Originally published in 1949 (London: Faber), this new edition seeks in the author's words 'to present Fernão Mendes Pinto (1509-83) to the British public'. Pinto led a life of adventure for twenty years from 1537, during which he visited Arabia, India, Indonesia, Burma, China, Japan and other countries in the Orient. His lively account of these years, which included numerous shipwrecks as well as encounters with pirates and slavers, was given in his posthumously published book, *Peregrinações* (Peregrinations), which forms the basis for Collis's account of Pinto's exploits.

Travellers' Accounts. Pre-20th century

118 Studies in the Portuguese Discoveries, I. Proceedings of the first Colloquium of the Centre for the Study of the Portuguese Discoveries.
Edited by T. F. Earle, Stephen Parkinson. Warminster, England: Aris & Phillips with the Comissão Nacional para as Comemorações dos Descobrimentos Portugueses, c.1992. 123p. maps. bibliog. (Studies in the Portuguese Discoveries, no. 1).

A varied collection of six papers from a colloquium on the Portuguese Discoveries. The papers discuss the role of Prince Henry, the Portuguese in the Maldive Islands, mixed race groups during the early period of Portuguese expansion, Portuguese shipbuilding, astronomical navigation and the computerized analysis of *Ásia* by João de Barros (1497-1562) in its 2,000 page edition of 1945.

119 Journal of a visit to Madeira and Portugal, 1853-1854.
Isabella de França. Funchal, Madeira: Junta Geral do Distrito Autónoma de Funchal, 1970. 269p.

A large-format edition of 'the most complete documentary of Madeiran life of the middle of the last century'. The text and accompanying twenty-four watercolours comprise the journal of an English woman who married a Madeiran landowner. The journal recounts their journey from London to Funchal, the capital of Madeira in the first chapter; the remaining five chapters include three on Madeira and two on Lisbon, including an excursion to Sintra. The Franças died in Southampton, England in the 1880s.

120 Intrepid itinerant: Manuel Godinho and his journey from India to Portugal in 1663.
Manuel Godinho, edited with an introduction and notes by John Correia-Afonso, translation by Vitálio Lobo, John Correia-Afonso. Bombay: Oxford University Press, 1990. 253p. maps.

This is a translation of the Padre Manuel Godinho's *Relação do novo caminho que fez por terra e mar vindo da India para Portugal no anno de 1663* (Relation of the new route which he took across land and sea whilst coming from India to Portugal in the year 1663). Godinho had gone to India as one of Portugal's many evangelizers and his entertaining chronicle is one of many produced by such early travellers to Portugal's overseas outposts.

121 The voyage of Pedro Álvares Cabral to Brazil and India from contemporary documents and narratives.
Translated, with introduction and notes by William Brooks Greenlee. London: Hakluyt Society, 1938. 228p. maps. bibliog. (The Hakluyt Society, Second Series, No. LXXXI).

After almost eighty pages of prefatory introduction to the voyage and to the biography of Pedro Álvares Cabral, this volume comprises sixteen contemporary documents in English translation. These all relate to the momentous voyage from Lisbon in March 1500 during which Brazil was discovered by the Portuguese. The documents include texts written by both Portuguese and Italians between 1500 and 1502. Several contemporary maps are also reproduced.

Travellers' Accounts. Pre-20th century

122 An overland journey to Lisbon at the close of 1846; with a picture of the actual state of Spain and Portugal.
T. M. Hughes.   London: Henry Colburn, 1847. 2 vols.

The 19th century saw many British gentlemen visit Portugal and record their experiences for posterity, as does Hughes who travelled through France and Spain to Lisbon. Amongst other lively accounts of Portugal are those of William Baxter, *The Tagus and the Tiber* (1852) and Charles Johnson, *Travels in Portugal* (1875). Military men such as John Alexander, nobility who included the Earl of Carnarvon, clerics like Joseph Oldknow, writers such as Alfred, Lord Tennyson and William Makepeace Thackeray, as well as the infirm, represented by Henry Matthews, all left their published memoirs of Portugal. These and other 19th-century travels are all documented in the *Lisbon* volume in the World Bibliographical Series, vol. 199, 1997, item nos. 241-78.

123 Builders of the oceans.
K. David Jackson, paintings by Ilda David.   Lisbon: Assírio & Alvim, 1997. 114p. bibliog. (Notebooks on the Portuguese Pavilion, Expo 98).

The author here provides a brief survey of the Portuguese maritime explorations, particularly in Asia. The abstract paintings frankly add nothing to the text other than that their title is the same as that of the book. Jackson makes heavy use of quotations from contemporary accounts, including obscure sources in Indo-Portuguese and Japanese. In *Into the rising sun: Vasco da Gama and the search for the sea route to the East* (New York: TV Books, 1999. 175p. map. bibliog.), its author, Luc Cuyvers, likens Vasco da Gama's 27,000-mile journey to the Indies to the Apollo moon-shots of the 1960s, as both were nationally orchestrated projects. Published to accompany a television series, the book is well illustrated by colour photographs of Portuguese outposts in Africa and Asia.

124 They went to Portugal too. Papers from Rose Macaulay's original manuscript for *They went to Portugal*, omitted when the projected two volume work was published as one volume in 1946, at a time of severe post-war paper rationing, here printed for the first time.
Rose Macaulay, introduction by Susan Lowndes, edited by L. C. Taylor.   Manchester, England: Carcanet Press in association with Calouste Gulbenkian Foundation, 1990. 338p. map. bibliog. (Aspects of Portugal).

As its somewhat rambling subtitle explains, this is a sequel to the classic *They went to Portugal* (London: Jonathan Cape, 1946; Harmondsworth, England: Penguin Books, 1985. 443p. bibliog.). Utilizing her extensive reading of personal memoirs and related publications and documents, Macaulay recounts the experiences in Portugal of eleven categories of British traveller or resident, moving chronologically from mediaeval traders through the Armada of 1588, the 1755 Lisbon earthquake and 19th-century British military involvement to her own Lisbon memoirs of the 1940s. Exploits of famous names such as Sir Francis Drake and Sir George Canning here sit alongside the biographies of more obscure but, nonetheless, fascinating Britons who visited Portugal.

Travellers' Accounts. Pre-20th century

125 Sketches and adventures in Madeira, Portugal and the Andalusias of Spain.
By the author of 'Daniel Webster and his contemporaries', [i.e. Charles W. March]. London: Sampson, Low, 1856. 445p.

An account of a journey from Southampton to Madeira and onward to Portugal and Spain. The first ten chapters cover Madeira, whilst the next four describe the journey and stay in Lisbon and its environs, including Sintra. The author is somewhat scornful of Portugal, whose 'glories are all in the past' and terms such as 'degenerate' and 'crumbling' are used to describe the capital and its hinterland.

126 Portugal e descobrimento do Atlântico. Portugal and the discovery of the Atlantic.
Alfredo Pinheiro Marques. Lisbon: Imprensa Nacional-Casa da Moeda, 1990. 117p. maps. bibliog.

The purpose of this volume is 'to try to provide an up-to-date synthetic summary of the essential questions and moments in the conquest of the Atlantic'. Produced to accompany the launch in 1989/90 of coins to commemorate the Portuguese era of Discoveries, the text concentrates on the Atlantic islands of the Canaries, Azores and Madeira from their earliest identification on maps to their exploitation by the Portuguese. The book also explains developments in Portuguese astronomical navigation and a detailed chronology is supplied. The text is enhanced by a number of colour photographs of contemporary charts and documents.

127 Copy of a letter of the King of Portugal sent to the King of Castile concerning the voyage and success of India.
Translated by Sergio Pacifici, introduction by John Parker. Minneapolis, Minnesota: Minnesota University Press, 1955. 24p. maps.

The importance of this anonymous *Letter*, first published in Rome in 1505, is that it contains the first printed reference to the discovery of Brazil as well as an account of the four earliest voyages to India by the Portuguese.

128 The travels of Fernão Mendes Pinto.
Fernão Mendes Pinto, edited by Rebecca D. Catz. Chicago, Illinois; London: University of Chicago Press, 1989. 663p. map. bibliog.

Supported by thirty pages of introduction and many more pages of notes, this is a translated edition of the *Peregrinações* (Peregrinations) of Fernão Mendes Pinto (c.1510-83) which were written in 1578 but only published in 1614. Catz sees Pinto's work as a satire on Portuguese behaviour in the East, written for his children, a view not accepted by all scholars, many of whom have seen the work as an essentially serious work of description. Either way it is a fascinating account of Asia as found by 16th-century Portuguese travellers.

Travellers' Accounts. Pre-20th century

129 The voyages and adventures of Ferdinand Mendez Pinto, the Portuguese.
Fernão Mendes Pinto, introduction by Arminius Vambery, translated by Henry Cogan. London: Fisher Unwin, 1891. 464p. (The Adventure Series).

An abridged, illustrated translation of the *Perigrinações* (Peregrinations) of the multi-faceted traveller and trader, Fernão Mendes Pinto (c.1510-83). Pinto travelled through numerous countries in South East Asia including Japan, China and Malaya, as well as India and Persia. He endured many shipwrecks before renouncing his worldly life and writing this adventure-packed autobiography.

130 William Beckford & Portugal: an impassioned journey, 1787, 1794, 1798. Exposição, exhibition, Palácio de Queluz, Maio-Novembro, 1987.
Maria Laura Bettencourt Pires. Lisbon: Instituto Português do Património Cultural, 1987. 197p. bibliog.

William Beckford, author of *Vathek*, fled to Portugal to escape a moral scandal and spent three periods in the country, in 1787, 1793-95 and 1798-99. Whilst gaining wide acceptance amongst Lisbon society, he failed to gain the full approbation of the Portuguese monarchy, partly due to the machinations of the expatriate British community. This catalogue of an exhibition in honour of Beckford is written in parallel Portuguese and English texts and includes a number of contemporary illustrations.

131 The travels of the Infante Dom Pedro of Portugal.
Francis M. Rogers. Cambridge, Massachusetts: Harvard University Press, 1961. 424p. bibliog.

The Infante Dom Pedro (Prince Pedro, 1392-1449) was a brother of Henry the Navigator. An account of Pedro's three years of travel from 1425 were published by Gómez de Sanisteban as an early 16th-century chapbook, which went through more than 100 editions in Iberia. Rogers provides a detailed introduction to the book as well as an English translation of the text and a commentary. Pedro's travels took him through much of Europe to the Near East and the Indies. Rogers also assesses the impact of the book on subsequent Portuguese chroniclers and on later writers such as Oliveira Martins and Guillaume Apollinaire.

132 Portuguese pilgrims and Dighton Rock: the first chapter in American history, with 164 illustrations.
Manuel Luciano da Silva. Bristol, Rhode Island: Nelson D. Martins, 1971. 99p. bibliog.

In the early 16th century, after Gaspar Corte-Real was lost on a voyage from the Azores, his brother Miguel set out to find him but he, too, never returned. However, the Dighton Rock in Massachusetts was found to bear inscriptions which many, including the author, take as proof that Miguel Corte-Real reached New England in 1511, well before the Pilgrim Fathers. With many drawings and photographs, as well as comparisons with Portuguese inscriptions found in Africa, Dr Silva furnishes a wealth of evidence to support his contention.

Travellers' Accounts. 20th century

133 In the wake of the Portuguese navigators: a photographic essay.
Michael Teague. Manchester, England: Carcanet, in association with Calouste Gulbenkian Foundation, 1988. 121p. map. (Aspects of Portugal, no. 1).

Following a colour map of the major Portuguese voyages of discovery and an introductory essay by the author, there follow four sections of his atmospheric black-and-white photographs, each headed by a small colour photograph. The sections are entitled 'Africa', 'Brazil', 'India' and 'East', and their purpose is to 'tell something of the story of a heritage'. In other words, they depict former Portuguese colonial lands, their people and the Portuguese legacy, both in terms of buildings and of other artefacts.

134 Portugal, the pathfinder: journeys from the medieval toward the modern world, 1300-ca1600.
Edited by George D. Winius. Madison, Wisconsin: Hispanic Seminary of Medieval Studies, 1995. 428p. 21 maps. bibliog.

In this volume Winius aims to redress the balance towards Portugal from what he sees as a pro-Spanish bias in the attribution of responsibility for the 'discovery' of new lands and consequential creation of the modern world. There are eighteen contributions in this compendium, four by Winius himself, the rest by other accomplished historians. A fascinating epilogue by Alfredo Pinheiro Marques charts the decline in Columbus's fortunes once the Portuguese discovery of the route to the Indies had been made known. He emphasizes Columbus's error in believing that the route there lay by sailing west from Europe. However, the Portuguese also erred; the discoveries of a Portuguese who had to sail under the Spanish flag are recorded in *Magellan's voyage: a narrative account of the first circumnavigation*, edited by Antonio Pigafetta (London: Constable, 1994. 208p.).

20th century

135 Portuguese journey.
W. T. Blake. London: Alvin Redman, 1963. 167p. map.

Major W. T. Blake was the former aviation correspondent of a number of British newspapers and the author of many books of travels. He was lame so his wife, who is referred to throughout only as 'R', acted both as chauffeur and, somewhat bizarrely, as the author's eyes for sights which required the climbing of steps or stairs. In the book's nineteen chapters an account is given of a journey beginning and ending in Tuy on the northern Portuguese border with Spain and passing through Oporto, Santarém, Lisbon, the Algarve and numerous other locations en route. The author is not afraid to express his opinion, particularly about Oporto, and his frequent complaints about the quality and price of gin and tonic, his predilection for country-house hotels and his propensity to hire local guides make this book almost as interesting as an account of upper middle-class Britons abroad as a description of Portugal.

Travellers' Accounts. 20th century

136 Playtime in Portugal: an unconventional guide to the Algarves.
John Gibbons. London: Methuen & Co., 1936. 184p. 2 maps.

The author claims that this is the first book by an Englishman exclusively on southern Portugal, although about a quarter of it covers the Lisbon area and the arduous third-class railway journey there from France. It is a most informative and sympathetic introduction to the country by a writer who was to spend a number of years living there. Illustrated by black-and-white photographs it interweaves Portuguese history with an entertaining account of the author's railway journey down to the Algarve and along the coast, both westwards to Lagos and eastwards to Vila Real de Santo António.

137 My tour in Portugal.
Helen Cameron Gordon (Lady Russell). London: Methuen & Co., 1932. 287p. map.

Lady Russell could not be described as a typical tourist and although she does offer some perceptive comments on what she sees as she travels around, she tends to overlook the harsher side of life in 1930s Portugal. She is, perhaps, most at home in her account of the Lisbon area and of its expatriate British community, written during a stay of more than a month at Estoril. Her narration is interspersed with Portuguese history and is illustrated by black-and-white photographs.

138 Backwards out of the big world: a voyage into Portugal.
Paul Hyland. London: Harper Collins, 1996. 269p. map. bibliog.

After reaching Lisbon by cargo boat, Hyland set off on a route ostensibly up the River Tagus to the Spanish border, before returning to Lisbon and the most westerly point of mainland Europe at Cabo da Roca. Whilst he visits such tourist magnets as Sintra, Tomar, Évora and Santarém, he also calls at some less well-known towns such as Idanha-a-Velha, Pego and Abrantes. The book includes more than two dozen black-and-white photographs of his travels which are interspersed with much historical and cultural information on Portugal.

139 Pleasure by the busload.
Emily Kimbrough, drawings by Mircea Vasiliu. New York: Harper & Brothers Publishers, 1961. 276p. map. bibliog.

A humorous account of a journey undertaken by five adults, including the American authoress, in a Volkswagen Microbus across the length and breadth of Portugal. Although the writer devotes much of her account to the interactions within the group of travellers, she does also convey something of the history and everyday life of Portugal as it was in the 1960s.

140 Fabled shore: from the Pyrenees to Portugal.
Rose Macaulay. Oxford: Oxford University Press, 1986. 248p. 2 maps.

In a work first published in 1949 (London: Hamish Hamilton Limited, reprinted 1973. 200p. map), Macaulay describes her travels down the Spanish Mediterranean coast before entering Portugal at Vila Real do Santo António, in the Algarve. She then journeyed by car, along the full length of the Algarve coast to Cape St. Vincent. In five chapters she describes a coastline still relatively unscathed by mass tourism. The monochrome photograph illustrations are of the standard National Tourist Office type.

141 Through Spain and Portugal.
Ernest Peixotto. New York: Charles Scribner's Sons, 1922. 281p.

Peixotto visited the major towns of tourist interest in the central and northern regions of Portugal. These include Lisbon, Leiria, Buçaco, Coimbra, Oporto, Guimarães and Braga. The account is illustrated by sixty-two of the writer's own drawings.

142 Daytrips, Spain and Portugal: 50 one-day adventures by car, rail or ferry.
Norman P. T. Renouf. Norwalk, Connecticut: Hastings House/ United Publishers' Group, 1997. 368p. maps.

Descriptions of eight trips in Portugal are included in this volume and these range across the country. The mixture of private and public transport routes is an unusual but welcome innovation, particularly in a travel book aimed primarily at a North American audience. The more expansive sub-title used on the book's cover is *50 one-day adventures by rail, bus or car including walking tours and side trips to Gibraltar and Morocco*.

143 Things seen in Portugal: the garden of the West, a land of mountains and rivers, of the vine, the olive and the cork tree, and of ancient buildings richly carved, picturesque peasantry & hardy fishermen.
M. F. Smithes. London: Seeley Service, 1931. 156p. map.

Smithes provides here a less than critical account of a traveller's experiences in interwar Portugal. The volume's thirty-two photographs provide a view of the country before mass tourism took a hold.

144 A philosopher in Portugal.
Eugène E. Street. London: T. Fisher Unwin, 1903. 248p.

By the same author who produced *Portuguese life in town and country*, this work recounts in twelve chapters the adventures of 'The Philosopher', a third-person creation, as he travels through Portugal on the tourist trail. Descriptions of such sites as Sintra, Queluz and Oporto are interspersed with digressions on such topics as the Portuguese character, bullfighting and the Portuguese language. Some of the diversions are esoteric, such as a discourse on the art of patching old clothes, which arises out of the Philosopher's keen observation.

145 No garlic in the soup.
Leonard Wibberley. London: Faber & Faber, 1960. 189p.

An entertaining account of how an Irish-American author took his wife and four children to live near Estoril for what he himself admits were rather vague reasons: life in Portugal would be cheap; it would be a change from the routine of the United States; he wanted to be cosmopolitan and it would benefit his children to travel. Although he admires the integrity and achievements of the prime minister, Salazar, he ultimately finds the

Travellers' Accounts. 20th century

bureaucracy and limitations on personal freedom of his dictatorship enough to prompt his return home.

Albuquerque: Caesar of the East.
See item no. 256.

The Portuguese Columbus.
See item no. 257.

Ferdinand Magellan.
See item no. 258.

Christopher Columbus and the Portuguese.
See item no. 259.

The brothers Corte-Real.
See item no. 265.

John of Empoli and his relations with Afonso de Albuquerque.
See item no. 269.

The career and legend of Vasco da Gama.
See item no. 272.

Flora and Fauna

146 The beginning of the Portuguese mammalogy.
Carlos Almaça. Lisbon: Universidade de Lisboa, 1991. 20p. bibliog.

This volume comprises a paper presented by Almaça at the First European Congress of Mammalogy, held in Lisbon in 1991. The text examines the history of Portuguese mammalogy and the teaching and study methods employed in the past. It is accompanied by twenty-two pages of plates, some of which are in colour. Almaça is also the author of *A natural history museum of the 18th century: the Royal Museum and Botanical Garden of Ajuda* (Lisbon: Museu Nacional de História Natural, Museu e Laboratório Zoológico e Antropológico, Museu Bocage, 1996. 28p.). The Ajuda botanic garden, adjacent to the royal palace of the same name, lies in the western outskirts of Lisbon and was established by order of the Marquis of Pombal in 1768-72. Its four hectares of vegetation remain the oldest such garden in Portugal.

147 An atlas of wintering birds in the western Algarve.
Mark Bolton. Upton, England; Portimão, Portugal: A Rocha Trust, 1987. 82p. (A Rocha Occasional Publication, no. 1).

This illustrated volume demonstrates both the geographical and the seasonal distribution of those bird species which winter in southern Portugal. The area's proximity to both Africa and the Mediterranean means that the Algarve is an attractive location for birdwatchers from northern Europe.

148 The complete Portuguese Water Dog.
Kathryn Braund, Deyanne Farrell Millar. New York: Howell Book House, 1986. 288p. (A Howell Dog Book of Distinction).

An illustrated handbook to the Portuguese Water Dog breed, which is visually similar to the poodle but has semi-webbed feet. Traditionally these dogs aided Portuguese fishermen in retrieving fish and submerged nets. The book covers all aspects of the breed, from caring and grooming the dog, to its dietary requirements. In addition, advice is provided on how it may be trained and bred successfully. Another volume on the same

Flora and Fauna

subject is Len Port's *Bica, the Portuguese Water Dog* (Lagoa, Portugal: Vista Ibérica, 1997. 25p.).

149 A birdwatching guide to the Algarve.
Kevin Carlson, Christine Carlson. Chelmsford, England: Arelquin, 1995. 52p. maps.

As well as being a tourist haven, many of the less popular areas of the Algarve are important birdwatching sites. Illustrated by both colour photographs and by sketches, this guide is a useful introduction to both coastal and inland locations.

150 Portugal: a country of forests.
Direcção Geral das Florestas. Lisbon: Direcção Geral das Florestas, 1992. 60p. maps.

A full-colour work which aims to publicize the work of its corporate author, the Portuguese Forestry Service. Many aspects of its work are covered, including conservation, dealing with fires, and its role in hunting and in forest industries. As well as explaining the work of the various divisions of the service, the book provides accounts of conservancy in each area of Portugal. Some thirty-six per cent of Portugal comprises forest and the Setúbal area is the most extensively covered, whilst Braganza (Bragança) and Lisbon are the least well endowed. A substantial 'country report' on Portuguese forests is also to be found in the European Commission's *Study on European forestry information and communication system reports on forestry inventory and survey systems* (Luxembourg: Office for Official Publications of the European Community, 1997, p. 861-904. maps. bibliog.).

151 The adventures of plants and the Portuguese discoveries.
José Mendes Ferrão. Lisbon: Institute of Tropical Scientific Research/ National Commission for the Commemoration of the Portuguese Discoveries/ Berardo Foundation, 1994. 78p.

An often neglected aspect of the Portuguese overseas explorations is the flora and medicinal plants which the voyagers came across on their travels which were unknown to Europeans. This slim volume seeks to redress that deficiency with an authoritative text on the botanical discoveries of these travellers, which is enhanced by a number of illustrations.

152 Birds of Iberia.
Clive Finlayson, David Tomlinson. Fuengirola, Spain: Mirador Books, 1993. 220p. map. bibliog.

The authors, both experienced birdwatchers, here provide a full-colour survey of more than 150 species of Iberian birds. The abundant excellent photographs are accompanied by a text arranged primarily by bird-types which include water birds, birds of prey, land birds and songbirds. A geographical index includes numerous references to Portugal and to habitats and bird-watching sites, in areas such as the Alentejo, the Algarve, the Berlengas islands and the Gerês national park in the north of the country.

Flora and Fauna

153 Trees of Monserrate.
João Sande Freitas, Raul Constâncio.   Lisbon: Edições Inapa/ Associação Amigos de Monserrate, 1997. 129p.

The Amigos de Monserrate, or Friends of Monserrate, exist to preserve the palace and gardens of Monserrate, which lie in the hills above the town of Sintra. The estate, near Sintra, is best-known in Britain for being the home of the writer William Beckford during his sojourns in Portugal in the 1790s. In this volume its magnificent trees and natural flora are depicted and described in a series of texts by various authors, including Emma Andersen Gilbert. However, it is the superb photographs of Raul Constâncio which are the highlight of the book.

154 The royal horses of Europe: the story of the Andalusian and the Lusitano.
Sylvia Loch.   London: J. A. Allen, 1986. 256p. maps. bibliog.

The authoress, Lady Loch, ran a school of Portuguese horses in Portugal, before she returned to England and founded, with her husband, the Lusitanian Stud and Equitation Centre. The Lusitanian horse, formerly known as the Portuguese Andalusian, is bred principally in the Alentejo and the Ribatejo areas, south-east of Lisbon. This well-illustrated book traces the breed back to pre-Roman times and includes accounts of the horse's role in bullfighting, as well as in war and dressage. The breed's influence in Britain and the Americas is also explained.

155 Algarve plants and landscape: passing tradition and ecological change.
D. J. Mabberley, P. J. Placito, with photographs by the authors and drawings by Rosemary Wise.   Oxford: Oxford University Press, 1993. 100p. maps. bibliog.

Covering wild and cultivated plants, this comprehensive volume is aimed at both residents and visitors to the Algarve. It is written as a continuous narrative but with the intention that individual chapters should also be self-contained. As well as the individual plant species, the ecology of the various regions of the Algarve is described and streets, parks and gardens are covered as well as the countryside. As well as 279 small colour photographs of plants, there are 269 other figures comprising monochrome photographs, maps, drawings and a number of 19th-century aquatints.

156 Wild flowers of the Algarve.
Mary McMutrie.   Printed at Vila Real de Santo António, Portugal: Empresa Litográfica do Sul, 1988. 15p.

A handy guide to forty-two species of wild flower to be found in the Algarve, which claims to be the first such pocket guide to the subject. Each flower is illustrated by a colour drawing and a brief description which gives the Latin name and flowering date, as well as a brief description of the flower and of its typical habitat. A glossary of botanical terms and an index by Latin name complete the volume.

Flora and Fauna

157 A birdwatchers' guide to Portugal and Madeira.
C. C. Moore, Gonçalo Elias, Helder Costa, illustrations by Tony Disley. Perry: Prion, 1997. 144p. maps. (Birdwatchers' Guides).

The mainland of Portugal is a surprisingly rich territory for birdwatchers. The location and mild climate of the Algarve, for example, make it a site rich in maritime species. Likewise, the Portuguese Atlantic island of Madeira is a focus for a number of African birds. With fine illustrations by Tony Disley, this handbook provides a useful guide for the ornithologist.

158 Bats of Portugal: zoogeography and systematics.
Jorge M. Palmeirim. Lawrence, Kansas: University of Kansas Museum of Natural History, 1990. 53p. maps. bibliog. (Miscellaneous Publication, no. 82).

Allegedly the first thorough review of the subject since 1910, this study, also published in Portuguese, aims to bring together all the available published information on Portuguese bats. It also seeks to summarize new distribution records, assess bat distribution patterns, analyse taxonomic status and provide morphological descriptions. There are twenty-four bat species in Portugal, twenty-one of which are covered here. These are, in descending order of importance, those pervasive in Iberia, those only found in the south, those found only in the north and those whose distribution varies by season. An extensive bibliography completes the volume.

159 Flowers of south-west Europe: a field guide.
Oleg Polunin, B. E. Smythies. London; New York; Toronto, Canada: Oxford University Press, 1973. Reprinted, 1988. 480p. maps. bibliog.

With eighty pages of colour illustrations and more than sixty pages of line drawings and maps, this compendium of the flora of south-west Europe remains the best introduction in English to Portuguese flowers. It is aimed at those travelling in Iberia and south-west France with sections on each of the regions therein. Thus there are sections on the Algarve, the Serra da Arrábida to the south of Lisbon, the Pinhal de Leiria and the coastal Beira of central Portugal, as well as on the northern *serras*, or mountain ranges. A full index is provided which utilizes both botanical and popular names of flowers.

160 The Estrela Mountain Dog and its background.
Roger F. Pye. Oporto, Portugal: Published by the author, 1980. 110p. 3 maps.

A finely produced work on the rugged Estrela Mountain Dog whose home environment is the rugged Estrela mountain range in the northern Portuguese interior. Illustrated by twenty-five photographs and some drawings, this is an authoritative text on the dog's behavioural and breeding characteristics by a founder of the Estrela Mountain Dog Association.

Flora and Fauna

161 Where to watch birds in Spain and Portugal.
Laurence Rose.   London: Hamlyn, 1995. 215p. maps. (Hamlyn Birdwatching Guides).

Three hundred and eight of the 'important bird areas', as defined by Grimmet and Jones in their 1989 compilation, are located in Iberia and Rose's book is based on these. More than thirty pages of the volume are devoted to sites in Portugal, Madeira and the Azores. For each site the types of bird to be seen, the timing of their presence and means of access by road or on foot are supplied. The volume is illustrated and also provides some brief guidance on accommodation in the areas in question.

162 Breeding birds of the Algarve.
G. A. Vowles, R. S. Vowles, illustrated by J. M. Benington.
Newent, England: Centro de Estudos Ornithológicos [sic], 1994.
364p. maps. bibliog.

Emanating from what must be the only Portuguese-named ornithological centre in Gloucestershire, this work is an authoritative guide to 154 species of birds known to breed in the Algarve region. Information is also provided on other non-breeding species including escaped exotic birds. The book's five chapters comprise four brief essays on 'The Algarve', 'Conservation', 'Birdwatching in the Algarve', 'Atlas Techniques' and, the body of the book, 'Breeding Birds of the Algarve'. A monochrome drawing of each species, a distribution map and details of habitat, food, breeding habits and distinctive features are included. Six appendices complete the volume.

163 Mediterranean wild flowers.
Text and drawings by Christopher Grey Wilson, colour paintings by Marjorie Blamey.   London: Harper Collins, 1993. 560p. maps. bibliog. (Collins Field Guide).

Although the title does not immediately suggest it, this is actually a guide which covers the flora of the non-Mediterranean country of Portugal from sea level to 1000 metres. It is a most attractively illustrated handbook in which the range of 'flowers' covered includes fruit trees, grasses, flowering trees and ferns.

The Pope's elephant.
See item no. 186.

The Portuguese meat and livestock industry.
See item no. 456.

Prehistory and Archaeology

164 Roman Portugal.
Jorge de Alarcão. Warminster, England: Aris & Phillips, 1988. 2 vols. maps. bibliog. (Archaeology Guides to the Roman World).

This is a comprehensive review of Roman remains in Portugal and the first such work in English. Volume I is an introduction to the subject whilst the three separate fascicules of volume II provide a thorough gazetteer to the Roman sites in the country. The three fascicules cover, firstly, Oporto, Braganza and Viseu in northern Portugal, then the central regions around Coimbra and Lisbon, and finally, the sites and finds in the south of the country, specifically around Évora, Lagos and Faro. The third fascicule contains maps at 1:250,000 of the locations listed in the gazetteer. The gazetteer entries are in both English and Portuguese.

165 Portugal, 1001 sights: an archaeological and historical guide.
James M. Anderson, M. Sheridan Lea. Calgary, Canada: Calgary University Press; London: Hale, 1995. 180p. 5 maps. bibliog.

Following a brief history of Portugal from palaeolithic times, this fascinating review of 1,001 archaeological sites ranges over the whole country. Eighty-seven monochrome photographs illustrate the subject to which Anderson has devoted more than a decade of his life in Portugal itself. Although necessarily brief, the entries are sufficient both to provide an overview of Portuguese archaeology and to stimulate further reading. The diverse subjects covered include cave paintings and Roman villas, as well as the more commonly found artefacts.

Prehistory and Archaeology

166 Encounters and transformations: the archaeology of Iberia in transition.
Edited by Miriam S. Balmuth, Antonio Gilman, Lurdes Prados-Torreira. Sheffield, England: Sheffield Academic Press, 1997. 170p. maps. bibliog. (Monographs in Mediterranean Archaeology, no. 7).

This volume brings together a number of papers from the First International Conference in America on Iberian Archaeology, held at Tufts University. Its fourteen papers include Portuguese archaeological discoveries of groundstone tools and a study of western Iberia at the end of the Bronze Age.

167 Mirobriga: investigations at an Iron Age and Roman site in southern Portugal by the University of Missouri-Columbia, 1981-1986.
Edited by William R. Biers, with contributions by William R. Biers, Jane C. Biers, Albert Leonard Jr., Kathleen Warner Slane, with a technical report by Maura F. Cornman, Craig E. Oder. Oxford: BAR, 1988. 398p. 3 maps. bibliog. (BAR International Series, no. 451).

The Mirobriga site, mentioned by Pliny the Elder, lies 15km from the Atlantic near Santiago do Cacém, some 140km south-east of Lisbon. Its origins have been traced back to the 9th century BC and there is much evidence of Roman occupation, but the site was in decline by the latter part of the 4th century AD. This thorough report of an archaeological survey is presented in five chapters entitled 'The survey', 'The excavations in the circus', 'The baths', 'The pottery from Mirobriga' and 'Mirobriga and its history'. Six appendices go into further detail about the finds and the geology of the site, whilst 245 illustrations, many photographic, depict unearthed building-foundations and artefacts. There are numerous appendices listing the finds in detail.

168 Social complexity and the development of towns in Iberia: from the Copper Age to the second century A.D..
Edited by Barry Cunliffe, Simon Keay. Oxford: Oxford University Press for the British Academy, 1995. 476p. maps. bibliog. (Proceedings of the British Academy, no. 86).

The seventeen papers in this volume derive from the British Academy symposium *The origins of urbanization in Iberia* held in 1994. Abstracts are provided at the rear of the volume which includes studies of emergent Iron Age urban centres in southern and central Portugal, and of the Portuguese *castros* or fortified settlements, which date from the late Bronze Age onwards and are to be found in the north of the country.

Prehistory and Archaeology

169 The archaeology of Iberia.
Edited by Margarita Díaz-Andreu, Simon Keay. London; New York: Routledge, 1997. 314p. maps. bibliog. (Theoretical Archaeology Group).

A compilation of selected papers from the Theoretical Archaeology Group (TAG) conference, held at Southampton in 1992, and attended by British, Spanish and Portuguese delegates. Most of the fifteen chapters cover Iberia as a whole but two are solely on Portugal: 'The Neolithic/Chalcolithic transition in Portugal' (chapter 7); and 'The dynamics of change in northwest Portugal during the first millennium B.C.' (chapter 8). The work claims to be groundbreaking in its application of theoretical frameworks to archaeological evidence discovered in Iberia.

170 Two industries in Roman Lusitania: mining and garum production.
J. C. Edmondson. Oxford: BAR, 1987. 355p. maps. bibliog. (BAR International Series, no. 362).

The seven chapters and six appendices of this work commence with a description of the Roman province of Lusitania, which straddled modern-day Portugal and western Spain. Whilst the value of metal to the Romans is self-evident, that of *garum*, or fish-paste, is less so. However, it was widely used both as a condiment and as a medicine and therefore played a significant part in the Lusitanian economy. The volume covers both the practicalities of mining and *garum* production as well as its place in Roman commerce.

171 An archaeometallurgical survey for ancient tin mines and smelting sites in Spain and Portugal: mid-Central Western Iberian geographical region, 1990-1995.
Craig Merideth. Oxford: Archaeopress, 1998. 205p. maps. bibliog. (BAR International Series, no. 714).

This five-year survey covers the period from 2000 BC to the 4th century AD. It assesses the surface evidence of use of cassiterite ores which were used in the production of bronze. Information is provided from laboratory analyses of slag, mineral and metal deposits. The volume is illustrated by line-drawings and forty-eight photographs, mostly in black-and-white.

172 A guide to the Megalithic monuments of the Évora region.
António Carlos Silva, Rui Parreira, in collaboration with Miguel Lago da Silva. Évora, Portugal: Câmara Municipal de Évora, 1992. 47p. maps. bibliog.

An illustrated guide, which is also available in Portuguese and French, to the so-called *pedras talhas* (hewn stones) of the Évora area in southern central Portugal. These are variously dated to between 4000 and 2000 BC but their purposes are often unclear. More than 150 dolmens have been found in the area, whilst other stones occur singly or in groups, which may have ritualistic significance.

Prehistory and Archaeology

Ancient languages of the Hispanic peninsula.
See item no. 293.

History

General

173 A short history of Portugal.
Caetano Beirão, translated from the Portuguese by Frank R. Holliday. Lisbon: Edições Panorama, 1960. 164p.

In seven chapters Beirão covers the history of Portugal from the formation of the county of Portucale to the election of Admiral Américo Tomás as President of the Republic in 1958. The fact that the last section of the book is entitled 'Peace and prosperity' is indicative of the author's uncritical account of Salazar's New State.

174 A concise history of Portugal.
David Birmingham. Cambridge, England: Cambridge University Press, 1993. 209p. 2 maps. bibliog. (Cambridge Concise Histories).

Arranged into seven chapters, accompanied by a short introduction and forty-three black-and-white illustrations, this book surveys more than 2,000 years of Portuguese history. However, all but the first chapter cover the period from the regaining of Portuguese independence from Spain in 1640 to the modern era which means that its title is a little misleading in its comprehensiveness. A family tree of the Portuguese monarchy and a list of the Republic's presidents are also provided.

175 The history of Spain and Portugal, from B.C.1000 to A.D.1814.
Mrs M. M. Busk. London: Baldwin & Craddock, 1833. 364p. (Library of Useful Knowledge).

Published under the auspices of the Society for the Diffusion of Useful Knowledge, this history of Iberia is perhaps most useful for its near-contemporaneous study of the Peninsular War which occupies more than fifty pages (p. 274-326). Mrs Busk judges Portugal's independence from foreign powers to be a more prize-worthy achievement than the country's historical conquests.

History. General

176 The Portuguese knights of the Order of the Garter.
Manuel Côrte-Real. Lisbon: The British Historical Society of Portugal, 1992. 63p. bibliog.

The English Order of the Garter was created by King Edward III in 1344. Amongst the overseas recipients of this signal honour the Portuguese were one of the most numerous nationalities, with fifteen recipients. All of the Portuguese recipients receive here a brief biographical description and all, except for the one non-monarch, D. Álvaro Vaz de Almada, are also portrayed either in colour or monochrome. King João I was the first overseas nominee to the Order, in 1400, although Queen Filipa (Philippa of Lancaster), had been made a Lady of the Garter as early as 1378. The last Portuguese recipient was the country's last monarch, Manuel II, in 1909. Eight colour photographs reproduce the Garter Plates of Portuguese recipients displayed in St George's Chapel, Windsor, England.

177 Portugal: a short history.
H. V. Livermore. Edinburgh: Edinburgh University Press, 1973. 213p. 4 maps.

This is the shortest of three general histories of Portugal by Harold Livermore. The other two are *A history of Portugal* (Cambridge, England: Cambridge University Press, 1947. 502p. 7 maps. bibliog.) and its revised abridgement, entitled *A new history of Portugal* (London: Cambridge University Press, 1966. 365p. 7 maps. bibliog.). Though obviously omitting the turbulent period following the 1974 Revolution, *Portugal: a short history* is nevertheless an authoritative and detailed account, illustrated by numerous photographs. To avoid repetition of his earlier works, the author here consciously places greater emphasis on the evolution of Portuguese society.

178 The history of Portugal and Spain.
William Mavor. London: Richard Philips, 1803. 354p. (Universal History, Ancient and Modern from the Earliest Records of Time to the General Peace of 1801, vol. 15).

Portugal occupies the first 110 pages of this pocket-size history of Iberia. The country's development over some 700 years from the times of the Counts of Portugal to the early 19th century is covered by the author, who was an amateur historian, a Berkshire vicar and chaplain to the Earl of Dumfries.

179 Portugal and the Portuguese world.
Richard Pattee. Milwaulkee, Wisconsin: The Bruce Publishing Co., 1957. 350p. map. bibliog.

A portrait of contemporary Portugal and its colonial territories across the world, admirably covered in ten chapters. The story of Portugal's origins, its period of global expansion and its subsequent decline is told in the first four chapters. Subsequent chapters include an admirable explanation of the *Estado Novo* of Salazar and coverage of the state-Church relationship in Portugal.

History. General

180 A history of Spain and Portugal.
Stanley G. Payne. Madison, Wisconsin: University of Wisconsin Press, 1976. 2 vols. 12 maps. bibliog.

A thorough and well-illustrated history of the Iberian countries by a leading American historian, which concentrates on Iberia rather than the overseas territories. The first volume covers up to the 17th century, whilst the second brings the story up to the modern era. Older, but nonetheless still respected, classic English-language histories of Portugal are William Atkinson's *A history of Spain and Portugal* (Harmondsworth, England: Penguin Books, 1960. 382p. map. bibliog. [The Pelican History of the World]) and Harold Livermore's *A new history of Spain and Portugal* (Cambridge, England: Cambridge University Press, 1966. 365p. 7 maps. bibliog.).

181 Portugal: a companion history.
José Hermano Saraiva, edited and expanded by Ian Robertson, L. C. Taylor. Manchester, England: Carcanet, in association with Calouste Gulbenkian Foundation, Instituto Camões, Instituto da Biblioteca Nacional e do Livro, 1997. 222p. 15 maps. bibliog. (Aspects of Portugal).

Specifically written for foreigners, this excellent history of Portugal by one of that country's leading authorities is supplemented by some seventy pages by Ian Robertson and L. C. Taylor. Their additions include fifteen annotated maps, a glossary, biographies, a historical gazetteer and an extensive English-language bibliography, all of which are designed to assist the newcomer to Portuguese history. Saraiva's own text covers Portuguese history from ancient times to 1987 in ten concise chapters, accompanied by sixty-four illustrations.

182 Iberia & the Mediterranean.
Edited by Benjamin F. Taggie, Richard W. Clement. Warrensburg, Missouri: Central Missouri State University, 1989. 344p.

An anthology of twenty-eight of the fifty-seven papers given at 'Mediterranean XI', an international symposium held in 1988, somewhat perversely, in the non-Mediterranean city of Budapest, in land-locked Hungary. Sixteen of the papers, nine in English, deal with aspects of Portugal ranging from history and cosmology to literature and religion. Specific topics include the *Estado Novo*, the Inquisition, the counter-reformation, Manuel de Mello, Eça de Queiroz and Antero de Quental.

183 Historical dictionary of Portugal.
Douglas L. Wheeler. Metuchen, New Jersey; London: The Scarecrow Press, 1993. 228p. 2 maps. bibliog. (European Historical Dictionaries, no. 1).

Compiled by the long-time Coordinator of the International Conference Group on Portugal, this is much more than a useful alphabetical guide to Portuguese historical events and figures. It also includes an historical chronology, lists of monarchs and presidents, as well as an informed introduction. Its extensive bibliography (p. 184-283), divided into twenty-eight subject or chronological groupings, provides an excellent stepping-stone to further study of Portuguese history.

History. Mediaeval and Renaissance period (1147-1639)

Muslim occupation (711-1147)

184 Muslim Spain and Portugal: a political history of al-Andalus.
Hugh Kennedy. Harlow, England: Addison Wesley Longman Higher Education, 1996. 342p. maps. bibliog.

Basing his work on Arab as well as western sources, Kennedy provides a fascinating perspective on Iberian history from 711 to the fall of Granada in 1492. His exposition of the various factions within both the Arabs and the Christians is particularly illuminating and is aided by dynastic charts. The book is arranged into chapters which cover the different Moorish regimes, including those of the Amirs, Umayyads, Almoravids and Almohads.

Mediaeval and Renaissance period (1147-1639)

185 King Dinis and the Alfonsine heritage.
Sheila R. Ackerlind. New York; Bern; Frankfurt am Main, Germany; Paris: Peter Lang, 1990. 220p. bibliog. (American University Studies, Series IX History, vol. 69).

King Dinis of Portugal (1279-1325) was the grandson of Alfonso X, *The Learned* of Castile and León (1252-84) and both were major patrons of the arts and poetry in the Galician-Portuguese language. Sheila Ackerlind assesses the influence of Alfonso on Dinis in the fields of translation, law, historiography, poetry and learning in general, an effect which she discerns as still evident on Portuguese culture some seven centuries later. She also covers Dinis's founding of the Universities of Coimbra and Lisbon as well as his declaration of Portuguese as the language for Portugal's judicial and legal proceedings. Important areas such as art, music and architecture are not covered here, however, and the fact that the work is based on a thesis presented in 1972 means that some of the content is a little dated.

186 The Pope's elephant.
Silvio Bedini. Manchester, England: Carcanet, 1997. 302p. (Aspects of Portugal).

Bedini recounts the amazing story of how King Manuel I of Portugal shipped an Indian elephant, called Hanno, to the new Pope, Leo X, in 1514. This gift was so successful in gaining papal support for the Portuguese monarch's plans for the spice islands that in 1515 Manuel also despatched a rhinoceros from his Lisbon menagerie to the Pope. However, the ship conveying the animal sank and the Pope had to make do with its embalmed body.

History. Mediaeval and Renaissance period (1147-1639)

187 Medieval Iberia: readings from Christian, Muslim and Jewish sources.
Edited by Olivia Remie Constable. Philadelphia, Pennsylvania: University of Pennsylvania Press, 1997. 426p. bibliog.

The nine sections of this volume each contain a number of essays on mediaeval Iberia. These range in chronological sequence from the Visigothic period to the 15th century and Muslim Granada. Portuguese subjects which are covered in detail are the siege of Lisbon (1147), Fernão Lopes's account of the wedding of King João I and the treatment of Portugal's Jews. There is also much analysis of the Almoravids and Almohads as well as of the Christian reconquest of Iberia.

188 Proceedings of the International Colloquium on The Portuguese and the Pacific, University of California, Santa Barbara, October, 1993.
Edited by Francis A. Dutra, João Camilo dos Santos. Santa Barbara, California: Center for Portuguese Studies, University of California, Santa Barbara, 1995. 450p. maps. (Publications of the Center for Portuguese Studies).

The 1993 Colloquium on The Portuguese and the Pacific was organized by the University of California, the Calouste Gulbenkian Foundation and various other Portuguese bodies. It was held over three days to mark the 450th anniversary of the death of João Rodrigues Cabrilho, the first European known to have visited California. Twenty-four papers by scholars from the United States, Europe and Asia are here collected and their topics include commercial, anthropological, religious, cartographic and artistic aspects of the Portuguese presence in the Pacific, mostly in the 16th century. This range of subjects and the diversity of the geographical areas covered underline the breadth of Portuguese exploratory activity.

189 The earliest Arthurian names in Spain and Portugal.
David Hook. St Albans, England: David Hook, 1991. 25p. map. (Fontaine Notre Dame, no. I).

David Hook here trawls through historical documents to locate early Iberian usage of the names found in Arthurian literature. The earliest such references date from around 1170. Hook speculates on whether such events as the arrival of English crusaders to assist in the reclamation of Lisbon and other towns from the Moors in the mid-12th century may have also served as the conduit for the arrival of Arthurian legends. Earlier works on this theme include Maria Rosa Lida de Malkiel, 'Arthurian literature in Spain and Portugal' in R. S. Loomis's *Arthurian literature in the Middle Ages* (Oxford: Clarendon Press, 1959, p. 406-18) and *The Arthurian legend in the literatures of the Spanish peninsula* by W. J. Entwistle (London: Dent, 1925. Reprinted, New York: Phaeton, 1975, p. 12).

190 The Portuguese in the 16th century: areas and products.
Joaquim Romero Magalhães, translation by the British Council, Lisbon. Lisbon: Comissão Nacional para as Comemorações dos Descobrimentos Portugueses, 1998. 101p. maps. bibliog.

The author here assesses the changes wrought in 16th-century Portugal and overseas by that country's momentous overseas discoveries. More than sixty full-colour facsimiles of contemporary maps, engravings and drawings capture the spirit of the Age of the Discoveries as well as of the diverse races, landscapes, fauna and products which were found by the Portuguese maritime explorers in Africa, Asia and South America. The accompanying text is an admirably concise account of the process of discovery, the resultant trading relationships between Portugal and these outposts, and the impact of such transactions on Portuguese society.

191 A society organized for war: the Iberian municipal militias in the central Middle Ages, 1000-1284.
James F. Powers. Berkeley, California; Los Angeles, California; London: University of California Press, 1988. 365p. 5 maps. bibliog.
This book's eight chapters are arranged into two parts which cover, firstly, 'The evolution of the Peninsular municipal military services' and, secondly, 'The organization for war and its social and economic influences'. The municipal militias of Iberian towns and cities were particularly strong and were engaged heavily in the struggle to clear the Moors from Portugal and Spain.

Independence and consolidation (1640-1799)

192 The bride of two kings: a forgotten tragedy of the Portuguese Court.
Edmund d'Auvergne. London: Hutchinson, 1910. 320p.
Prompted by a Spanish manuscript of 1701, found in the British Museum, the author relates the story surrounding Maria Francesca Luísa de Sabóia who married the disabled King Afonso VI of Portugal. In 1667, shortly after she had left him, Afonso was overthrown by his brother Pedro, who became Prince Regent and also took his brother's wife as his own. D'Auvergne tells the story of court intrigue surrounding this 'bride of two kings'.

193 The English contingent, 1661-1668, in Portugal.
P. H. Hardacre. *Journal of the Society for Army Historical Research*, vol. 38 (1960), p. 112-25. map.
In a relatively unknown manifestation of the Anglo-Portuguese alliance, Charles II of England despatched three regiments of former Cromwellian soldiers to Lisbon to assist Portugal in its attempts to retain its recently won independence from Spain. Firstly under the Earl of Inchiquin but later, and more successfully, under Count Schomberg, these forces took part in the battles of Ameixial and Estremoz. Wellington allegedly drew on Schomberg's strategies during the Peninsular War. Hardacre draws on the reports of Fanshawe, the British envoy, for contemporary information.

Early 19th century

194 New lights on the Peninsular War. International Congress on the Iberian Peninsula. Selected papers, 1780-1840. The Calouste Gulbenkian Center, Lisbon, Portugal, 24th-26th July, 1989.
Edited by Alice D. Berkeley. Lisbon: The British Historical Society of Portugal, 1991. 368p. maps. bibliog.

Thirty-one conference papers are here reproduced, of which nineteen are in English. These include studies of the Lines of Torres Vedras, the battles in Portugal between Wellington and Masséna, the flight of the Portuguese royal family to Brazil and more esoteric subjects, such as Americans in Oporto in the early 18th century. Virtually all of the contributions gathered here are by European scholars, as eighteen other papers by North Americans were published in the *Proceedings* of the 20th Consortium on Revolutionary Europe at Florida State University (1989), at which event they were represented.

195 Wellington's Peninsular victories.
Michael Glover. Moreton-in-Marsh, England: The Windrush Press, 1998. reprint. 166p. (Great Battles).

Originally published in 1963 (London: Batsford), this is a detailed analysis of Wellington's victories against four different French commanders. One of the battles described is that of Buçaco in 1810, the others being Vitoria, Salamanca and the Nivelle. Glover describes the prelude to Buçaco and covers the creation of the Lines of Torres Vedras, 1810/11, built to protect Lisbon.

196 Napoleon and Iberia: the twin sieges of Ciudad Rodrigo and Almeida, 1810.
Donald D. Horward. Tallahassee, Florida: University Presses of Florida, 1984. 419p. 13 maps. bibliog.

The twin sieges recounted in this volume were crucial in buying time for the Allied forces facing French Marshal Masséna as he advanced towards Lisbon. Using Masséna's archives, as well as knowledge gleaned from seven topographical visits to the battlefields, Horward shows how the works carried out to complete the Lines of Torres Vedras, an array of man-made obstructions before Lisbon, were dependant on the three-month delay caused to the French at Almeida, near the Spanish border, and at Ciudad Rodrigo. The time gained also allowed Allied reinforcements to land at Lisbon and force back the French who were then, themselves, besieged at Almeida.

197 The migration of the Royal Family of Portugal to Brazil in 1807/08.
Kenneth H. Light. Rio de Janeiro: Published by the Author, 1995. unpaginated. bibliog.

An account of the flight of the Portuguese Royal Family, before the advance of Napoléon's armies, from Portugal to Brazil in 1807. The family and its entourage were conveyed by the British Royal Navy to Rio de Janeiro in the Portuguese colony of Brazil. Based on reproductions of sixteen ships' logs held in the Public Record Office in London,

History. Early 19th century

including the captains' reports from the escort vessels, *HMS Bedford* and *Marlborough*, this large-format volume includes parallel texts and a preface and notes in Portuguese and English.

198 The War in the Peninsula.
Major-General Sir William Napier, edited and introduced by Brian Connell.   London: The Folio Society, 1973. 331p. 28 maps.

An admirably concise version of Major-General Napier's 19th-century account of the Peninsular War, originally published in six volumes. Although Napier himself produced a single-volume abridgement in 1852, neither that nor any edition of Napier's work had been in print since the early years of the 20th century before Connell's new edition appeared in 1973. It consists of eighteen chapters derived from Napier's opinionated original work in which the likes of Beresford and Canning were freely denigrated. Chapters 7-9 are of particular relevance to Portugal, covering the battle of Buçaco, the lines of Torres Vedras and Masséna's retreat. Copious maps depict, *inter alia*, the battlelines at Buçaco, Torres Vedras, Pombal and around Oporto.

199 Wellington's Peninsular War: battles and battlefields.
Julian Paget.   London: Leo Cooper, 1990. 284p. maps. bibliog.

Written by a former army officer, this book replaces Weller's *Wellington in the Peninsula* (see item no. 202) as the leading modern study of the Peninsular War. It covers twenty-eight of the campaign's battles, each of which is accompanied by a map and advice on the location and landmarks for modern visitors to the scenes of conflict. Six of the Portuguese battles are recorded in detail, these being Roliça, Vimeiro, Oporto, Buçaco, Torres Vedras and Almeida. There is also a substantial account of the Lines of Torres Vedras and their strategic importance.

200 Battle studies in the Peninsula: a historical guide to the military actions in Spain, Portugal and southern France, between June 1808 and April, 1814, with notes for wargamers.
Richard Partridge, Michael Oliver.   London: Constable, 1998. 284p. 49 maps. bibliog.

A successful combination of historical study and war-gaming suggestions from two members of the Southend Wargamers' Club. In eight chapters, eight Peninsula War battles are described from the strategic point of view, each accompanied by many maps. The Portuguese battles of Roliça (17 August 1808) and Vimeiro (21 August 1808) are amongst those covered.

201 The Battle of Buçaco.
Alberto Araújo e Silva, translated by Ernesto S. J. Leal.   Buçaco, Portugal: Military Museum and Memorials of Buçaco, c1985. 49p.

The Battle of Bussaco (Buçaco) took place on 27 September 1810 during Wellington's campaign against the French who had invaded Portugal in 1807. They were expelled in 1809 and after an abortive attempt in 1809, they invaded again in 1810. Buçaco lies in hilly country, inland from the central University town of Coimbra. The French army of 64,000 men was here repulsed by 53,000 Portuguese and British forces. This book is an admirably concise account of the background to and the events of the battle, together with

History. Mid- and late 19th century

a description of the museum, the memorial obelisk, erected in 1873, and surviving features of the landscape. The text is accompanied by a number of colour and black-and-white illustrations.

202 Wellington in the Peninsula, 1808-1814.
Jac Weller. London: Kaye & Ward, 1962. 395p. 22 maps. bibliog.

Fifty-eight of the author's photographs of the present-day appearance of the Peninsular War battle sites underline the extent of his research. Much topographical detail is supplied and there is detailed coverage of the military campaign in Portugal, including the battles of Buçaco and Roliça, as well as a lengthy account of the construction and strategic importance of the Lines of Torres Vedras, built by Wellington to protect Lisbon from the advancing French army.

Mid- and late 19th century

203 The civil war in Portugal and the siege of Oporto.
A British Officer of the Hussars who served in the Portuguese Army during the Peninsular War. London: Edward Moxon, 1836. 285p.

An account of the Portuguese civil war, otherwise known as the War of the Two Brothers, between King Pedro IV and Dom Miguel, the would-be usurper of the throne. Oporto, a traditional liberal stronghold, was unsuccessfully besieged by Miguel's Absolutist forces in 1832/33. The author, resident in Oporto at the time of publication, provides a detailed account of the background to the war and to the events which occurred in its duration from 1831 to 1834.

204 A year in Portugal.
George Bailey Loring. New York: George Putnam's Sons, 1891. 313p.

Loring was the United States' Minister in Portugal and he here recounts his year in Lisbon, together with his visits to Spain and the Mediterranean. This deluxe edition includes accounts of Coimbra, Alcobaça, Sintra, Mafra, Pombal and Torres Vedras, as well as the Portuguese capital itself.

Early 20th century (1900-26)

205 Revolutionary Portugal, 1910-1936.
V. de Bragança Cunha. London: James Clarke & Co. Ltd, [c. 1938]. 282p.

A sequel to the same author's *Eight centuries of Portuguese monarchy* (London: Stephen Swift, 1911. 265p.). Following a substantial historical introduction, six chapters review the period from the assassination of King Carlos in 1908 to 1936, although the emphasis is very much on the 1910 Republican Revolution and its immediate aftermath. The author makes little secret of his pro-monarchical stance and his disdain for the Portuguese Republicans but his book is, nevertheless, one of the most detailed contemporary English-language accounts of the period. A major deficiency of the book is its lack of an index but whilst it also lacks a bibliography, there are many footnote references to other English-language sources.

206 The tragedy of Portugal, as shown in the sufferings of the Portuguese political prisoners: royalists, republicans, socialists and syndicalists. Six articles reprinted by permission from 'The Daily Chronicle' and one from the 'Contemporary Review'.
Philip Gibbs, with an introduction and notes by E. M. Tenison. London: L. Upcott Gill & Sons, 1914. 80p. bibliog.

The six articles from *The Daily Chronicle,* published in December 1913, are entitled 'Lisbon under the Republic', 'The rule of the *carbonarios*', 'The prisons of Oporto', 'The Limoeiro and the *penetenciaria* of Lisbon', 'The *Aljube* of Lisbon and the *penetenciaria* of Coimbra' and 'Evidence of Dr Cunha e Costa, the famous Republican lawyer', whilst that from *The Contemporary Review* is 'The tyranny in Portugal', dated January 1914. The articles purport to be independent accounts of the treatment of political prisoners in Portugal in the chaos after the 1910 Republican revolution. On a similar theme, from the same publisher, is Adeline, Duchess of Bedford's *Political prisoners in Portugal* (1913) and *Portuguese political prisoners, a British national protest*, compiled by the British Protest Committee (1913. 5th ed.).

207 The social origins of democratic collapse: the first Portuguese Republic in the global economy.
Kathleen C. Schwartzman. Lawrence, Kansas: University Press of Kansas, 1989. 224p. bibliog. (Studies in Historical Social Change).

A thorough study of the fall of democracy in May 1926, when the military intervened to put an end to the chaotic First Portuguese Republic which had existed since the overthrow of the monarchy in 1910. In the intervening period Portugal experienced forty-five prime ministers and nine Presidents of the Republic. Drawing parallels with the demise of the Second French Republic (1857), the Italian Republic (1922) and the Weimar Republic (1933), the author chronicles the failure of the Portuguese bourgeoisie to achieve a cohesive system of government prior to the imposition of the authoritarian regimes which were to rule the country for almost fifty years.

History. *Estado Novo* (1926-74)

Estado Novo (1926-74)

208 Flight into Portugal.
Ronald Bodley. London: Jarrolds, 1947. 224p.
Illustrated by twenty-five photographs, this book tells of Ronald Bodley's escape to Lisbon from France as the Germans advanced through that country in 1940. Interwoven with his account of his stay in wartime Lisbon and at Sintra, where he was upset at the sight of large numbers of desperate refugees, is an account of Portuguese history and culture. Before escaping on a ship to New York, Bodley travelled around Portugal, visiting Coimbra, the abbey at Batalha and the Alentejo region amongst other locations.

209 Portugal now.
Ralph Fox. London: Laurence & Wishart, 1937. 80p.
In what he describes as 'random notes' arising from a visit to Portugal, Fox surveys the country under Salazar at a time when it housed exiles from the Spanish Civil War (1936-39). Salazar is portrayed as having the 'ideas of an Irish country priest' and his alleged economic successes are here questioned, as is his support for the Franco rebellion in Spain in 1936.

210 Portugal from monarchy to pluralist democracy.
Walter C. Opello Jr. Boulder, Colorado; San Francisco, California; Oxford: Westview Press, 1991. 176p.
Opello's central thesis in this volume places a good deal of emphasis on the fact that Portugal was one of Europe's earliest nation states and that the early establishment of its empire and consequential wealth afforded the Portuguese monarchy an exaggerated degree of power. This situation is seen as causing the country's economic backwardness and the delay in the arrival of democracy in Portugal until 1974.

211 Fascism and resistance in Portugal: Communists, Liberals and military dissidents in the opposition to Salazar, 1941-1974.
D. L. Raby. Manchester, England; New York: Manchester University Press, 1988. 288p. map. bibliog.
Reconstructing the history of opposition movements in dictatorial states is not an easy task and Raby is obliged to make heavy use of interviews with participants in events to supplement his nevertheless thorough trawl through archives, newspapers and other printed sources. The book's eight chapters include two each specifically on the Portuguese Communist Party and on the actions of the military dissidents Henrique Galvão and Humberto Delgado. There is slighter coverage of the African Wars of the 1960s and early 1970s, which is not unreasonable in a work whose main thrust is to analyse the internal dissidence of mainland Portugal.

History. Contemporary era (1974 to date)

1974 Revolution

212 Conflict and change in Portugal, 1974-1984. Conflitos e mudanças em Portugal, 1974-1984.
Edited by Eduardo de Sousa Ferreira, Walter C. Opello Jr.   Lisbon: Teorema, 1985. 342p. bibliog.

Papers from the Third International Meeting on Modern Portugal, held at Durham, New Hampshire, 1984, comprise the majority of this compilation of twenty articles, seven of which are in English. The meeting was organized by the International Conference Group on Portugal, a North American-based grouping of academics from many countries. The subject is the effect of the 1974 Portuguese Revolution, ten years on, with particular reference to government, labour, migration and international relations.

213 Revolution and counter-revolution in Portugal.
Martin Kayman.   London; Wolfeboro, New Hampshire: Merlin Press, 1987. 265p.

A four-part treatise on the Portuguese Revolution of 1974 which the author sees as a stage in a continuum of the country's history from the 19th century onwards. The book's four parts cover, initially, the underlying themes in Portuguese history which came to a head in 1974, then move on to describe the Revolution of 1974 up to March 1975. The third section covers the 1975 counter-revolutionary period, whilst the final part addresses the years after the defeat of the revolutionaries and the beginnings of the Portuguese capitalist democracy.

Contemporary era (1974 to date)

214 Portugal's Revolution: ten years on.
Hugo Gil Ferreira, Michael W. Marshall.   Cambridge, England; London; New York; New Rochelle, New York; Melbourne, Australia; Sydney: Cambridge University Press, 1986. 303p. bibliog.

Produced on what must be the lowest grade paper ever used by Cambridge University Press, this book merits a better format for its publication of extensive verbatim interviews with leading lights of the Armed Forces' Movement which swept aside the Salazar/Caetano regime in April 1974. The central section of interviews is prefaced by a scene-setting chapter and completed by an analysis of the major socio-political changes in the period from 1974 to 1984.

History. Contemporary era (1974 to date)

215 The new Portugal: democracy and Europe.
Edited by Richard Herr. Berkeley, California: University of California at Berkeley, 1992. 205p. (International and Area Studies, Research Studies, no. 86).

A publication based on the conference 'Portugal since the Revolution' held at Berkeley in 1990, organized by the Iberian Studies Group of the Center for Western European Studies. Its three sections cover 'The Transition', 'The Background' and 'The Culture', with chapters written mostly by Portuguese academics. The final section also includes a Conclusion which puts forward the view that Portugal's African colonial heritage brings to Europe a unique perspective and that its democracy now appears to be firmly established, following the 1974 Revolution.

216 Portugal in the 1980s: dilemmas of democratic consolidation.
Edited by Kenneth Maxwell. New York; Westport, Connecticut; London: Greenwood Press, 1986. 254p. map. bibliog. (Contributions in Political Science, no. 138, Global Perspectives in History and Politics).

Eight essays, each by a different author, attempt to provide 'a collective overview of contemporary Portugal', at the beginning of its second decade of democracy. The writers are drawn from North America and Europe and include Francisco Pinto Balsemão, a former prime minister of Portugal. They address the position of Portugal in an international context, as well as its economy and internal politics. The editor identifies the need to come to terms with its historical heritage and with its reduced physical dimensions as the major issue facing Portugal in the late 1980s.

217 Modern Portugal.
Edited by António Costa Pinto. Palo Alto, California: The Society for the Promotion of Science and Scholarship, 1998. 312p.

In fourteen chapters, mostly written by Portuguese academics, this book surveys a wide range of political, economic, social and cultural issues of the period from the 1970s onwards. The book is aimed at the general reader as well as the specialist, and provides an English-speaking audience with an authoritative, inside view of developments in recent Portuguese history, politics, economics and sociology, as well as literature and art.

The history of the Jews of Spain and Portugal.
See item no. 369.

Military dress of the Peninsular War.
See item no. 659.

Visita ao Museu Militar.
See item no. 703.

Society for Spanish and Portuguese Historical Studies Bulletin.
See item no. 738.

Overseas territories

General

218 The Portuguese seaborne empire, 1415-1825.
C. R. Boxer. Manchester, England: Carcanet in association with the Calouste Gulbenkian Foundation, 1991. 2nd ed. 426p. 7 maps. bibliog. (Aspects of Portugal).

A reprint of the 1969 edition of Boxer's classic account of the formation and operation of Portugal's extensive maritime empire. A short new preface includes a brief survey of the literature published on the subject since 1969. The first section of the book comprises a more or less chronological account of the establishment of the empire, whilst the second part employs a more thematic approach, in which trade and shipping are important subjects.

219 Portugal and its empire: the truth.
António de Figueiredo. London: Victor Gollancz, 1961. 159p. bibliog.

A groundbreaking work which its author claims is 'the first book on contemporary Portuguese politics ever written in any language by a Portuguese born and educated under the Salazar regime' (p. 21). Figueiredo was a poor Portuguese who emigrated at the age of seventeen to Mozambique where his self-taught knowledge of English gained him employment in a British-owned bank. His sympathy for the local Africans' plight led him to support of General Delgado, the focus of dissent against the Salazar regime, and thus to arrest and exile. The book initially describes the socio-political condition of contemporary Portugal before addressing the role and state of its overseas empire.

220 Portugal and her overseas provinces.
Luís C. Lupi. Lisbon: Agência-Geral do Ultramar, 1961. 45p.

A classic defence of Portuguese colonialism which derives from what must have been a lengthy speech at the Cambridge University Liberal Club. The first section explains 'How and why the Portuguese sought independence through expansion across the seas' and the second 'Why and how the Portuguese must safeguard their overseas territories in order to survive as a nation within the framework of western civilization'. Much is made of Portuguese miscegenation, non-discrimination and the nation's paternalistic concern for the native population in the face of Russian, and particularly Chinese, expansionism in Africa.

221 Discovery in the archives of Spain and Portugal: quincentenary essays, 1492-1992.
Edited by Laurence J. McCrank. New York; London; Norwood, Australia: The Haworth Press, 1993. 590p. bibliog.

Divided into three sections, this substantial volume addresses, firstly, the mediaeval foundations of the Age of Discoveries through assessments of the methods and content of selected Iberian archives. The second part concentrates on Columbus, whilst the third and

History. Overseas territories. Africa

most voluminous section includes more than 100 pages on 'Portugal and its seaborne empire'. This section comprises four essays on 'Sources in Portuguese and Goan archives and libraries', 'Archival evidence of the Portuguese expansion in Africa', 'Sources for Portuguese West African history in the Vatican and related collections' and a study of Portuguese archival documentation of the Cape Verde islands.

222 The first Portuguese colonial empire.
Edited by Malyn Newitt. Exeter, England: Exeter University Press, 1986. 103p. 2 maps. bibliog. (Exeter Studies in History, no. 11).

A collection of four essays on Portugal's early expansionism, with particular reference to the nation's exploits in India and south-east Asia. Whilst the essays are useful contributions to Portuguese colonial history, the book has the appearance of duplicated typescript.

223 A history of Portuguese overseas expansion, 1400-1670.
Malyn Newitt. London: UCL Press, 1999. 352p. maps. bibliog.

Malyn Newitt here provides an up-to-date assessment of Portugal's three centuries of expansionism, based on maritime supremacy in the Atlantic and Indian Oceans. The book is aimed at undergraduates and provides an informed introduction to the predominantly state-sponsored enterprises that shaped the seaborne empire of the Portuguese.

224 A world on the move: the Portuguese in Africa, Asia and America, 1415-1808.
A. J. R. Russell-Wood. Manchester, England: Manchester University Press, 1992. 289p. 9 maps. bibliog.

A masterly study of the breadth of Portuguese expansionism which is a worthy adjunct to Boxer's seminal *Portuguese seaborne empire* (see item no. 218). The work serves as a counterpoint to the 1992 adulation of Columbus and Spanish exploration by underlining the Portuguese contribution to the Age of Discoveries. Innovatively, the approach is to study the movement of people, commodities, flora and fauna, styles, mores and ideas through the Portuguese overseas process of expansion rather than to present a purely conventional military or political history.

Africa

225 Portugal and Africa.
David Birmingham. Basingstoke, England: Macmillan, 1999. 216p.

Like Duffy's *Portuguese Africa* (see item no. 227), this work's coverage is not as broad in subject coverage as its title implies. It has an overwhelming emphasis on Angolan colonial and post-colonial history and even includes a chapter on Angolan fiction, while the space allocated to Mozambique and Portugal's other west African territories is slight.

History. Overseas territories. Africa

226 Counterinsurgency in Africa: the Portuguese way of war, 1961-1974.
John P. Cann. Westport, Connecticut: Greenwood Press, 1997. 226p. 4 maps. bibliog. (Contributions in Military Studies, no. 167).

During a period of NATO service at Oeiras in Portugal, the author developed an admiration for his host country's attempts to retain its colonies by military means. He judges as successful the Portuguese army's adoption of the British tactics in its colonies of using small-scale operations to counter guerrilla activity rather than the employment of massive firepower, as used by the Americans in Vietnam. He argues that the Army's containing measures, which saw much lower death rates and costs than in similar conflicts in Algeria, Vietnam or Indo-China, could have brought about a political settlement to the conflict. However, Cann considers that, after the 1974 Portuguese Revolution, the politicians in Lisbon failed to capitalize on the thirteen years of successful counterinsurgency on three fronts in Africa to achieve an advantageous and peaceful solution.

227 Portuguese Africa.
James Duffy. Cambridge, Massachusetts: Harvard University Press, 1959. 389p. maps.

A groundbreaking study of Portugal's African territories written shortly before the outbreak of African rebellions in the early 1960s. The thirteen chapters are acknowledged by Duffy to be heavily biased towards Angola and Mozambique, to the detriment of the smaller west African colonies of Guinea-Bissau, Cape Verde and São Tomé e Príncipe. Amongst the topics covered are: missionaries and slavery in the colonies; the involvement of Livingstone in Portuguese Africa; international disputes, notably with Britain; and the native policies and administration of the colonies by Portugal.

228 Portugal and Africa, 1815-1910: a study in uneconomic imperialism.
R. J. Hammond. Stanford, California: Stanford University Press, 1966. 384p. 7 maps. (A Publication of the Food Research Institute, Stanford University).

In eleven chapters, Hammond traces a century of Portuguese policy and attitudes towards its colonies in Africa. As the author himself describes it, the book is an account of the 'Scramble for Africa' from a Portuguese perspective and, as such, it provides a counterpoint to the more widely studied British viewpoint. Hammond makes heavy use of the archives of the British Foreign and Colonial Offices, The Public Record Office in London as well as Portuguese Foreign Ministry records, although these last were not available for scrutiny for the post-1850 period.

229 The decolonization of Portuguese Africa: metropolitan revolution and the dissolution of empire.
Norrie MacQueen. London; New York: Longman, 1997. 266p. 5 maps. bibliog.

A study, in seven chapters, which claims to be the first 'up-to-date comprehensive analysis of the collapse of Portugal's 500 year-old empire in Africa'. As its title implies, it also addresses the political situation in metropolitan Portugal, tracing the story from the

History. Overseas territories. Africa

Estado Novo of 1926 to the present day. MacQueen points out how the Portuguese colonial situation varied from that of Britain or France in its historical duration, its higher proportion of emigrants from the homeland and its consequently greater numbers of poor whites in the colonies.

230 Dictionary of Portuguese-African civilization.
Benjamín Núñez. London; Melbourne, Australia; Munich; New Jersey: Hans Zell, 1995-96. 2 vols. maps. bibliog.

The first volume of this work is sub-titled *From discovery to independence* (532p.) and it comprises some 3,000 entries covering the period from 1415. The second volume is entitled *Biographies from ancient kings to presidents* (478p.). The author took from 1978 to 1989 to compile the alphabetical entries which make up each of the volumes and a further five years to organize them for publication. The work, which is particularly useful on the non-political front, with its copious details of African flora, fauna and geography, suffers from a number of typographical and other errors. It is nevertheless a monumental work of scholarship which covers all areas of Portugal reached by the Portuguese and not just its formalized colonies.

231 Politics in the Portuguese empire: the state, industry and cotton, 1926-1974.
M. Anne Pitcher. Oxford; New York: Clarendon Press, Oxford University Press, 1993. 322p. 3 maps. bibliog.

A well-researched and detailed study of the Portuguese colonial cotton industry which was based on African raw materials. Despite the advantages of protectionism and favourable colonial policies, the Portuguese textile industry was in a depressed state by 1974. Pitcher seeks to explain this paradoxical state of affairs and in doing so uncovers inconsistencies and incoherence in the government's policies, which were exacerbated by bureaucracy, corruption and industrial inefficiency.

232 Portugal, Spain and the African Atlantic, 1343-1490: chivalry and crusade from John of Gaunt to Henry the Navigator.
Edited by P. E. Russell. Aldershot, England; Brookfield, Vermont: Variorum, 1995. 327p in various paginations. maps. bibliog. (Variorum Collected Studies Series CS496).

A most useful compilation of previously disparate contributions from the renowned historian, Peter Russell, which includes sixteen papers published between 1938 and 1992, and in one case previously unpublished. The first ten articles look at English involvement, both diplomatic and military, in Portugal during the period 1343 to c.1400, including studies of John of Gaunt, Fernão Lopes and Portuguese students at Oxford University. The remaining seven papers assess the work of Prince Henry the Navigator and the 15th-century Portuguese maritime explorations.

History. Overseas territories. Asia

233 The Portuguese period in East Africa.
Justus Strandes, edited by J. S. Kirkman, translated by Jean F. Wallwork. Nairobi: East African Literature Bureau, 1971. 325p. map. bibliog.

A translation of *Die Portugiesenzeit von Deutsch- und Englisch-Ostafrika*, which recounts two centuries of Portuguese presence in Mozambique and the adjoining area of East Africa. A chronology and notes on the monetary system and topography, as well as a number of contemporary illustrations, are included in the volume.

234 Visit to the Portuguese possessions in south-western Africa.
G. Tams, translated from the German, with an introduction and annotations by H. Evans Lloyd. London: T. C. Newby, 1845. 2 vols.

The German author here provides an objective account of his visit to Angola and the Congo. He provides first-hand evidence of continuing slave trade activity, involving observations of United States ships engaged in their transatlantic transportation.

235 Portuguese rule and Spanish Crown in South Africa, 1581-1640.
Sidney R. Welch. Cape Town; Johannesburg, South Africa: Juta, 1950. 634p. bibliog.

Between 1580 and 1640, mainland Portugal was under the Spanish Crown but, as Welch shows, this had little impact on Portuguese activity in southern Africa. Indeed, Welch sees this as an era of particularly outstanding Portuguese envoys in the region. In twenty-seven chapters he describes the Portuguese trading activities in Mombassa, Mozambique, the Cape and Zambezi regions, as well as Madagascar.

Asia

236 'Regent of the sea': Cannanore's response to Portuguese expansion 1507-1528.
Geneviève Bouchon, translated from the French by Louise Shackley. Delhi; Oxford; New York: Oxford University Press, 1988. 254p. maps. bibliog. (French Studies in South Asian Culture and Society, no. 2).

A translation of the French original published in 1975 but not updated for this translation. The book uses oriental as well as western sources to trace the history of the port of Cannanore, near Calicut, on the Malabar coast of India. Bouchon seeks to compare Indian sources for a complementary view to that which has come to us from the Portuguese chroniclers. She pays particular attention to the activities of Mamale de Cananor, leader of the local Eli kingdom's Islamic community in the early 16th century, who was known as the 'Regent of the sea' and who sought to exploit the death of the Portuguese governor, Afonso de Albuquerque, to local advantage.

History. Overseas territories. Asia

237 Portuguese merchants and missionaries in feudal Japan, 1543-1640.
C. R. Boxer. London: Variorum Reprints, 1986. various paginations. (Collected Studies Series CS232).

A compilation of nine articles by the leading authority on Portugal's Asian exploits. The topics covered include obscure matters such as Japanese grammars produced by Portuguese travellers, but also embrace the mainstream religious and trade topics promised by the book's title. The articles were published between 1929 and 1984, with five of them having first been printed in the *Transactions and Proceedings of the Japan Society of London*.

238 The Portuguese in India: being a history of the rise and decline of their eastern empire.
Frederick Charles Danvers. New Delhi: Asian Educational Services, 1988. 2 vols. maps. bibliog.

This is a reprint of the fine 1894 edition (London: W. H. Allen, 2 vols), which was illustrated by contemporary engravings and maps. After a brief history of Portugal, the bulk of the text covers Portuguese activities in the Indian Ocean area from the late 15th century up to 1893. Necessarily there is emphasis on the early period of discovery and growth but Danvers' detailed coverage of the decline of Portuguese power is less familiar territory even for most modern-day readers.

239 A Spaniard in the Portuguese Indies: the narrative of Martín Fernández de Figueroa.
Martín Fernández de Figueroa, edited by James B. McKenna. Cambridge, Massachusetts: Harvard University Press, 1967. 288p. map. bibliog.

A facsimile and accompanying critical essay of the first printed account of the Portuguese conquest of Goa. The work also includes an English translation of a work which throws much light on Portuguese Goa in the early years of the 16th century. The editor demonstrates the faithfulness of the author's account which belies the fanciful accounts of some later historians.

240 Encountering Macau: a Portuguese city-state on the periphery of China, 1557-1999.
Geoffrey C. Gunn. Boulder, Cologrado: Westview Press, 1996. 211p. (Transitions: Asia and Asian America).

This work seeks to cover the entire period of Portuguese involvement in Macao, from the early 16th century to the present. As such it goes beyond traditional studies of the enclave which concentrate on the period up to the 17th-century economic collapse. Gunn stresses the 19th- and 20th-century economic and political developments, drawing parallels with other south-east Asian developing economies such as that of Hong Kong. The book is marred by a number of textual inaccuracies and errors of citation.

History. Overseas territories. Asia

241 History of the Portuguese navigation in India, 1497-1600.
K. M. Mathew. Delhi: Mittal Publications, 1988. 352p. bibliog.

A revised version of the author's doctoral thesis, which was presented in 1978. Part I concerns Portuguese nautical knowledge and cartography. Part II concentrates on the maritime aspects of the Portuguese presence in the Indian Ocean, with chapters on the voyage of Vasco da Gama (1497/98) as well as on Portuguese naval policy, organization and armaments. Local evidence of coastal forts, of shipwrecks and of Portuguese shipbuilding in India is also studied.

242 Portuguese and the Sultanate of Gujarat, 1500-1573.
K. S. Mathew. Delhi: Mittal Publications, 1986. 263p. map. bibliog.

This is a groundbreaking study of the influence of the Portuguese on the history of the Indian Gujarat region. Drawing on the 16th-century chronicles of João de Barros, Gaspar Correia and Diogo do Couto, Mathew interweaves their accounts with the exploits of local figures such as Khwaja Safar and Malik Ayaz to demonstrate the interdependence of European and Indian sources for those seeking to explain the history of the region. Numerous contemporary documents are transcribed in the final section of the book.

243 The Ottoman response to European expansion: studies on Ottoman-Portuguese relations in the Indian Ocean and Ottoman administration in the Arab lands during the sixteenth century.
Salih Özbaran. Istanbul: The Isis Press, 1994. 222p. 4 maps. bibliog. (Analecta Isisiana, XII).

Özbaran brings together here sixteen essays written by him in English and published over the previous twenty years or so. The essays are presented in two groups, the first entitled 'Characteristics of an empire' and the second covering the 'vicissitudes' of Ottoman-Portuguese relations, including assessments of conflicts in the Red Sea, Persian Gulf and Indian Ocean areas in the 16th century. The author concludes that whilst Portuguese seamanship was better than that of the Ottoman navies, it was not sufficiently superior to consolidate its advantage in the Gulf and Red Sea in particular.

244 Port cities and intruders: the Swahili coast, India and Portugal in the early modern era.
Michael N. Pearson. Baltimore, Maryland; London: The Johns Hopkins University Press, 1998. 202p. maps. bibliog. (The Johns Hopkins Symposia in Comparative History, no. 23).

Pearson here chiefly covers the period up to 1700 in a study which tries to place Portuguese activity on the East African and Indian coasts within the context of the world economy. He concludes that in India, the Portuguese tried to monopolize a previously peaceable trading system and also introduced bigotry to a tolerant social system. In Africa, he sees the Portuguese as failing in their monopolistic goals and being obliged to operate on a more cooperative basis, an attitude which he feels was more productive in the long term.

History. Overseas territories. Asia

245 The Portuguese in India.
M. N. Pearson. Cambridge, England: Cambridge University Press, 1987. 178p. 3 maps. bibliog. (The New Cambridge History of India, I,1)

In seven chapters Pearson shows how the Portuguese, lured by the prospect of spices, first landed in India in May 1498 and retained a presence there until December 1961 when they were evicted by force from their territories of Diu, Damão and Goa by Nehru. Pearson shows, however, that long before then their role in Indian trade had been usurped by the British and Dutch who used their acumen to develop their commerce, rather than squander their profits on a sumptuous court and religious excess as occurred in Portugal. From an essentially pro-Indian stance, he also highlights the difference between the Portuguese 'civilizing mission' and the more focused commercialism of their latter-day European rivals.

246 Ribeiro's 'History of Ceilão', with a summary of De Barros, De Couto, Antonio Bocarro and the Documentos Remettidos, with the Parangi Hatane and Konstantinu Hatane. Translated from the original Portuguese and Sinhalese.
P. E. Pieris. Colombo, Sri Lanka: The Colombo Apothecaries' Co. Ltd, 1909. 2nd ed. 416p.

This is the first English version of Captain João Ribeiro's history of Ceylon, translated from the Lisbon edition (1836). Pieris's translation, however, incorporates only an abridged version of part three of the book. Ribeiro was on the island of Ceylon from 1640 but his *History* dates from 1685. Summaries are also provided of accounts from other early Portuguese travellers, as well as an English version of the Sinhalese *Hatane* texts.

247 Slavery in Portuguese India, 1510-1842.
Jeanette Pinto. Bombay, India: Himalaya Publishing House, 1992. 154p. map. bibliog.

Whilst the slave trade between Portuguese Africa and Brazil is relatively well-documented, this illustrated account of slavery in Portugal's Indian territories of Goa, Diu and Damão confirms the prevalence of the activity in Asian areas of Portugal's colonial empire. Pinto includes a number of contemporary source documents as well as a substantial bibliography.

248 Macau, the imaginary city: culture and society, 1557 to 1996.
Jonathan Porter. Boulder, Colorado: Westview Press, 1996. 240p. maps. (New Perspectives on Asian Studies).

A wide-ranging cultural history of the Portuguese enclave of Macao, in China. Using Chinese as well as Portuguese sources, Porter approaches his subject from a thematic rather than strictly chronological angle. The breadth of his knowledge is impressive and includes details of flora and fauna as well as more traditional historical subject matter.

History. Overseas territories. Asia

249 The survival of Empire: Portuguese trade and society in China and the South China Sea. 1630-1754.
George Bryan Souza. Cambridge, England; London; New York; New Rochelle, New York; Melbourne, Australia; Sydney: Cambridge University Press, 1986. 282p. 9 maps. bibliog.

The Portuguese community and its trading activity continued into the 18th century in China and, indeed, in Macao until the present day. Developing his work from his doctoral thesis, Souza shows how Portuguese pragmatism enabled them to continue even after the demise of Portuguese sea-power in the East. Extensive use is made of archives in Goa, The Netherlands, Britain and Portugal, as well as translated, rather than original, Chinese sources.

250 Improvising empire: Portuguese trade and settlement in the Bay of Bengal, 1500-1700.
Sanjay Subrahmanyam. Delhi: Oxford University Press, 1990. 269p. bibliog.

A compilation of journal articles, originally published by the author in the period 1985-88 in sources such as the *Indian Economic and Social History Review*. Overall, Subrahmanyam seeks to re-examine Portugal's policy and objectives in the Bay of Bengal. His studies show that the Europeans' motivations were primarily those of commercial profit and advantage, which they frequently implemented by means of coercion and force.

251 The Portuguese empire in Asia, 1500-1700: a political and economic history.
Sanjay Subrahmanyam. London; New York: Longman, 1993. 320p. 10 maps. bibliog.

The author seeks to show that most histories of Portuguese involvement in Asia, which emphasize the initial discoveries of Afonso de Albuquerque, undervalue the more important subsequent involvement of the newcomers in developing trade in Asia. The book's title belies the fact that the text covers not only the activities of the Portuguese in Asia but also in East Africa. Subrahmanyam's wide grasp of both European and Asian history make this a work which illuminates the study of both continents and underlines their interrelationship.

252 India and the West: the first encounters: a historical study of the early Indo-Portuguese cultural encounters in Goa.
Joseph Velinkar. Mumbai, India: Heras Institute of Indian History and Culture, St Xavier's College, 1998. 222p. 2 maps. bibliog. (Studies of the Heras Institute, no. 26).

In nine chapters the author covers a wide range of Indo-Portuguese contacts in the 16th and 17th century. The subjects covered include history, society, religion, economics, culture and literary developments. The book is illustrated by twelve monochrome and eight colour plates, as well as six 19th-century drawings.

History. Overseas territories. Brazil and the Americas

253 Embassies and illusions: Dutch and Portuguese envoys in K'ang-hsi, 1666-1687.
John E. Wills. Cambridge, Massachusetts: Council on East Asian Studies, Harvard University, 1984. 303p. bibliog. (Harvard East Asian Monographs, no. 113).

An account of Portuguese and Dutch contact with the Chinese emperor (K'ang-hsi), which includes extensive accounts of the embassies of Manoel de Saldanha (1667-70) and of Bento Pereira de Faria (1678). These provide details of Portuguese activity in Canton and Macao in particular.

Brazil and the Americas

254 Christopher Columbus and the participation of the Jews in the Spanish and Portuguese discoveries.
Mayer Kayserling, translated from the author's manuscript, with his sanction, and revision by Charles Gross. North Hollywood, California: Carmi House Press, 1989. 189p. bibliog.

Originally published in 1894 (New York: Longmans, Green), this is a translation of Kayserling's (1829-1905) *Christoph Columbus und der Anteil der Juden an den spanischen und portugiesischen Entdeckungen*. Despite its age, it remains a classic study of an often overlooked area of the Age of Discoveries.

255 The making of Brazil: Portuguese roots, 1500-1822.
N. P. Macdonald. Lewes, England: The Book Guild, 1996. 520p. 2 maps. bibliog.

In fifty chapters, grouped into nine parts, Macdonald traces the roots of Portuguese history before devoting the majority of the volume to the years between the Portuguese discovery of Brazil in 1500 and 1822, when Brazil gained independence from Portugal. Macdonald openly attempts to emphasize the Portuguese involvement in the development of the Americas to counterbalance what he sees as a general bias towards the attribution to Spaniards of the glory for its role in the New World. He covers the arrival of African slaves as well as Portuguese emigrants and charts their interactions with the indigenous populations.

Intrepid itinerant.
See item no. 120.

In the wake of the Portuguese navigators.
See item no. 133.

The adventures of plants and the Portuguese discoveries.
See item no. 151.

History. Overseas territories. Brazil and the Americas

Dictionary of Portuguese-African civilization.
See item no. 230.

Albuquerque: Caesar of the East.
See item no. 256.

Ferdinand Magellan.
See item no. 258.

Christopher Columbus and the Portuguese.
See item no. 259.

The brothers Corte-Real.
See item no. 265.

The career and legend of Vasco da Gama.
See item no. 272.

The quest for eastern Christians.
See item no. 376.

Vanguard of empire.
See item no. 480.

Bibliographie des voyages en Espagne et en Portugal.
See item no. 748.

Biographies and Autobiographies

256 Albuquerque: Caesar of the East. Selected texts by Afonso de Albuquerque and his son.
Afonso de Albuquerque, edited and translated, with an introduction and notes by J. Villiers, T. F. Earle. Warminster, England: Aris & Phillips, 1990. 308p. maps. bibliog. (Hispanic Classics).
A parallel-text, bilingual edition of selections from the letters of Afonso de Albuquerque and of the commentaries of his son. The critical apparatus includes photographs and plans as well as explanatory notes and background material on the life of Afonso, who spearheaded much of Portugal's expansion in the East. This is the first English version of Albuquerque's works since brief extracts were published in 1929 by Edgar Prestage. The texts now published include accounts of the conquests in Ormuz (1507), Malacca (1511), Benasterim (1512), Aden (1513) and India (1512), including Goa (1515).

257 The Portuguese Columbus: secret agent of King John II.
Mascarenhas Barreto, translated by Reginald A. Brown.
Basingstoke, England: Macmillan, 1992. 572p. maps. bibliog.
An abridged translation of *O Português Cristóvão Colombo: agente secreto do rei Dom João II*, which originally appeared in 1988 (Lisbon: Edições Referendo), but which was developed from a thesis written in 1971-72. The delay in publication was caused by the author's attempts to solve the riddle of Columbus's signature on which his case for Columbus' Portuguese nationality largely rests. Its claims, which include an allegation that Columbus was an agent of Portugal planted in the Spanish court to deflect Spanish interest from the Indies, are seen by some critics as fanciful.

258 Ferdinand Magellan.
E. F. Benson. London: John Lane, The Bodley Head, 1929. 262p. (The Golden Hind Series).
A biography of the Portuguese-born explorer, Fernão de Magalhães (c.1480-1521) who in his early years saw military service for Portugal in north Africa. However, his plans for exploration were rejected by Portugal's King Manuel I. Consequently, he entered the

service of the rival Spanish Crown and, in 1520, he rounded the southern tip of South America through what is now known as the Straits of Magellan. He met his death at the hands of Filipino natives in 1521 but one of his ships succeeded in completing the world's first circumnavigation in 1522.

259 Christopher Columbus and the Portuguese.
Rebecca Catz. Westport, Connecticut; London: Greenwood Press, 1993. 133p. bibliog. (Contributions to the Study of World History, no. 39).

Christopher Columbus resided in Portugal between 1476 and 1485. In this book, Rebecca Catz seek to redress what she sees as the pro-Spanish bias of historians who discuss the opening up of the Atlantic and the Americas. To this end, she covers the Portuguese discoveries of the Azores and Madeira, as well as the debt which she perceives that Columbus owed to the Portuguese maritime explorers.

260 Every inch a king: a biography of Dom Pedro I, Emperor of Brazil.
Sérgio Corrêa Costa. London: Robert Hale, 1972. 230p. bibliog.

A reprint of the 1950 edition of a biography of Pedro IV, King of Portugal, who was a member of the Portuguese royal house which was exiled in Brazil following the French invasion in 1807. Pedro became Emperor of Brazil and abdicated the Portuguese throne in 1826 in favour of his daughter, Maria da Glória. He fought a successful civil war in Portugal (1831-34) with his brother, D. Miguel, who had usurped the Portuguese throne in 1828.

261 John James Forrester, Baron of Portugal, 1809-1861.
John Delaforce. Printed at Maia, Portugal: Published by the Author, in association with Christie's Wine Publications, 1992. 128p. bibliog.

John James Forrester was a Yorkshireman who became Baron de Forrester in 1855 and was, like this book's author, a leading figure in the port wine trade in Oporto, following his marriage into the Fladgate family of wine shippers. He was also a talented amateur artist, photographer and cartographer and examples of his work are included in this book. Forrester died when his boat, carrying sixteen people, capsized in the rapids of Cachão da Valeira in the upper Douro valley in 1861. As is described here, Forrester was allegedly weighed down by gold coins in his money belt and was, consequently, one of three passengers to drown; his body was never found.

262 Damião de Góis: the life and thought of a Portuguese humanist, 1502-1574.
Elizabeth Feist Hirsch. The Hague: Martinus Nijhoff, 1967. 243p. bibliog. (Archives Internationales d'Histoire des Idées, International Archives of the History of Ideas, no. 19).

Damião de Góis, who died in 1574, was Portugal's leading Renaissance humanist and a friend of Erasmus. He wrote celebrated chronicles of the Portuguese kings, D. Manuel and João III. This book's twelve chapters chronicle the many visits he made to European countries, including Italy, the Low Countries, Poland and Russia as well as the period of

Biographies and Autobiographies

five months spent as Erasmus's guest. His successful career came to an unfortunate end when he was condemned by the Portuguese Inquisition as a heretic and died, two years later, in 1574.

263 William Beckford: an English *fidalgo*.
Malcolm Jack. New York: AMS Press, 1996. 170p. bibliog.

A biography of the wealthy writer and dilettante, William Beckford which places particular emphasis on his life between his mid-twenties and early forties, a period which includes his visits to Portugal between 1787 and 1798. This stage of his life is seen to be the key to explaining Beckford's transformation from the flamboyant author of *Vathek* and the architect of Fonthill to his end as a reclusive book-collector in Bath. The author views Portugal, which Beckford first visited by chance when bad weather caused him to land in Lisbon en route to Jamaica, as central to the development of Beckford's artistic life. A broader biography of Beckford is B. Fothergill's *Beckford of Fonthill* (London; Boston, Massachusetts: Faber & Faber, 1979. 387p.), while J. Lees-Milne's *William Beckford* (Tisbury, England: Compton Russell, 1976. 124p.) and R. J. Gemmett's *William Beckford* (Boston, Massachusetts: Twayne Publishers, 1977. 189p. [Twayne's English Authors Series, no. 204]) are also useful studies which cover the writer's Portuguese sojourns.

264 Mário Soares: portrait of a hero.
Hans Janitschek, with a foreword by Edward Kennedy. London: Weidenfeld & Nicolson, 1985. 116p.

Illustrated by many black-and-white photographs of Mário Soares, many of which show him with world dignitaries, this is a friendly biography of Portugal's former President and Prime Minister. It tells of Soares's early years as a left-wing youth movement activist, and his involvement in the presidential campaigns of 1949 for General Norton de Matos and of 1958 for the ill-fated General Delgado. The bulk of the book, however, describes his triumphant return from exile in Paris in 1974 and his rise to the status of international statesman.

265 The brothers Corte-Real.
Francisco Fernandes Lopes, translated by M. Freire de Andrade. Lisbon: Instituto de Investigação Científica e Tropical, Edições Culturais da Marinha, 1991. 22p. map. bibliog.

This work was previously published in 1957 (Lisbon: Agência-Geral do Ultramar/ Centro de Estudos Históricos Ultramarinos). João Vaz and his sons, Vasco Anes, Gaspar and Miguel Vaz Corte-Real were all noteworthy sailors in the early period of the Portuguese epoch of the Discoveries. Gaspar Corte-Real is believed in some quarters to have reached Newfoundland in the late 15th century (see item no. 132).

266 Dom Pedro: the struggle for liberty in Brazil and Portugal, 1798-1834.
Neill Macaulay. Durham, New Hampshire: Duke University Press, 1986. 361p. maps. bibliog.

In 1807 the Portuguese King, João VI, and his Court fled to Rio de Janeiro, with British assistance, to escape the invading French army. Macaulay tells how João returned to

Portugal in 1821, leaving his son, Pedro in Brazil. In 1822 Pedro proclaimed Brazilian independence from Portugal and became Emperor Pedro I. Having renounced the Portuguese throne, which he had inherited in 1826, he was forced to return to Portugal to defeat his brother, Miguel, who had seized the crown in 1828. Following a civil war from 1831-34, Miguel was finally banished and Pedro's daughter, Maria, became Queen of Portugal.

267 Pedro Nunes, 1502-1578: his lost algebra and other discoveries.
Edited and translated by John R. C. Martyn. New York; Washington, DC; Baltimore, Maryland; Bern; Frankfurt-am-Main, Germany; Berlin; Vienna, Paris: Peter Lang, 1996. 158p. bibliog. (American University Studies, Series IX, History, Vol. 182).

A fascinating biography of Pedro Nunes whose accomplishments included mathematical prowess, navigational skills and the authorship of Greek and Latin poetry. Martyn also includes an English version of Nunes's supposedly lost treatise on algebra of 1533, used by him to tutor the princes of the Portuguese royal household in Évora, in whose public library the manuscript was rediscovered. Nunes's private life is also fascinating; although half-Jewish he was a friend of Prince Henrique the Inquisitor and his daughter was accused of slashing the face of a member of the court.

268 Pombal, paradox of the Enlightenment.
Kenneth Maxwell. Cambridge, England: Cambridge University Press, 1995. 200p. bibliog.

A high-quality biography of the effective ruler of Portugal during the reign of King José I, Sebastião José de Carvalho e Melo (1699-1782), who became the Marquês de Pombal in 1769. With a text illustrated by eleven colour plates and forty-seven other illustrations, Maxwell assesses the life of a man seen by some as an enlightened absolutist and by others as a tyrant. Pombal is best remembered abroad for his calm reaction to the destruction of Lisbon by earthquake in 1755, although he also attempted to revitalize the Portuguese economy and industry, as well as combat the influence in Portugal of the Jesuits. On the King's death in 1777, Pombal fell from power.

269 John of Empoli and his relations with Afonso de Albuquerque.
Laurence A. Noonan. Lisbon: Instituto de Investigação Científica Tropical, 1989. 240p. 2 maps. bibliog.

Giovanni da Empoli (1483-1517) was a Florentine trader who accompanied Afonso de Albuquerque (1453-1515) on his groundbreaking explorations of Asia. His two letters to his father are here transcribed in their original Italian as well as in an annotated English version. The first, from 1503, describes his trip from Lisbon to India, whilst the second (1514) describes a visit made in 1513/14 to Malacca, again in a Portuguese fleet. He participated in such momentous events as the Portuguese capture of Goa and Malacca, as well as in the early attempts to establish trade with China. His letters provide rare first-hand narratives from a participant who was not constrained by the secrecy of the Portuguese, who wished to retain their navigational and commercial supremacy.

Biographies and Autobiographies

270   Biographies of Prince Edward and Friar Pedro.
André de Resende, edited and translated by John R. C. Martyn. Lewiston, New York; Queenston, Canada; Lampeter, Wales: Edwin Mellen Press, 1997. 226p.

The first English edition of the biographies of Prince Duarte (Edward) and of Friar Pedro Porteiro written by André de Resende (1498-1573), tutor to the Prince. The original titles were, respectively, *Vida do Infante D. Duarte* and *Santa vida e religiosa conversação do Frei Pedro*. Friar Pedro's early years were unconventionally spent as a ship's cabin-boy and his life-story is accompanied by a detailed account of Prince Duarte's upbringing and of life at Court. Both are furnished in parallel texts in Portuguese and English. Brief details of Resende's own life precede the texts and these include references to his friendship with Erasmus and his travels through western Europe.

271   Internationalism and the three Portugals: the memoirs of Francis Millet Rogers.
Francis Millet Rogers, edited by Sheila Rogers Ackerlind.   New York; San Francisco, California; Bern; Baltimore, Maryland; Frankfurt-am-Main, Germany; Berlin; Vienna, Paris: Peter Lang, 1992. 386p. bibliog. (American University Studies, IX, History, vol. 131).

Ackerlind here publishes the autobiography of her father, the one-time Harvard Professor of Romance Languages, Francis M. Rogers (1914-89) who was a renowned Lusophile. The content includes Rogers's account of visits to the 'three Portugals', namely the Azores, Madeiras [*sic*] and Portugal itself, as well as to Brazil. His experiences during the Second World War are also recounted.

272   The career and legend of Vasco da Gama.
Sanjay Subrahmanyam.   Cambridge, England: Cambridge University Press, 1997. 400p. 4 maps. bibliog.

A study of the life of Vasco da Gama and of the conjectures and myths that were created in his lifetime and which have since proliferated around him. The author sees the legend as having started even before Vasco da Gama died and also asserts that the renowned voyager himself participated in its creation. In this he was in tune with the intention of King Manuel I (1495-1521) to build up Portuguese success in finding the real route to the Indies, in contrast with the Spaniards' claims for Christopher Columbus.

273   Dom Pedro, the magnaminous.
Mary Wilhelmine Williams.   New York: Octagon Books, 1966. 414p. map. bibliog.

A reprint of Williams's 1936 biography of D. Pedro, the son of Portugal's King Pedro IV. The younger Pedro assumed the imperial throne of Brazil, as Pedro II of Brazil, when his father abdicated in 1831. The book's nineteen chapters cover a visit by D. Pedro to Portugal, Brazil's relations with its former colonial master, and the royal family's banishment from Brazil in 1889. Pedro's final years were spent in Cannes, France, after an initial period of exile in Portugal which is chronicled here.

Dias and his successors.
See item no. 116.

Intrepid itinerant.
See item no. 120.

A list of the writings of Charles Ralph Boxer.
See item no. 761.

Emigrants from Portugal

274 **Portuguese emigration to the United States, 1820-1930.**
Maria Ioannis Benis Baganha. New York; London: Garland Publishing, 1990. 421p. map. bibliog. (European Immigrants and American Society).

This is a revised version of the author's 1988 doctoral thesis. Its four chapters cover the creation of the Portuguese migratory system, the socio-political framework of Portuguese emigration to the United States, the nature of Portuguese society and a survey of Portuguese emigration to the United States between 1820 and 1930. During this period more than 250,000 Portuguese are thought to have made the journey across the Atlantic, with male, unskilled labourers in the vanguard. Later, many Portuguese emigrants became industrial workers or farmers.

275 **Men who migrate, women who wait: population and history in a Portuguese parish.**
Caroline B. Brettell. Princeton, New Jersey: Princeton University Press, 1986. 329p. map. bibliog.

A study based on the peasant community of 2,000 people in Lanheses, in the Alto Minho region of northern Portugal, which has been affected by large-scale emigration, particularly to France. The phenomenon of emigration, with the intention of return, was particularly strong in Portugal and Brettell investigates associated phenomena such as late age of marriage, numerical dominance of female inhabitants and fertility rates. The study draws on local archives as well as direct study and is illustrated by black-and-white photographs of present-day life in Lanheses.

276 We have already cried many tears: the stories of three Portuguese migrant women.
Caroline B. Brettell. Prospect Hills, Illinois: Waveland Press, 1995. 151p. maps. bibliog.

This is a re-edition, with an updated preface, of a work by Brettell first published in 1982 (Cambridge, Massachusetts: Schenkman Publishing Company, 151p. 4 maps. bibliog.). The book recounts the experiences of three Portuguese women who emigrated to France, with varying degrees of success. The women are all from the north of Portugal; from Beira Alta, Minho and Oporto respectively. All three express a sense of freedom at having escaped many of the constrictions of conservative Portuguese lower-class life.

277 Regional emigration and remittances in developing countries: the Portuguese experience.
Rick Chaney. New York; Westport, Connecticut; London: Praeger, 1986. 258p. bibliog. (Praeger Special Studies).

The author's work in the 1970s with Portuguese immigrants in Toronto, Canada, excited his interest in the topic of this book. This experience was supplemented by ten months of study in Portugal. Curiously, the start of the text is an extensive 'Conclusion' which includes the finding that, in Chaney's view, migration is a region-to-region phenomenon rather than a country-to-country one. The work concludes with a discussion of remittance policies in Portugal.

278 Portuguese migration in global perspective.
Edited by David Higgs. Toronto, Canada: Multicultural History Society of Ontario, 1990. 207p. bibliog.

Starting in the pre-1800 era, the eleven essays in this book look at Portuguese emigration throughout the world, including migration to Canada, the United States and South Africa. In addition, the essays, derived from a 1988 conference, assess the impact of emigration on Portugal itself. The bibliography concentrates on Portuguese immigration to Canada and the texts are illustrated by some black-and-white photographs.

279 With hardened hands: a pictorial history of Portuguese immigration to Canada in the 1950s.
Domingos Marques, Manuela Marujo. Etobicoke, Ontario: New Leaf Publications, 1993. 144p. map. bibliog.

This volume comprises an initial chapter addressing 'three decades of failed attempts to encourage emigration from Portugal to Canada', followed by a photographic essay which charts the first significant arrivals in 1953 and how they established themselves in their new surroundings. A short 'Afterword' addresses the literary accounts of Portuguese immigration to Canada. Such works countered the generally happy picture revealed in the photographic record, which mostly comprised images sent home to relatives with the intention of demonstrating how successfully the immigrants had settled in Canada.

280 Inside ethnic families: three generations of Portuguese Canadians.
Edite Noivo. Montreal: McGill-Queen's University Press, 1997. 164p. bibliog. (McGill-Queen's Studies in Economic History, Series Two).

Developed from a doctoral thesis, this study of family life amongst Portuguese emigrants to Canada uses case-studies of three generations of an immigrant family. Noivo concludes that the gulf between the idealism of the immigrants and the realities of their experiences in their new home lead them to live a 'necessary illusion' in order to survive.

281 My people, my country: the story of the Malacca Portuguese community.
Bernard Sta Maria. Malacca, Malaysia: The Malacca Portuguese Development Centre, 1982. 236p. map. bibliog.

The author, a Malaysian Opposition politician, traces the origins of the Malacca Portuguese community back to its origins in the early 16th century, before the Dutch took over the territory in 1641. Frequently citing original source documents, he relates the community's troubled history through the Dutch, British and Japanese occupations to its contemporary struggle for representation within an independent Malaysia.

Immigrants in Portugal

282 Growing up English: memories of Portugal, 1907-1930.
D. J. Baylis (née Bucknall). Lisbon: The British Historical Society of Portugal, 1997. 99p.

Joyce Bucknall's autobiographical account of her childhood in Portugal provides an insight into the privileged life of an expatriate family of cork traders. Born in 1907, she spent much of her life in the Lisbon area until she finally left in 1930. The book also provides an account of the social conditions of the workers on the cork-tree estates of the Alentejo in the post-revolutionary period, as well as some vivid accounts of walking through Lisbon under gunfire during the frequent periods of half-hearted military coups after the 1910 Revolution.

283 Closing the migratory cycle: the case of Portugal.
Edited by Eduardo de Sousa Ferreira, Guy Clausse. Saarbrücken, Germany; Fort Lauderdale, Texas: Breitenbach, 1986. 249p. bibliog. (Sozialwissenschaftliche Studien zu Internationalen Problemen. Social Science Studies on International Problems, Bd. 111).

With contributions from fifteen experts, this compilation centres on the phenomenon of the *retornados*, those Portuguese citizens who, having emigrated to the country's African territories, returned to Portugal following the upheavals unleashed by the 1974 Portuguese Revolution. The huge number of *retornados* placed huge strains on an impoverished western European nation and created a rare sociological case of a mass immigration of former emigrants.

Immigrants in Portugal

284 Transportation and deportation: the expulsion of the gypsies of England, Spain and Portugal.
Sharon Floate, Antonio Gómez Alfaro, Elisa Maria Lopes da Costa. Hatfield, England: University of Hertfordshire Press, [2000]. c.200p. maps.

Originally projected for publication in 1999, this internationally cooperative work, produced under the auspices of the Gypsy Research Centre of the Université René Descartes, Paris, is now expected to appear in 2000. The studies include assessments of various Portuguese plans to banish gypsies to the country's former colonies of Angola and Brazil.

285 Buying a home in Portugal.
David Hampshire. London: Survival Books, 1998. 204p. maps.

A thorough, practical guide to the complex process of purchasing a property in Portugal. The book is aimed at the British purchaser and the whole process is covered, from the initial search for a property to moving in and settling down in Portugal. The bureaucracy and the financial regulations are explained and a glossary of Portuguese terms is provided.

286 The English in Portugal, 1367-1387. Extracts from the Chronicles of Dom Fernando and Dom João.
Fernão Lopes, introduction, translation and notes by Derek W. Lomax, R. J. Oakley. Warminster, England: Aris & Phillips, 1988. 368p. 4 maps. bibliog.

The editors here seek to bring to the English-speaking reader the work of one of Europe's major court chroniclers, Fernão Lopes (c.1385-c.1460). Preceded by a brief introduction, royal family trees and four maps, are the English versions of the Chronicle of Dom Fernando I (1367-83) and both parts of the Chronicle of his successor to the Portuguese Crown, Dom João I (1385-1433). Both monarchs had turbulent reigns involving conflict within Portugal and with its Castilian neighbours. João married Philippa of Lancaster and sired offspring who included Prince Henry the Navigator and Dom Duarte (1433-38).

287 British community handbook.
d'Arcy Orders. Lisbon: APN Publications, 1990. rev. ed. 107p.

This handbook covers virtually everything that might be of use to the expatriate Briton in Portugal, with entries on topics as diverse as the Portuguese Alcoholics' Anonymous organization, Sintra Dogs' Home, the Scottish Country Dance Group and Vilamoura Cruising Club. The information is grouped into sections entitled 'General', 'Clubs, Sports & Leisure', 'Schools', 'Churches', 'Embassies', 'Hospitals', 'Fire Departments' and 'Police Departments'. Whereas Orders emphasizes the Lisbon area, Edward Eves's *Portugal's foreign community handbook* (Lagoa, Portugal: Vista Ibérica Publicações, c.1995) has more information on the Algarve.

Immigrants in Portugal

288 Live & work in Spain and Portugal.
Jonathan Packer. Oxford: Vacation Work, 1998. 2nd ed. 319p. maps.

A mine of information for those intending to stay in or emigrate to Portugal. The section on Portugal (p. 187-309) has two sub-sections on living in Portugal and working in Portugal. The former covers background on the country, entry regulations, daily life and retirement needs. The latter addresses employment law and how to set up a business. The book lacks an index, which would have been useful in such a fact-filled volume.

289 Your home in Portugal.
Rosemary de Rougemont. London: Longman, 1988. 185p. maps. (Allied Dunbar Money Guides).

A guide to buying property in Portugal which looks at locations, types of property and the legal aspects of such a transaction. Its sixteen chapters include descriptions of the Portuguese banking and taxation systems, as well as advice on making a will in Portugal, acquiring health insurance and settling into Portuguese society.

290 Living in Portugal: the essential guide for property purchasers and residents.
Susan Thackeray. London: Hale, 1990. 3rd ed. 284p. maps.

Previously published as *Living in Portugal: a complete guide* (London: Robert Hale, 1985. 240p. maps), this book is illustrated by black-and-white photographs and provides a practical guide to residing in Portugal. The author emigrated, with her husband, from Montréal to the Algarve in the early 1980s. Despite her own origins, the text is orientated towards the British *émigré* with advice on such topics as British taxation, bringing pets to Portugal and the compatibility of British electrical equipment with the Portuguese power supply system. Thackeray goes on to explain concisely the workings of Portuguese bureaucracy and how to deal with the country's utility companies, shops and banks. She also provides many other useful hints to smooth the emigrant's integration into Portuguese society.

291 The slave trade: the history of the Atlantic slave trade.
Hugh Thomas. London: Picador, 1997. 925p. maps. bibliog.

In the four centuries from 1492 some ten million Africans were transported as slaves to the Americas, with the Portuguese and Brazilians amongst the most assiduous shippers. This tome is divided into six 'Books' and is illustrated by numerous black-and-white photographs. Coverage includes an analysis of the Portuguese trade in which such figures as the Lisbon-based Florentine, Bartolommeo Marchioni, and the Brazilian Felix de Sousa were prominent.

The migration of the Royal Family of Portugal to Brazil in 1807/08.
See item no. 197.

Race Relations

292 Many races, one nation: the traditional anti-racialism of Portugal's civilizing methods.
António Alberto de Andrade. Lisbon: Agência Geral do Ultramar, 1956. 52p.

An apologia for Portugal's colonial expansion in Africa. The author cites numerous instances of Portugal's civilizing influence on African peoples while avoiding contradictory historical evidence. The book is illustrated with black-and-white photographs, most of which seek to represent European and African Portuguese in harmony in schools, the army and society. Parts of historical documents are also transcribed, including a number from the 18th century, the 1928 Labour Code for Portuguese Africa and extracts from the Portuguese Constitution operative in the 1950s.

Language

General

293 Ancient languages of the Hispanic peninsula.
James M. Anderson. Lanham, Maryland; London: University Press of America, 1988. 144p. 13 maps. bibliog.
Effectively updating Antonio Tovar's classic, *The ancient languages of Spain and Portugal* (New York: Vanni, 1961. 138p.), this volume is arranged into nine chapters covering the pre-Roman languages of Iberia. The chapters comprise an introduction and survey of ancient Iberian writing, followed by chapters on the languages of eastern Iberia, the southern peninsula, southern Portugal, the Hispano-Celtic languages, Basque, ancient Iberian relationships and the demise of the ancient Hispanic languages. There are many reproductions of inscriptions and copious transliterations are recorded, many of which are grave markers. Chapters 4 to 6 are the most relevant to Portugal.

294 On Portuguese simple sounds, compared with those of Spanish, Italian, French, English, etc.
H.I.H. Prince L-L. Bonaparte. London: The Philological Society, c.1880. 19p.
Prince Bonaparte was a leading philologist of his day and in this work he attempts to 'enumerate, describe and classify' the sounds of Portuguese. His study is based on his own contact with 'cultivated society in Lisbon' and on his study of João de Deus's *Dicionário prosódico* (Lisbon, 1878). Following the text are tables which identify the fifteen vowel sounds in question, followed by a short extract from Camões's *Lusíadas*, with a phonetic transcription and translation into English. Amongst the Prince's other researches on the Portuguese language is *Portuguese vowels according to Mr R.G. Vianna, Mr H. Sweet and myself* (London: The Philological Society, c.1884. 5p.) which, after a brief introduction, lists thirty-three vowel sounds in a comparative chart which conveys the findings of Bonaparte and two other philologists, Vianna and Sweet.

Language. General

295 A survey of English language teaching and learning in Portugal.
British Council, for English Language Promotion Unit. London: British Council, 1991. 51p. map.

Describing itself as 'A guide to the market', this book contains nine chapters which describe in detail the place of English in the Portuguese school and higher education systems, as well as in the private sector. Portuguese education is seen as undergoing a period of radical reform both to its structure and the curriculum, whilst a growth in private language schools is also detected. There are also chapters on teacher training, English-language publishing, bookshops and libraries, as well as available examinations on the English language. Thirteen appendices include many useful addresses, such as those of language schools and universities offering English courses.

296 The Portuguese language.
J. Mattoso Câmara Jr, translated by Anthony J. Naro, with an annotated bibliography of the writings of Joaquim Mattoso Câmara Jr, compiled by Anthony J. Naro, John Reighard. Chicago, Illinois; London: The University of Chicago Press, 1972. 270p. bibliog. (The History and Structure of Languages).

Mattoso Câmara, who died in 1970, was Brazil's leading philologist of his day. In the ten chapters of this work he covers the Portuguese language in general, its phonology and morphology, its adverbs, verbs, periphrastic structures, connectives, lexicon and sentence structures. He deals with both European and Brazilian Portuguese in a text which is essentially a narrative rather than a quick-reference grammar.

297 Theoretical issues and practical cases in Portuguese-English translations.
Malcolm Coulthard, Patricia Anne Odber de Baubeta. Lewiston, New York; Queenston, Canada; Lampeter, Wales: The Edwin Mellen Press, 1996. 189p.

Deriving from a conference, this volume comprises twelve essays in English and seven Shakespeare songs translated into Portuguese. Major names such as the historian, Harold Livermore, and the translator, Giovanni Pontiero, are amongst the contributors who address both practical problems of translating Portuguese and a number of theoretical issues. Whilst the stress is on literary translations, there are also essays on such fields as the translation of advertisements.

298 Portuguese vocables in Asiatic languages. From the Portuguese original of Monsignor Sebastião Rodolfo Dalgado.
Sebastião Rodolfo Dalgado, translated into English, with notes, additions and comments by António Xavier Soares. New Delhi: Asian Educational Services, 1988. 520p. bibliog.

With more than 200 pages of introduction before the 520 pages of text, this is a translation of *Influência do vocabulário português em línguas asiáticas*, published in 1936 (Baroda, India: Oriental Institute). It examines the etymology of oriental languages to reveal Portuguese elements in their vocabulary.

Language. General

299 Studies on the acquisition of Portuguese. Papers presented to the First Lisbon Meeting on Child Language, with Special Reference to Romance Languages, University of Lisbon, June 14-17, 1994.
Edited by Isabel Hub Faria, Maria João Freitas. Lisbon: Edições Colibri, APL- Associação Portuguesa de Lingüística, 1995. 214p. bibliog.

A compilation of fourteen papers from the first Lisbon Meeting on Child Language, all of which relate to the Portuguese language and its acquisition by children. The volume's aim is threefold: to stimulate Portuguese research into child language; to capture public interest in the topic; and to increase the international profile of the Portuguese language.

300 The subject in Brazilian Portuguese.
Solange de Azambuja Lira. New York; Washington, DC; Baltimore, Maryland; San Francisco, California; Bern; Frankfurt am Main, Germany; Berlin; Vienna, Paris: Peter Lang, 1996. 101p. bibliog.

A quantitative study of the structure and position of the subject in spoken Brazilian Portuguese, which seeks to explain why the pronominal subject is more common than the zero subject. The work is based on the study of spontaneous vernacular speech by a sample of thirty speakers of both sexes and a range of ages, hailing from differing strata of society in Rio de Janeiro.

301 Issues in the phonology and morphology of the major Iberian languages.
Edited by Fernando Martínez-Gil, Alfonso Morales-Front.
Washington, DC: Georgetown University Press, 1997. 694p. bibliog.
(Georgetown Studies in Romance Linguistics).

One of the five sections of this large tome covers Portuguese. This includes articles by respected scholars on stress, prosody, intonation, morphology, apocope and lentition in the Portuguese language.

302 501 Portuguese verbs fully conjugated in all the tenses in a new easy-to-learn format, alphabetically arranged.
John J. Nitti, Michael J. Ferreira. Hauppage, New York: Barron's Educational Series, 1995. 533p.

The essence of this volume is a list of verbs, with all tenses conjugated and a small number of samples of usage. It is preceded by a short introduction which explains the use of diacritics, subject pronouns, moods, tenses and pronunciation. European Portuguese is the norm used. Nitti's shorter compilation, *201 Portuguese verbs fully conjugated in all the tenses in a new easy-to-learn format, alphabetically arranged* (Hauppauge, New York: Barron's Educational Series, 1974. 223p.), is also still in print.

Language. General

303 Portuguese.
Stephen Parkinson. In: *The Romance languages*. Edited by Martin Harris, Nigel Vincent. London; New York: Routledge, 1997, 2nd rev. ed., p. 131-70. maps.

A masterly and concise description of the Portuguese language is provided here by Stephen Parkinson in this 500-page volume. He identifies two dialects of Portuguese in the north of the country and a further two in the central-southern regions of Portugal. In addition, there is copious information on the phonology, lexicography and orthography of the language, as well as details of verb formations, contractions and many other aspects of Portuguese grammar. The essay also covers Galician, from which Portuguese sprang but which is now classified as a language of Spain. The first edition of this compendium appeared in 1988 (London: Croom Helm).

304 Portuguese palaeography.
P. P. Shirodkar. Goa, India: Mrs Sulabha P. Shirodkar, 1997. 222p.

A collection of over 3,000 difficult palaeographic words, phrases and abbreviations form the basis of this useful guide to those working in Portuguese archives. Prakashchandra P. Shirodkar is an eminent scholar, who has worked in the Historical Archives of Goa since 1976. The entries are arranged in alphabetical order of their Portuguese transcription, with the original manuscript version alongside. Three brief appendices give examples of epitaphs, ancient Roman numerals and other numerical representations.

305 Linguistic minorities of the European Economic Community: Spain, Portugal, Greece. Summary of the report.
Miquel Siguan. Luxembourg: Office for Official Publications of the European Communities, 1990. 61p. (European Commission Document).

Although the section on Portuguese is very brief, it is nonetheless important for being a concise summary of the linguistic cohesiveness that exists within the frontiers of Portugal. Indeed, Siguan asserts that 'Portuguese is probably the most linguistically uniform country in the whole of the EC and even in the whole of western Europe'. The only significant variant which he notes is 'mirandês', a purely oral development of Asturian-Leonese spoken in villages around the border town of Miranda do Douro in northern Portugal.

306 Bungs, bribes and bad language: some strategies of Portuguese and Spanish conspiratorial talk.
Robin Warner. Bristol, England: University of Bristol, Department of Hispanic, Portuguese and Latin American Studies, 1996. 18p. bibliog. (Occasional Papers Series, no. 17).

A fascinating analysis of a covertly recorded conversation between conspirators seeking to fix Portuguese football matches occupies a half of this study. Warner shows how the interlocutors avoid incriminating specifics such as names and also do not seek clarifications to the degree that would be expected in normal conversation. As such the conversation is classed as 'successfully bad communication'.

Language courses

307 Hugo's advanced Portuguese course.
Maria Fernanda Allen. Woodbridge, England: Hugo's Language Books, 1999. 157p. (Hugo's Advanced Series).

A language course, comprising ten modules, aimed at the student who has mastered the author's companion volume *Portuguese in three months* (London: Hugo/Dorling Kindersley, 1997. new ed. 254p.). The advanced volume includes both explanations and practice exercises and is also available with four supplementary audio cassettes. Also from the Hugo stable is *Hugo's speak Portuguese today* (London: Hugo/Dorling Kindersley, 1989), which provides thirteen Portuguese conversations on an audio cassette.

308 Get by in Portuguese: the all-in-one language and travel guide.
Peter Bull, Matthew Hancock. London: BBC Books, 1998. 128p. + audio cassette.

Accompanies a language course for travellers broadcast by the BBC. It comes with an optional audio cassette and booklet for oral practice. Curiously, an earlier work with the same main title, but different authors, is also published by the BBC (see item no. 319).

309 Barron's travel wise Portuguese.
José A. Palma Caetano, adapted by John J. Nitti. Hauppauge, New York: Barron's Educational Series, 1998. 292p.

Unusually for a language-teaching book, the text is accompanied by colour photographs. As well as the course itself, there is a section on Portuguese grammar and also a small dictionary section.

310 A Portuguese primer.
R. Anthony Castagnaro. New York; Bern; Frankfurt-am-Main, Germany; Paris: Peter Lang, 1989. 401p. (American University Studies, Series VI, Foreign Language Instruction, vol. 9).

'Intended primarily as a beginning language textbook in North American colleges', this extensive primer is arranged into twenty chapters, following a brief introduction. Although it covers both European and Brazilian usage, its stress is on the latter. Pronunciation guidance is by approximation to English sounds rather than to the International Phonetic Alphabet. Each chapter combines explanation with exercises, some of which are reading exercises, which also seek to impart Luso-Brazilian culture; others are practical translations or suggestions for discussion or essay. Vocabulary is dispersed throughout the volume with no overall dictionary provided.

311 Portuguese.
Manuela Cook. Sevenoaks, England: Hodder & Stoughton, 1987. 226p. (Teach Yourself Books).

Optionally accompanied by an audio cassette, this volume is aimed at those with no previous knowledge of Portuguese. It uses European Portuguese as the norm but also

Language. Language courses

includes Brazilian variants. Its stress is on everyday situations that might be encountered by a visitor but it also seeks to furnish the user with the ability to write a simple letter in Portuguese. Exercises in grammar and comprehension are provided in the ten sections of the book, each of which deals with a particular context, such as eating out or purchasing items. Appendices list verb forms and Portuguese-English vocabulary.

312 Quick & easy Portuguese.
Manuela Cook. Sevenoaks, England: Hodder & Stoughton, 1988. unpaginated. (Teach Yourself Books).

A simplified companion volume to the *Portuguese* volume by the same author (see item no. 311). It comprises twenty units on specific topics such as 'Driving a car', 'Accommodation' and 'The weather', each of which has between three and seven subsections. Each section also includes practical exercises and the book also has a brief section on pronunciation, grammar and vocabulary.

313 A practical grammar of Portuguese and English, exhibiting in a series of exercises, in double translation, the idiomatic structure of both languages, as now written and spoken.
Rev. Alexander J. D. D'Orsey. London: Trübner & Co., 1868. 298p.

A companion to D'Orsey's *Colloquial Portuguese* (see item no. 346), this work follows the models of Arnold and Ollendorf in presenting and teaching grammar. Thus, each lesson has three parts, comprising: examples in English and Portuguese; Portuguese text illustrative of the lesson, for translation into English; and English text for translation into Portuguese.

314 A grammar of the Portuguese language.
Joseph Dunn. Washington, DC: National Capital Press, 1928. 667p.

A comprehensive descriptive grammar of Portuguese, written by a Professor of Celtic at the Catholic University of America. Dunn covers both contemporary usage and 'obsolete forms to enable ... [one] to read the poets of the classic period' in Portuguese. European Portuguese is the norm but Brazilian and colloquial variants are also cited. The author uses an adaptation of the International Phonetic Association's alphabet to convey pronunciation accurately. Orthographically, he follows the rules laid out by the Portuguese Government's Commission in 1911, with its 1927 modifications.

315 Linguaphone curso de português. (Linguaphone Portuguese course.)
Course written by Antonio Fornazaro. London: Linguaphone Institute, 1991. 2 vols.

This two-volume course comprises the course itself (343p.), replete with drawings of linguistic situations, and a handbook (382p.), written by Ana Paula Ramos da Silva and edited by John C. Pride. These are supplemented by audio cassettes. The course comprises forty units, divided into four levels, each of which has its own test. Both European and Brazilian Portuguese are covered.

Language. Language courses

316 Discovering Portuguese: a BBC course in Portuguese, for beginners.
Alan Freeland, edited by Terry Doyle. London: BBC Books, 1995. rev.ed, 1995. Reprinted, 1997. 196p. + 2 audio cassettes.

A basic course in Portuguese, with two accompanying cassettes, which include recordings of Portuguese people in their natural environments rather than purely studio recitations of phrases. It seeks to give the user sufficient foundation in the language to be able to develop still further. Its two main sections comprise six chapters on specific topics, such as greetings or travel, and twelve chapters entitled 'Antologia' on aspects of Portuguese culture, including codfish, emigration and ceramic tiles. Illustrated by many small photographs and drawings, the volume ends with some fifty pages of vocabulary, grammar, aids to pronunciation and keys to exercises.

317 A new method for learning the Portuguese language.
E. F. Grauert. New York: D. Appleton & Company, 1906. 346p.

A pioneering grammar of Portuguese for English speakers, originally compiled in 1863 when Portuguese orthography was 'as yet, in a very unsettled state' by an author who had formerly resided in Brazil and hence uses that country's version of Portuguese as standard. After an introduction to the pronunciation and orthography of Portuguese, the book comprises two main sections on 'Principal sentences' and 'Subordinate sentences'. The volume concludes with an extensive dictionary of Portuguese-English and English-Portuguese words.

318 Taking Portuguese further.
Hugo. London: Dorling Kindersley, 1998. unpaginated.

This course book is intended as a sequel to Hugo's *Portuguese in three months* (see item no. 307) and is thus aimed at those with a reasonable knowledge of Portuguese so that they can develop their understanding and ability to speak the language. The book comprises reading and listening texts, notes and word lists, with explanations of grammar and a variety of exercises, some of which are intended for oral work. Extracts are taken from contemporary newspapers, magazines and other sources to add relevance to the exercises. It is also available with a set of fourteen audio cassettes. From the same publisher come *Hugo advanced Portuguese* and *Hugo on the move: Portuguese* (London: Dorling Kindersley, 1998), which comprises a workbook, four audio cassettes and sixteen checkcards. The tapes include conversations and spoken explanations.

319 Get by in Portuguese: a beginner's course for holiday makers and business people. Course book.
Penny Newman, language consultant Manuela Cook, produced by Christopher Stone. London: BBC Books, 1997. reprint. 80p. map.

The revised version of a book which accompanied a five-programme BBC Radio language course, first transmitted in 1982. The volume consists of five chapters, entitled 'Meeting people', 'Finding somewhere to stay', 'Getting around', 'Eating out' and 'Going shopping'. Each chapter comprises keywords, conversations, explanation and exercises on the theme in question. The work aims to enable the reader to use the language in typical holiday and business situations. It is completed by test and reference sections as well as lists of 'emergency' words and phrases. The book is also available as the *Get by in Portuguese travel pack* with two audio cassettes. Another BBC course book

Language. Language courses

is *BBC talk Portuguese* by Cristina Mendes Llewellyn (London: BBC Publications, 1998. 127p.), which is optionally available with two cassette tapes, and provides a themed approach to speaking Portuguese.

320 Colloquial Portuguese: a complete language course.
João Sampaio, Barbara McIntyre. London; New York: Routledge, 1995. 302p. (The Colloquial Series).

The aim of this book 'is to provide ... a sound base of conversational Portuguese in a relatively short period of time, sufficient to cope in general holiday/ business situations'. The course is arranged into twelve chapters, followed by a brief reference grammar, a key to the exercises, a Portuguese-English and English-Portuguese glossary, a topic index and a grammatical index. Two audio cassettes are an optional accompaniment to the volume. A companion volume is *Colloquial Portuguese of Brazil: the complete course for beginners* by Esmenia Simões Osborne, João Sampaio, Barbara McIntyre (London; New York: Routledge, 1987. 302p. [The Colloquial Series]). This is arranged into twelve chapters, each of which is entitled by a Portuguese colloquial phrase. The chapters themselves use numerous drawings to illustrate the text and include exercises, dialogue, vocabulary and grammar. At the end are sections of grammar reference, a key to the course exercises and a glossary of English-Portuguese and Portuguese-English terms.

321 Bem-vindos, a Portuguese language course. (Welcome.)
Cintia Stammers, Juliet Perkins, Carmo Ponte, illustrated by Irene Guerreira. Hanley Swan, England: The Self Publishing Association, 1992. 182p. 2 maps.

Specifically aimed at students from the age of fourteen upwards as well as at adults, this beginners' course in Portuguese includes GCSE topics. It aims to develop listening, reading, speaking and writing skills in its thirty units. The index clearly expounds what is covered in each unit and the text is enhanced by 'realia' – reproductions of such items as Portuguese transport timetables, advertisements and tickets. Another course, from Portugal itself, is *A practical guide to colloquial Portuguese* by D. Teixeira Tamulonis (Cascais, Portugal: Delfina Teixeira Tamulonis, 1997. 3 vols), which is heralded as 'a new method, a totally new approach' to the rapid learning of Portuguese by adults, especially business people and diplomats. Its stress is on oral communication skills and the three volumes are accompanied by three audio cassettes. The volumes incorporate a textbook, an exercise book, explanations in English, Portuguese/English vocabulary and a key to the exercises. Vol. 1 is sub-titled 'Conversando' (Conversation), vol. 2 'Debate' (Discussion) and vol. 3 'Intervenção' (Intervention).

322 Instant Portuguese.
Dorothy Thomas. Whitley Bay, England: Dot Publications, 1994. 80p.

An inexpensive but very useful book, aimed at those who may be learning a language for the first time. Its method is akin to that found in the Oxford Pictorial or the Usborne children's books, namely to use drawings of people, objects or situations with appropriate vocabulary linked to specified parts of the illustrations. There is, however, no overall dictionary section for rapid reference.

Language. Language courses

323 Beginner's Portuguese: an easy introduction.
Sue Tyson-Ward. London: Hodder Headline, 1996. 197p. map. (Teach Yourself Books).

This introduction to European Portuguese is arranged into twenty clearly laid-out thematic chapters, covering topics such as meeting people, the family and eating out. These chapters are divided into Part 1, on grammar, and Part 2, on practising the language in 'real life' situations. As well as being illustrated by drawings which include facsimiles of menus, timetables and other realia, the effort of learning is also lightened by the inclusion of wordsearches in Portuguese. A key is provided to the practical exercises as is a brief Portuguese-English vocabulary section. An optional audio cassette is also available to facilitate pronunciation drills. From the same author comes *Time for Portuguese* (Cheltenham, England: Stanley Thornes Publications, 1999), which claims to be a twenty-minute a day language course and is accompanied by two audio cassettes.

324 Brazilian Portuguese: a complete course for beginners.
Sue Tyson-Ward. London: Hodder Headline, 1997. 216p. (Teach Yourself Books).

Portuguese is spoken worldwide by almost twenty times as many people as inhabit Portugal itself. The majority of these non-European speakers are Brazilian and, here, Sue Tyson-Ward provides a basic self-tuition course to this strain of the language. The volume is illustrated by line drawings and includes grammatical explanations, pronunciation aids and exercises.

325 Portuguese verbs and essentials of grammar: a practical guide to the mastery of Portuguese.
Sue Tyson-Ward. Lincolnwood, Illinois: Passport Books, 1997. 140p.

This work is divided into two parts. The first, subdivided into seventeen sections, covers Portuguese verbs, whilst the second covers major grammatical concepts of the language in a further seventeen sections. The author highlights the benefits of collecting together in distinct sections all the relevant information on each concept, such as reflexive verbs or radical-changing verbs, as opposed to what she sees as the traditional approach of inserting bits on each concept through many chapters of a grammar. The book covers both European and Brazilian Portuguese usage.

326 A Portuguese grammar, with the Portuguese words properly accented according to the latest and best authorities.
Anthony Vieyra. London: J. Collingwood, 1827. 10th ed., revised and improved. 391p.

A frequently republished Portuguese grammar book, aimed primarily at English merchants, this work first appeared in the late 18th century. It is arranged into four parts of which the first concerns grammar, the second syntax and the third is a vocabulary, with conversational phrases, which prides itself especially on coverage of the worlds of commerce, navigation and war. The revised fourth part includes extracts from modern Portuguese writers which are intended to compensate for the difficulty of obtaining Portuguese imprints in Britain.

Language. Language courses

327 Conversational Brazilian Portuguese.
Edwin B. Williams, Marialice Pessoa. New York: R. D. Cortina Co./ Henry Holt, 1977. 186p. (An Owl Book).
Utilizing the 'Cortina Method' of tuition, based on repetition of oral drills, this course in Brazilian Portuguese is aimed at a North American audience. It is intended both for use in schools and for self-study.

328 An introductory Portuguese grammar.
Edwin B. Williams. New York: Dover Publications, 1976. 168p.
A photographic reprint of the original 1942 edition of Williams's grammar of Portuguese, the intention of which was to offer 'to the beginner, the elements of the everyday language of Portugal and Brazil'. The book has an introduction to Portuguese pronunciation then twenty-five chapters, each of which comprises grammatical explanations followed by exercises. Appendices include verb conjugations and Portuguese-English and English-Portuguese glossaries. Its format is very similar to that of the later, but more comprehensive, grammar by R. C. Willis (see item no. 329).

329 An essential course in modern Portuguese.
R. Clive Willis. London: Harrap, 1971. Reprinted, 1984. rev. ed. 523p.
A thorough grammar of the Portuguese language which was first published in 1965 and has remained a standard teaching aid and work of reference ever since. Its forty lessons, which assume no previous knowledge of the language, include vocabulary and exercises and its two appendices comprise regular-verb tables and a short exposition of the differences between European Portuguese, which is the volume's norm, and the Brazilian version of Portuguese. The book is particularly strong on the pronunciation of the language with the International Phonetic Alphabet used extensively to this end.

330 A computer-validated Portuguese-English transformational grammar.
James Larkin Wyatt. The Hague; Paris: Mouton, 1972. 439p. bibliog.
Wyatt bases this groundbreaking transformational grammar on a corpus of spoken Brazilian Portuguese derived from an immigrant to the United States. The bulk of the book consists of chapter five, a computer print-out of the results of a programme automating one-string and two-string grammatical transformations, which is described in the first four chapters.

Dictionaries

331 Hugo Portuguese dictionary. Portuguese-English: English-Portuguese.
Compiled by Maria Fernanda Allen. London: Hugo's Language Books, 1995. 629p.

A compilation, comprising some 40,000 entries and 70,000 translations, aimed at tourists, business travellers and students alike. The dictionary is thus particularly strong on the vocabulary of commerce. It is prefaced by a pronunciation guide and the entries give examples of idiomatic and colloquial usage. Brazilian Portuguese variants are given and stress marks are provided to assist with pronunciation. The volume is a paperback and its low purchase price makes it remarkably good value.

332 Langenscheidt universal Portuguese dictionary.
Claudina Marques Coelho. Berlin; Munich: Langenscheidt, 1984. 248p. + 399p.

A genuinely pocket-sized dictionary from the authoritative Langenscheidt publishing house. It appears to have been reprinted since its copyright date although no later date appears on the volume. Unusually in such dictionaries, the Portuguese-English section is considerably more expansive than the preceding English-Portuguese section. Despite its title, less easily pocketed is the *Langenscheidt's pocket Portuguese dictionary, Portuguese-English, English-Portuguese* by the Edições Melhoramentos Editorial Staff, from Brazil (796p.). As with the *Universal* dictionary, current editions bear a date (1989) which appears to refer to the original date of publication and not to the latest reprinting.

333 Business Portuguese glossary. English-Portuguese, Portuguese-English.
P. H. Collin. Teddington, England: Peter Collin, 1998. 170p.

Aimed at the budget end of the market, this is a 5,000-word dictionary of business terms arranged into English-Portuguese and Portuguese-English sections.

334 Collins gem Portuguese dictionary; Portuguese-English, English-Portuguese.
Edited by Mike Harland, Brazilian consultant, Euzi Rodrigues Moraes. London; Glasgow, Scotland: Collins, 1986. rev. ed. 340p. + 287p.

This pocket-sized volume has 40,000 references and 70,000 translations as well as thousands of idioms and constructions. Abbreviations and acronyms are also included and the International Phonetic Alphabet is employed to aid pronunciation. The vocabulary covers both Brazilian and European Portuguese usage. A companion volume is *Collins gem Portuguese phrase finder cassette pack* (Glasgow, Scotland: HarperCollins, 1996. 256p. + 40 minute audio cassette). The tape includes conversations with a shopkeeper, a receptionist and a waiter. It covers phrases which would be useful in situations as diverse as the office and the seaside and also includes short conversations.

Language. Dictionaries

335 Dicionário Inglês-Português. (English-Portuguese dictionary.)
Edited by Antônio Houaiss, Ismael Cardim. Rio de Janeiro: Record, 1982. new ed. 928p.

A comprehensive dictionary of Portuguese, with the Brazilian variant of the language being its standard. Curiously for an English-Portuguese dictionary, its preface is only given in Portuguese, as indeed is that of the *Dictionary of metaphoric idioms, English-Portuguese, Dicionário das expressões idiomáticas, metafóricas inglês-português* (São Paulo, Brazil: Editora Pedagógica e Universitária, 1990. 283p.) by Sidney Camargo and Marina Steinberg which seeks to prevent users making mistakes by literally translating idiomatic phrases. The entries are in alphabetical order of the keyword in the English idioms listed.

336 Hugo practical dictionaries: Portuguese-English, English-Portuguese.
Antônio Houaiss, Ismael Cardim. New York: Hugo, 1994. 283p. + 426p.

Something of a hybrid publication in that it comprises abridged versions of two quite distinct dictionaries. The Portuguese-English section is based on the authors' *Webster's Portuguese-English dictionary*, whilst the lengthier English-Portuguese section is abridged from James L. Taylor's *Webster's English-Portuguese dictionary*. This results in a whole which, though authoritative, is unbalanced in terms of detail, as its pagination indicates. It also lacks the overall consistency of a work compiled by a single team. Brazilian Portuguese is accorded primacy.

337 NTC's compact Portuguese & English dictionary.
NTC Publishing Group. Lincolnwood, Illinois: NTC Publishing Group, 1995. 792p.

An unadorned but nevertheless solid Portuguese and English dictionary, with simulated pronunciation for each word defined. It is a re-edition of the *Pequeno dicionário Michaelis* (São Paulo, Brazil: Edições Melhoramentos, c.1980).

338 Living language Portuguese dictionary. Portuguese-English. English-Portuguese.
Revised and updated by Jura Oliveira, based on the original by Oscar Fernández. New York: Crown Publishers Inc., 1993. 225p. optional audio cassette. (The Living Language Series).

An updated version of the *Living language common usage dictionary*, first published in 1965 which in its current form contains more than 18,000 Portuguese words, including up-to-date terminology from the fields of technology, business and the media. Brazilian usage is its norm but European Portuguese variants are also given. Definitions are supported by illustrative sentences or idiomatic expressions, which in many cases allow the publishers to claim that it is both a phrasebook and a conversation guide, as well as a dictionary. Curiously, the 1,000 most common Portuguese terms are capitalized to facilitate rapid location.

Language. Dictionaries

339 The Oxford Duden pictorial Portuguese-English dictionary.
Oxford University Press/ Bibliographisches Institut AG. Oxford: Clarendon Press, 1992. Reprinted, 1996. unpaginated.

The title of this bulky compendium is somewhat misleading in that this is not strictly a Portuguese-English dictionary but rather a collection of drawings to which are attached the appropriate Portuguese and English descriptive terms. Using the illustrations from the original German *Bildwörterbuch* produced by the Bibliographisches Institut, this comprehensive dictionary provides Portuguese terms for thousands of items grouped into 384 categories of subject as diverse as bird names, textile machinery and astronomy. Drawings are provided, typically of sixty or seventy objects in each category, and their Portuguese and English names are provided. Brazilian Portuguese is accorded primacy but European Portuguese terms are also given. A very detailed index is provided of the English and Portuguese terms used in the dictionary.

340 A Portuguese-English dictionary.
James L. Taylor, with corrections and additions by the author and Priscilla Clark Martin. London; Toronto, Canada; Wellington, New Zealand; Sydney: George G. Harrap & Co., 1975. 4th revised printing. 655p.

The first comprehensive Portuguese-English dictionary published since 1887, Taylor's dictionary first appeared in 1958 and it remains the classic Portuguese-English dictionary of the modern era. Brazilian Portuguese is accorded primacy. The introduction includes sections on orthography and pronunciation, while appendices, by James S. Holton, cover verbs. These appendices cover regular verbs and those with orthographic or radical changes, as well as irregular verbs.

341 Collins Portuguese dictionary.
John Whitlam, Vitoria Davies, Mike Harland. Glasgow, Scotland: HarperCollins, 1991. Reprinted, 1996. 382p. + 367p.

This medium-sized dictionary covers Brazilian as well as European Portuguese, with the former given primacy. It has some 80,000 references and 110,000 translations and prides itself on its inclusion of business and computing terms, in particular. There are also sections covering abbreviations, acronyms, geographical names, irregular verbs and nouns, as well as a pronunciation guide. A smaller work, *Collins pocket dictionary, Portuguese-English, English-Portuguese,* in the same format and by the same authors, is also published (617p.); this is also known by the Portuguese title *Dicionário escolar.*

342 The Oxford colour Portuguese dictionary.
Portuguese-English compiled by John Whitlam, English-Portuguese compiled by Lia Correia Raitt. Oxford; New York: Oxford University Press, 1999. 436p.

This is a re-titling of *The Oxford paperback Portuguese dictionary* by the same compilers and publishers (1996. 436p.) which differs only in having each of the entry-words printed in colour (namely blue). This additional visual aid embellishes a handy plastic-bound dictionary containing some 40,000 words and phrases accompanied by a pronunciation guide, dictionary and a section on Portuguese irregular verbs. Brazilian, rather than European, Portuguese is given primacy.

Language. Phrasebooks

Phrasebooks

343 AA essential Portuguese phrase book.
Automobile Association/ First Edition Translations. Basingstoke, England: AA Publishing, 1997. 151p.

Based on a Dutch-Portuguese phrasebook, this volume comprises fifteen sections covering normal tourist situations, such as seeking accommodation, eating and drinking. As might be expected, motoring situations are also covered. Portuguese words are helpfully shown in red, while the English text is black. The book also includes a pronunciation table.

344 Berlitz Portuguese phrase book.
Berlitz. Princeton, New Jersey: Berlitz, 1998. 224p. map. (Berlitz Phrase Book and Dictionary Series).

The cover describes this as a 'phrase book and dictionary', although the title-page restricts itself to the words 'phrase book'. After a helpful guide to the pronunciation of Portuguese, the book is laid out in thematic sections covering everyday tourist situations. The page edges are colour coded for easy reference and a small dictionary section completes the volume.

345 Collins Portuguese phrase book & dictionary.
Collins. Glasgow, Scotland: HarperCollins, 1999. rev. ed. 192p.

A thoroughly revamped edition of an established phrasebook and dictionary which now includes an expanded food and drink section by the cookery writer Edite Vieira Phillips, who receives a degree of acknowledgement not granted to the authors of the fourteen main sections of the publication. These cover matters such as car travel, shopping and getting around by public transport. There are also brief sections on Portuguese grammar and pronunciation.

346 Colloquial Portuguese; or, The words and phrases of everyday life, compiled from dictation and conversation for the use of English tourists and visitors in Portugal, the Brazils, Madeira and the Azores, with a brief collection of epistolatory phrases.
Rev. Alexander J. D'Orsey. London: Trübner & Co., 1868. 3rd rev. ed. 126p.

The premise of the first edition of this book (1854) had been to record the author's own experience of the Portuguese language in his role as a chaplain at Madeira to provide a basic guide for fellow English-speakers in giving 'orders to servants'. However, this third edition is a more professional work which benefits from the involvement of A. C. da Costa Ricci, 'Professor' of Portuguese at King's College, London. After some initial chapters on such matters as pronunciation and grammar, the bulk of the volume is arranged into thematic sections of practical vocabulary and phrases on topics such as domestic servants, horses, invalids, ladies' dress and going to the dentist's.

Language. Phrasebooks

347 How to eat out in Portugal & Brazil. How to understand the menu and make yourself understood. Dictionary and phrase book for the restaurant.
Claudia Fernandes.   Rome: Gremese Editore, 1998. 190p.

A pocket-sized guide to dining in Portugal and Brazil. As well as explaining the make-up of typical Portuguese dishes, this volume also includes general phrases for the visitor to employ, as well as sections on Portuguese grammar and vocabulary.

348 Holiday Portuguese.
Hilary Fleming, Iza Moneiro Rainbow.   London: Hodder & Stoughton, 1995. 90p. maps. (Teach Yourself).

Originally published in 1989 as *Portuguese in a week* (London: Headway/ Hodder & Stoughton, 90p.), which comprised seven chapters, entitled Monday to Sunday, respectively. Within each chapter of *Holiday Portuguese* are various themes such as 'Hello and goodbye' and 'Arriving at the hotel'. The volume describes itself as 'more than just a phrase book', which is a justifiable assertion given its inclusion of lessons and exercises. It also includes colour photographs and other illustrations to accompany the chapters and the vocabularies.

349 Portuguese phrase book.
Alan Freeland, consultant Graça Martins.   London: BBC, 1995. rev. ed. Reprinted, 1997. 298p.

A pocket-sized phrase book for the British traveller, originally published in 1992. It is divided into thematic sections, each of which commences with a brief introduction to the topic in question. The volume is completed by a 5,000-word 'mini-dictionary'.

350 Portuguese phrase book.
Compiled by Lexus Ltd with Ana de Sá Hughes, Mike Hyland. London; New York; Stuttgart, Germany; Moscow: Dorling Kindersley, 1999. 129p. (Eyewitness Travel Guides).

A pocket phrasebook divided into nineteen sections, which include motoring, hotels and dining out. It shares the same compilers as the Rough Guide phrasebook (see item no. 351). The volume employs European Portuguese and utilizes a phonetic guide to pronunciation. It is completed by metric and other conversion tables, as well as a mini-dictionary.

351 Rough Guide Portuguese phrase book.
Compiled by Lexus.   London: Rough Guides, 1996. 262p.

This book is unusual in that it is really a dictionary rather than a phrasebook. After a brief exposition of the basics of the Portuguese language, the rest of the volume comprises an English-Portuguese and a Portuguese-English dictionary, followed by a 'menu reader' covering the language of food and drink. The dictionary entries do include conversational phrases but finding the phrase that you want can be difficult.

Portuguese, Brazilian and African studies.
See item no. 621.

Language. Phrasebooks

Portuguese language and Luso-Brazilian literature.
See item no. 746.

Religion and Religious Buildings

352 The making of an enterprise: the Society of Jesus in Portugal, its empire and beyond, 1540-1750.
Dauril Alden. Stanford, California: Stanford University Press, 1996. 707p. 7 maps. bibliog.

A massive work of scholarship, to be completed by a second volume, *Destruction of an enterprise*. In twenty-five chapters, arranged in five sections, the author traces the development of the Jesuit Order's so-called Portuguese Assistancy which included the country's overseas territories. Alden is dismissive of earlier published works on the Jesuits and bases his own on extensive use of archival sources both within and outside Portugal. He identifies many of the previously concealed financial benefactors of the Order, as well as studying many controversies arising between the Jesuits, the State and commercial enterprises.

353 Spanish and Portuguese Jewry before and after 1492.
David Fitz Altabe. Brooklyn, New York: Sepher-Hermon Press, 1993. 154p. bibliog.

The author examines the prelude and aftermath of a turbulent period in the history of Iberian Jewry. In 1492 Fernando and Isabella, the Spanish monarchs, expelled the Jews and many of them fled to the then more tolerant Portugal. However, in late 1496 and 1497, the Portuguese king, Manuel I, himself implemented a policy of forced conversion of a Jewish population, estimated to be as high as ten per cent of the national total.

354 Churches of Portugal.
Carlos de Azevedo, photographs by Chester E. V. Brummel. New York: Scala Books, 1985. 199p. map. bibliog.

After a substantial textual introduction (p. 11-40) to Portuguese church history and architecture from the Visigothic to the Baroque period, the remainder of this volume comprises an amalgam of colour and monochrome photographs of ecclesiastical buildings in Portugal. The work aims 'to provide basic information ... and does not pretend to be a profound technical survey'. Whilst most of the churches illustrated are celebrated tourist

Religion and Religious Buildings

sights, a number of more obscure locations such as Aveiro, Melgaço and Tavira are also included.

355 Fatima, a close encounter of the worst kind?
David Barclay. Irchester, England: Mark Saunders Publications, 1987. 196p. bibliog.

In this revisiting of the events of 1917 at Fátima, when three peasant children witnessed visions of the Virgin Mary, Barclay adopts a stance which differs from that of most books on the allegedly miraculous happening. He muses on whether the events at Fátima and the world events linked to them, such as the influenza pandemic of 1917, were in fact the 'product of an alien contact rather than a religious experience'. The bibliography includes as many references to flying saucers, UFOs and humanoids as to religious material.

356 El libro de los acuerdos; being the records and accompts of the Spanish and Portuguese Synagogue of London from 1663 to 1681.
Translated from the original Spanish and Portuguese by Lionel D. Barnett. Oxford: Oxford University Press for the Board of Elders of the Congregation, 1931. 143p.

Under the relatively tolerant rule of both Cromwell and Charles II, the Congregation of Spanish and Portuguese Jews flourished in London. The *Libro* comprises decrees, inventories of the Congregation's possessions and records of income and expenditure, all recorded during a time of expansion of the Community's activities.

357 Hebrews of the Portuguese nation: conversos and community in early modern Amsterdam.
Miriam Bodian. Bloomington, Indiana: Indiana University Press, 1997. 219p. bibliog. (The Modern Jewish Experience).

The *conversos* were descendants of baptised Jews who, in the late 16th and 17th century, left Portugal and settled in various European cities, including Venice, Hamburg, Bordeaux, London and Amsterdam. By the mid-18th century there were 3,000 Portuguese Jews in Amsterdam where they formed a community of international importance as merchants and printers. Bodian recounts, from the rich resources of Amsterdam archives, how the immigrants retained their Portuguese identity, even after they largely adopted the Dutch language in the early 19th century.

358 Liturgies of the Spanish and Portuguese Reformed Episcopal Church.
Edited by Colin Buchanan. Bramcote, Nottingham, England: Grove Books, 1985. 41p. (Grove Liturgical Study, no. 43).

After a brief 'Introduction', this publication comprises translations of four rites, two each from the Spanish Reformed Episcopal Church and the Lusitanian Church. The Spanish rites are, in the first case, derived from the 1889 *Prayer Book* and, in the second instance, comprise the 1984 *Rite*. The Portuguese texts are taken from the 1882 *Prayer Book* and the 1969 *Rite* of the Lusitanian Church, respectively. Both Churches were founded in

Religion and Religious Buildings

1880 by former Roman Catholics and, in 1980, they both became provincial dioceses of the Anglican Communion.

359 Vestígios hebraicos em Portugal: viagem de uma pintora. Jewish vestiges in Portugal: travels of a painter.
Laura Cesana. Lisbon: Fundação Calouste Gulbenkian, 1997. 159p. map.
With a text in both English and Portuguese, this large hardback volume by the painter, Laura Cesana, records aspects of Jewish life still evident in Portugal.

360 The fire of tongues: António Vieira and the missionary Church in Brazil and Portugal.
Thomas M. Cohen. Stanford, California: Stanford University Press, 1998. 262p. bibliog.
A renowned preacher, António Vieira (1608-97) believed that Portugal was destined to lead the Roman Catholic Church in its task of converting the Jews of Europe and the indigenous peoples of the New World to the 'one true faith'. Cohen traces Vieira's two spells in Brazil (1653-61 and 1681-97), which were punctuated by four years (1663-67) in the custody of the Inquisition. The book's title derives from Vieira's belief in the Jesuits' 'fire of tongues' or mastery of languages in the quest to convert native peoples.

361 The churches in Portugal: the pathway to the future.
Commission on Inter-Church Aid, Refugee and World Service.
Geneva: World Council of Churches, 1984. 36p. map.
This volume seeks to 'describe the life and witness of the historic Protestant Churches in Portugal' through a text written by the Portuguese Churches themselves. The Churches described include the Lusitanian Catholic-Apostolic Evangelical Church, the Portuguese Methodist Church, the Evangelical Presbyterian Church in Portugal, the German Evangelical Church of Lisbon and the Salvation Army in Portugal. Accounts of ecumenical initiatives within Portugal are also described and the addresses of the various Protestant Churches in Portugal are listed.

362 A travel guide to Jewish Europe.
Ben E. Frank. Gretna, Louisiana: Pelican, 1996. 599p. maps.
The section of this book (p. 227-40) which covers Portugal provides pointers to surviving buildings with Jewish connections throughout the country, covering towns such as Estremoz as well as Lisbon. In addition to providing historical information, for example on the use of the Rossio square in Lisbon for *autos-da-fé*, current information is provided on the availability in Portugal of kosher food and the location of functioning synagogues.

363 Under the bright wings.
Peter Harris, illustrated by Susan Rubira. London; Sydney; Auckland, New Zealand: Hodder & Stoughton, 1993. 176p. bibliog.
The author, formerly a clergyman on The Wirral, and a keen ornithologist, emigrated in 1983 to the Alvor area of the Algarve in southern Portugal, with his wife and family. There, attached to the Igreja Lusitana (Anglican Church of Portugal), he established *A*

Religion and Religious Buildings

Rocha Christian Field Study Centre and Bird Observatory, where he combines his Christian ministry with his passion for birdwatching. This book tells the story of nine years of life in Portugal, illustrated by line drawings.

364 As cartuxas de Portugal: the charterhouses of Portugal.
Edited by James Hogg. Salzburg, Austria: Institut für Anglistik und Amerikanistik, Universität Salzburg, 1984. 148p. bibliog. (Analecta Cartusiana, no. 69).

A somewhat disjointed work which initially comprises two essays in Portuguese on the Évora and Lisbon charterhouses of the Carthusians, followed by seventy-five monochrome photographs of the Évora complex, founded in 1587 and boasting the largest cloister in Portugal. There follows an essay on Carthusian life in Portugal today, in Portuguese, and a history of the Carthusian Order in Portugal in German. Finally, the only contribution to bear an author's name is an essay in English by James Hogg on 'The charterhouses of Portugal'.

365 A genealogy of ecclesiastical jurisdictions: schematic outline illustrating the development of the Catholic Church in territories assigned to Portugal by Treaty of Tordesillas in 1494.
Harrie Huiskamp. Kampen, The Netherlands: Uitgeverij Kok, 1994. 315p. maps. (Kerk en Theologie in Context, no. 23).

A monumental work which traces the development of the Catholic Church in those countries which lie to the east of the demarcation line between Spain and Portugal, agreed in the Treaty of Tordesillas in 1494, but only ratified by the Pope in 1506. Extensive use is made of genealogical-type charts and maps to show the historical origins of present-day ecclesiastical jurisdictions in Africa, Australasia, Asia and South America. Countries such as New Zealand and Sudan are included because, even though they were not settled by the Portuguese, they fell within the area assigned to Portugal at Tordesillas.

366 The Sephardim of England: a history of the Spanish and Portuguese Jewish community, 1492-1951.
Albert M. Hyamson. London: Methuen & Co. Ltd, 1951. 468p.

A work which claims to be the first full-length study of the English population of Sephardic Jews, whose origins can be traced back to the diaspora provoked by the expulsion of the Jews from Spain in 1492 and from Portugal in 1496/97. As Hyamson writes, 'it was from the exiles of Portugal of 1496 more than from those of Spain four years earlier that the new Sephardi settlements in England ... were drawn'. The twenty chapters and more than fifty accompanying illustrations and photographic plates trace the story in chronological sequence. The six appendices include lists of Elders and a glossary.

367 Fatima: a story of hope.
Colin Jeffrey, Paul Dunn. Composed at Old Woking, England: Unwin Bros, c.1970. 68p.

The visions of the Virgin Mary experienced by three peasant children from 13 May 1917 at Cova da Iria in central Portugal have given rise to a substantial literature in English, of which this is one of the typically unquestioning examples. In sixteen chapters it traces the cult from its origins in 1917 to the creation of the imposing pilgrimage centre at Fátima, erected in 1921 as a focus for adherents. The text also describes the three secrets allegedly revealed by the Virgin to the three children, Francisco, his sister Jacinta and their cousin Lúcia. These were respectively: a vision of hell; a prophecy that communism would spread from Russia to engulf the world unless devotion was made to the Immaculate Heart of Mary; and the secret of world peace. This last secret was placed in a sealed envelope by Lúcia, long after 1917, to be opened by the Bishop of Leiria in 1960. Its contents had not been made public at the time of publication.

368 The laws and charities of the Spanish and Portuguese Jews Congregation of London.
Neville Laski. London: The Cresset Press, 1952. 224p.

Laski, a Queen's Counsel and an Elder of the Bevis Marks synagogue in London, here depicts life in the Congregation from 1663-77 and also describes the legal and charitable aspects of the activities of the Jewish community in that city into the 20th century. The book also commemorates the 250th anniversary in 1951 of the consecration of the Bevis Marks synagogue.

369 The history of the Jews of Spain and Portugal, from the earliest times to their final expulsion from those kingdoms, and their subsequent dispersion; with complete translations of all the laws made respecting them during their long establishment in the Iberian peninsula.
E. H. Lindo. London: Longman, Brown, Green & Longman, 1898. 384p.

After an introduction to the early settlement of the Jews in Spain and Portugal in chapter I, it is in the latter part of the volume (chapter XXVII, p. 303 onwards) that the history of the Jews in Portugal is most thoroughly covered. Emphasis is on the early periods of history, with more recent times covered only in a somewhat discursive and arbitrary manner.

370 Two Portuguese exiles in Castile: Dom David Negro and Dom Isaac Abravanel.
Elias Lipiner, translated from the Portuguese by Menahem Pariente. Jerusalem: The Magnes Press, The Hebrew University, 1997. 173p. bibliog. (Hispania Judaica, X).

Two historically separate instances of Portuguese Jews being forced into exile in Castile are here recounted. After a background chapter, 'The Jews of Portugal: an overview', Lipiner describes the experiences of Rabbi David Negro, who was tried for his involvement in the 1383 rebellion in Portugal, and of Isaac Abravanel (1437-1508), who was obliged to flee the court of King João II of Portugal following his involvement in a conspiracy. These episodes are used to illustrate the precarious existence of even high-ranking Jews in Portugal. The latter half of the book comprises transcriptions and photographic reproductions of contemporary documents.

Religion and Religious Buildings

371 The Jews of Spain and Portugal and the Inquisition.
Frederic David Mocatta. London: Longmans, Green & Co., 1877. 99p.

Developed by the author from a lecture, this is an extended essay on the relationship between the Jews of Iberia and the Inquisition. Mocatta sees the Iberian Jews as enjoying a period of privilege for much of the Middle Ages, compared with their fellow-believers elsewhere in Europe. He goes on to describe how the *marranos* (crypto-Jews) maintained Christian appearances whilst covertly keeping alive their Jewish faith. Mocatta also refers to the *auto-da-fe* ceremonies held in Portugal.

372 When men walk dry: Portuguese messianism in Brazil.
Carole A. Myscofski. Atlanta, Georgia: Scholars Press, 1988. 209p. bibliog. (American Academy of Religion Academy Series, no. 61).

In the 16th century Portugal was the source for a number of messianic cults. These included Isaac Abranavel's forecast of the arrival of a Redeemer in 1503 and the beliefs that arose around the return of King Sebastian of Portugal, lost in the Battle of Alcácer-Kibir in 1578. Other messianic beliefs related to the alleged existence of Prester John, a Christian leader in Abyssinia and to the visions of Portugal's first monarch, Afonso Henriques. These messianic ideologies resurfaced three times in North-East Brazil in 1817, 1838 and 1883 and are here traced back to their Portuguese origins.

373 Fatima has the answer.
Simon O'Byrne. Printed at Kildare, Ireland: Leinster Leader, 1986. 111p. bibliog.

The author is an American-educated Irish priest who sets out to explain why devotion to Our Lady is essential and why he believes that Man must practise mortification in reparation for his sins. In twenty-eight short sections, of which only six describe the events at Fátima in 1917 and their aftermath, O'Byrne somewhat incredulously concludes that the allegedly miraculous events have 'blessed Portugal with great peace and prosperity'. O'Byrne also wrote *Our Lady at Fátima* (Dublin: Adam & Eve Counselling and Consultation Centre, 1990).

374 The expulsion 1492 chronicles: an anthology of medieval chronicles relating to the expulsion of the Jews from Spain and Portugal.
Selected and edited by David Raphael. North Hollywood, California: Carmi House Press, 1992. 203p.

A collection of contemporary source materials documenting the expulsion of the Jews from Spain in 1492 and from Portugal in 1496/97. Documents originally written in Hebrew, Latin, Portuguese and Spanish are included. Amongst those relevant to Portugal are the chronicles of King João II by Garcia de Resende and Rui de Pina, the chronicles of King Manuel by Damião de Góis and Jerónimo Osório, Abraham Zarco's *Book of genealogies* and Samuel Usque's *Consolation for the tribulations of Israel*.

Religion and Religious Buildings

375 The chapel of Saint John Baptist and its collections in São Roque church, Lisbon.
Maria João Madeira Rodrigues. Lisbon: Inapa, 1988. 253p. bibliog.

With many colour photographs, this work illustrates the magnificent 18th-century decoration of S. Roque, an externally plain Jesuit church in Lisbon whose interior ornament, much of it gilded carving, was chiefly the work of Italians. St Rock was a Venetian saint, whose cult was deemed to afford protection against plague. Although King Manuel I obtained a relic of the saint, it was not till later in the 16th century that the present church was constructed. As well as describing the artistic work in the church, this book also includes an inventory of the church, which includes items now lost.

376 The quest for eastern Christians: travels and rumor in the Age of Discovery.
Francis M. Rogers. Minneapolis, Minnesota: University of Minnesota Press, 1962. 221p. 2 maps. bibliog.

A companion to the author's earlier *Travels of the Infante Dom Pedro of Portugal* (see item no. 131), this book provides an unusual perspective on Portuguese overseas exploration in the 15th and 16th centuries. Firstly its aim is not to study the history or politics of the explorations, but to assess the religious aspect of their motivation. Rogers is fascinated by the Portuguese quest for Christianity beyond their immediate Islamic neighbours. Secondly, the author's study is also innovative for being based on a painstaking study of contemporary texts, mostly in Latin, culled from American and European libraries.

377 The third secret of Fátima.
Brother Michel de la Sainte Trinité. Chulmleigh, England: Augustine Publishing, 1986. 37p.

Amongst the voluminous literature relating to the alleged appearances of the Virgin Mary at Fátima in 1917, this is an important contribution. This translation abridges the 600-page third volume of the author's *Toute la verité sur Fatima*. In 1941, Sister Lúcia, one of the peasant children who witnessed the vision, revealed that there were three secrets revealed by the Virgin; two of these were publicised in 1942, but the third was not to be revealed until Lúcia was dead or until '1960 at the latest'. Although Pope John XXIII read the sealed third secret in 1959, it was not publicly revealed at the time of writing. Brother Michel here suggests that the secret concerned a crisis of faith in the Catholic Church but exhorts the Church to make public the full 'secret'. Other Augustine Publishing titles include *Fatima, the great sign*, *Fatima in Lucia's own words*, *Devotion to the Immaculate Heart of Mary*, *When millions saw Mary* and *Our Lady of Fatima's peace plan from heaven*.

378 Reluctant cosmopolitans: the Portuguese Jews of seventeenth-century Amsterdam.
Daniel M. Swetschinski. London: The Littman Library of Jewish Civilization, 1999. 352p.

Following the Treaty of Utrecht (1579), which declared religious tolerance in the Netherlands, Portuguese *marranos* (crypto-Jews) migrated to Amsterdam and by 1608

Religion and Religious Buildings

there were two Portuguese synagogues there. The newcomers' wealth was largely invested in trade and commerce and these activities, as well as their internal quarrels, are chronicled in this book. By 1675 Amsterdam boasted the most magnificent synagogue in Europe and the city had become a centre of Jewish learning and printing.

Portuguese merchants and missionaries in feudal Japan, 1543-1640.
See item no. 237.

Anticlerical satire in medieval Portuguese literature.
See item no. 530.

Society

General

379 Revolution at the grassroots: community organizations in the Portuguese Revolution.
Charles Downs. Albany, New York: State University of New York Press, 1989. 215p. bibliog. (SUNY Series in Urban Public Policy).

Downs presents a study of the 1974 Portuguese Revolution as experienced in the industrial city of Setúbal, south of Lisbon. He spent three years in Portugal, 1975-78, and during that time he studied the grassroots political movements of the Setúbal area. His conclusion was that such movements were an important component of the revolutionary process but he was less sure that they would maintain their importance in the period after the transition to democracy.

380 Liberal revolution, social change and economic development: the region of Viana, (N.W. Portugal) in the first three quarters of the nineteenth century.
Rui Feijó. New York; London: Garland Publishing Inc., 1993. 236p. maps. bibliog. (Modern European History Spain and Portugal: A Garland Series of Outstanding Dissertations).

This is a published version of the author's thesis, written at the end of 1983. Its six chapters cover Portuguese socio-political developments between 1807 and 1870 and, in particular, their effects in Viana do Castelo. A wide spectrum of social phenomena is covered, including marriage, celibacy, fertility, emigration, agrarian problems, land ownership and legal matters. He concludes that liberalism failed to deliver major change to the Viana area, where land redistribution and socio-economic change were only accomplished on a moderate scale.

Society. General

381 Queerspace: a history of urban sexuality.
Edited by David Higgs. London: Routledge, 1999. 224p. maps.

Higgs provides an assessment of gay city life and its varied meeting places in Lisbon, as well as in London, Amsterdam, Rio, San Francisco, Paris and Moscow. Compared with most of the above cities Portuguese attitudes are still conservative but gay bars and an annual gay and lesbian festival, started in 1997, are now growing in both acceptability and popularity. The book makes use of personal recollections and creative literature as well as legal pronouncements on homosexuality from the countries in question.

382 The structure of Portuguese society: the failure of fascism.
Diamantino P. Machado. New York; Westport, Connecticut; London: Praeger, 1991. 216p. bibliog.

In seven chapters, and a postscript, the author seeks to fulfil a two-fold aim. Firstly, he aims to examine the nature of Portuguese society and the role of the State between 1926 and the 1974 Revolution, the period of the *Estado Novo*. Secondly, he investigates the causes of the 1974 Revolution and subsequent developments, up to 1976. He concludes that there never was a transition to real socialism in the wake of the Revolution; the conflict was 'not class against class, but faction against faction within the old hegemonic class'.

383 Social inequality in a Portuguese hamlet: land, late marriage and bastardy, 1870-1978.
Brian Juan O'Neill. Cambridge, England; New York; New Rochelle, New York; Melbourne, Australia; Sydney: Cambridge University Press, 1987. 431p. map. bibliog. (Cambridge Studies in Social Anthropology, no. 63).

A study in eight chapters, deriving from a 1982 doctoral thesis, of the mountain village of Fontelas, near Vila Real in northern Portugal. The author seeks to disprove the findings of previous studies of similar villages which asserted that such populations enjoyed egalitarian social structures. O'Neill finds that a clear hierarchy exists in the village, that religion is only cursorily acknowledged and that rates of illegitimacy are exceptionally high. His study, which makes heavy use of church records, addresses three main topics: land tenure, cooperative labour and forms of marriage and inheritance.

384 Sons of Adam, daughters of Eve: the peasant worldview of the Alto Minho.
João de Pina-Cabral. Oxford: Clarendon Press, 1986. 258p. map. bibliog.

An anthropological study of the peasant communities of Paço da Barca and Couto de S. Fins in the Alto Minho region of northern Portugal. After an introductory chapter, the author addresses the subjects of 'household and family', 'men, women and sexuality', 'household and community', 'coping with evil' and 'life and death'.

385 Les personnes agées dans le monde. The elderly all over the world: Portugal.
Maria de Lourdes Baptista Quaresma. Marcinelle, Belgium; Paris: Centre International de Gerontologie Sociale/ International Center of Social Gerontology, 1980. 97p. bibliog. (Les Monographies du C.I.G.S/ I.C.S.G. Monographs Series).

This assessment of the welfare of the elderly in Portugal reaches the somewhat facile conclusion that 'we have a long way to go' before arriving at satisfactory social welfare for the elderly. Nevertheless, it ranges over many features of the problem of the aged in society, including the demographic, socio-economic, health and legal aspects. The text is in both French and English and is supported by statistics.

Inside ethnic families.
See item no. 280.

Linguistic minorities of the European Economic Community.
See item no. 305.

Social anthropology

386 Reclaiming English kinship theory: Portuguese refractions of British kinship theory.
Mary Bouquet. Manchester, England; New York: Manchester University Press, 1993. 260p. bibliog.

Bouquet examines the pre-eminence of British scholarship in the development of kinship theory, as exemplified by the export of English theory to Portugal. From a Portuguese perspective, Bouquet challenges the dominance of Anglo-Saxon theory in the field of social anthropology and argues, specifically, that English texts of kinship theory betray an arrogance and preparedness to judge others whilst resisting attempts to address the anthropology of their own land.

Statistics

387 Anuário estatístico de Portugal. Statistical Yearbook of Portugal.
Instituto Nacional de Estatística.   Lisbon: Instituto Nacional de Estatística, 1991- . annual.

This annual compilation has appeared since 1991 (covering 1990) and is now a completely bilingual Portuguese and English publication. The attractively presented 1997 volume (published 1998, 368p.) has twenty-four statistical sections which cover social, demographic, environmental, industrial and economic data which for the most part was collected in 1995/96. Comparisons with earlier years are also provided and the final section consists of international comparisons between Portugal, other European countries, Japan and the United States.

Gender and Women's Studies

388 **Women of the *praia*: work and lives in a Portuguese coastal community.**
Sally Cole. Princeton, New Jersey: Princeton University Press, 1991. 189p. 3 maps. bibliog.

In 1984-85 the author, a United States graduate student, spent thirteen months in Vila Chã, a community of 3,000 people lying 23km north of Oporto on the Atlantic coast. She entered into the life of the local womenfolk in a quest to ascertain the position of women in southern European rural society. In this illustrated volume, Cole examines the change in women's role from their past direct participation in fishing to their increasing absorption into the present-day fish processing, textile and other industries. She also describes the tensions between the local fishing community and neighbouring agricultural workers.

389 **The employment of women in Portugal.**
Manuela Silva. Luxembourg: Office for Official Publications of the European Communities, 1984. 218p. bibliog. (European Commission Document).

Written by a former Secretary of State for Planning in the Portuguese government, this volume has thirteen sections. These include statistical and descriptive information on women's wages, legal status, demographic distribution, employment and training. By the 1970s female employment was growing at a faster rate than male employment in sectors such as catering, distribution and the hotel and service industries. However, some sectors remain male bastions, such as building and mining. The author is concerned that, despite the great advances made in legislating for the increased employment of women, the decades of ingrained sexual discrimination in Portugal will mean that achieving equality of opportunity will be a lengthy process.

Gender and Women's Studies

390 Women in Portugal.
Maria Manuela Stocker de Sousa, Maria Cristina Perez Dominguez.
Brussels: Commission of the European Communities, 1982. 59p.
(Supplement No. 11 to Women in Europe).
A comprehensive survey of the status of Portuguese women across a broad spectrum of environments, including education, family life, the law, politics, contraception, civic affairs, employment, advertising and emigration. There is also a review of Portuguese women's associations. The authors, not surprisingly, conclude that there is still much progress to be made in the emancipation of Portuguese women. Such advances as had been made by 1990 are reviewed in *Portugal: status of women* by Maria Reynolds de Sousa, Dina Canço (Lisbon: Commission for Equality and Women's Rights, Prime Minister's Office, 1991). A retrospective comparison of women's rights can be had by consulting *The legal situation of the Portuguese woman*, published by the Office of the Secretary of State for Information and Tourism (Lisbon: General Direction for Information, 1971. 24p.), which traces the status of Portuguese women from the 1933 Constitution to the time of writing, with paternalistic emphasis on medical and welfare provision.

Men who migrate, women who wait.
See item no. 275.

Sons of Adam, daughters of Eve.
See item no. 384.

Women, literature and culture in the Portuguese-speaking world.
See item no. 529.

Gender, ethnicity and class in modern Portuguese-speaking culture.
See item no. 536.

The feminine in the poetry of Herberto Helder.
See item no. 588.

The hegemonic male.
See item no. 660.

Politics

391 Political parties and democracy in Portugal: organizations, elections, and public opinion.
Edited by Thomas C. Bruneau. Boulder, Colorado: Westview Press, 1997. 144p.

The five chapters of this illustrated book constitute what its editor claims is the first book in English or Portuguese 'to devote itself to the political parties of Portugal' in the period since the 1974 Revolution. After the editor's 'Introduction', Carlos Cunha writes on the Portuguese Communist Party, Juliet Antunes Sablosky assesses the Portuguese Socialist Party, 'The Right' is covered by Maritheresa Frain and the work concludes with an essay on public opinion surveys and election results by Mário Bacalhau. Bacalhau concludes that the revolutionary fervour of the 1970s has been replaced by a four-party system in which two of the parties alternate in power.

392 Politics in contemporary Portugal: parties and the consolidation of democracy.
Thomas C. Bruneau, Alex Macleod. Boulder, Colorado: Lynne Rienner, 1986. 236p. bibliog.

This study is based not only on printed and archival resources but also on numerous interviews with leading politicians, including Francisco Pinto Balsemão, Marcello Caetano and Diogo Freitas do Amaral. Between 1976 and 1986 no Portuguese government survived for more than two years so, not surprisingly, the authors see political instability as the biggest threat to democracy, a threat exacerbated by the alienation of grassroots supporters caused by the centralization of power within the parties. President Eanes is identified as offering a unifying factor through his stance of aloofness from party politics.

Politics

393 Transitions from dictatorship to democracy: comparative studies of Spain, Portugal and Greece.
Ronald H. Chilcote, Stylianos Hadjiyannis, Fred A. López III.
New York; Philadelphia, Pennsylvania; Washington, DC; London: Crane Russak, 1990. 217p. bibliog.

Written chiefly by American academics, these five essays form a retrospective assessment of post-1974 developments in Portugal, Greece and southern Europe. The approach is much indebted to the Marxist theorist of the state, Nicos Poulantzas, whose 1976 volume, *The crisis of dictatorships* (London: NLB), itself analysed the Portuguese political situation. Here many of Poulantzas's theories regarding the bourgeoisie, capitalism and the working classes are reexamined in the light of some fifteen years of Portuguese democracy.

394 The Portuguese Communist Party's strategy for power, 1921-1986.
Carlos A. Cunha. New York; London: Garland Publishing Inc., 1992. 431p. bibliog. (Modern European History: Spain and Portugal. A Garland Series of Outstanding Studies and Dissertations).

The Portuguese Communist Party (PCP) was founded in 1921 and was for many years a focal point of resistance to the authoritarian regime which operated in Portugal from 1926 to 1974. This book is a revised version of the author's 1987 doctoral thesis. About a half of its content covers the post-1974 Revolution period, whilst the preceding section is divided between an introductory history of the Portuguese political system and a study of the PCP from 1921 to 1974.

395 The Portuguese military and the State: rethinking transitions in Europe and Latin America.
Lawrence S. Graham. Boulder, Colorado; San Francisco, California; Oxford: Westview Press, 1993. 152p. bibliog.

Comparisons are drawn here between the role of the military in Portuguese politics and the armed forces' involvement in regimes in Latin America, Eastern Europe and elsewhere in southern Europe, such as Spain and Greece. The absence for so many years, during the Salazar era, of a civilian opposition in Portugal, with mass support and strong leadership, is seen as affording the Portuguese military a key role in ensuring the transition to democracy, a process which is viewed as having taken fifteen years, up to 1989. António Rangel Bandeira's *Military interventions in Portuguese politics: antecedents of the Armed Forces Movement* (Toronto, Canada: Brazilian Studies, 1975. 91p.) seeks to show how the army's role in Portugal throughout the 20th century laid the foundations for its *coup d'état* of 1974.

396 The revolutionary Left in Portugal.
Introduction by Tom Harrison. London: I-CL, 1977. 24p.

A collection of interviews with unnamed representatives of three of the leading left-wing political organizations which were active at the height of the 1974/75 lurch towards revolutionary socialism in Portugal. The interviews, conducted between July and September 1975, are with the PRP (Partido Revolucionário do Proletariado; Proletarian Revolutionary Party), the PRT (Partido Revolucionário dos Trabalhadores; Workers'

Revolutionary Party) and the LCI (Liga Comunista Internacional; International Communist League). The interviews clearly demonstrate the extent to which Portugal veered towards Marxist-Leninism in reaction to decades of political repression under Salazar.

397 The changing architecture of Iberian politics, 1974-1992: an investigation on the structuring of democratic political systemic culture in semiperipheral southern European societies.
José M. Magone.   Lewiston, New York; Queenston, Canada; Lampeter, Wales: Mellen University Press, 1996. 653p. bibliog.

Originally written as a thesis for the University of Vienna, this large tome covers the period of Portuguese and Spanish accession to the European Community. Portugal is classed as a semiperipheral country in which the European Parliament is forecast to have an important role in determining the long-term nature of Portuguese democracy. Less than perfect English, a lot of theoretical content and a wealth of jargon make this work heavy going and the perfunctory index does little to enhance its accessibility.

398 European Portugal: the difficult road to sustainable democracy.
José M. Magone.   Basingstoke, England: Macmillan Press, 1997. 217p. bibliog.

Based on democratization theory, the author assesses in ten chapters Portugal's developing democracy up to 1995, with an appendix covering the 1996 elections. He sees popular participation in Portuguese institutions as essential in building a truly qualitative and sustainable democracy. By studying Portugal against a backdrop of world developments, Magone sees the Portuguese Revolution as the harbinger of a wave of democratization which swept Europe after 1974. Almost thirty charts and tables enhance the text.

399 The challenges of democratic consolidation in Portugal: political, economic, and military issues, 1976-91.
Paul Christopher Manuel.   Westport, Connecticut; London: Praeger, 1996. 103p. bibliog.

Manuel divides the period of study into three sections. Firstly 1976-79 is defined as a period of political and economic instability, following the 1974 Revolution. Secondly, the National Assembly is seen as resolving the military challenge to its authority, while, finally, from 1983 to 1991 political stability and economic growth were achieved. The author concludes that 'the outlook for the continuation of democracy in Portugal is excellent'.

400 Uncertain outcome: the politics of the Portuguese transition to democracy.
Paul Christopher Manuel.   Lanham, Maryland; New York; London: University Press of America, 1995. 197p. map. bibliog.

Following an explanation of the origins of the 1974 Portuguese Revolution, the author delineates four phases in the transition to democracy up to the swearing in of Mário Soares, the socialist leader, as prime minister by the then recently-elected President, Ramalho Eanes on 23 July 1976. He sees institutional stability as returning, following the

Politics

failed *coup d'état* of 25 November 1975, when military forces of the Left were outmanoeuvred by centrists.

401 Nationalism and the nation in the Iberian peninsula: competing and conflicting identities.
Edited by Clare Mar-Molinero, Angel Smith. Oxford; Washington, DC: Berg, 1996. 281p. bibliog.

A collection of papers, most of which derived from a conference on Nationalism and National Identity in the Iberian Peninsula, held at the University of Southampton in 1995. Two of the papers address Portuguese culture. The first, 'Nationalising cultural politics: representations of the Portuguese "Discoveries" and the rhetoric of identitarianism, 1880-1926' by Abdool Karim A. Vakil (p. 33-52, bibliog.), shows how 19th- and 20th-century Portuguese politicians sought to manipulate the legend of the 15th- and 16th-century Discoveries to their own ends. The second essay, 'The people and the poet: Portuguese national identity and the Camões tercentenary, 1880' by Alan Freeland (p. 53-67, bibliog.), demonstrates how the celebrations sought to revive national consciousness and recapture the country's historical importance.

402 The making of Portuguese democracy.
Kenneth Maxwell. Cambridge, England: Cambridge University Press, 1995. 250p. bibliog.

Maxwell sees the period 1974-76, during which Portugal was in revolutionary ferment, as a time which, twenty years later, is to some degree sublimated in the national consciousness. The schisms of that time and the fact that the military were dominant are seen as leading to a 'bowdlerization of the revolution'. Maxwell revisits this period of internal upheaval and collapse of empire and demonstrates how events in Portugal had major implications for democracy in neighbouring Spain and in Africa, as well as influencing Eurocommunism, the Cold War and the collapse of dictatorships in eastern Europe.

403 Portugal: ancient country, young democracy.
Edited by Kenneth Maxwell, Michael H. Haltzel. Washington, DC: The Woodrow Wilson Center Press, 1990. 122p. bibliog.

A distinguished array of contributors figure in this collection of papers from a 1987 conference sponsored by the West European Program of the Woodrow Wilson Center for Scholars. The collaborators include the socialist politician, Mário Soares and the philosopher, Eduardo Lourenço who contributed the volume's concluding chapter. The nine other chapters cover politics, economics, banking, foreign policy and cultural issues. The contributors are united by their enthusiasm for the future of Portugal and especially for European integration.

404 Democratization and social settlements: the politics of change in contemporary Portugal.
Daniel Nataf. Albany, New York: State University of New York Press, 1995. 289p. bibliog.

An American academic, Daniel Nataf, here seeks to show that the political and social rupture caused by the 1974 Portuguese Revolution led to the subsequent establishment of democracy and the market economy. He sees the Revolution as not only destroying the pre-existing political institutions but also uprooting traditional social relations. He uses government statistics, including censuses, business and trade union documents, as well as information from myriad political parties, to support his theses. Three stages are discerned: first, from the Revolution to 11 March 1975 when the proletariat made gains as the bourgeoisie resisted; second, from 12 March to 25 November 1975 when the bourgeoisie consolidated its position; and from 26 November 1975 to 25 April 1976 when the radicals were purged and the bourgeoisie reasserted itself.

405 Salazar's dictatorship and European fascism: problems of interpretation.
António Costa Pinto. Boulder, Colorado: Social Science Monographs, 1995. 230p. bibliog.

A study of Portugal in the context of 20th-century European totalitarian regimes. The author sees Portuguese monarchists and Catholic groups pre-empting the rise of genuine fascism in their country in the 1920s, leading to the emergence of the authoritarian corporatist regime of Salazar. An impressive bibliography supports the text.

406 The transition to democracy in Spain and Portugal.
Howard J. Wiarda, Ieda Siqueira Wiarda. Washington, DC: American Enterprise Institute for Public Policy Research, 1989. 416p. (AEI Studies, no. 482).

This volume provides a concise assessment of Portugal's first fifteen years of democracy, following the 1974 Revolution. Howard Wiarda is also the author of *Iberia and Latin America: new democracies, new policies, new models* (Lanham, Maryland: Rowman & Littlefield, 1996. 118p.), itself a shorter reworking of his *The Iberia-Latin America connection: implications for U.S. foreign policy* (Boulder, Colorado: Westview Press; Washington, DC: American Enterprise Institute, 1986. 482p.) which included William Perry's 'The fabric of Luso-Brazilian relations' (p. 408-26).

Foreign Relations

General

407 Synergy at work: Spain and Portugal in European foreign policy.
Edited by Franco Algieri, Elfriede Regelsberger. Bonn: Europe Union Verlag/ Institut für Europäische Politik, 1996. 334p. (Analysen zur Europapolitik des Instituts für Europäische Politik, Band 10).

An assessment of Spanish and Portuguese foreign policy since their accession to the European Community in 1986. The editors demonstrate how the Iberian countries, both relatively isolated politically from the 1930s till the 1970s, have, nevertheless, integrated themselves harmoniously into the EC.

408 Portugal, the U.S. and N.A.T.O.
Luc Crollen. Louvain, Belgium: Leuven University Press, 1973. 162p. bibliog. (Department of Political Science, Studies in International Relations, no. 1).

A study of small power behaviour within and in relation to the NATO international alliance. After examining the motives for Portugal's joining the Organization, the author concludes that Salazar was initially attracted primarily by NATO's anti-communist stance. Portugal remained in NATO for this reason even after NATO declared itself powerless to intervene in Portugal's African conflicts. Crollen argues, nevertheless, that the country's NATO relationship with the Great Powers facilitated its retention of its African colonies for, he asserts, 'There is no hope for Portugal outside NATO'.

Foreign Relations. General

409 Lusophone Africa, Portugal and the United States: possibilities for more effective cooperation.
Kimberly A. Hamilton. Lisbon, Washington, DC: Luso-American Development Foundation; Center for Strategic and International Studies, 1992. 57p. (Significant Issues Series, vol. 14, no. 11).

Papers from a 1991 conference, attended by a hundred experts and held in Lisbon, are collected together here into four chapters and three appendices. As well as assessing the position of Portugal as a potential conciliator in African conflicts, owing to her long colonial involvement in the continent, the papers address the issue of trilateral economic collaboration between the United States, Portugal and Lusophone Africa, namely the former Portuguese colonies of Angola, Mozambique, Cape Verde, São Tomé e Príncipe and Guinea-Bissau.

410 European destiny, Atlantic transformations: Portuguese foreign policy under the Second Republic, 1974-1992.
Scott B. MacDonald. New Brunswick, New Jersey; London: Transaction Press, 1993. 176p. bibliog.

The eight chapters of this volume, covering post-Revolution Portugal, fill what MacDonald sees as a gap in North American studies. Portugal's foreign policy is complicated by its historical connections with Africa and Asia, together with its desire to play a full part in the European Community. As far as its transatlantic relations are concerned, MacDonald believes that Portugal faces the 'danger of becoming too European'.

411 Portugal, an Atlantic paradox: Portuguese/U.S. relations after the E.C. enlargement.
José Calvet de Magalhães, Álvaro de Vasconcelos, Joaquim Ramos Silva. Lisbon: Instituto para Estudos Estratégicos e Internacionais/ Institute for Strategic and International Studies, 1990. 139p. bibliog.

The authors are experts on diplomatic relations, international security and economic cooperation and they look at all of these aspects of the bilateral relations between Portugal and the United States. Portugal's joining the European Community in 1986 is seen as causing a realignment of the country's foreign relations which the authors are keen should not undermine its historical transatlantic links which, on the fall of the Salazar/ Caetano regime in 1974, were the target of much left-wing opposition.

412 Portuguese defense and foreign policy since democratization.
Edited by Kenneth Maxwell. New York: Camões Center for the Study of the Portuguese-Speaking World, Columbia University, 1991. 92p. (Camões Center Special Report, no. 3).

A work comprising five chapters based on various seminars held in Washington, DC and in Portugal. These assess the changes in Portuguese security and foreign policies resulting from the collapse of the authoritarian regime in Portugal, accession to the European Communities and the fall of communism in eastern Europe. Portugal's flirtation with 'Atlantic neutrality' in the immediate aftermath of the 1974 Revolution is also described.

Anglo-Portuguese alliance

413 The Anglo-Portuguese alliance: its roots and contemporary relevance.
Manuel Côrte-Real. Reading, England: University of Reading Graduate School of European and International Studies, 1987. 11p. (University of Reading Papers in European and International Social Science Research, no. 16).

A succinct summary of Anglo-Portuguese relations from their mediaeval origins to the present day is provided by the Portuguese Embassy's Counsellor in London, Manuel Côrte-Real. He traces the origins of the 1386 Treaty of Windsor, whose 600th anniversary is marked by this review, and examines later developments such as the 17th-century trade agreements, the Peninsular War and the two countries' relationship during the two World Wars.

414 Our oldest ally.
Harry J. Greenwall. London: W. H. Allen & Co., 1943. 112p.

Written at the height of the Second World War, this volume nevertheless attempts to take a balanced look at Portugal's *Estado Novo* in the context of European fascism. The author, a journalist with twenty-one years' experience of visiting Portugal, much admires the 'disciplined democracy' of 1940s' Portugal and, after a chapter on the origins of the Anglo-Portuguese alliance gives a cogent description of the workings of the corporative state, though he perhaps goes too far in describing the Portuguese Nationalist Party as akin to Winston Churchill's Liberal Unionists.

415 The oldest ally: Britain and the Portuguese connection, 1936-1941.
Glyn Stone. Woodbridge, England: Boydell Press for the Royal Historical Society, 1994. 228p. bibliog.

Stone attempts to explain why two countries such as Portugal and Britain, geographically apart as well as ideologically and socially at odds with each other, should have had such close ties between 1936 and 1941. It was the Spanish Civil War (1936-39) and the Second World War (1939-45) which acted as the catalyst. The Azores, Madeira and Portugal's overseas colonies held a strategic importance to Britain in the Second World War and Salazar is here depicted as one of the few world leaders who expected the Allies to win the war and was thus considered to be loyal to the British cause. On a broader theme is Stone's *The Great Powers and the Iberian peninsula, 1931-1941* (Basingstoke, England: Macmillan, 1993. 356p. [The Making of the Twentieth Century]).

Mário Soares.
See item no. 264.

Building popular power.
See item no. 490.

Constitution and Law

416 Campaign against repression in Portugal.
British Committee for Portuguese Amnesty. London: British Committee for Portuguese Amnesty, 1963. 8p.

One of a series of pamphlets from the British Committee for Portuguese Amnesty, produced in support of those whose views led them into difficulties and imprisonment during the Salazar regime. Other titles include *Portugal: women in prison* (1964, 16p.) and *Portugal: the price of opposition*, by Helen B. Ward (1963, 16p.).

417 Constitution of the Portuguese Republic. First revision 1982.
Directorate-General of Diffusion. Lisbon: Directorate-General of Diffusion, 1984. 160p.

This volume provides an English version of the Constitution of 2 April 1976, promulgated after the Portuguese Revolution of 25 April 1974, which swept aside the corporate state of the Salazar and Caetano governments. There are four parts to the Constitution: Fundamental rights and duties; Economic organisation; Organisation and political power; and Safeguards and revision of the constitution. Also incorporated is the revision of 30 September 1982. An English translation of the second revision of the Constitution appeared in 1989 (Lisbon: Direcção-Geral da Comunicação Social. 164p.). For those concerned with the legalities of doing business with Portugal, *Portugal: practical commercial law* by C. Jenkins (London: Longman, 1993) is invaluable.

418 Portugal: the Constitution and the consolidation of democracy, 1976-1989.
Edited by Kenneth R. Maxwell, Scott C. Monke. New York: Camões Center, Columbia University, 1991. 62p. (Camões Center Special Report, no. 2).

A study which claims to be 'the first comprehensive discussion available in English on the Portuguese constitutional experience'. The conference papers presented cover the 1976 Constitution, framed after the 1974 Revolution, and the revisions of 1982 and 1989.

Constitution and Law

The last revision is shown as assisting the process of creating a mixed economy along the lines of other European Community members.

Doing business in Portugal.
See item no. 448.

Diário da República.
See item no. 714.

Administration and Local Government

419 Putting citizens first: the Portuguese experience in administrative reform.
Atila Apoge, Liz Dacier. Paris: Organisation for Economic Cooperation and Development, 1996. 159p. bibliog. (Public Management Occasional Papers, no. 13).

Following the passing of the 1976 Constitution, Portuguese state administration went under a period of reform which is here studied up to early 1995. The two main stimuli to reform were the democratic processes after the 1974 Revolution and Portugal's accession to the European Community in 1986 which necessitated further administrative changes to meet the country's need to compete and integrate with its new partners. Portugal's approach of 'selective radicalization' to break the former centralized bureaucracy is here seen as a successful and innovative method for bringing administration closer to its goal of meeting the population's needs.

420 Local development: restructuring, locality and economic initiative in Portugal.
Stephen Syrett. Aldershot, England; Brookfield, Vermont; Singapore; Sydney: Avebury, 1995. 372p. maps. bibliog.

The author, an American academic, provides an insight on the local economic initiatives witnessed in Portugal from the early 1980s. He provides an excellent overview of local government and initiatives such as cooperatives and self-help initiatives, with particular reference to Castanheira de Pêra in central Portugal. The local council there was a prime example of a body taking an initiative to develop the local economy in the wake of the collapse of the local industry, in this case, the woollen industry.

Economy

421 A history of Portuguese economic thought.
António Almodovar, José Luís Cardoso. London; New York: Routledge, 1998. 144p. bibliog. (Routledge History of Economic Thought).

The authors here present a survey of Portuguese economic thought from 1500 to the 1960s. They admit that the country itself is still in the 'infancy of economic thought' but they assess such aspects as the impact of Keynesian and other foreign theories on Portugal.

422 The Portuguese economy towards 1992. Proceedings of a conference sponsored by Junta Nacional de Investigação Ciêntífica e Tecnológica and Banco de Portugal.
Edited by João Ferreira do Amaral, Diogo Lucena, António S. Mello. Boston, Massachusetts; Dordrecht, The Netherlands; London: Kluwer Academic Publishers, 1992. 258p. bibliog.

Based on a conference held at Vimeiro, Portugal in 1991, these eleven papers address a wide range of issues related to the proposed European economic integration in 1992. The authors are predominantly Portuguese with a smaller number of British and North American contributors. The diverse topics include studies of Portuguese business cycles, financial liberalization, life insurance, wages, the labour market, emigrants' remittances, labour supply, telephone services and trade. The Portuguese economy is seen as being semi-developed, yet highly open to external factors.

423 Issues in Portuguese economic integration.
João Confraria. Birmingham, England: Research Centre for International Strategy, Department of Commerce, University of Birmingham, 1994. 21p. bibliog. (Occasional Papers in Industrial Strategy, no. 24).

A study of the evolution of Portuguese economic policy and of economic performance in the period from 1960. It thus covers both the period of Portugal's membership of EFTA (European Free Trade Area) and its integration into the European Union, from 1986 onwards. From 1960 to 1974 high GDP growth rates and low inflation were maintained but from 1974 and 1985 both indicators markedly worsened. While unemployment and inflation dropped after 1986, the recovery in GDP was arrested from 1991 onwards. The work is supplemented by a number of graphs and tables recording economic, trade and employment patterns from 1960 to 1993.

424 The development of the Portuguese economy: a case of Europeanization.
David Corkill. London; New York: Routledge, 1999. 259p. bibliog. (Contemporary Economic History of Europe Series).

Seen as a 'latecomer modernizer', Portugal is here portrayed as having made good use of its membership of the European Community to facilitate its rapid development from an economically backward region of western Europe to one which is on course for convergence with its European partners. Using case-studies, the author demonstrates the unevenness of the various sectors of the Portuguese economy and also points to potential problems which may beset the country once it joins the European single currency.

425 The Portuguese economy since 1974.
David Corkill. Edinburgh: Edinburgh University Press, 1993. 172p. map. bibliog.

In five chapters, the author covers Portugal's emergence from dictatorship, through the political crises of 1968-85, to the period of boom and consumerism under Cavaco e Silva (1985-91). Corkill aims to fill the need for a 'concise general introduction to Portugal's economy'. Despite the progress made, he points out the underlying dangers to Portugal from regional inequalities and the lack of economic planning and of the setting of clear priorities.

426 Country studies: Portugal.
Directorate-General for Economic and Financial Affairs of the Commission of the European Communities. Luxembourg: Directorate-General for Economic and Financial Affairs of the Commission of the European Communities, 1991. 39p. (Economic Papers, Country Studies, no. 2).

Comprising two parts and a statistical annex, this volume reviews the performance of the Portuguese economy with particular reference to the period from Portugal's accession to the EC in 1986. The modernization of the country's financial system is acknowledged but fears are expressed over the threats to the economy of inflation and public debt. Priorities for the future are defined as including the control of inflation, a tightening of fiscal policy and an active incomes policy. A further expressed concern is the instability of the Persian

Economy

Gulf, given that Portugal has the highest dependency on oil imports of any EC member state.

427 Portugal, 1998-99.
The Economist Intelligence Unit. London: The Economist Intelligence Unit, 1998. 45p. map. (Country Profile).

The Economist's Country Profile series provides annual information on the underlying political and economic condition of Portugal. This is supplemented by quarterly updates which concentrate on current trends in the economy. The volume holds a wealth of statistical data as well as authoritative analysis to justify its high price.

428 Portrait of the regions, volume 3: Portugal, Spain, Italy, Greece.
Eurostat/ Commission of the European Communities. Luxembourg: Commission of the European Communities, 1993. 333p. maps. bibliog.

Belying the EC's reputation for dull and inaccessible publications, this colourful, glossy hardback compendium provides an overview of Portugal's economic and social state (p. 1-46). Good use is made of clear, colourful charts and diagrams, accompanied by photographs. These demonstrate trends in demography, industrial production, unemployment, pollution, agriculture and countless other indicators of economic performance. The text comprises seven chapters devoted respectively to northern Portugal, the centre of the country, Lisbon and the Tagus valley, the Alentejo, the Algarve, the Azores and Madeira. The volume is intended to supplement the *Eurostat Statistical Yearbook of the Regions*.

429 North and central Portugal in the 1990s: a European investment region.
Jorge Gaspar, Alan Williams. London: The Economist Intelligence Unit, 1991. 114p. maps. bibliog. (Special Report, no. M604) (EIU European Investment Regions Series).

In seven chapters the authors cover a wide spectrum of the Portuguese economy with seven appendices addressing issues such as foreign exchange, tax system, mergers and acquisitions in more detail. The volume covers the area from Aveiro and Viseu north to the Spanish border (see item no. 430 for the southern region of Portugal). The Oporto area is seen as the engine of development in northern Portugal in what is an optimistic analysis of Portugal's economic future.

430 Southern Portugal in the 1990s: a European investment region.
Jorge Gaspar, Alan Williams. London: The Economist Intelligence Unit, 1992. 135p. maps. bibliog. (Special Report, no. M610) (EIU European Investment Regions Series).

A companion volume to item no. 429, this volume covers the area south from Leiria and Castelo Branco to the Algarve, including the Lisbon area and the Azores and Madeira. With its youthful workforce, Lisbon is viewed as well-placed to lead national expansion which has been stimulated by privatization and European Community assistance. The volume comprises an objective and up-to-date survey of the region's economic situation and future.

Economy

431 Portugal to 1993: investing in a European future.
Mark Hudson. London: Economist Intelligence Unit, 1989. 147p. map. (Special Report, no. 1157) (EIU Economic Prospects Series).

Hudson recognizes the problems facing Portugal which include a high level of dependency on tourism and emigrants' remittances as well as reliance on food and fuel imports and a large overseas debt. Nevertheless he forecasts growth and increasing foreign investment which will take Portugal ahead of Greece in terms of GDP per head. Amongst Hudson's earlier contributions on the same theme are *Portugal to 1990: the challenge to modernisation* (EIU Special Report, no. 237).

432 Portugal and EC membership evaluated.
Edited by José da Silva Lopes. London: Pinter Publishers; New York: St Martin's Press, 1993. 256p. (EC Membership Evaluated Series).

A compilation of twenty-one essays by native Portuguese academics and economists, which is divided into three sections. These cover the economic, political and social aspects of the entry of Portugal into the EC in 1986. The volume would have been enhanced by a unifying concluding chapter of somewhat greater length than the three-and-a-half-page introductory essay.

433 The Portuguese economy: a picture in figures. XIX and XX centuries with long term series.
João Luís César das Neves. Lisbon: Universidade Católica Editora, 1994. 256p. 2 maps. bibliog. disk.

The author, a Portuguese professor and sometime advisor to his country's prime minister, provides a statistical analysis of the Portuguese economy since the 1830s. The volume includes fifty-seven textual tables and charts, as well as a disk of statistical data. Its text comprises three sections: an introduction; an analysis of the Portuguese developmental process; and a presentation of the long-term series of statistics of the Portuguese economy.

434 OECD economic surveys, 1997-98: Portugal.
Organisation for Economic Cooperation and Development. Paris: OECD, 1998. 118p.

A concise and authoritative survey of the contemporary economic situation in Portugal, which has been regularly published since the 1960s. The volume has numerous coloured charts and graphs to display trends in economic performance and a useful summary chapter.

435 Foreign economic relations of the European Community: the impact of Spain and Portugal.
Alfred Tovias. Boulder, Colorado; London: Lynne Rienner, 1990. 137p. bibliog.

Tovias is a Senior Lecturer in International Relations at the Hebrew University of Jerusalem. He assesses the effect of the 1986 accession of the Iberian countries on the European Community's external economic policy. Both countries are portrayed as

Economy

reluctant to open up the EC's trade to more competition, given their own economic states. He also concludes that the diversity of the five southern members of the EC will preclude a collective lobby from those countries with regard to Latin America, the Middle East or the United States.

Finance and Banking

436 Portugal, a new era.
William Chislett. London: Euromoney Publications in association with Finantia, KPMG Peat Marwick, Pereira, Leal & Partners, Sociedade Financeira Portuguesa-Banco de Investimento SA, 1991. 177p.

Illustrated by colour photographs, this is a comprehensive, fourteen-chapter, review of the contemporary financial scene in Portugal by a former *Financial Times* journalist and Iberia specialist. After an historical and geographical introduction, further chapters cover the domestic economy, agriculture, foreign investment, banking, capital markets, the corporate sector and privatization, commercial property and the legal, tax and accounting environments. Finally, the country's economic prospects for the 1990s are considered. By the same author is *Portugal: investment and growth* (London: Euromoney Publications, 1997. 185p.).

437 The development of accounting in Portugal and the establishment of the Aula do Commercio.
Maria Leonor Fernandes Ferreira, Moyra Kedslie, Manuel A. C. V. de Freitas. Hull, England: University of Hull, School of Management, 1995. 22p. bibliog. (Working Paper Series No. HUSM/MK/21).

This small tome tells how Portugal, despite being a 'follower rather than a leader' in accounting, was the setting for the groundbreaking Aula do Commercio, a college of commerce founded in 1759. Its mentor was the Marquis of Pombal, Portugal's *de facto* ruler during the reign of King José I and the monarch's own interest in the project extended to his regular attendance to observe the examination process. The output of qualified bookkeepers allowed Portugal to end its reliance on foreign accountants.

Finance and Banking

438 **The Portuguese financial system.**
Bjorn Lygum, Daniel Ottolenghi, Alfred Steinherr. *Cahiers BEI, EIB Papers*, no. 7 (1988), p. 5-66.

A review of the development of the Portuguese financial system and its prospective integration into the European financial markets. This process is seen as liberalizing the movement of capital as a consequence of the country's opening up to market forces. Further modernization is prescribed and the danger to the banking and other sectors of the public sector deficit is noted. In *Corporate acquisitions and mergers in Portugal: a practical guide to the legal, financial and administrative implications* (London; Dordrecht, The Netherlands; Boston, Massachusetts: Graham & Trotman, 1993. 125p. [European Business Law & Practice Series; European Law Library]), Ronald Charles Wolf provides a guide on how to do business in Portugal. The author, an American lawyer based in Portugal, sees the two major drawbacks as the relatively small returns on investment in Portugal and having to master the Portuguese language.

439 **Problems of medieval coinage in the Iberian area, 2.**
Edited by Mário Gomes Marques, M. Crusafont i Sabater. Avilés, Spain: Sociedad Numismática Avalesina/ Instituto de Sintra, 1986. 460p. maps. bibliog.

A compendium of revised papers from the second Symposium on Problems of Medieval Coinage in the Iberian Area, held in Avilés, Asturias, Spain in December 1986. Of the twenty-five papers, more than a quarter deal explicitly with Portugal and cover the period from the 11th to the mid-15th century. All of the papers are in English, but résumés are also provided in both Spanish and Portuguese. Numerous monochrome plates, illustrations, charts and tables complete the volume.

Trade, Commerce and Business

440 Portuguese trade in Asia under the Habsburgs, 1580-1640.
James C. Boyajian. Baltimore, Maryland; London: The Johns Hopkins University Press, 1993. 356p. map. bibliog.

A detailed study of Portuguese trade with Asia during the period of Spanish occupation of the Portuguese throne. In eleven chapters, the author shows how the capital investment of private Portuguese merchants actually exceeded by far that of the Crown as well as that of more celebrated bodies such as the Dutch East India Company. Back in Portugal, however, the rising merchant class were held down by the dominant landed aristocracy, the Inquisition and the monarchy. Boyajian also shows how the demise of Portuguese trade with Asia was accelerated by Dutch naval blockades rather than by superior trading practices.

441 Country profile: Portugal.
London: British Overseas Trade Board/ Department of Trade and Industry, 1990. 43p. map. biblelog.

An update of *Portugal: a country profile*. It is effectively a handbook of practical information for businesses seeking to trade with Portugal. As well as giving a brief overview of the country and its economic situation, it furnishes the reader with details of Portuguese marketing methods, legal constraints and even such details as Portuguese vehicle-driving arrangements and burial arrangements for expatriates. Many useful addresses are supplied, both in Britain and in Portugal, to assist companies in dealing with Portugal.

442 1386-1986, Portugal, business partners in Europe.
Edited by Martin Cabral. London: De Montfort Publishing for The Anglo-Portuguese Foundation, 1986. 156p. map.

A glossy volume, with many colour photographs, produced to commemorate the 600th anniversary of the Treaty of Windsor, by which Richard II and King João I of Portugal cemented the Anglo-Portuguese alliance. After a brief essay on the Treaty, its six chapters

Trade, Commerce and Business

include two chapters on the past, 'Land and people' and 'Transition and continuity'; the others cover 'The EEC', 'Basic resources', 'Life-style' and 'Arts and letters'.

443 Duns Pep 7.500: principais empresas de Portugal, 1998. (Major Portuguese companies.)
Dun & Bradstreet Portugal. Lisbon: Dun & Bradstreet Portugal, c.1998. various paginations.

This large directory is arranged into five sections. These comprise: details of Portuguese firms ranked by their sales value; details of financial, insurance and related companies; an alphabetical list of companies consisting of 7,500 entries; a list of companies by economic sector; and statistics. Details provided for each firm include name, address, names of leading management figures as well as sales figures and employee numbers. Although the text is in Portuguese, the content of the entries for each firm is relatively self-explanatory.

444 Export Directory of Portugal, including Azores, Madeira and Macao.
Interpropo. Lisbon: Interpropo, 1960- . annual. map.

The 1998 edition of the above title is the 38th edition, published in 1997, with bilingual Portuguese and English text. Its core is an extensive alphabetical listing of Portuguese companies, followed by a listing of products and services and a classified list of companies by product. Finally, there is a substantial section of glossy adverts for Portuguese companies. The prefatory material includes basic statistics such as the 1996 GDP, unemployment and inflation rates and a map. Portugal's major exporting sectors are shown to be the metal products/ transport equipment/ machinery industries, followed by the textiles/ clothing/ leather and footwear industries. The directory's importance is supported by its proud announcement that it 'represents the Portuguese economy in the Library of the European Union'.

445 Kompass. Repertório da indústria, comércio e serviços de Portugal. Register of Portuguese industry, trade and services, 1996.
Kompass Portugal. Lisbon: Kompass Portugal, c.1996. 5th ed. 2 vols.

These two large volumes of more than 1,200 pages in total are entitled, respectively, *Informação das empresa [sic]. Company information*, and *Produtos e serviços. Products and services*. Volume 1 comprises a list of companies by district, starting with Lisbon and then alphabetically arranged. Addresses, company activities, sales, management structure and employee numbers are amongst the details given. There is also a trademark index and lists of firms' representatives. In volume 2 there are lists in Portuguese and English of the products and services offered by Portuguese companies.

446 Trade and finance in Portuguese India: a study of the Portuguese country trade, 1770-1840.
Celsa Pinto. New Delhi: Concept Publishing Co., 1997. 315p. bibliog. (Xavier Centre of Historical Research Studies Series, no. 5).

A study of the Portuguese participation in the Asiatic trade system during the period when mercantilism was giving way to free trade. The Pakistani author also provides a useful bibliographical essay.

447 Portuguese U.K. Chamber of Commerce yearbook/ directory, 1997/8.
Portuguese UK Chamber of Commerce. London: Portuguese UK Chamber of Commerce, 1997. 103p.

A useful handbook which would be greatly improved by an alphabetical subject index, to complement the unordered list of contents which is the only key to its contents. Nevertheless, the volume is packed with information which includes company details, trade contact names and addresses and details of the Chamber's membership which includes major Portuguese and British firms.

448 Doing business in Portugal.
Price Waterhouse. London: Price Waterhouse, 1992-95. 219p. + supplement 70p.

The five chapters and appendices of the main volume of this title provide an account of Portugal's physical geography and history as well as helpful summaries of its legal system and economic development. The remainder of the volume is an admirable, practical handbook for anyone intending to trade with Portugal. The supplement brings the information up-to-date by recording changes in procedures and regulations as well as recording new statistical data.

449 The Anglo-Portuguese Alliance and the English merchants in Portugal, 1654-1810.
L. M. E. Shaw. Aldershot, England; Brookfield, Vermont; Singapore; Sydney: Ashgate, 1998. 232p. map. bibliog.

In 1654 Oliver Cromwell concluded an Alliance, here reproduced, with King João IV of Portugal, which was to endure until 1810. The Alliance helped to ensure Portuguese independence whilst also expanding Anglo-Portuguese trade. Although never organized into a Company, English traders filled the vacuum created by the demise of the New Christians in Portugal, caused by the actions of the Inquisition. It was only after 1770 that the English influence in Portugal waned, due to measures taken by Pombal against foreign traders.

450 Trade and power: informal colonialism in Anglo-Portuguese relations.
S. Sideri. Rotterdam, The Netherlands: Rotterdam University Press, 1970. 256p. bibliog.

Despite one or two lapses in the written English of this book, it is nevertheless a coherent study of Anglo-Portuguese trade in the context of international trade theory. Sideri sees

Trade, Commerce and Business

the Methuen Treaties of the 18th century as reinforcing the specialization of production in each country, to the detriment of Portugal and to the benefit of Britain. An extensive bibliography completes the work.

451 Lisbon World Expo '98 projects.
Edited by Luíz Trigueiros, Cláudio Sat, with Cristina Oliveira, translation by Mark Cain. Lisbon: Blau, 1996. 216p. (Blau Monographs).

A substantial and colourful overview of twenty-six of the architectural projects associated with Lisbon's Expo '98 event is provided here. The twofold purposes of the event – to increase awareness of the world's oceans and to regenerate the derelict docklands and industrial areas of Lisbon's north-east fringes – are depicted here in the form of drawings and models. Expo '98 itself was a popular and successful event, the legacy of which includes a modern international railway station, shopping and cinema complexes, new apartments and the Parque das Nações (Nations' Park), a new site for the Feira Internacional de Lisboa (Lisbon International Fair), an international business and commercial convention and exhibition centre.

Business Portuguese glossary.
See item no. 333.

Industry

452 Textiles and training in Portugal.
Jaime Serrão Andrez, Mário Caldeira Dias. Berlin: CEDEFOP-European Centre for the Development of Vocational Training, 1987. 167p. bibliog.

The Portuguese textile industry was selected by CEDEFOP as the first area to be studied as part of a European project on vocational training and its relationship with the employment market. As a major sector in the Portuguese economy, the textile industry is seen to be in need of large-scale restructuring to compete with output from developing countries. Given this need, the historical lack of importance accorded to vocational training in the Portuguese textile industry is seen as a key area to be addressed.

453 The public enterprise in Portugal and Spain: analysis from the point of view of competition policy.
I. Jalles/ Commission of the European Communities. Luxembourg: Office for Official Publications of the European Communities, 1988. 212p.

A study of the organization and operation of state-owned enterprises and of their importance to the Portuguese economy is here accompanied by an analysis of competition in various industrial sectors, in the context of Portugal's entry into the EC in 1986. The sectors covered include the coal industry, petroleum, fertilizers, cement, cellulose and paper, iron, beer, transport, communications and the mass media.

454 Packaging in Spain and Portugal.
B. Keskin. London: Pira International, 1996. 200p.

This covers Portugal and Spain in separate sections, giving an overview of each country's economy and legislation before moving on to cover in detail the various aspects of the packaging industry. These include not only paper and board packaging but also metal and glass formats. In addition, the recycling aspects of the industry are covered and profiles of packaging companies are provided.

Industry

455 Packaging in Europe: Spain and Portugal. The market and the suppliers in the 1990s.
Graham Lewis. London: The Economist Intelligence Unit, 1992. 126p. (Special report no. R162).

Part two of this survey covers Portugal's packaging industry in great detail. Everything from glass bottles to fruit-juice cardboard packaging is covered. Appendices provide statistical information as well as details of relevant associations.

456 The Portuguese meat and livestock industry.
Meat and Livestock Commission. Bletchley, England: Meat and Livestock Commission Economic Information Service, 1983. 42p. maps.

This report paints a general picture of Portugal as a country with a strong agricultural tradition, yet dependant on imports for more than a half of its foodstuffs, not least due to its backward methods and profusion of smallholdings. At the time of writing the Portuguese economy was subject to serious inflationary pressure and the approaching absorption of the country into the European Community was seen as likely to increase competitive pressure. Statistics of meat and livestock production are provided and coverage also includes feedgrains.

457 The Iberian construction industry: a guide for UK professionals.
S. D. Reynolds, S. Sheppard. London: Construction Industry Research and Information Association, 1989. 107p. bibliog. (Construction Industry Research and Information Association, no. 67).

In this second volume in a series on the construction industries of the European Communities, Portugal occupies the latter section (p. 69 onwards). There are seven chapters in each section and these cover: the background of the Portuguese building industry; the construction market; the legal and institutional framework; the contracting industry; resources for construction; building teams and professionals; and the impact of European integration. Appendices provide details of relevant organizations, a glossary and list of abbreviations, and a bibliography.

An analysis of the hotel industry of Portugal.
See item no. 107.

Agriculture and Fishing

458 Production, marketing and consumption of animal products in Portugal.
Francisco X. M. Avillez, Stylianos D. Katranidis. Kiel, Germany: Wissenschaftsverlag Vaul Kiel, 1992. 163p. bibliog. (Economics of Animal Production in Mediterranean EC Countries, vol. 4).

This is a report, in less than perfect English, funded by the Volkswagen Foundation, on recent trends in the livestock sector in Portugal. Its ten chapters cover consumer demand, marketing, production, income, investment, ecology and government policy in the livestock sector. At the time of writing forty-five per cent of Portuguese consumers' expenditure on food and drink was on animal products and demand for meat was rising, especially for beef and veal. Herds were small and Portuguese productivity was low but a growth in the size of dairy farms and of cattle herds was predicted. An earlier analysis of Portuguese agricultural policy by Avillez, with Timothy J. Finan and Timothy Josling, is *Trade, exchange rates, and agricultural pricing policy in Portugal* (Washington, DC: World Bank, 1988. 127p. bibliog. [World Bank Comparative Studies]). This examines the effects of the switch of government support for large Alentejan *latifundia* to smaller northern farms in the 1960s, followed by the post-1974 Revolution period and its emphasis on cheap food for urban dwellers. Finally, the reduction in consumer subsidies in the 1980s is assessed.

459 Today there is no misery: the ethnography of farming in northwest Portugal.
Jeffrey W. Bentley. Tucson, Arizona; London: The University of Arizona Press, 1992. 177p. 2 maps. bibliog. (Arizona Studies in Human Ecology).

Bentley, a Honduras-based anthropologist, bases this study of agricultural ethnography on the *freguesia* (parish) of Pedralva in the Minho district of north-western Portugal. Although it is an area blighted by male emigration to France from 1964 onwards and threatened by Portugal's entry into the European Community, Bentley's first-hand experience of the resilience, adaptability and hard work of the locals leads him to a more optimistic prognosis of this agricultural community's future than that put forward by Portuguese agricultural planners and economists.

460 The revolution within the Revolution: workers' control in rural Portugal.
Nancy Gina Bermeo. Princeton, New Jersey: Princeton University Press, 1986. 263p. 7 maps. bibliog.

Bermeo studies the emergence of workers' control in Portuguese agriculture following the 1974 Portuguese Revolution, before moving on to address its consequences. The third and final section of the book covers workers' control and 'the problem of articulation'. This involves an assessment of the interaction between the workers' movement and the State and political parties. The Portuguese rural struggle is seen as a precursor of other proletarian conflicts in Europe and Latin America, in particular.

461 Crisis and change in rural Europe: agricultural development in the Portuguese mountains.
Richard Black. Aldershot, England; Brookfield, Vermont; Hong Kong; Singapore; Sydney: Avebury, 1992. 208p. maps. bibliog.

In seven chapters, Black looks at the impact of accession to the European Community on rural Portugal and, in particular, on the mountainous Serra do Alvão region, near Mondim de Basto in the province of Trás-os-Montes. This is an area of high emigration, economic backwardness and conservatism. Basing his study on direct contact with the local peasantry, Black concludes that a new European Communities' policy for upland areas is required to provide a future for such areas as the one studied.

462 Pre-bureaucratic Europeans: a study of a Portuguese fishing community.
Jan Brøgger. Oslo: Norwegian University Press, 1989. 150p. map. bibliog. (The Institute for Comparative Research in Human Culture, Institut for sammenlignende kulturforskning, Serie B).

What should have been a groundbreaking study of the Nazaré fishing community on the coast, north of Lisbon, has been the target of much criticism for its thesis that the villagers live in a state of 'medieval innocence', largely unaffected by capitalism and materialism. The community's avoidance of the travails of modern 'bureaucratic' existence is chiefly attributed to its matriarchal society. The book has been republished as *Nazaré: women and men in a pre-bureaucratic Portuguese fishing village* (Fort Worth, Texas: Holt, Rinehart & Winston, 1992. 135p. bibliog.).

463 Portuguese agriculture after accession.
Bureau Européen de Recherches S.A. London: Agra Europe, 1986. 50p. map. bibliog. (Agra Europe Special Report, no. 29).

The Brussels-based Bureau Européen de Recherches here assesses the background and expected impact of Portuguese accession to the European Communities on the country's agricultural sector. Supported by forty-two tables of data, the book's chapters cover four subject areas, after an introduction and general overview of Portuguese agriculture. These are the accession arrangements for Portugal, the effect of enlargement on the EEC and on

Portuguese agriculture, the Portuguese food industry and the potential benefits to Portugal of the EEC's structural policies.

464 Port o'call: memories of the Portuguese White Fleet in St John's, Newfoundland.
Priscilla Doel. St John's, Canada: Institute of Social and Economic Research, Memorial University of Newfoundland, 1992. 204p. map. bibliog. (Social and Economic Studies, no. 49).

Inspired by a visit to Newfoundland, Doel set about conducting a series of interviews with sailors and locals, upon which evidence most of this book was subsequently based. In the late 1950s some sixty or more Portuguese fishing vessels, the so-called 'White Fleet', would use the port facilities of St John's after sailing from Portuguese bases which included Aveiro, Lisbon, Viana do Castelo and Figueira da Foz. International fishing legislation has since prevented the Portuguese fleet from landing in Canada so the story is necessarily one of reminiscence. The author also drew on Portuguese as well as Canadian sources to complete her story.

465 Structural change and small-farm agriculture in northwest Portugal.
Eric Monke, Francisco Avillez, José Pimentel Coelho, Dennis Cory, Manuela Ferro, Timothy Finan, Roger Fox, João Jesus, Manuela Jorge, Mark Langworthy, Margarida Marques, Francisco Martins, Manuela de Medeiros, Scott Pearson. Ithaca, New York; London: Cornell University Press, 1993. 223p. map. bibliog. (Food Systems & Agrarian Change).

A collection of ten essays, each by three of the book's fourteen contributors and edited by Eric Monke. These studies assess the present and future prospects of agriculture in the Entre Douro e Minho region of northern Portugal as it confronts the consequences of the country's accession to the European Community. The book concludes that 'small-farm agriculture has a bright future, even in a newly industrializing economy'.

466 Agriculture and the regions: the situation and developments of the enlarged Community. The regional impact of the Common Agricultural Policy in Spain and Portugal. Summary report for the Regional Policy Directorate General of the Commission of the European Communities.
L. Mykolenko, Th. de Raymond, P. Henry. Luxembourg: Commission of the European Communities, 1987. 31p. maps. bibliog.

Produced by the authors for SEDES (Société d'Étude pour le Développement Économique et Social), this report assesses the impact on Portugal of accession to the European Communities (EC) and the implications for the EC's Common Agricultural Policy (CAP). The authors suggest that the previous bias of the CAP towards the agricultural products of northern and central Europe must be corrected to take more account of the southern European output of such produce as fruit, vegetables and wine.

Agriculture and Fishing

467 **The cork.**
Manuel Alves de Oliveira, Leonel de Oliveira. Lisbon: Grupo Amorim; Lancaster, Pennsylvania: Cork Institute of America, 1995. 159p.

Portugal is the world's largest supplier of cork and this volume is written by experts of Portuguese origin. Cork derives from the bark (*suberose parenchyma*) of the cork oak tree, which is a member of the beech family. This illustrated book outlines the origins of cork production, drawing heavily on Portuguese experience, as well as its method of manufacture and its multifarious uses. The volume is accompanied by a cork slipcase.

468 **Agricultural policy in Portugal.**
Organisation for Economic Cooperation and Development. Paris: Organisation for Economic Cooperation and Development, 1975. 44p.

At the time of writing some thirteen per cent of the Portuguese GDP was generated by agriculture and thirty per cent of the national labour force was employed in the sector. Part I of the volume describes 'The state of agriculture', whilst part II addresses 'Agriculture policy, aims and measures'. The history of national Development Plans for agriculture is traced back to 1958 and up to the Fourth Plan (1974-79) which modestly sought to raise agricultural production and standards of living whilst also improving the trade balance. These plans were to be thrown into chaos in the mid-1970s by the lurch towards the nationalization of large estates and the resultant decline in production, caused by the Portuguese Revolution of 1974.

469 **Portuguese agriculture in transition.**
Scott R. Pearson, Francisco Avillez, Jeffrey W. Bentley. Timothy J. Finan, Roger Fox, Timothy Josling, Mark Langworthy, Eric Monke, Stefan Tangermann. Ithaca, New York; London: Cornell University Press, 1987. 283p. 2 maps.

This book records the activities of the joint University of Arizona and Stanford University project carried out as part of PROCALFER (Portugal Program of Soil Correction, Fertilizer and Forages). The writers are social scientists who here record their findings after five years of research in a book which the preface claims 'will be a definitive work on Portuguese agriculture for some years to come'. The authors conclude that new technology will be necessary for Portuguese agriculture to survive within the European Community's Common Agricultural Policy.

470 **North Portuguese agriculture in the European context: progress and prospect.**
Tim Unwin. Egham, England: Department of Geography, Royal Holloway and Bedford New College, 1989. 41p. bibliog. (Papers in Geography, no. 6).

The aim of this study is to examine the 'likely future structure of agriculture in northern Portugal in the context of the country's accession to the European Community in 1986 and the creation of a Single European Market in 1992'. This is achieved by reviewing developments, both positive and negative, in the landholding, production and commercialization of agricultural products in the period from the 1970s. The broad effect

Agriculture and Fishing

on agriculture of the performance of the Portuguese economy as a whole is also assessed. Unwin also emphasizes the clash between the economic imperative of larger and more efficient agricultural units and the traditional way of life of the northern Portuguese farming population.

Communications

471 O selo base português: evolução formal. Ordinary Portuguese stamps: formal evolution. Le timbre ordinaire portugais: évolution formelle.
J. Martins Barata, José Pedro Roque Martins Barata. Lisbon: Correios e Telecomunicações de Portugal, 1976. unpaginated.

A short, trilingual book which traces the history of the Portuguese stamp from 1853, when the first stamp issue appeared. Accompanying the nineteen sections of text, which trace the evolution of stamp design in chronological sequence, are nearly sixty individual stamps which are printed as enlarged colour reproductions. These range from the first issues of 1853 to the definitives issued in 1973-74. The English text is somewhat stilted but is, nevertheless, informative. *Provisional town postmarks of Portugal, 1879-1912* by David L. Gordon (Beckenham, England: Portuguese Philatelic Society, 1985. 160p.) provides a survey of the wide range of postal cancellations marks used in Portuguese towns in the decades straddling 1900. Many examples are illustrated by facsimiles.

472 Stanley Gibbons stamp catalogue. Part 9, Portugal & Spain.
London: Stanley Gibbons, 1996. 4th ed. 448p.

The most authoritative English-language guide to Portuguese stamps. As well as providing details on and illustrations of all stamp issues from mainland Portugal, it also includes the country's dependencies and former colonies. Current market values are provided for all stamps and the other information supplied includes details of perforations, watermarks, shades, errors, forgeries and date of issue.

473 Western European broadcasting, deregulation and public television: the Portuguese experience.
Nelson Traquina. Columbia, South Carolina: Association for Education in Journalism and Mass Communication, 1998. 44p. bibliog. (Journalism & Mass Communication Monographs, no. 167).

Written by a Professor from the Universidade Nova de Lisboa, this slim volume reviews the deregulation of Portuguese TV, following the legalization of private television companies in 1990 and the abolition of the licence fee in 1991. SIC became the first independent rival to the former state-run monopoly, RTP, in 1992. Portugal is seen to have been slow in developing and executing its national media policy. Traquina also calls for a resurrection of the financially distressed RTP and a restoration of balance towards public television. The volume includes useful statistics of such matters as cinema attendance, national sources of non-factual TV programmes and TV advertising revenue.

O bilhete postal ilustrado e a história urbana da Grande Lisboa. The illustrated postcard and the urban history of Lisbon metropolitan area.
See item no. 20.

Transport

Aerial

474 Lisbon Airport, 1942-1992.
Aeroportos e Navegação Aérea. Lisbon: Inapa/ANA, 1992. 189p.
A publication produced to mark the golden anniversary of Portela de Sacavém, the current international airport of Lisbon, which is operated by the Aeroportos e Navegação Aérea (ANA) undertaking. In addition to recording the history and future plans of the airport, this profusely illustrated quarto volume also depicts and describes scenes from the wider field of Portuguese aviation history, going back to the 1920s. ANA also produce a free colour newspaper for Lisbon airport users called *Imagem* (Image), as well as a regularly-updated paperback guide to the city for visitors which is available free of charge to passengers arriving at the airport.

475 Precision astrolabe: Portuguese navigators and transoceanic aviation.
Francis M. Rogers. Lisbon: Academia Internacional da Cultura Portuguesa, 1971. 397p. map. bibliog.
Inspired by the navigational methods employed during the historic trans-Atlantic air-crossing from Lisbon to Rio de Janeiro by Sacadura Cabral and Gago Coutinho in 1922, the author reviews historic types of marine sextants and their use. He then assesses how various early trans-oceanic aviators navigated before looking in detail at the methods and instrumentation used by Cabral and Coutinho. He shows how these two Portuguese aviators produced an artificial-horizon sextant so good that it was taken up by more technologically advanced countries. Finally, he compares the methods devised by the two aviators with those used at the time of writing by Portuguese Boeing 707 pilots and merchant shipping captains.

Maritime

476 Cacilheiros. (Lisbon river ferries.)
Luís Miguel Correia.   Lisbon: Edições e Iniciativas Náuticas, 1996.
151p. map. bibliog.

An informed and very attractive survey of the river ferries of Lisbon from their origins in the 19th century to the present day. Strictly speaking, the 'cacilheiros' are the ferries which link Lisbon to Cacilhas, directly across the river Tagus from the capital. However, the term now has a wider usage to cover all the Lisbon river ferries, wherever they serve. Full details are given of all the ferries operated by the Transtejo company since 1975, including the British-built catamarans introduced in 1995. The author's excellent colour photographs complement historical pictures and watercolours of bygone days.

477 Cais e navios de Lisboa. Lisbon docks and ships.
Luís Miguel Correia.   Lisbon: Edições e Iniciativas Náuticas, 1996.
93p.

With parallel texts in both Portuguese and English, this is an attractive large-format collection of some of the 60,000 colour slides taken by the author since 1975, though most of those represented are photographs taken in the 1980s and 1990s. His subject matter embraces all types of ships in the Tagus and the extensive docks of Lisbon, ranging from ferry-boats, sail-training vessels, container ships and naval vessels to luxury passenger liners.

478 Veleiros de Portugal. Sailing vessels in Portugal.
Francisco Correia Figueira, translated by Wendy Graça.   Lisbon: Edições Inapa, 1994. Reprinted, 1998. 125p. bibliog. (Colecção Símbolos Portugueses).

An atmospheric compilation of excellent photographs of 19th- and 20th-century sailing vessels pictured around the Portuguese coastline. The accompanying textual descriptions are in both Portuguese and English. Fifty-four fine colour drawings by Telmo Gomes adorn his *Embarcações portuguesas da tradição portuguesa. Regional boats in the Portuguese tradition* (Lisbon: Edições Inapa, 1997. 120p. bibliog.). Sections on boats of the north, centre, south and autonomous regions of Portugal precede coverage of trawlers and cod luggers. Opposite each illustration is a brief Portuguese and English description. Gomes's *Portuguese ships, 14th-19th century* (Lisbon: Edições Inapa, 1995. 133p.) is an equally attractive and colour-illustrated volume.

479 Atlantic Spain and Portugal.
Edited by Oz Robinson, Mike Sadler, for the RCC Pilotage Foundation.   St Ives, England: Imray, Laurie, Norie & Wilson, 1990. 2nd ed. 190p. maps.

The first edition of this work (1988) was simply attributed to the RCC (Royal Cruising Club) Pilotage Foundation, which is a charity established to produce mariners' guides such as this. Based on charts from the Spanish and Portuguese hydrographic authorities, this volume provides coloured charts of the Atlantic coast of Portugal, from Galicia to the Algarve-Spanish border. Details are provided of beacons, buoys, harbour approaches and

Transport. Terrestrial

signals, as well as of other navigational aids. Brief information is supplied on shore facilities at the various marinas and small-vessel docks along the length of the Portuguese coast. Numerous colour photographs, many of them aerial views, are also provided.

480 Vanguard of empire: ships of exploration in the Age of Columbus.
Roger C. Smith. New York; Oxford: Oxford University Press, 1993. 316p. bibliog.

A study of shipbuilding and advances in shipping technology during the era of Discoveries. The Portuguese, with their Atlantic fishing tradition, were at the forefront of such developments and their monarchs were the first to support oceanic exploration in the 15th century. Smith uses printed sources, as well as marine archaeology, to expand the boundaries of knowledge not only of shipbuilding, but also of navigation, manning and provisioning, rigging and maritime artillery. The book contains a number of line drawings as well as a glossary of Portuguese and Spanish nautical terms.

Terrestrial

481 European railway atlas: Spain, Portugal, Italy, Greece.
M. G. Ball. Shepperton, England: Ian Allen, 1993. 66p. maps.

A two-coloured book of A4-size maps which includes the entire Portuguese railway system (p. 7, 8, 17-18, 25-27, 33-34) at a scale of approximately 1 inch to 12 miles, although an additional inset map at 1 inch to 6 miles scale is provided of the Lisbon region. Every station is shown and categorized, while the railway lines are differentiated according to whether they are electrified, main lines or secondary lines, or standard or narrow-gauge. A gazetteer facilitates location of all the stations, whilst the addition of the relevant timetable number alongside each line makes the book a useful complement to the national timetable (see item no. 484). A very detailed two-sided map of the country's railways is *Portugal, railway map* (Exeter, England: Quail Map Company, 1984). The main map is at a scale of approximately 1:275,000 while the many regional insets are shown in more detail still.

482 A guide to Portuguese railways: Caminhos de Ferro Portugueses.
David Clough, Martin Beckett, Michael Hunt. Leigh, England: Fearless Publications, 1991. 64p. map.

A thorough guide to Portugal's contemporary railway system. After a brief introduction, the book comprises nine sections, six of which cover broad- and narrow-gauge stock, with the remainder covering the Estoril line, track machines and steam locomotives. Details are given of each locomotive or unit's size, power and performance, as well as its operational base and fleet number. The volume, which is illustrated by monochrome photographs, would have benefited greatly from more thorough proof-reading. A revised edition has been advertised (1998) but at the time of writing had yet to appear.

Transport. Terrestrial

483 Narrow gauge railways of Portugal.
W. J. K. Davies.   East Harling, England: Plateway Press, 1998.
312p. 30 maps. bibliog.

A detailed guide to the narrow-gauge railway lines of Portugal and to their rolling stock and locomotives, illustrated by copious black-and-white photographs and a number of line drawings. The seven chapters necessarily concentrate almost exclusively on the lines of northern Portugal where the more rugged terrain favoured narrow-gauge development. However, even ephemeral lines elsewhere, such as that of the 19th-century Larmanjât steam monorail system from Lisbon to Sintra and Torres Vedras, are covered. Five appendices cover topics such as locomotive numbering, postal services, timetables, museums and typical railway buildings.

484 Guia horário oficial. (Official timetable guide.)
Lisbon: Caminhos de Ferro Portugueses, twice yearly. maps.

This is the timetable of the Portuguese national railway company CP, which is now also accessible via the internet. Traditionally it is issued in book form twice a year, in May and September, with coverage of all national and international services, including a clear diagrammatic map at the head of each page of the timetable section. The timetable for every route is accompanied by a cumulative distance measurement, in kilometres, from the point of origin to the final destination of the service. The timetables are preceded by a full index of all Portuguese railway stations, which also supplies details of their facilities, such as left-luggage offices, refreshment services and staffed ticket-offices. An English-language explanation of the many symbols and pictograms used in the timetable is provided.

485 Spain & Portugal by rail.
Norman Renouf.   Chalfont St Peter, England; Old Saybrook, Connecticut: Bradt Publications; The Globe Pequot Press, 1994.
326p. 6 maps.

Portugal receives very disappointing coverage from this volume, occupying only p. 245-65. Lisbon and Oporto are the only Portuguese cities to merit an entry, with details being given of their major tourist attractions and useful plans provided of their respective international railway stations, Santa Apolónia and Campanhã. Brief information on hotel accommodation, transport to the city centres and journey times to other cities is provided.

486 Spain and Portugal.
D. Trevor Rowe.   London: Ian Allan, 1970. 112p. maps.
(Continental Railway Handbooks).

A heavily illustrated guide to the railways of Iberia aimed at the railway enthusiast but, nevertheless, also very useful for the general visitor. Details are provided of the Portuguese rail network, its motive power and signalling systems. Though now somewhat dated, the book still provides a useful background for present-day visitors to Portugal who have an interest in railways.

Transport. Terrestrial

487 European loco pocket book, volume 2: France, Greece, Portugal, Spain.
Neil Webster, Philip Wormald. Batley, England: Metro Enterprises, 1993. 2nd ed. 128p. (European Report).

Originally published in 1990 as volume 3 of the same title in a slightly different format, this illustrated pocket-sized book lists all the currently operating diesel and electric locomotives of CP, Caminhos de Ferro Portugueses (Portuguese Railways). Details are supplied of the builders, construction dates, size, performance and power specification of each locomotive. In addition, some brief guidance on ticketing arrangements is also given.

Daytrips, Spain and Portugal.
See item no. 142.

The Portuguese seaborne empire, 1415-1825.
See item no. 218.

Port to port.
See item no. 671.

Labour and Employment

488 Workers in Europe: study booklets in European trade unionism, 3. Spain and Portugal.
Basil Bye, Mel Doyle. London: The Workers' Educational Association, c.1978. 20p.

This A4-size volume traces the origins of Portuguese labour movements back to 1926 and the start of the 'fascist' period which was to last until 1974. The founding of Intersindical in 1970 and its growth into a major focus of workers' resistance is also chronicled. Finally, a thorough analysis is provided of the moves towards workers' control in the Setenave shipyards at Setúbal, after the 1974 Revolution. At the time, such movements provided an inspirational model for other European leftist organizations.

489 The trade union movement in Portugal.
European Trade Union Institute. Brussels: European Trade Union Institute, 1988. 57p. bibliog. (Info 23).

In fourteen sections this small volume tells the story of Portugal's two major trade union confederations, after briefly outlining the development of labour movements from the 1820 Revolution onwards. The two bodies in question are the UGT (*União Geral de Trabalhadores* – General Workers' Union), which was aligned to the European Trade Union Confederation, and the more radical CGTP-IN (*Confederação Geral dos Trabalhadores: Inter-Sindical Nacional* – General Confederation of Workers: National Inter-Union Organization) which remained unattached to pan-European bodies. The text shows how the Portuguese trade union movement is relatively young and still tainted by the many decades of corporatism imposed by Salazar. Topics covered include collective bargaining, trade union representation on other bodies, relations amongst trade unions, and relations between them and the political parties.

Labour and Employment

490 Building popular power: workers' and neighborhood movements in the Portuguese Revolution.
John L. Hammond. New York: Monthly Review Press, 1988. 301p. map. bibliog.

A study of the ultimately unsuccessful working-class movements which arose out of the sudden political freedoms engendered by the 1974 Portuguese Revolution, an event which its author claims was the only 20th-century revolution in western Europe at the time of writing. Hammond describes the rise and fall of the Portuguese fascist regime before recounting the wave of workers' takeovers of their workplaces and of community action, both in the cities and rural areas. The book ends with an account of the reassertion of order, in November 1975, by factions of the army on an increasingly chaotic socio-political situation.

491 Occupational segregation in Portugal, 1991/92. Final report.
Margarida Chagas Lopes, Cândida Ferreira, Heloisa Perista. Manchester, England: Manchester School of Management, 1992. 77p. bibliog.

A study of the Portuguese National Institute of Statistics's (Instituto Nacional de Estatística) *Inquérito permanente ao emprego* (Permanent inquiry into employment, 1980) and *Inquérito ao emprego* (Inquiry into employment, 1989). It addresses occupational segregation in the labour market in general as well as in specific occupations, before looking at the issues of measurement and policy. Amongst its findings, well-supported by tables of data, is the view that women are still under-represented in occupations of strategic importance. A companion study is *Wage determination and sex segregation in employment in Portugal* by Margarida Chagas Lopes, Heloisa Perista (Manchester, England: Manchester School of Management UMIST, 1993. 76p. bibliog.) which analyses pay determination in the sectors of agriculture, manufacturing and construction, private services, public services and telecommunications, and also addresses gender inequality in the civil service and banking. The Portuguese Commission for Equality and Women's Rights, established in 1991, had not addressed equal pay, but the authors are more hopeful that the Commission for Equality at Work and Employment will do so effectively.

492 Policies on labour relations and social dialogue in European countries: the Portuguese and German cases.
Rainer Pischai, and others. Baden Baden, Germany: Nomos, 1997. 176p. bibliog.

Two of the four chapters of this book relate directly to Portugal, whilst a third offers a general European overview. The two specific approaches to Portugal are 'Social dialogue in Portugal' and 'Labour market policies in Portugal'.

493 Labour market studies: Portugal.
Quarternaire Portugal and Centro de Estudos de Economia Industrial, do Trabalho e da Empresa. Luxembourg: Office for Official Publications of the European Communities, 1997. 203p. bibliog.

Financed by the Commission of the European Communities, this study assesses the rapidly changing labour market in Portugal over the decade following the country's joining the European Communities in 1986. It presents a scene of economic modernization, decline in traditional fields such as labour-intensive agriculture and the rise of new manufacturing industries.

494 Child workers in Portugal: a report on child labour in Portugal for Anti-Slavery International.
Suzanne Williams. London: Anti-Slavery International, 1991. 80p. 2 maps. (Child Labour Series, no. 12).
The author, a social anthropologist, based this report on a three-week visit and survey, backed up by questionnaires. The towns and cities detailed are largely in northern Portugal, including Braga, Guimarães, Barcelos and Oporto, but other places such as Aveiro and Lisbon are also covered. Twenty-four child-workers were interviewed and on the basis of her brief sojourn, the writer drew up nine recommendations. As well as the eight chapters, the book has two appendices which include a statement on child labour by the Portuguese government.

Live & work in Spain and Portugal.
See item no. 288.

Living in Portugal.
See item no. 290.

Architecture and Planning

495 Álvaro Siza: architecture writings.
Antonio Angelillo. Milan, Italy: Skira Editore, 1997. 207p.

A compendium of numerous extracts from the writings of the architect Álvaro Siza which expound his architectural philosophy as well as express his views on projects which he has undertaken.

496 Álvaro Siza, 1954-1988.
Architecture + Urbanism, no. 6 (June 1989), 244p. bibliog.

The whole of this issue of the journal, *A+U*, is devoted to an appraisal of the work of the celebrated Portuguese architect Álvaro Siza. The volume comprises three essays about his work, illustrations and plans of thirteen of his projects, sketches of fourteen works by Siza himself and eight drawings, also by Siza. The illustrations are mostly in full colour and the text is in English and Japanese. The volume is completed by a chronological list of Siza's works from 1954-88 and a bibliography.

497 Casas atlánticas, Atlantic houses: Galicia y norte de Portugal, Galicia and northern Portugal.
Antonio Armesto, Quim Padró, translated by Graham Thomson.
Barcelona, Spain: Editorial Gustavo Gili, 1996. 144p. bibliog.

Describing itself as an 'anthology of good architecture', this attractive volume provides architectural appraisals of nine modern houses built in northern Portugal, as well as thirteen in Galicia, Spain. Among those whose domestic architecture is represented here are the Portuguese architects Álvaro Siza Vieira and Fernando Távora. Each building is described in English and Spanish, as well as being depicted both by colour and monochrome photographs and by architectural drawings and plans.

Architecture and Planning

498 Tomás Taveira.
Andrea Bettella, art editor. London: Academy Editions, 1994. 144p. (Architectural Monographs, no. 37).

A large-format colour introduction to the work of the architect Tomás Taveira, best known for his massive and strikingly colourful Amoreiras shopping complex in Lisbon. Although there are two brief introductory essays, the volume mostly comprises fifteen sections of reproductions of plans and architectural drawings. Most of the projects described are in the Lisbon area.

499 Tomás Taveira: architectural works and designs.
Introduction by Geoffrey Broadbent. London: Academy Editions/ St Martin's Press, 1990. 272p.

A large-format book which describes twenty-five projects of the Portuguese architect, Tomás Taveira, accompanied by colour photographs and architectural drawings, plans and elevations. The projects include both those actually completed, such as the strikingly massive Banco Nacional Ultramarino building in Lisbon, and ones that remain on the drawing board, such as the development of the Cais do Sodré railway station buildings, also in the capital. A further two chapters cover 'recent projects' and 'Design projects'. A more concise survey of Taveira's output is by Andrea Bettella, *Tomás Taveira* (London: Academy Editions, 1994. 144p. – see the *Lisbon* volume in the World Bibliographical Series, vol. 199, 1997, item no. 508).

500 The fire of excellence: Spanish and Portuguese oriental architecture.
Miles Danby, photography by Matthew Weinreb. Reading, England: Garnet Publishing, 1997. 236p. map. bibliog.

Oriental architecture is here taken to mean work deriving its style from anywhere east of Spain and Portugal, or around the Mediterranean. The oriental Mudejar style is seen by Danby as surviving in the famous Portuguese Manueline architecture of the late 15th and early 16th centuries. This large tome is magnificently illustrated by plans and colour photographs and its coverage includes buildings in Lisbon, Évora, Beja and Buçaco. Modern structures are also included, such as the Campo Pequeno bullring (1892) and Rossio railway station (1889) in Lisbon.

501 Architecture.
José Manuel Fernandes, translated by Reginald Albert Brown. Lisbon: Comissariado para a Europália 91- Portugal/ Imprensa Nacional-Casa da Moeda, 1991. 168p. bibliog. (Synthesis of Portuguese Culture).

Illustrated by fifty colour photographs, this book provides an excellent survey of Portuguese architectural history and not the generic study of worldwide architecture which its title may imply. Its seven chapters look at the recurrent characteristics of Portuguese architecture as well as its chronological development. There is also a section on major Portuguese architectural works as well as assessments of the house and the city in Portuguese architecture.

Architecture and Planning

502 Queluz: the palace and gardens.
Maria Inês Ferro. London: Scala Books/ Instituto Português do Património Arquitectónico, 1997. 128p.

A colourful guide to the 18th-century rococo palace and gardens of Queluz, some 15km north-west of Lisbon. The text is in four sections covering the palace's construction, life at Queluz, the interiors and the gardens. The palace was developed by D. Pedro, later Pedro III of Portugal, from a pre-existing residence of the Marquês de Castelo Rodrigo. The impressive formal gardens and each of the major rooms are described and illustrated by copious colour photographs which also depict many of the palace's artistic works.

503 Álvaro Siza, city sketches. Stadtskizzen. Desenhos urbanos.
Edited by Brigitte Fleck, texts by Álvaro Siza, Wilfried Wang, translated into English by Robin Benson. Basel, Switzerland; Berlin; Boston, Massachusetts: Birkhäuser Verlag, 1994. 248p.

Texts in English, Portuguese and German support the black-and-white reproduction of numerous architectural sketches of Álvaro Siza. Monochrome photographs further illustrate the architect's work in Évora, Berlin, Macau, The Hague, Venice, Madrid, Lisbon, Paris, Barcelona and Oporto. Many of the sketches are very rudimentary and thus the accompanying explanatory texts by Siza are an indispensable element of the compilation. Also by Fleck is *Álvaro Siza* (London: E & F. N. Spon, 1995. 143p. bibliog. [Architecture Collection]). This is illustrated by colour and monochrome photographs, as well as plan drawings. In a text aimed at non-specialists, Siza's work is presented in chapters on 'Porto, city of granite', 'Matosinhos', 'The small works', 'The competitions', 'Monotony and imagination', 'The Porto School', 'Chiado and the strategy of discovery' and 'Projects of the 1990s'.

504 The work of Álvaro Siza: architecture and design.
Philip Jodidio. Cologne, Germany: Benedikt Taschen Verlag, 1999. 176p.

This sizeable volume is an attractively illustrated review of the work of Álvaro Siza. The text, by Philip Jodidio, covers the varied output of Siza and includes both the more celebrated large-scale architectural commissions and his smaller-scale design work.

505 Lisboa e o aqueduto: Lisbon and the aqueduct.
Ana Paula Moita, Ana Vilas Boas, Leonilde Viegas, Maria de Lurdes Baptista, Maria de Lurdes Ribeiro. Lisbon: Câmara Municipal de Lisboa, Departamento de Património Cultural, Divisão de Arquivos, Arquivo Fotográfico, 1997. 101p. map. bibliog.

A volume produced to accompany an exhibition of photographs of the Águas Livres aqueduct, which first supplied water to Lisbon in 1748. It was one of the few major structures of Lisbon to survive the 1755 earthquake, although a small part was blown up in the 1940s to make way for a road. Forty-two monochrome photographs of the structure and related works are here reproduced with textual accompaniment and an introductory essay. An appendix illustrates and describes twenty-six of the public fountains and water sources which delivered the aqueduct's water to the citizens of Lisbon. The text throughout is in Portuguese and English, the latter being very far from perfectly rendered.

Architecture and Planning

506 Património mundial. World heritage. Portugal.
Maria João Pinto-Coelhom, preface by Vítor Serrão, translated by David Alan Prescott. Lisbon: Estar Editora, 1997. 150p. map.

In addition to a parallel English-Portuguese rendition of this book's preface, the final section (p. 123-50) consists of three English texts and two English documents. The former cover 'Urban and environmental lighting', 'Heritage: the metaphor of time' and 'Intervention on heritage'; the latter comprise the 'Convention concerning the protection of world cultural and national heritage' and 'Formulation of the candidature dossier: Portugal'. The rest of the book comprises accounts, with aerial and other colour photographs of the existing UNESCO world heritage sites in Portugal, in Lisbon and at Batalha, Tomar, Angra (Azores), Évora, Alcobaça and Sintra. Further sites are in the process of consideration for the UNESCO accolade, including the centres of Oporto, Santarém and Elvas, as well as Lisbon's Baixa district and its Castelo de São Jorge (St. George's Castle).

507 Cidades Indo-Portugueses. Indo-Portuguese cities. Contribuições para o estudo do urbanismo português no Hindustão Ocidental. A contribution to the study of Portuguese urbanism in the Western Hindustan.
Walter Rossa. Lisbon: Comissão Nacional para as Comemorações dos Descobrimentos Portugueses, 1997. 117p. map. bibliog.

The text of this book is in both Portuguese and English and is accompanied by numerous colour reproductions of town plans and maps, as well as by photographs. Six cities in present-day India, all of which were formerly occupied by the Portuguese, are the subject of this pioneering study. These are Cochin, Diu, Damão, Goa, Chaul and Bassein, whose periods under Portuguese rule extended in the case of Diu, Damão and Goa until 1961.

508 Architectural practice in Europe: Portugal.
Royal Institute of British Architects. London: Royal Institute of British Architects, 1991. 128p. maps. bibliog.

Portugal has proportionately more architects than the British Isles, even though it has a small, albeit growing, construction industry and its engineers have traditionally done much of the design and project supervision work which is traditionally executed by architects in Britain. An increasing number of British architects have become involved in Portugal, particularly on tourist and commercial projects, as the profession's involvement in construction has grown in recent years. In addition to examining the architect's role in Portugal, this book provides succinct summaries of the country's geography, economy and transport infrastructure, its political, educational and legal systems, as well as its company taxation and employment law provisions.

509 Arcos de Lisboa. (Lisbon's arches.)
José Sá e Silva, photographs by Jorge Ribeiro. Lisbon: Câmara Municipal/ Edições Inapa, 1997. 197p. bibliog.

Fully illustrated by colour photographs, this volume is a survey of every conceivable type of archway to be found in Lisbon. These architectural features are presented in groups which include manifestations as diverse as railway bridges and doorways. More than 120 of the capital's public archways and arcades are also depicted in *Arcos e arcadas de*

Architecture and Planning

Lisboa (Archways and arcades of Lisbon) by Baltazar de Matos Caeiro (Sacavém, Portugal: Distri Editora, 1991. 142p. 5 maps. bibliog.), details of which may be found in the *Lisbon* volume in the World Bibliographical Series, vol. 199, 1997, item no. 492. Lisbon's architecture of the decade up to 1998 is attractively illustrated by monochrome photographs and descriptions in Paulo Santos's *Lisbon: a guide to recent architecture* (London: Ellipsis London, 1998. 235p. map). The buildings shown range from public toilets and bus stations to bars and housing projects. They are presented in nine geographical groups.

510 Álvaro Siza: works & projects, 1954-1992.
Edited by José Paulo dos Santos, introductions by Peter Testa, Kenneth Frampton. Barcelona, Spain: Editorial Gustavo Gili, 1993. 311p. bibliog.

Siza's career is here surveyed in a sumptuously illustrated compendium arranged into three main sections. These cover, in turn, private houses, public buildings in Portugal, and public buildings in the rest of Europe. Each section is accompanied by excellent colour photographs, as well as architectural plans and elevations. There are also brief notes of Siza's furniture, as well as a chronology of his life and work. In *Poetic profession: Álvaro Siza*, by Kenneth Frampton, Nuño Portas, Alexandre Alves Costa and Pierluigi Nicolin (Milan, Italy: Electa/ The Architectural Press, 1986. 188p.), many of Siza's early projects are recorded in predominantly monochrome photographs. These include works in Matosinhos and Évora in Portugal as well as some overseas commissions, in Berlin and elsewhere. The text is provided in both English and Italian and the volume concludes with a critical anthology of the architect's work.

511 Into the city: Álvaro Siza.
Álvaro Siza, edited by Marc Dubois, photographs by Giovanni Chiaramonte. New York: Whitney Library of Design, 1998. 95p.

Here Siza Vieira comments on seven of his major building ventures; these include a water tower, a house, a museum, university offices and an urban renewal project in Portugal and Spain, as well as a Dutch public housing project in The Hague. The book includes photographs of architectural models, working drawings and pictures of the completed buildings in question.

512 Álvaro Siza.
Peter Testa. Basel, Switzerland; Boston, Massachusetts; Berlin: Berkhäusen, 1996. 192p. bibliog.

An assessment, in parallel German and English texts, of the work of architect, Álvaro Siza Vieira, liberally accompanied by plans and drawings. This book covers many of Siza's projects, mostly in Portugal, including sites in Oporto, Maia and Leça, but also some of his work in Germany.

513 1986-1995: Álvaro Siza.
Edited by Luiz Trigueiros. Lisbon: Editorial Blau, 1995. 214p. (Blau Monographs).

Siza's more recent output is described in this substantial landscape-format volume with numerous colour photographs, as well as some plans, elevations and photographs in black-and-white. Parallel texts in Portuguese and English provide fairly minimal information to support the images. Amongst the projects covered are works for the Portuguese universities of Coimbra and Aveiro, the rebuilding of the fire-gutted Chiado district of Lisbon and overseas commissions in The Netherlands, Barcelona and elsewhere. There are also similar Blau Monographs on two other Portuguese architects, Fernando Távora and Eduardo Souto Moura.

Churches of Portugal.
See item no. 354.

Housing

514 Housing in Portugal: an overview.
Vítor Neves.   Glasgow, Scotland: Centre for Housing Research and Urban Studies, University of Glasgow, 1997. 61p. maps. (Occasional Paper, no. 37).

Written by an academic from the University of Coimbra in Portugal, this book's five chapters and two appendices address the problem of Portugal's chronic housing shortages, which are particularly severe in urban areas. Neves attributes the shortage to questions of tenure and affordability rather than to deficiencies of the construction industry. In particular, only four per cent of the country's stock is made up of social housing.

Your home in Portugal.
See item no. 289.

Living in Portugal.
See item no. 290.

The Iberian construction industry.
See item no. 457.

Architectural practice in Europe: Portugal.
See item no. 508.

Education and Training

515 Teachers and trainers in vocational training. Volume 2: Italy, Ireland and Portugal.
Teresa Ambrosio, Nora M. T. Byrne, Teresa Oliveira, Kenneth W. Page, Pierluigi Richini, Project coordinator Africa Melis. Berlin: CEDEFOP-European Centre for the Development of Vocational Training, 1995. 139p. bibliog.

Portuguese vocational training is surveyed on p. 99-139. The volume provides a description of the national programme in Portugal for the regulation and training of teachers and trainers of young people, as well as of the opportunities available for the continuing in-service development of these deliverers of vocational training. Based on studies made in 1982 is *Training of trainers in Portugal* by Mário Gil Videira Vicente (Berlin: CEDEFOP, European Centre for the Development of Vocational Training, 1990. 50p.), which looks first at the profiles of trainers in Portugal: their qualifications, geographical distribution, age and professional attainments. There then follows an account of the role of the Portuguese Institute of Employment and Vocational Training (IEFP). Concern is expressed at the lack of a career structure, the predominance of male trainers and the fact that half of all trainers in Portugal have never received teaching training. There is also a plea for schools to deliver basic technology training for trainers.

516 Educational reform under political transition: a study of change in Portuguese education in the 1970s.
Maria Emília Catela. Stockholm: Institute of International Education, 1990. 216p. bibliog. (Studies in Comparative and International Education, no. 19).

The Swedish International Development Agency and the Institute of International Education assisted in Portugal's evaluation of the 1975 reforms of its junior secondary school education. These reforms were framed at the height of Portugal's lurch to the Left after the 1974 Revolution and their prime aim was to eradicate perceived 'discriminatory distinctions' and traces of 'capitalist social organization' in the Portuguese education system. This survey reveals that these reforms led to an incoherent system and to a low

Education and Training

level of student performance. The report is backed by extensive tables of statistics and a substantial bibliography.

517 Profiles of language education in 25 countries: overview of phase 1 of the IEA Language Study.
Edited by Peter Dickson, Alister Cumming. Slough, England: National Foundation for Educational Research, 1996. 134p.

The International Association for the Evaluation of Educational Achievement (IEA) was founded in 1959 and has fifty-five member countries. The section on Portugal (p. 86-90) by Maria Filomena Matos addresses national language policy, the education system and educational trends in Portugal. The influx of ex-colonial citizens has brought about an increase in bilingual teaching.

518 Survey of education in Portugal.
Michael H. Higgins, Charles F. S. de Winton. London: George Allen & Unwin Ltd, 1942. 75p. bibliog.

Although now somewhat dated, this remains a useful survey of the Portuguese education system by a lecturer at the London School of Economics and a counterpart from Lisbon's Technical University. After a chapter tracing the evolution of Portuguese education from the Middle Ages to the Renaissance, the next four sections cover primary, secondary and technical education in the subsequent years, with emphasis on the contemporary set-up. The final chapter covers the 'classical university'.

519 Theses in Hispanic studies, approved for higher degree by British and Irish universities, 1983-1987, with some additional earlier material.
Margaret Johnson. *Bulletin of Hispanic Studies* (Liverpool), vol. LXVI, no. 4 (1989), p. 417-46.

One of an irregular series of lists which provide access to British university theses relating to Portugal. Earlier lists, by a variety of compilers, appeared in vol. 49 (for theses up to 1971), vol. 52 (for 1972-74), vol. 56 (for 1975-78) and vol. 61 (for 1979-82). Comparable listings for American theses appear in the journal *Hispania* (q.v.) under the title 'Dissertations in Hispanic and Luso-Brazilian languages and literatures'. For older theses, E. Kettenring, *A bibliography of theses and dissertations in Portuguese topics completed in the United States and Canada, 1861-1983* (Durham, New Hampshire: International Conference Group on Portugal, 1984) is particularly useful.

520 Vocational training in Portugal.
Artur Mota, Eduardo Marçal Grilo. Berlin: CEDEFOP-European Centre for the Development of Vocational Training, 1985. 170p. map. bibliog.

Following a brief background description of Portugal and its economic framework, this volume describes the Portuguese educational and training system, from pre-school level through to higher education and, beyond, to cover apprenticeships and continuing education. The limited nature of existing vocational training is acknowledged and proposals are made for improvement which include the setting of higher standards, and more precise regulations, especially for the financing and assessment of vocational

Education and Training

training. Further details of the Portuguese Vocational Guidance Institute, founded in 1925, and the Employment and Vocational Training Institute, set up in 1979, are to be found in *A summary report on the services available for the unemployed and especially the long-term unemployed in Denmark, the Federal Republic of Germany, France, Italy, the Netherlands, Portugal, Spain and the United Kingdom* by Volker Köditz (Berlin: CEDEFOP, 1990. 63p. + 36p.).

521 Europe at school: a study of primary and secondary schools in France, West Germany, Italy, Portugal & Spain.

Norman Newcombe.   London: Methuen, 1977. 264p.

The author of this survey visited two of Portugal's cities, Braga and Évora, to research the section on the country's primary education. As Newcombe's remarks are based on observations at particular schools, they have the validity of close observation but, arguably, his findings may not be typical of the primary school system of Portugal as a whole. As the chapters are thematic, across the five countries studied, it is necessary to use the index entry for each school to elicit information derived from Portugal alone. Topics covered include syllabuses, buildings, the teaching profession and pastoral care. An appendix briefly outlines the 'Curriculum in Portugal'.

522 Classification of educational systems: Iceland, New Zealand, Portugal.

Organisation for Economic Cooperation and Development.   Paris: Organisation for Economic Cooperation and Development, 1975. 78p.

The section of this book on Portugal provides, in tabular form, an analysis of Portuguese education from nursery school level, through the six compulsory years from age seven to thirteen, to higher education. Details are given of entry requirements for each level as well as general descriptions of each tier of the system.

523 From higher education to employment, volume IV: Portugal, United Kingdom, Sweden, Switzerland.

Organisation for Economic Cooperation and Development.   Paris: Organisation for Economic Cooperation and Development, 1992. 241p.

With full text in both English and French, the section on Portugal (p. 5-55) describes recent changes in the Portuguese higher education system. These include growth in the number of universities, the creation of polytechnics and the granting of degree awarding rights to private institutions. An account is then given of the relationship between Portuguese higher education and the employment market, as well as an assessment of the factors of social and regional mobility on the transition from education to work, or 'active life' as it is termed here.

Education and Training

524 New information technology in education in Portugal.
J. Tomás Patrocínio, Luís Valadares Tavares. Luxembourg: Office for Official Publications of the European Communities, 1993. 112p. maps.

This publication is largely devoted to an account of the MINERVA programme which sought to develop information technology (IT) within Portuguese schools and colleges. Its outcome was to produce a large number of IT-aware teachers and trainers able to implement a Portuguese educational curriculum which itself is being developed to address the country's need for a generation with sufficient information technology skills to compete in the modern world.

Textiles and training in Portugal.
See item no. 452.

The Times Higher Educational Supplement.
See item no. 740.

Science and Technology

525 Science in Portugal.
Coordination by José Mariano Gago. Lisbon: Comissariado para a Europália 91-Portugal/ Imprensa Nacional-Casa da Moeda, 1991. 172p. (Synthesis of Portuguese Culture).

One in a series of eleven volumes which covers the spectrum of Portuguese arts and sciences. This volume has three sections. Part I comprises three essays on 'History, institutions, scientific output'. Part II is entitled 'Four examples' and is made up of essays on the contemporary state of Portuguese chemistry, social science, the science of language and biomedical science. Part III is a 'Guide to Portuguese institutions of scientific research and postgraduate study'. It largely consists of a directory of Portuguese scientific institutions which includes location details and information on their research specialities. Gago has also edited a more extensive survey of Portuguese science in Portuguese in his *O estado das ciências em Portugal* (The current state of the sciences in Portugal) (Lisbon: Publicações Dom Quixote, 1992. 455p.).

526 Reviews of national science and technology policy: Portugal.
Organisation for Economic Cooperation and Development. Paris: OECD, 1993. 161p. bibliog.

The volume is the record of a rigorous review of Portugal's achievements in science and technology policy by an outside panel of experts. Portugal is judged to lag behind the rest of western Europe in experimental research and development but its efforts to invest more funds in this area are acknowledged.

527 Science and technology in southern Europe: Spain, Portugal, Greece and Italy.
Carlos Otero Hidalgo. London: Cartermill Publishing, 1997. 309p. bibliog. (The Cartermill Guides).

Chapter 2 (p. 111-57) of this work surveys the state of science and technology research in Portugal. Aimed at financiers, policy analysts, decision-makers, scholars and students, the text identifies the leading Portuguese research institutions, their research strengths,

Science and Technology

funding arrangements, international partnerships and future prospects. Despite a quadrupling of investment in the 1980s, Portuguese research and development is still at the bottom end of the European Communities' rankings. Apart from Greece, Portugal has the highest percentage of government-financed research and the lowest industrially-financed research in the EC. A review of the early history of Portuguese science is to be found in *The rise of scientific Europe, 1500-1800* by D. C. Goodman and Colin A. Russell (London: Hodder & Stoughton, 1999. 416p. bibliog.).

528 30 anos de engenharia civil 1968/1998. 30 years of civil engineering 1968/1998.
José Eduardo Cansado de Carvalho de Matos e Silva. Lisbon: AJE Sociedade Editorial, 1998. 280p.

A bilingual, Portuguese and English, text which aims 'to show the public the almost anonymous and ignored activity carried on by engineers, in particular that of civil engineers'. Forty-five projects are detailed, each illustrated by a colour photograph, drawings and a descriptive text. These are arranged into fifteen categories of three projects each, mostly projects in Portugal but some in Macao. English was chosen as the shared language of the work so as to spread the word about Portuguese engineering to as wide an audience as possible. There is also an extensive curriculum vitae of the author.

Pedro Nunes, 1502-1578: his lost algebra and other discoveries.
See item no. 267.

Precision astrolabe.
See item no. 475.

New information technology in education in Portugal.
See item no. 524.

Literature

Literary history and criticism

529 Women, literature and culture in the Portuguese-speaking world.
Edited by Cláudia Pazos Alonso, with assistance by Glória Fernandes. Lewiston, New York; Queenston, Canada; Lampeter, Wales: The Edwin Mellen Press, 1996. 202p.

A collection of twelve essays based on a conference held at the University of Newcastle-upon-Tyne, England in 1994. The essays explore literary discourses by and about women in the Portuguese-speaking world. They are divided into four sections, covering 'Women in recent Portuguese cultural history', 'Portugal', 'Brazil' and 'Lusophone Africa'. Amongst the Portuguese women writers studied are Florbela Espanca and Maria Velho da Costa.

530 Anticlerical satire in medieval Portuguese literature.
Patricia Odber de Baubeta. Lewiston, New York; Queenston, Canada; Lampeter, Wales: The Edwin Mellen Press, 1992. 356p. bibliog.

The author here draws upon a very wide range of documents, including sermons, confession manuals, historical chronicles, doctrinal works and other sources to compare the representation of clerics in such material with that to be found in mediaeval Portuguese literature. She shows that the reality of clerical behaviour and performance, as revealed by the documentary evidence, is far different from that derived from an uncritical reading of the satirical literature of the period.

Literature. Literary history and criticism

531 Dictionary of the literature of the Iberian peninsula.
Edited by Germán Bleiberg, Maureen Ihrie, Janet Pérez. Westport, Connecticut; London: Greenwood Press, 1993. 2 vols.

More than 140 contributors' articles are included in this dictionary, on which Bleiberg began work in the 1970s. While a number of the entries for Spanish-language authors are derived from earlier works, those for the Portuguese writers are newly published here. Galician literature is also covered. In the alphabetical entries, each writer's biographical details are supplemented by a review of his or her output and a short bibliography. The work is aimed at both specialists and those with no previous knowledge of the field.

532 History of literature.
Maria Leonor Carvalhão Buescu, translated by Trevor O'Hara. Lisbon: Comissariado para a Európália 91 Portugal/ Imprensa Nacional-Casa da Moeda, 1991. 102p. bibliog. (Synthesis of Portuguese Culture).

Despite its generic title, this is a history of Portuguese literature in twelve chronological chapters. Although the work was written by a leading Portuguese critic, execrable English at times renders the text unintelligible. Dated, but more readable, is the classic *Characteristics of Portuguese literature*, by Fidelino de Figueiredo, translated by Constantino José dos Santos (Coimbra, Portugal: Imprensa da Universidade, 1916. 41p.). Figueiredo attempts to provide an alternative to the traditional literary history by providing a thematic rather than historical approach. The seven sections within his appraisal are entitled 'The cycle of Discoveries', 'Predominance of lyricism', 'Frequency of the epic taste', 'Scarcity of the drama', 'The absence of both the critical and the philosophical spirit', 'Aloofness from the public' and 'A certain mysticism of thought and sentiments'.

533 The post-colonial literature of Lusophone Africa.
Patrick Chabal, with Moema Parente Angel, David Brookshaw, Ana Mafalda Leite, Caroline Shaw. Evanston, Illinois: Northwestern University Press, 1996. 314p. map. bibliog.

In many ways a supplement to Russell Hamilton's pioneering and more wide-ranging *Voices from an empire* (see item no. 537), this is a collection of six essays on Portuguese African literature since the 1974 Portuguese Revolution. The first three essays survey the scene in Mozambique, Angola and Guinea-Bissau respectively. The second part of the book has essays on the written and oral literature of the archipelagos of Cape Verde and São Tomé e Príncipe. The bibliography lists the principal literary and critical works published about or by Portuguese-African authors since 1974.

534 After the Revolution: twenty years of Portuguese literature, 1974-1994.
Edited by Helena Kaufman, Anna Klobucka. Lewisburg, Pennsylvania: Bucknell University Press; London: Associated University Presses, 1997. 252p. bibliog.

A compilation of ten essays, several of which are jointly written by a total of eleven academics, of whom four practise in Portugal, the remainder in the United States. Collectively the book fills a gap in English-language appreciations of modern Portuguese literature in the period after the 1974 Revolution. The essays appear in three parts. After two introductory essays on the socio-political and cultural aspects of modern Portugal, the second part comprises three overviews of, respectively, poetry, drama and the essay in Portugal. The final part consists of five essays on topics which include fiction and women's writing.

535 The Babel guide to the fiction of Portugal, Brazil & Africa in English translation.
Ray Keenoy, David Treece, Paul Hyland, illustrations by Jackie Wrout. London: Boulevard Books, 1995. 161p. bibliog.

Provides summaries and reviews to the major works of Portuguese fiction which have been translated into English since their original publication. Works from Portugal, Brazil, Angola and Mozambique are included. The useful appendix listing the translations is, unfortunately, flawed by the absence of any place of publication or ISBN details. The jaunty tone of the reviews may not be to everyone's taste, but they do undoubtedly provide a stimulus to the reader to explore the world of Lusophone literature through English translations of its masterpieces.

536 Gender, ethnicity and class in modern Portuguese-speaking culture.
Edited by Hilary Owen. Lewiston, New York; Queenston, Canada; Lampeter, Wales: The Edwin Mellen Press, 1996. 235p.

The ten papers in this volume derive from a colloquium held in Belfast, Northern Ireland in 1993. The purpose of the colloquium was to find 'new ways of working with modern Portuguese, Brazilian and African culture, whilst questioning the relevance and applicability for Lusophone culture of the critical theories for which modern English- and French-speaking academics fall heir'. In fact, virtually all of the papers address literary issues, although one or two of the papers do take the application of theory to the boundaries of ready comprehension. An index would have been a useful addition to the volume.

537 Transculturation and resistance in Lusophone African narrative.
Phyllis Peres. Gainesville, Tallahassee, Tampa, Boca Raton, Pensacola, Orlando, Miami, Jacksonville, Florida: University Press of Florida, 1997. 131p. bibliog.

This book's broad title is belied by its content which actually concentrates on Angolan fiction from the mid-1960s to the mid-1990s. Particular emphasis is placed on the work of Luandino Vieira, Uanhenga Xitu, Pepetela and Manuel Rui to which Peres applies 'a postcolonial theoretical perspective'. A wider approach is that of *Voices from an empire: a history of Afro-Portuguese literature* by Russell G. Hamilton (Minneapolis, Minnesota: University of Minnesota Press, 1975. 450p. bibliog. [Minnesota Monographs in the Humanities, vol. 8]). This was a groundbreaking English-language survey of the Portuguese literature of Africa. Although largely written before the 1974 Portuguese Revolution, Hamilton looked forward to a period of uncensored output and the publishing of previously suppressed works, as the former Portuguese colonies in Africa gained their independence. The work is arranged into four sections, covering respectively Angola, Mozambique, the Cape Verde islands and the São Tomé and Príncipe archipelago. All the quotations and book titles are supported by English-language translations.

Literature. Literary history and criticism

538 The question of how: women writers and new Portuguese literature.
Darlene J. Sadlier. New York; Westport, Connecticut; London: Greenwood Press, 1989. 141p. bibliog. (Contributions in Women's Studies, no. 109).

Sadlier attempts to describe the flowering of Portuguese feminist writing which occurred in the wake of the liberating 1974 Revolution. Following a brief introduction, five chapters address, in chronological sequence, the *Novas cartas portuguesas*, and individual works by Fernanda Botelho, Lídia Jorge, Hélia Correia and Teolinda Gersão, who are described as a 'group of middle class women who have political attitudes that are in some ways opposed to the dominant culture'. Consequently the volume omits the conservative Agustina Bessa-Luís, 'arguably the most influential woman of letters in contemporary Portugal'. An appendix, 'Feminism in Portugal: a brief history', and a bibliography complete the volume.

539 Modern Spanish and Portuguese literatures.
Compiled and edited by Marshall J. Schneider, Irwin Stern. New York: Continuum, 1988. 615p. (A Library of Literary Criticism) (A Frederick Ungar Book).

Almost 100 pages of this useful compendium are devoted to Portuguese literature. The approach is to reprint verbatim extracts or translations from critical appraisals of major authors which have been culled from monographs and periodical articles. Sixteen modern writers from Portugal are studied, with both poetry and prose represented. Those assessed include Fernando Namora, Fernando Pessoa, José Régio and Miguel Torga. No female writers are included and José Saramago's rise to fame apparently came too late for his name to be included here.

540 A revisionary history of Portuguese literature.
Edited by Miguel Tamen, Helena C. Buescu. New York: Garland Publishing, 1999. 238p. bibliog. (Garland Reference Library of the Humanities, vol. 2122) (Hispanic Issues, vol. 18).

To date, a thorough English-language history of Portuguese literature has not been published. Whilst this collection of chronologically arranged chapters by diverse authoritative Portuguese literary critics is the nearest yet to filling that void, its tendency to concentrate on certain writers to the detriment of others (such as Gil Vicente) means that it cannot be considered to be truly comprehensive. It provides the best English-language introduction to many Portuguese writers but the fact that half of the twelve chapters cover just the 19th and 20th centuries exacerbates the unevenness of coverage inevitable in a work by so many hands.

541 Eleven essays on Spain, Portugal & Brasil [sic], 1951-1955.
J. B. Trend. Cambridge, England: R. I. Severs, 1951-55. 11 parts in 1. bibliog.

These eleven essays by the distinguished historian J. B. Trend include 'Introduction to Portugal', 'Medieval lyrics in Spain and Portugal', 'Modern poetry from Brasil [sic] in Portuguese' and 'Portuguese poems'.

542 **Roads to today's Portugal: essays on contemporary Portuguese literature, art and culture.**
Edited, with an introduction by Nelson H. Vieira. Providence, Rhode Island: Gávea-Brown, 1983. 157p.

A most useful English-language survey of contemporary Portuguese literary, artistic and cultural activity which also includes Cape Verdean poetry and Azorean literature. The book has eight chapters and thirteen monochrome reproductions of Portuguese works of art. The chapters which, after a brief historical introduction, comprise six on literature and one on art, are concise review articles which serve as valuable introductions to their themes for English-language speakers.

Major authors

Eugénio de Andrade

543 **Inhabited heart: the selected poems of Eugénio de Andrade. Bilingual edition.**
Eugénio de Andrade, translated by Alexia Levitin, with an introduction by Pilar Gómez Bedate. Van Nuys, California: Perivale Press, 1985. 81p.

This selection was made in conjunction with the poet himself and therefore constitutes Eugénio de Andrade's favourite poems. The poems cover the period 1948-84 and are presented in chronological order. Portuguese text is printed opposite the English translation whilst a brief, but useful, introduction defines Andrade as a 'post symbolist' poet. To commemorate the choice of Portugal as the theme at the Frankfurt Book Fair, Andrade's 5 *poemas, poèmes, poems, poesie, Gedichte* (Lisbon: Campo das Letras, 1997. 75p. bibliog.) was published, with each of the selected poems printed in each of the five languages indicated in the title. It is translated by Alexis Levitin, as are Andrade's *Memory of another river* (Minneapolis, Minnesota: New Rivers Press, 1988) and *The shadow's weight* (Providence, Rhode Island: Gávea Brown, 1996).

António Lobo Antunes

544 **Act of the damned.**
António Lobo Antunes, translated by Richard Zenith. New York: The Grove Press, 1995. 246p.

Translated from *Autos dos danados* (1983), this novel portrays the shortcomings of the ruling classes in Portugal under the Salazar regime, up to the 1974/75 revolutionary period. The narrator is a dentist, estranged from his corrupt family who were seeking to safeguard their wealth by transferring it abroad. Other translations of Antunes's novels

175

Literature. Major authors. Luís Vaz de Camões

include *Fado alexandrino* (translated by Gregory Rabassa, 1996). The Grove Press also has plans for further translations of Antunes's novels under the titles *The inquisitor's manual, Getting to know the inferno, Elephant's memory, Return of the caravels* and *Treatise on the natural order of things.*

545 An explanation of the birds.
António Lobo Antunes, translated by Richard Zenith. New York: The Grove Press, 1991. 261p.

The narrator of this blackly comic novel, Rui, is a political historian who is estranged from his father and his first wife. Over the course of a long weekend, he takes his second wife, a Marxist, away to terminate their relationship. It is a translation of *Explicação dos pássaros* and its text is arranged into chapters entitled from 'Thursday' to 'Sunday'. The birds of the title are those that the narrator's father foretold would peck at his corpse. Indeed, Rui does die but not before suffering the indignity of his wife's leaving him before he can abandon her.

546 Fado alexandrino. (Alexandrine fado.)
António Lobo Antunes, translated by Gregory Rabassa. New York: Grove Weidenfeld, 1990. 497p.

Translated from a Portuguese original of the same title, this lengthy novel is divided into three parts, covering 'Before the Revolution, 'The Revolution' and 'After the Revolution'. Also available to an English-speaking readership is *South of nowhere*, translated by Elizabeth Lowe (London: Chatto & Windus, 1983. 154p.), which is a translation of *Os cus de Judas*, first published in 1979 (Lisbon: Editorial Vega). The narrator is sent from Lisbon by troop-ship to Angola, as part of the Portuguese forces trying to suppress the native independence movement. In chapters which are alphabetized from A to Z rather than numbered, the narrator captures the experience of those involved in Portugal's fruitless colonial wars of the 1960s and 1970s.

Luís Vaz de Camões

547 Epic & lyric.
Luís Vaz de Camões, edited by L. C. Taylor, translations by Keith Bosley, illustrations by Lima de Freitas. Manchester, England: Carcanet, in association with the Calouste Gulbenkian Foundation, 1991. 116p. bibliog. (Aspects of Portugal).

A combination of translations of extracts from Camões's 16th-century epic, *Os Lusíadas* (The Lusiads), and from his lyric poetry, which combine to provide an admirable introduction for English readers to Portugal's national poet. The texts are accompanied by illustrations and by historical texts on Camões by Roy Campbell, Elizabeth Barrett Browning and Herman Melville, together with modern essays by Maurice Bowra, Helder Macedo and Luís de Sousa Rebelo. Melville's and Ezra Pound's views of Camões are assessed in two thought-provoking works by Norwood Andrews: *Melville's Camões* (Bonn: Bouvier, 1989. 170p. [Studien zur Germanistik und Komparatistik]); and *The case against Camões: a seldom considered chapter from Ezra Pound's campaign to discredit*

Literature. Major authors. Fernando Pessoa. General

rhetorical poetry (New York: Peter Lang, 1988. 146p. [Utah Studies in Literature and Linguistics, no. 27]).

548 The Lusiads.
Luís Vaz de Camões, translated, with an introduction and notes by Landeg White. Oxford; New York: Oxford University Press, 1997. 258p. 3 maps. bibliog. (World's Classics).
This translation of Camões's epic poem, *Os Lusíadas*, claims to be the first English version for some fifty years. It describes itself as 'an untrammelled, unrhymed' translation which aims to avoid the allegedly academic tone of previous efforts. It also endeavours to keep the flavour of the original, not least by its avoidance of the constraints of rhyme. Nevertheless, this English version does retain the eight-line stanzas of the original Portuguese.

Fernando Pessoa

General

549 Always astonished: selected prose.
Fernando Pessoa, translated by Edward Honig. San Francisco, California: City Lights, c.1988. 134p.
A compilation of essays, journal extracts and other prose by Fernando Pessoa (1888-1935), Portugal's leading 20th-century poet. This anthology includes Pessoa's explanation of his use of heteronyms, or alternative personalities, under whose names he published much of his work. Also included here are extracts from the poet's journal, a lengthy missive to the Italian, Marinetti, on the Futurist movement and Pessoa's short story, *The anarchist banker*.

550 The book of disquiet.
Fernando Pessoa, edited by Maria José de Lancastre, translated by Margaret Jull Costa. London: Serpent's Tale, 1991. 262p. map.
This is a translation of Pessoa's *O livro do desasossego*, a posthumous work in prose which is presented as a diary in 523 sections written between 1913 and 1934. Its author is ostensibly one Bernardo Soares and it records his lonely life and routines in Lisbon. Two other translations of the same work also appeared in 1991 by Carcanet Press and Quartet Books. The former, entitled *The book of disquietude by Bernardo Soares, assistant bookkeeper in the city of Lisbon*, has subsequently been published in a revised edition (Manchester, England: Carcanet in association with Calouste Gulbenkian Foundation, 1996. 323p. [Aspects of Portugal]). The Quartet edition is *The book of disquiet: a selection*, translated and introduced by Iain Watson (London: Quartet, 1991. 195p.).

Literature. Major authors. Fernando Pessoa. General

551 A centenary Pessoa.
Fernando Pessoa, edited by Eugénio Lisboa, with L. C. Taylor, translations and poetry by Keith Bosley, prose by Bernard McGuirk, Maria Manuel Lisboa, Richard Zenith. Manchester, England: Carcanet, in association with The Calouste Gulbenkian Foundation, The Instituto Camões, The Instituto da Biblioteca Nacional e do Livro, 1995. 335p. bibliog. (Aspects of Portugal).

Probably the best single-volume English-language introduction to the multiplicity of persona which made up Fernando Pessoa, Portugal's leading 20th-century poet. In addition to a number of translations of Pessoa's work, this compendium also includes critical and biographical information, and an excellent bibliography. As well as black-and-white photographs of Pessoa at various stages of his life, colour reproductions of artistic representations of the poet adorn the volume.

552 English poems.
Fernando Pessoa. Lisbon: Olisipo, 1921. 2 vols.

Portugal's greatest 20th-century poet was actually born in South Africa, in 1888, and wrote many poems in English, particularly in his early career. Here volume 2 comprises *Epithalamium* (1913) whilst the later *Antinous* (1915) constitutes volume 1. A more comprehensive compilation is *Poemas ingleses: Antinous, Inscriptions, Epithalamium, 35 sonnets e Dispersos* (English poems: Antinous, Inscriptions, Epithalamium, thirty-five sonnets and uncollected works), edited by Jorge de Sena (Lisbon: Edições Ática, 1974. 229p. [Obras Completas de Fernando Pessoa, XI]). This includes, in parallel English and Portuguese texts, *Epithalamium* and *Antinous/ Antinóo* as well as *Inscriptions* (1920), *35 sonnets* and a number of uncollected poems dating back to Pessoa's childhood in 1901. His English poems are often mannered and few would claim them to be masterpieces. Nevertheless, they are an important element in Pessoa's development and provide some early clues to the emergence of his heteronyms.

553 Fernando Pessoa & Co: selected poems.
Fernando Pessoa, edited and translated from the Portuguese by Richard Zenith. New York: Grove Press, 1998. 290p. bibliog.

The title is a reference to Pessoa's use of heteronyms (or differing literary identities) the authors of his poetry. Here the main heteronyms (Alberto Caeiro, Ricardo Reis, Álvaro de Campos and Fernando Pessoa himself) are represented in separate sections. Pessoa was born in South Africa but his English-language verse is here omitted. This selection mostly comprises poems not previously published in English translation and provides an excellent demonstration of the poet's range and originality.

554 Message.
Fernando Pessoa, introduction by Helder Macedo, translation by Jonathan Griffin. London: The Menard Press/ King's College London, 1992. 105p.

A parallel text edition in English and Portuguese of Pessoa's *Mensagem* (Message), a collection of forty-four poems, the only such compilation published during Pessoa's own lifetime, in 1934. The death of the translator, Jonathan Griffin, had resulted in the English versions used here being in an incomplete state and these were therefore polished for

Literature. Major authors. Fernando Pessoa. Critical works

publication by Professor Macedo of King's College London. These patriotic verses are particularly appreciated by those well versed in the history of Portugal.

555 Selected poems.
Fernando Pessoa, translated by Jonathan Griffin. Harmondsworth, England: Penguin Books, 1982. 2nd ed. with a new supplement. 159p. (Penguin Twentieth-Century Classics).

When Fernando Pessoa, Portugal's most celebrated 20th-century poet, died in 1935, he left much of his verse unpublished. This is Jonathan Griffin's revision and expansion of his own 1974 edition of the *Collected poems*, which takes into account this newly discovered work by Pessoa by including twenty-seven extra poems written in Pessoa's own name. The poems from the 1974 edition, which are reproduced here, are arranged into four categories, namely poems written in Pessoa's own name and works attributed by the poet to his three main heteronyms (or alter egos), namely Alberto Caeiro, Ricardo Reis and Álvaro de Campos.

556 Fernando Pessoa, a galaxy of poets, 1888-1935.
St Pancras Library. London: London Borough of Camden in association with the Portuguese Ministries of Foreign Affairs and Culture, 1985. 119p. bibliog.

Although at first sight this may appear to be simply the catalogue of an exhibition held at St Pancras Library, London, it is also a most useful introduction to the poet. It comprises an essay by José Blanco on Pessoa and his heteronyms, a chronology of his life, letters by Pessoa, a critical and poetical anthology, a bibliography and a number of colour and monochrome reproductions of paintings and sculptures of the poet. The section on the exhibition itself reproduces, albeit in small format, a number of Pessoa manuscripts, printed texts and photographs.

Critical works

557 Fernando Pessoa: voices of a nomadic soul.
Zbigniew Kotowicz. London: Menard Press, 1996. 108p. bibliog.

This book provides a most useful introduction to Portugal's major modern poet. Pessoa's life is recounted and his work is placed in literary context before the curious phenomenon of his heteronyms is explained. Much of the poet's work was unpublished at his death and Kotowicz here provides a stimulating assessment of the role of editors and others in putting together the disparate material left by Pessoa. He pays particular attention to Pessoa's *Livro do desassossego* (Book of disquietude). Kotowicz's book is illustrated by some 'modern' drawings and an appendix includes an English translation of Pessoa's *A Tabacaria* by Suzette Macedo.

Literature. Major authors. José Maria Eça de Queiroz

558 **The presence of Pessoa: English, American and southern African literary responses.**
George Monteiro. Lexington, Kentucky: University Press of Kentucky, 1998. 164p. (Studies in Romance Languages, no. 43).

A groundbreaking study of the influence of Fernando Pessoa (1888-1935), Portugal's leading 20th-century poet, on English-language writers over three continents. Amongst those studied here are Allen Ginsberg, John Wain, Joyce Carol Oates, D. H. Lawrence and Lawrence Ferlinghetti. The volume also includes an unpublished and unfinished biographical study of Pessoa by Roy Campbell.

559 **An introduction to Fernando Pessoa, literary modernist: Modernism and paradoxes of authorship.**
Darlene J. Sadlier. Gainesville, Florida: University Press of Florida, 1998. 168p. bibliog.

In this most useful introduction to Fernando Pessoa for an English-speaking audience, Sadlier ranges across the full spectrum of the author's output. In particular, she addresses Pessoa's innovative use of literary heteronyms and assesses how these seemingly paradoxical identities interacted and responded to each other.

560 **Fernando Pessoa, the bilingual Portuguese poet. A critical study of 'The mad fiddler'.**
Anne Terlinden. Brussels: Facultés Universitaires Saint-Louis, 1990. 235p. bibliog. (Publications des Facultés Universitaires Saint-Louis, Travaux et Recherches, no. 20).

The Belgian author, an academic based in the United States, uses the extensive corpus of English-language work by Portugal's major 20th-century poet, Fernando Pessoa, to demonstrate the 'English facet' of his writing. Born and brought up as a child in South Africa, Pessoa (1886-1935) subsequently wrote 'The mad fiddler', a collection of mystical poems, between 1911 and 1917. Terlinden not only links these poems to later themes found in Pessoa's Portuguese poems attributed to his heteronyms, but also uncovers a French aspect of his work, revealed both in his writing in that language and in his assimilation of French Symbolism.

José Maria Eça de Queiroz

561 **Cartas de amor de Anna Conover e Mollie Bidwell para José Maria Eça de Queiroz, cônsul de Portugal em Havana. Original letters in English.** (Love letters written by Anna Conover and Mollie Bidwell to José Maria Eça de Queiroz, Portuguese consul in Havana, 1873-74.)
Edited by A. Campos Matos, translations by Alice Lamath Ferreira. Lisbon: Assírio & Alvim, 1998. 189p.

Eça's period as consul in Havana, Cuba brought him into contact with two North American ladies who became ardent admirers of the then unknown Portuguese writer.

Literature. Major authors. José Maria Eça de Queiroz

These curious episodes are captured here for the first time in thirty-three letters, printed both in Portuguese and in their original English. Written over a five-month period, seven of the letters are from young Mollie Bidwell, from Pittsburgh, and a further five are from her parents. The remaining twenty-one letters are from Annie Bidwell, a married mother of two from New York and these cover a thirteen-month period. Contemporary illustrations of the protagonists and of some of the correspondence are included.

562   The city and the mountains.
José Maria de Eça de Queiroz, translated by Roy Campbell. Manchester, England: Carcanet in association with The Calouste Gulbenkian Foundation, 1994. 216p. (Aspects of Portugal).

A new edition of a translation first published in 1955 of Eça's *A cidade e as serras*, a novel edited by his son in 1901, following the novelist's death in 1900. The protagonist, a wealthy provincial man, moves to Paris where he lives a life of sophistication in his Champs Elysées apartment. A most useful English-language introduction to the work of Eça in particular and to Portuguese Realism in general is to be found in *The age of Realism*, edited by F. W. R. Hemmings (Harmondsworth, England: Penguin Books, 1974. 414p. [Pelican Guides to European Literature]).

563   The illustrious house of Ramires.
José Maria Eça de Queiroz, translated by Ann Stevens, with an introduction by V. S. Pritchett.   London: Quartet Books, 1998. 309p. (Quartet Encounters).

A re-edition of a translation, which first appeared in 1968, of *A ilustre casa de Ramires*, which is here combined with a helpful introductory essay by V. S. Pritchett culled from his *The myth makers* (London: Chatto & Windus, 1979). The central character of the novel is Gonçalo Ramires, a ruined aristocrat who seeks solace in reliving the martial exploits of his Visigothic ancestors through writing about them. As such, many critics have seen him as a quixotic metaphor for Portugal herself at the time of writing. Following a much-exaggerated scuffle from which he emerged victorious, Gonçalo achieves ill-deserved fame as a novelist and makes an advantageous marriage.

564   The Maias.
José Maria Eça de Queiroz, translated by Patricia McGowan Pinheiro, Ann Stevens.   Harmondsworth, England: Penguin Books, 1998. 633p. bibliog. (Penguin Classics).

This translation of *Os Maias* (1888) was first published in 1965 (London: Bodley Head). It is here preceded by a short introduction to the author by Nigel Griffin who sees Eça's work as reminiscent of Balzac's *Comédie humaine*. A more recent translation by Patricia McGowan Pinheiro (Manchester, England: Carcanet, 1993) is described in the *Lisbon* volume in the World Bibliographical Series, vol. 199, 1997, item no. 564. The novel chronicles the moral decline of the Maia family in contemporary Lisbon. An English-language critique of this novel is to be found in *An introduction to fifty European novels* by Martin Seymour-Smith (London; Sydney: Pan Books, 1979. 528p. bibliog. [Pan Literature Guides]).

Literature. Major authors. Mário de Sá-Carneiro

565 The mandarin and other stories.
José Maria Eça de Queiroz, translated by M. Jull Costa, with an afterword by Robert Webb. Sawtry, England: Dedalus, 1993. 125p. (Dedalus European Classics).

Together with a translation of the novella *O mandarim* (1880), this volume provides English versions of an extract from the novel, *A relíquia* (The relic), and the short story, *José Matias*. The mandarin tells the humorous and fantastic story of Teodoro, a minor clerk in Lisbon, whose reading of cheap books leads him to confront a timeless moral dilemma and ensuing guilt. He succumbs to the Devil's temptation of acquiring huge wealth by the act of ringing a bell, knowing that the act condemns a man to death in faraway China. An earlier edition of *The mandarin and other stories*, comprising the title story with *Peculiarities of a fair-headed girl, A lyric poet* and *José Matias*, was translated by Richard Franko Goldman (London: The Bodley Head, 1966. 185p.). *The relic* involves its narrator's attempt to ingratiate himself with a wealthy and religious aunt by visiting the Holy Land, whilst *José Matias*, written in 1897, concerns José's romantic love for Elisa. Webb's 'Afterword' is an excellent, brief survey of Eça's work.

566 The sin of Father Amaro.
José Maria Eça de Queiroz, translated by Nan Flanagan. Manchester, England: Carcanet in association with The Calouste Gulbenkian Foundation, 1994. 351p. (Aspects of Portugal).

This translation of the novel *O crime do Padre Amaro* (1875, 1876 and 1880) first appeared in 1962. The one-page introduction to the author and his work, which is provided here, is not particularly specific to this work and thus there is no mention of the textual problems deriving from the three variant versions of the novel. Indeed, the introduction dates the book at 1876 whilst the back of the title page implies we have here an 1874 edition. With anticlerical satire never far from the surface, the novel tells of the immoral behaviour of a cleric who seduces a young woman in the provincial town of Leiria.

Mário de Sá-Carneiro

567 The great shadow, and other stories.
Mário de Sá-Carneiro, translated from the Portuguese by Margaret Jull Costa. Sawtry, England: Dedalus, 1996. 249p.

This translation of the decadent short stories of Mário de Sá-Carneiro (1890-1916) derives from *The sky ablaze (Céu em fogo)*, stories written in Paris, where the writer resided and where he committed suicide by taking strychnine. The themes of death, madness and suicide pervade the narratives and their dark nature is epitomised by *The great shadow*, in which a curious *ménage à trois* leads to a violent death.

568 Lúcio's confession.
Mário de Sá-Carneiro, translated from the Portuguese by Margaret Jull Costa. Sawtry, England: Dedalus, 1993. 121p.

Written in 1913, three years before its young author committed suicide in Paris, this is a short novel set in the artistic circles of *fin-de-siècle* Paris and Lisbon. It explores Sá-

Carneiro's recurrent themes of abnormality, madness, sensual experience, decadence and death. The narrative revolves around the relationships of two Portuguese poets, Lúcio and Ricardo, the latter of whom marries the mysterious Marta who, in turn, becomes Lúcio's mistress.

José Saramago

569 All the names.
José Saramago, translated from the Portuguese by M. Jull Costa. London: The Harvill Press, 1999. 243p.

A translation of Saramago's *Todos os nomes*, a novel whose central character is Senhor José, a lowly clerk in a Portuguese registry office. Accidentally coming across the birth certificate of a woman, José becomes obsessive in his pursuit of details of her life in a narrative which can be read as a parable on the abuse of power.

570 Baltasar and Blimunda.
José Saramago, translated by Giovanni Pontiero. London: The Harvill Press, 1998. 343p.

A translation of Saramago's first successful work, *Memorial do convento*, his third novel, published in 1977. The novel is set around the building of the royal palace at Mafra on which work began in 1717. As well as portraying the austere King João V, the narrative involves all manner of fantastic happenings, a number of which are based on the historical figure of Gusmão, an early theorist of aviation. Central to the narrative is the affair between Baltasar, a one-handed soldier, and Blimunda, whose mother was taken from her by the Inquisition. This is Saramago's best-selling title in his native land.

571 Blindness: a novel.
José Saramago, translated from the Portuguese by Giovanni Pontiero. London: The Harvill Press, 1999. 309p.

Translated from *Ensaio sobre a cegueira* (Essay on blindness), this novel recounts an epidemic of 'white blindness' which breaks out and leads to the incarceration of its many victims in asylums. As urban civilised normality collapses, Saramago prompts his readers to re-examine their own comfortable routines and familiar surroundings. The translation was completed by Margaret Jull Costa, following the death of Giovanni Pontiero. Curiously, Harvill brought out this book in 1997 but have reissued it in a slightly smaller format but identical length in 1999; the same has occurred with other Saramago novels, such as *The year of the death of Ricardo Reis* and *The gospel according to Jesus Christ* (q.v.). Amongst Saramago's other novels is *The history of the siege of Lisbon* (see the *Lisbon* volume in the World Bibliographical Series, vol. 199, 1997, item no. 579).

572 The gospel according to Jesus Christ.
José Saramago, translated from the Portuguese by Giovanni Pontiero. London: The Harvill Press, 1999. 341p.

Published in 1991 as *O evangelho segundo Jesus Cristo*, and first issued in translation by Harvill in 1993, this controversial novel rewrites the New Testament with an account of how Jesus Christ cohabits with Mary Magdalene. As a result of the hostile critical reception accorded this book, Saramago vowed never to return to live in Portugal and, indeed, he continues to reside in Lanzarote in the Canaries.

573 Manual of calligraphy: a novel.
José Saramago, translated from the Portuguese by Giovanni Pontiero. Manchester, England: Carcanet, 1994. 223p. (From the Portuguese, no. 3).

The story of a resentful portrait painter whose distaste for his subjects leads to the collapse of his career and his move into the field of creative writing. He ultimately finds his true *milieu* in the sphere of revolutionary politics. This novel, first published in 1976 as *Manual de pintura e caligrafia* (Manual of painting and calligraphy), has thus been seen as reflecting Portugal's achievement of democracy in 1974 after years of suppression.

574 The stone raft.
José Saramago, translated from the Portuguese by Giovanni Pontiero. London: Harvill, 1994. 263p.

José Saramago won the Nobel Prize for Literature in 1998. This is a translation of his novel *A jangada de pedra* (1986), in which the Iberian peninsula is cast adrift when it breaks off from mainland Europe at its junction with the Pyrenees. Its five characters and their dog drift southwards, narrowly avoiding a collision with the Azores, before moving south between Africa and Latin America. Seen by some as an anti-European parable, its story also reflects the author's own abandonment of Portugal for a home in the Canary Islands. The book has also been published in the United States (San Diego, California; New York; London: Harcourt, Brace & Company, 1996. 292p.).

575 The tale of the unknown island.
José Saramago, illustrated by Peter Sis, translated by Margaret Jull Costa. New York; San Diego; London: Harcourt, Brace & Company; London: Harvill Press, 1999. 51p.

Following the untimely death of Giovanni Pontiero, Saramago's long-time English translator, Margaret Jull Costa has established herself as his successor. Her translation of *O conto da ilha desconhecida* (Lisbon: Pavilhão de Portugal Expo '98/ Assírio & Alvim, 1997. 35p.) is of a book which appears to be a children's fable but can also be seen as a deeper parable of life in which the narrative involves a man asking a king for a boat, before setting sail for an unknown island.

576 The year of the death of Ricardo Reis.
José Saramago, translated from the Portuguese by Giovanni Pontiero. London: Harvill Press, 1998. 358p.

A new edition of the 1992 translation of *O ano da morte de Ricardo Reis* but now in a smaller format. Reis was one of the heteronyms of Fernando Pessoa, the Portuguese poet. In this novel Reis is seen to have outlived his creator and to have returned to Lisbon during the 1930s, where he establishes himself as a locum doctor. In his meandering across a Lisbon backdrop, Reis encounters a cast which even includes the dead Pessoa but he also becomes romantically involved with a chambermaid and a woman with a crippled hand. The divergent social classes of these two lovers point to Saramago's concern with Portugal's socio-political tensions.

Gil Vicente

General

577 Three discovery plays. Auto da barca do inferno; Exortação da guerra, Auto da Índia. (Drama of Hell's boat; War exhortation; Drama of India.)
Gil Vicente, edited and translated by Anthony Lappin. Warminster, England: Aris & Phillips, 1997. 229p. bibliog.

Gil Vicente (c.1470-1536) was the major playwright of the era who wrote in both Portuguese and Castilian. This compilation of three of his early *autos* (short plays) comprises parallel Portuguese and English texts and has excellent critical apparatus, including an explanation of the historical context, a brief introduction to each work, textual variants and even a guide to pronunciation of Portuguese at the time of the plays' composition. All three plays were written in the reign of King Manuel, when the initial major Portuguese maritime discoveries were made, but the editor also traces emendations to the texts by both the author and the Portuguese Inquisition. Also of interest is Vicente's *The boat plays: The boat to heaven; The boat to hell; The boat to purgatory*, translated by David Johnston (London: Absolute Classics, 1997. 96p.). Johnston's tinkering with Vicente's original texts for dramatic ends is, however, significant.

Critical works

578 Gil Vicente and the development of the *comedia*.
René Pedro Garay. Chapel Hill, North Carolina: University of North Carolina, Department of Romance Languages, 1988. 220p. bibliog. (North Carolina Studies in the Romance Languages and Literatures, no. 232).

Gil Vicente, Portugal's major dramatist of the 15th century, wrote in both Portuguese and Castilian Spanish. After a survey of pre-16th-century comic theory and of the development of the *comedia* genre in Iberia, this study concentrates on the *Comedia de Rubena* and the *Comedia do viúvo*, both of which were written in Spanish. Garay concludes that Vicente, with Torres Naharro, was the father of the *comedia* genre in Iberia.

579 Gil Vicente.
Jack Horace Parker. New York: Twayne Publishers Inc., 1967. 169p. bibliog. (Twayne's World Authors Series, no. 29).

Although primarily known as a dramatist, Gil Vicente (c.1470-1536) was also, as Parker here shows, a notable goldsmith, master of the Portuguese Royal Mint, a member of the Lisbon town council and impresario at the royal court. Parker concludes that Vicente was really a consummate mediaeval figure rather than a profoundly innovative dramatist. The accompanying bibliography of works, criticism and background material is helpfully annotated.

580 The carnival stage: Vicentine comedy within the serio-comic mode.
José I. Suárez. Rutherford, New Jersey; Madison, Wisconsin; Teaneck, New Jersey: Fairleigh Dickinson Press; London; Toronto, Canada: Associated University Press, 1993. 172p. bibliog.
In three chapters, the author here traces the popular origins of the plays of Gil Vicente and concludes that the dramatist wrote both within the Western literary tradition of carnival and was also a precursor of the French writer, Rabelais. He also looks at the application of Menippean satire to Vicente's work and seeks the origins of Vicente's works in Iberian drama.

Other authors

Maria Isabel Barreno

581 New Portuguese letters: the three Marias.
Maria Isabel Barreno, Maria Teresa Horta, Maria Velho da Costa, prose translated by Helen R. Lane, poetry translated by Faith Gillespie, with Suzette Macedo. London: Readers International, 1994. 326p.
A new edition of a work first published in this translation in 1975 (London: Victor Gollancz, 432p.), which transformed the literary scene in Portugal in the immediate period before the 1974 Revolution. Published as *Novas cartas portuguesas* in 1972, its authors, the so-called 'Three Marias', were arrested on grounds of immorality. The work is a loosely connected collection of letters, poetry and prose, with a title which is an allusion to the *Letters of a Portuguese nun* (see item no. 608), a 17th-century classic. In fact, the book can be seen, to some extent, as a modern counterpart to that work in its exposition of the female condition in Portugal.

Al Berto

582 The secret life of images.
Al Berto, translated by Richard Zimler. Dublin: Mermaid Turbulence, 1997. unpaginated. (A Finis Terrae Volume).

Al Berto (1948-97) abandoned his career as a painter in Brussels in 1971 during his years of exile (1967-75) from the Salazar regime in Portugal. This is a collection of Al Berto's verse inspired by twenty-six works of art, both paintings and sculptures, which are reproduced in colour opposite Al Berto's texts. In the poems, the writer uses his own artistic experience to explore behind the surface of art to discern the 'secret life' of each image. The images range from works by Giotto and Cézanne to lesser-known pieces by Portuguese artists.

Sophia de Mello Breyner

583 Log book: selected poems.
Sophia de Mello Breyner, translated by Richard Zenith. Manchester, England: Carcanet, 1997. 111p. (From the Portuguese).

Born in Oporto in 1919, Sophia, as she is generally known, had a cosmopolitan upbringing which brought her into contact with French and Greek culture in particular. Thus her poems not only depict a Portuguese backdrop, but also allude heavily to Greek mythology. A recurrent theme in Sophia's poetry and in this anthology is the Portuguese maritime discoveries. This compilation comprises representative translations from a dozen collections which were originally published between 1944 and 1994. In addition, five unpublished poems are included as well as a perceptive introduction by the translator.

Mário de Carvalho

584 A god strolling in the cool of the evening: a novel.
Mário de Carvalho, translated by Gregory Rabasssa. London: Weidenfeld & Nicolson, 1997. 265p.

A translation of *Deus passeando pela brisa da tarde* by Carvalho (1944-) which won the 1996 Pegasus prize. Its backdrop is the Roman province of Lusitania, which embraced much of modern Portugal, in the 3rd century. The central figure is a city prefect who is struggling to repel the Moors and to deal with the rise of Christianity and social upheaval. The book has also been issued in paperback (London: Phoenix, 1997. 265p.).

Camilo Castelo-Branco

585 Visions of the self in the novels of Camilo Castelo Branco, 1850-1870.
David Gibson Frier. Lewiston, New York; Queenston, Canada; Lampeter, Wales: The Edwin Mellen Press, 1996. 472p. bibliog. (Hispanic Literature, vol. 29).

A fascinating study of Camilo Castelo Branco, a major 19th-century Portuguese novelist whose national fame has not travelled to the English-speaking world where his copious output of predominantly sentimental novels remains untranslated. In this thorough and persuasive work, Frier shows how Camilo escaped reality through his fiction because he was 'so engrossed by his own person'. Another essential source for the student of Camilo is the collection of perceptive papers in *Camilo Castelo Branco no centenário da morte. Colloquium of Santa Barbara* (Camilo Castelo Branco on the centenary of his death), edited by João Camilo dos Santos (Santa Barbara, California: Center for Portuguese Studies, University of California, 1995. 296p.).

António Ferreira

586 The muse reborn: the poetry of António Ferreira.
T. F. Earle. Oxford: Clarendon Press, 1988. 187p. bibliog.

A critical assessment of António Ferreira (1528-69), Portugal's major classicist poet and literary theorist. He wrote the first ode, sonnet sequence and verse tragedy to have survived in Portuguese. After an initial career in law and academia in Coimbra, he was obliged by the religious climate of the day to move to Lisbon. This study of Ferreira concentrates on the classical influences on the writer, including Horace's *Odes* and *Epistles*, Virgil, the Greek epigram and elegy, and the work of Petrarch.

587 The tragedy of Inês de Castro.
António Ferreira, translated into English, with introductory essays by John R. C. Martyn. Coimbra, Portugal: Universidade de Coimbra, 1987. 382p. bibliog. (Acta Universitatis Conimbrigensis).

Preceded by some 150 pages of introduction to Ferreira and his times, this is a parallel Portuguese and English text of Ferreira's drama on the tragic theme of Inês de Castro, the lover of the future King Pedro I. Caught up in the politics of her era, Inês was murdered, with the connivance of Pedro's father. This vernacular tragedy comprises 1,760 lines and is followed by seven appendices, which include a table of the author's correspondence.

Herberto Helder

588 The feminine in the poetry of Herberto Helder.
Juliet Perkins. London: Tamesis Books, 1991. 177p. bibliog.

After an introduction and biographical information on the poet, Herberto Helder (1930-), Perkins studies the Great Mother archetype in his work. She demonstrates that the mother-son relationship is central to the poet's creativity and that his poetry is a statement of 'religious coherence'.

David Mourão-Ferreira

589 Lucky in love.
David Mourão-Ferreira, translated from 'Um amor feliz' by Christine Robinson. Manchester, England: Carcanet in association with Calouste Gulbenkian Foundation, Instituto Camões, Instituto Português do Livro e das Bibliotecas, 1999. 282p.

A translation of *Um amor feliz*, which is set in Lisbon in 1986. The narrator of this novel personifies the idealism of many Portuguese at the time of the 1974 Revolution. As time passes in this tale of clandestine love, his political illusions dissipate as conformity reimposes itself. The approach is erudite at times with heavy use of the classical metaphor of Janus at the crossroads.

Fernando Gonçalves Namora

590 Mountain doctor.
Fernando Namora, translated from the Portuguese by Dorothy Ball. London: William Kimber, 1956. 200p.

An English edition of Fernando Gonçalves Namora's neo-Realist classic, *Retalhos da vida de um médico* (Pieces from a doctor's life, 1948). Namora was a doctor in the backward rural village of Monsanto in northern Portugal, close to the Spanish border. Much of his own experience comes through in this book in which each chapter is effectively a short story.

André de Resende

591 André de Resende's 'Poemata latina'/ Latin poems.
André de Resende, translated, edited and with an introduction by John R. C. Martyn. Lewiston, New York; Lampeter, Wales; Queenston, Canada: The Edwin Mellen Press, 1998. 549p. (Medieval and Renaissance Studies, vol. 18).

After a brief biography of the Portuguese humanist, André de Resende (1498-1573) and clarification of the manuscript sources, this volume reproduces many of his poems in both the original Latin and in English translation, but in sequential rather than parallel texts. These are arranged in two sections, the first being newly discovered works, while the second comprises works already in print. The poems cover a wide range of topics including autobiography, Portuguese history, classical, religious and moralizing themes, and poems addressed to Erasmus and to royal figures.

Literature. Other authors. Miguel Torga

Jorge de Sena

592 A poet's way with music: humanism in Jorge de Sena's poetry.
Francisco Cota Fagundes. Providence, Rhode Island: Gávea-Brown, 1988. 375p. bibliog.

This is a study of Jorge de Sena's *Arte de música* (Art of music). It is inspired by Sena's belief that humans were the 'noblest model for art'. Before an analysis of the individual poems, all of which are music-related, there are chapters on Sena's philosophy and his overall corpus of poetry. Fagundes, with James Houlihan, is also the translator of Sena's *Metamorphosis* (Providence, Rhode Island: Copper Beech Press, 1991).

593 By the rivers of Babylon and other stories.
Jorge de Sena, edited and with a preface by Daphne Patai. Edinburgh: Polygon; New Brunswick, New Jersey: Rutgers University Press, 1989. 155p.

Jorge de Sena (1919-78) was a major figure in 20th-century Portuguese letters, primarily as a poet and critic, but also as a translator and writer of prose fiction. He was also a political opponent of the Salazar regime. The eleven stories in this collection are taken from *Andanças do Demónio* (Wanderings of the Devil, 1960) and *Novas andanças do Demónio* (Further wanderings of the Devil, 1966) and can seem somewhat cerebral at times. Other English translations of Sena's prose work include *The wondrous physician*, translated by Mary Filton (London; Melbourne: J. M. Dent & Sons Ltd, 1986. 123p. [Everyman Fiction]). This is a translation of *O físico prodigioso*, which was first printed in a collection in 1966, then in 1977 as a monograph. It blends romance, chivalry and myth in portraying the adventures of a physician who, through a pact with the Devil, is able to become invisible, enact cures and raise the dead. *Signs of fire*, translated by John Byrne from *Sinais de fogo* (Manchester, England: Carcanet, 1998. 480p.) is a novel in which the protagonist, Jorge, is a student staying with his uncle in Figueira da Foz on the Portuguese coast. Set during the Spanish Civil War, the drama revolves around the uncle's harbouring of two Spaniards who are being sought by the Portuguese police. George Monteiro's *In Crete with the Minotaur and other poems* (Providence, Rhode Island: Gávea Brown, 1980. 77p.), is a parallel English and Portuguese collection of twenty-six of Sena's poems.

Miguel Torga

594 The creation of the world: the first day and the the second day.
Miguel Torga, translated by Ivana Rangel-Carlsen. Manchester, England: Carcanet, 1996. 125p. (From the Portuguese, no. 4).

Originally published in 1937 as *A criação do mundo*, this autobiographical book covers, as its 'first day', the childhood of the author in an illiterate peasant family in Portugal's rural Trás-os-Montes province, and as the 'second day', his period of servitude to his uncle and aunt on a remote Brazilian estate. Torga later returned to Portugal and became a doctor in his native village. He produced more than fifty books before his death in 1995.

Literature. Anthologies

595 Tales & more tales from the mountain.
Miguel Torga, translated by Ivana Rangel-Carlsen. Manchester, England: Carcanet, 1995. 215p.

A translated compilation of two of Torga's collections of short stories, *Contos de montanha* and *Novos contos de montanha*. These convey the rugged world of village life in Portugal's austere and mountainous northerly Trás-os-Montes region. This is a physically harsh and socially conservative area from which many people, especially men, were forced by economic necessity to emigrate. Their heroic, resilient lives are captured in Torga's understated prose, here translated from the fifth edition of the *Contos* (1982) and the thirteenth edition of *Novos contos* (1986). An earlier edition of Carlsen's translation of *Tales from the mountain* was published in 1991 (Fort Bragg, California: Q.E.D. Press, 151p.). *Contos da montanha* was first published in 1941 and was immediately banned by the Portuguese authorities. Two further editions did appear in 1955 and 1962, published in Brazil, but it was not until 1969 that Torga himself published another edition in his home country, with a preface that is here translated and reproduced.

Anthologies

596 Selections of nineteenth-century Portuguese prose.
Edited by Dorothy M. Atkinson. London; Toronto, Canada; Wellington; Sydney: George G. Harrap & Co., 1965. 106p.

Intended as an introduction to the breadth of style and subject matter of 19th-century Portuguese prose, this selection of Portuguese texts is aimed at the inquisitive English reader. The extracts are taken from Alexandre Herculano's historical novel *O bobo* (The fool), Camilo Castelo Branco's Romantic novel, *O amor de perdição* (Love of perdition), the philosophical prose of Antero de Quental, together with three extracts in varied styles by the novelist, Eça de Queiroz. A Portuguese-English vocabulary and explanatory notes are provided.

597 A horse of white clouds: poems from Lusophone Africa.
Selected and translated by Don Burness, with foreword by Chinua Achebe. Athens, Ohio: Ohio University Center for International Studies, 1989. 193p. (Monographs in International Studies, Africa Series, no. 55).

An edition, with parallel Portuguese and English texts, of sixty-six poems written by forty poets from Portuguese-speaking Africa. The poems, from the 19th and 20th centuries, are presented country by country in five sections covering São Tomé and Príncipe, Angola, Cape Verde, Guinea-Bissau and Mozambique. Although the texts are not accompanied by details of the publications from which they have been reprinted, there is a useful potted biography of each author at the end of the anthology. The English versions seek to capture the spirit of the original texts rather than provide slavishly accurate translations. A contrasting African anthology is *Shades of Adamastor, Africa and the Portuguese connection: an anthology of poetry*, edited by M. van Wyk Smith (Grahamstown, South Africa: Institute for the Study of English in Africa, Rhodes University/ National English

Literature. Anthologies

Literary Museum, 1988. 214p. bibliog.). Published on the 500th anniversary of Dias's rounding of the Cape, it comprises translations of extracts of *The Lusiads* and of works by Fernando Pessoa and J. Paço d'Arcos, before presenting works by more than fifty South African English-language poets on the themes of Dias, Vasco da Gama and the mythical creature, Adamastor, of *The Lusiads*.

598 Thirty-two 'cantigas d'amigo' of Dom Dinis: typology of a Portuguese renunciation.
Rip Cohen. Madison, Wisconsin: Hispanic Seminary of Medieval Studies, 1987. 140p. (Portuguese Series, no. 1).
An assessment of the first thirty-two of the collection of Galician-Portuguese poems of the Portuguese King, Dom Dinis (1261-1325), which are seen as an ordered series relating the history of renunciation. The *cantigas d'amigo* were parallelistic poems written as if by women, expressing the pains and sorrows of love. Classical poetic theory is applied to the poems in an attempt to convince the reader of the coherence of the collection.

599 Songs of a friend: love lyrics of medieval Portugal.
Translated by Barbara Hughes Fowler. Chapel Hill, North Carolina: University of North Carolina Press, 1996. 122p.
With eight illustrations, this is a compilation of 103 medieval *cantigas d'amigo* (songs of a friend), one of the main categories of the Galician-Portuguese lyric genre. The work of thirty-one writers is represented here, but only the English translation is given, not the original text. The *cantigas d'amigo* were love songs written during the 12th and 13th centuries and this collection is mostly derived from the 1926 Coimbra edition of J. J. Nunes's *Cantigas d'amigo dos trovadores galego-portugueses* (Songs of a friend by the Portuguese troubadours). There is some overlap with Zenith's anthology (see item no. 606).

600 Passport to Portugal.
Edited by M. Gerrard, T. MacCarthy. Huntingdon, England: Passport, 1994. 155p. (A Passport Anthology, no. 8).
Nineteen elements make up this anthology of modern Portuguese fiction, one of which is an interview with the novelist José Saramago, conducted during a visit to Manchester. The other elements are translations of prose by writers from Portugal, Angola and Mozambique. The absence of an introductory essay is an unfortunate aspect of the book and the three pages of brief biographical notes on some of the authors and translators do not compensate for this omission. Nevertheless, the anthology brings to the English reader a number of texts not otherwise readily accessible to the non-Portuguese reader.

601 The anarchist banker and other Portuguese stories, volume I.
Edited by Eugénio Lisboa. Manchester, England: Carcanet, in association with the Calouste Gulbenkian Foundation, Instituto da Biblioteca Nacional e do Livro, and the Instituto Camões, 1997. 201p. (From the Portuguese Series).
A collection of seven Portuguese short stories by Eça de Queiroz, Fialho de Almeida, António Patrício, Fernando Pessoa, Irene Lisboa, José Régio and José Rodrigues Miguéis.

Literature. Anthologies

The title story, *The anarchist banker*, is a rare prose work by the poet Fernando Pessoa, whilst the other contributors are all important 19th- and 20th-century contributors to Portugal's strength in the short story and *novella* genres. The second volume implicit in this work's title is actually entitled *Professor Pfiglzz and his strange companion, and other Portuguese stories* (see item no. 603).

602 The Dedalus book of Portuguese fantasy.
Edited by Eugénio Lisboa, Helder Macedo. Sawtry, England: Dedalus/ Hippocrene, 1995. 291p.

This anthology is the fruit of a joint initiative by the Calouste Gulbenkian Foundation in London and the Instituto Camões in Lisbon to bring Portuguese literature to an English audience. Indeed, several of the works included here would be considered less than well-known even in Portugal itself. This anthology comprises seventeen pieces by fourteen different authors including Manuel Pinheiro Chagas, Eça de Queiroz and Fialho de Almeida from the 19th century and Mário de Sá-Carneiro, Almada Negreiros and David Mourão-Ferreira from the 20th century. The term 'fantasy' is applied loosely and thus also includes tales of the macabre and the absurd.

603 Professor Pfiglzz and his strange companion, and other Portuguese stories, volume II.
Edited by Eugénio Lisboa. Manchester, England: Carcanet in association with Calouste Gulbenkian Foundation, Instituto da Biblioteca Nacional e do Livro, Instituto Camões, 1997. 202p. (From the Portuguese Series).

A companion volume to *The anarchist banker* (see item no. 601), this compilation comprises ten short stories by Domingos Monteiro, Branquinho da Fonseca, Miguel Torga, Joaquim Paço d'Arcos, Manuel da Fonseca, José Marmelo e Silva, Maria Judite de Carvalho, David Mourão-Ferreira and the author of the title work, Mário de Carvalho. It therefore differs from the earlier volume in being a collection of entirely 20th-century writing. The works have been translated by various hands and provide access to works which are otherwise inaccessible to English readers.

604 Spanish & Portuguese short stories.
London: Senate, 1995. 375p.

An anthology selected from *The Masterpiece Library of Short Stories, Vol.XVIII, Spanish and Portuguese*. It includes ten Portuguese stories, mostly from mainland Portugal and written in the late 19th century. The continental Portuguese authors represented are Alexandre Herculano, Rebelo da Silva, Júlio César Machado, Teófilo Braga, Eça de Queiroz, Fialho de Almeida and Afonso Botelho. The book lacks any introduction and, apart from the authors' birth and death dates, it provides no biographical or bibliographical information. Nevertheless, it provides English-language access to some otherwise very obscure Portuguese stories.

605 Modern Poetry in Translation. New series, no. 5. Summer 1994.
Edited by Daniel Weissbort. London: King's College, 1994. 185p.

This is a special issue of *Modern Poetry in Translation*, dedicated to the Galician-Portuguese troubadours of the 13th century, with an illuminating introduction by Richard

Literature. Literary works relating to Portugal published in English

Zenith which covers the history of the Galician-Portuguese language as a literary medium. The texts comprise twenty of the troubadours' songs (*cantigas*), translated in a lively fashion which captures their often earthy spirit. The same issue also includes two poems each by the 20th-century Portuguese poets, Fernando Pessoa and Sophia de Mello Breyner.

606 113 Galician-Portuguese troubadour poems.
Translated by Richard Zenith. Manchester, England: Carcanet, in association with Calouste Gulbenkian Foundation, Instituto Camões, 1995. 280p. bibliog.

A collection of 113 Galician-Portuguese poems of the 13th and early 14th century is presented here in parallel texts in the original language and in English. As the literary language of the Portuguese court, Galician Portuguese was even employed by Portuguese monarchs for poetic purposes. Prefaced by a masterly introduction (p. ix-xlii) which surveys the genre of the Galician-Portuguese lyric, this anthology demonstrates the full range of work which derived from imitation of Provençal court poetry.

Literary works relating to Portugal published in English

607 Torrent of Portyngale. Reedited from the unique MS in the Chetham Library, Manchester.
Edited by E. Adam. London: N. Trübner for the Early English Text Society, 1887. 120p.

An edition of a 15th-century English manuscript which recounts the chivalrous exploits of Torrent, a young knight, in his quest for the hand of Desonelle, daughter of the mythical King of Portugal, Calamond. After several encounters both with giants and with a hostile Calamond, Torrent finally succeeds in winning Desonelle's hand before he finally becomes the Emperor of Rome. The narrative backdrop ranges from Portugal to Norway, the Holy Land and back again.

608 Letters from a Portuguese nun.
Mariana Alcoforado, translated from the French and with an introduction by Olive Kennedy, illustrated by Richard Kennedy. Andoversford, England: The Whittington Press, 1986. 36p.

A large-format edition, with full-page sketches, of the five letters of Mariana Alcoforado addressed to a French soldier, Noël Bouton, Comte de Chamilly, written in 1667. He had served in Portugal, when the French had assisted the Portuguese consolidate their independence in battles against the Spaniards. The letters, first published in Paris in 1669, became a sensation across Europe and were subsequently taken up by the 19th-century Romantics. Earlier English editions include the classic translation by Edgar Prestage

Literature. Literary works relating to Portugal published in English

(London: David Nutt, 1893) and that by E. Allen Ashwin (Talybont, Wales: Walterson, 1929).

609 Mariana.
Mariana Alcoforado, edited and translated by Katherine Vaz. Hammersmith, England: Flamingo, 1998. 325p.

An American academic's new translation from the French of *The letters of a Portuguese nun*. The work comprises the allegedly genuine letters of Mariana Alcoforado, born of nobility and placed in a convent in Beja at the age of eleven, during the 17th century. She had a scandalous affair with a French army captain, Noël Bouton. After they were parted by his military career, she wrote these passionate epistles to him. The *Letters* became a Romantic focus and, to date, some 250 editions have appeared worldwide.

610 Death on the Douro.
Tony Aspler. London: Headline, 1997. 217p.

This is the third in a series of Tony Aspler's crime novels which are set against a background of wine-making, with the intrigue here occurring in Portugal's Douro valley in the north of the country, the source of grapes for the port wine industry.

611 Sonnets from the Portuguese, and other poems.
Elizabeth Barrett Browning. New York: Dover; London: Constable, 1995. 51p. (Dover Thrift Editions).

Published originally in an anonymous edition in 1847, this is a collection of forty-four love poems from Elizabeth Barrett Browning to her husband, Robert. Only after her death was Elizabeth Barrett Browning revealed to be the composer of the verses. It is assumed by some that the title is an allusion to the sonnets of Camões. Indeed, the format of the sonnets is not in the traditional English style of one fourteen-line stanza but rather, in the Portuguese mode, of two quatrains and two tercets.

612 Sharpe's enemy: Richard Sharpe and the defence of Portugal, Christmas, 1812.
Bernard Cornwell. London: Harper Collins, 1996. 351p. map.

Originally published in London (Collins, 1984), and Glasgow (Fontana, 1985), this is the fifth in a series of historical novels about Major Richard Sharpe. It is set on the Portuguese-Spanish border during the Peninsular War and the narrative requires him to rescue a group of ladies held hostage by a band of deserters, one of whom is Sharpe's enemy, Sergeant Hakeswill.

613 The peasant of Portugal.
Thomas De Quincey. London: Aporia Press, 1985. 36p.

This publication comprises *The peasant of Portugal: a tale of the Peninsula [sic] War* and an extract from *The stranger's grave*. The former work is extracted from *The literary souvenir; or, Cabinet of poetry and romance* (1827), utilizing the original spelling and punctuation. It tells, in prose, of the heroism of the supposedly Portuguese peasant, with the incongruous pseudo-Spanish name of Juan Taxillo, and his role in the defeat of a regiment of French *cuirassiers* during the Peninsular War.

Literature. Literary works relating to Portugal published in English

614 The river running by.
Charles Gidley. London: André Deutsch, 1981. 500p.

This is the first novel of Charles Gidley Wheeler, to give the author his full name. It concerns Bobby Teague, director of his family's port wine business in Oporto. The action, however, takes place in various parts of Portugal, including Lisbon and Cascais. The narrative, set mostly in the 1970s, involves Bobby's uneasy marriage and his relationship with a Portuguese 'fish-girl' called Natalia, who becomes the family maid.

615 Annals of the purple city.
Frederick Lees. Hong Kong; London: Crane Books, 1995. 290p.

An, at times, racy novel by a British ex-diplomat which is based on his experiences of the Portuguese colony of Macao in the 1950s. Indeed, Macao is the 'purple city' of the title. Lees attempts to fuse the traditions of the European novel with those of the Chinese classical novel, particularly with the latter's use of subplots, dreams and poetry. The novel tells of Diana, a beautiful Australian, and her relationships with four men: her English husband, a Eurasian lover, an expatriate Hong Kong homosexual and a Chinese millionaire of advancing years.

616 The Lisbon traviata.
Terrence McNally. New York: Dramatists' Play Service, 1992. rev. ed. 94p.

A play for four male characters, culminating in a homosexual stabbing, which was first produced in New York City in 1985. Throughout the drama a pirated copy of a rendition in Lisbon of *La Traviata* by Maria Callas appears as a symbol of the protagonists' evasion of real life. The fact that this performance was supposedly recorded in Lisbon's 'San Carlo' (i.e. São Carlos) opera house indicates a lack of deep knowledge of the city and that McNally is using Lisbon largely as an exotic touchstone.

617 The following story.
Cees Nooteboom, translated from the Dutch by Ina Rilke. San Diego, California; New York; London: Harcourt Brace & Company, 1994. 115p. (Harvest in Translation) (A Helen and Kurt Wolff Book).

Originally published as *Het volgende verbaal* (Amsterdam, 1991), this novel, by one of The Netherlands's most popular writers, won the European Literary Prize for Best Novel in 1993. It recounts the experiences of Herman Mussett who went to sleep one night in Amsterdam, dreaming of outer space, only to awaken in Lisbon, where he stays in a hotel in the Rua das Janelas Verdes before becoming involved in a drama of jealousy and revenge which ranges across a number of countries.

618 Taking lives.
Michael Pye. London: Phoenix, 1999. 370p. (Phoenix Paperbacks).

Pye is a resident of Portugal and that country forms the backdrop to this novel of suspense and violence. The plot involves a young Dutch serial murderer, Martin Arkenhout, who kills an art historian, Christopher Hart, but also assumes his victim's life, taking up the deceased's travels in Portugal. However, Arkenhout is himself pursued by John Costa.

Literature. Literary works relating to Portugal published in English

Costa is pursuing the real Hart, who is suspected of stealing a valuable manuscript. The hunter becomes the hunted and the novel ends with an unexpected twist.

619 A small death in Lisbon.
Robert Wilson. London: Harper Collins, 1999. 439p. map.

In this thriller the explanation for a murder in the late 1990s is found to be rooted in the 1941 activities of the German SS in Lisbon. At that time the Germans were fictitiously, if not in reality, involved in the activities of a Portuguese bank. As well as evoking wartime Lisbon, the storyline also encompasses the 1974 Portuguese Revolution.

620 The last Kabbalist of Lisbon.
Richard Zimler.   Woodstock, New York; New York: The Overlook Press, 1997. 318p.

An historical mystery story, supposedly recently found in a cellar in Istanbul. The novel is set in the 16th century in Portugal and tells of the death of one Abraham Zarco, a Lisbon kabbalist, who is found dead in a room with a young woman. His nephew, Berekiah, sets about resolving this mysterious situation against a backdrop of Jewish persecution during the reign of King Manuel I.

William Beckford & Portugal.
See item no. 130.

Bulletin of Hispanic Studies.
See item no. 725.

Hispania.
See item no. 728.

Luso-Brazilian Review.
See item no. 731.

Portuguese Literary and Cultural Studies.
See item no. 733.

Portuguese Studies.
See item no. 735.

Tesserae.
See item no. 739.

Portuguese language and Luso-Brazilian literature.
See item no. 746.

Literature. Festschriften

A new bibliography of the Lusophone literatures of Africa. Nova bibliografia das literaturas africanas de expressão portuguesa.
See item no. 755.

Festschriften

621 Portuguese, Brazilian and African studies: studies presented to Clive Willis on his retirement.
Edited by T. F. Earle, N. H. Griffin. Warminster, England: Aris & Philips, 1995. 410p.

A *Festschrift* dedicated to the former Professor of Portuguese at the University of Manchester, Clive Willis. It has five sections on 'Language', 'Medieval Portugal', 'Portugal and Europe in the early modern period', 'The eighteenth and nineteenth centuries' and 'The Portuguese-speaking world in the twentieth-century'. The breadth of these studies reflects the diversity of Willis's areas of expertise. The volume is completed by an 'Afterword' on 'Manchester's Hispanic connections, 1874-1939'.

622 Studies in Portuguese literature and history in honour of Luís de Sousa Rebelo.
Edited by Helder Macedo. London: Tamesis Books, 1992. 209p. bibliog. (Colección Tamesis, Serie A, Monografías, no. 147).

A collection of nineteen essays, eight in English, the rest in Portuguese, comprising a *Festschrift* to the distinguished Portuguese literary scholar, Luís de Sousa Rebelo, who spent many years as an academic at King's College London. The contributions, by British, North American, Brazilian and Portuguese academics, range over Portuguese literary history from the mediaeval to the contemporary era. A bibliography of the works of Rebelo completes the publication.

Arts

Visual arts

General

623 The Berardo Collection.
Sintra, Portugal: Sintra Museum of Modern Art, 1996. 418p.
The José Berardo Collection is the nucleus of the newly established Sintra Museum of Modern Art, located in the royal town of Sintra on the outskirts of Lisbon. The Collection, amassed from 1992, consists of world art produced from 1945 onwards. This volume includes essays by Sarah Wilson, Marco Livingstone, Ann Hendry, Robert Rosenblum and Alexandre Melo, as well as a foreword by José Berardo himself. Following these texts the bulk of the volume is taken up by numerous colour plates of works by, amongst others, Andy Warhol, Cindy Sherman and Francesco Clements. Biographies and exhibition histories of some 200 artists represented in the collection are also provided.

624 English art in Portugal.
Alice Berkeley, Susan Lowndes. Lisbon: Edições Inapa, 1994. 155p. bibliog. (Collection [sic] História da Arte).
One hundred and forty fine colour illustrations illuminate this well-researched and innovative study of English art in Portugal. The writers cover some 800 years of Anglo-Portuguese contact and genres as diverse as painting, furniture, architecture and ceramics. The text weaves the artistic examples into a narrative which also reveals the long history of Anglo-Portuguese relations. Amongst the subjects addressed are Catherine of Braganza, the British community in Oporto, 18th and 19th-century British travellers to Portugal and visits to Portugal by British royalty.

The Arts. Visual arts. General

625 Nove: nine Portuguese painters.
John Hansard Gallery. Southampton, England: John Hansard Gallery, 1986. unpaginated.

The Director of the John Hansard Gallery, Barry Barker, has here selected individual works by nine contemporary Portuguese artists to capture the essence of that country's modern painting. Whilst one of those chosen, Paula Rego, has now become a household name, the remainder – Pedro Casqueiro, Ilda David, Álvara Lapa, Graça Morais, Pedro Portugal, Pedro Proença, Pedro Cabrita Reis and Ruth Rosengarten – will not generally be known to an international audience. One work of each artist is here reproduced in colour. Prefatory essays by Eugénio Lisboa on 'Portuguese art at home and abroad' and by Manuel Villaverde Cabral on 'Authentication, democracy and modernity in Portugal' complete the volume.

626 The sacred and the profane: Josefa de Óbidos of Portugal, 1630-1684.
Josefa de Óbidos, edited by Maria de Lourdes Simões de Carvalho, Jordana Pomeroy, translated by Elisabeth Plaister, Gary Vessels, Hilde M. Novais. Lisbon, Washington, DC: Ministério da Cultura, Gabinete de Relações Internacionais/ The National Museum of Women in the Arts, 1997. 190p.

The catalogue of an exhibition of the work of Portugal's major female artist of the 17th century, organized by the Portuguese Gabinete de Relações Externas and the National Museum of Women in the Arts, and held at the National Gallery, Washington, DC in 1994. The exhibition was subsequently mounted in London. This volume comprises four essays and the catalogue, which includes numerous colour reproductions. Josefa de Ayala y Cabrera, though born in Seville in 1630, lived in Óbidos, central Portugal, from 1634. She died in 1684, having spent most of her life in a convent and, consequently, most of her pictures have religious themes, though she did also paint portraits for the Portuguese royal family of King Pedro II (1667-1706).

627 The age of the baroque in Portugal.
Edited by Jay A. Levenson. Washington, DC: National Gallery of Art; New Haven, Connecticut: Yale University Press, 1993. 303p. bibliog.

Produced to mark the first exhibition ever held in the United States of art exhibits taken solely from Portuguese collections. It includes eleven essays by experts in their respective fields, including the historian Kenneth Maxwell and the art critics Angela Delaforce and Helmut Wohl. The essays cover a diverse range of topics, including royal coaches, sculpture, 18th-century thought, Lisbon and Pombal, Baroque architecture, jewellery, the court at Queluz and silver table services. There follows a catalogue of the exhibition with colour photographs and accompanying details of each item. Furniture, jewellery, ceramics and sculptures are included amongst the exhibits.

628 The 25th of April in the Portuguese public art: forms of freedom.
Arlindo Mota, photographs by Pedro Soares. Lisbon: Published by the Authors, 1999. 166p.

During almost fifty years of authoritarian rule and censorship during the Salazar years, public art in Portugal was largely confined to unadventurous representations, often with nationalistic overtones. Produced in the twenty-fifth anniversary year of the liberating 1974 Revolution in Portugal, this large-format colour compendium shows many examples of modern Portuguese public art, created to commemorate the country's new freedom.

629 Who's who of the artists in Portugal: a biographical dictionary.
André Jean Paraschi. Torres Novas, Portugal: Sol Invictus, with the support of the Instalation [sic] Committee of the Institute of Contemporary Art/ Ministry of Culture, 1997. 96p.

The admirable intention of this volume, to provide a directory of contemporary Portuguese artists for an international audience, is let down by very poor use of English and copious errors in spelling. The first half of the volume comprises a directory of artists, many accompanied by monochrome photographs, and a selection of examples of the artists' signatures. The latter half of the volume consists of colour reproductions of works by many of the artists in question.

Paula Rego

General

630 The dancing ostriches from Disney's 'Fantasia'.
Paula Rego, introduction by Sarah Kent, essay by John McEwen. London: Saatchi Collections, 1996. various paginations.

Paula Rego was born in 1935 and after an education at the British St Julian's School at Carcavelos, near Lisbon, she was trained at the Slade School of Art in London in the 1950s. From 1976 she settled permanently in London. In this volume, inspired by Walt Disney's 'Fantasia', Rego's interpretation of the theme is typically striking. Her 'ostriches' are sturdy middle-aged women incongruously dressed in ill-fitting black tutus. The sequence of Rego's paintings on this theme is here reproduced in colour, following introductory essays by Sarah Kent and John McEwen.

631 Dog woman, 1994.
Paula Rego. London: Marlborough Fine Art (London) Ltd, 1994. unpaginated.

Devoid of any accompanying text, this is a colour catalogue of fourteen of Rego's pictures. These feature women, either singly or in pairs, mostly in slightly unusual postures such as leaning over a wall, sleeping or squatting.

The Arts. Visual arts. Paul Rego. Critical works

632   Nursery rhymes, 23 November-22 December 1989.
Paula Rego.   London: Marlborough Fine Art Ltd, Graphics Gallery, 1989. 31p. (Catalogue no. 7).
An illustrated catalogue of Rego's pictures drawn to accompany English nursery rhymes, the texts of which are also reproduced. A more extensive review on the same theme is to be found in *Nursery rhymes*, with an introduction by Marina Warner (London: Thames & Hudson, 1994. 70p.), which comprises twenty-six traditional English nursery rhymes. Each double-page spread comprises the text on the left and a print by Rego on the right. Most are monochrome, but a few are coloured illustrations. The rhymes include 'Humpty Dumpty', 'Jack and Jill' and 'Little Miss Moffat', while the illustrations typically verge on the grotesque.

633   Paula Rego.
Paula Rego.   London: Tate Gallery Publishing, 1997. 152p. bibliog.
Born in Portugal in 1935, Rego studied at the Slade School of Art in London before finally settling in London in 1976. This volume was published to accompany an exhibition of her output between 1959 and 1995, held in 1997, initially at the Tate Gallery, Liverpool and then at the Centro Cultural de Belém in Lisbon. It includes many of her drawings as well as full-colour photographs of many of her paintings. Four introductory essays by Fiona Bradley, her husband Victor Willing, Ruth Rosengarten and Judith Collins cast light on her approach to art, which has been termed 'gestural automatism'.

634   Pendle witches: a suite of twelve etchings with poems by Blake Morrison.
Paula Rego, Blake Morrison.   London; New York: Marlborough Graphics, 1996. 16p. (Catalogue no. 29).
This collaborative work is the catalogue of an exhibition held in London in October and November 1996 and then transported to New York for a show running from December 1996 to January 1997. The exhibition theme derives from the legendary Pendle witches of Lancashire, England.

635   Peter Pan & other stories.
Paula Rego.   London: Marlborough Fine Art, 1992. unpaginated.
Based on nursery rhyme themes, this is a collection of watercolour and ink-on-paper drawings produced by Paula Rego during 1992. The pictures are thus reproduced in a mixture of colour and monochrome. There is no textual elucidation of the works.

Critical works

636   Paula Rego: paintings 1982-83.
Edward Totah Gallery.   London: Edward Totah Gallery; Bristol, England: Arnolfini; Milan, Italy: Studio Marconi, c.1982. unpaginated.
Some of Paula Rego's early works, exhibited in Bristol in 1983 and in Milan and London in 1984, are covered in this sixteen-page review. Of the twenty-two works exhibited, nine

are reproduced here with 'transmuted' animals being the most recurrent theme. The introduction is by Rego's husband, Victor Willing.

637 Paula Rego: tales from the National Gallery.
Essays by Germaine Greer, Colin Wiggins. London: National Gallery Publications, 1991. 40p.

In 1990 Paula Rego was appointed the first National Gallery Associate Artist and this publication both acknowledges that fact and was produced to accompany a touring exhibition of England, from London to Plymouth, Manchester, Barnsley and back to the capital. The book includes sketches for paintings as well as colour reproductions of finished works. A brief biography of Rego is also provided.

638 Paula Rego: selected works 1981-1986. Gweithiau detholedig. A touring exhibition organised by Aberystwyth Arts Centre and Edward Totah Gallery, London. Arddangosfa deithiol a drefnwyd gan Ganolfan y Celfyddydau Aberystwyth a Oriel Edward Totah.
Alistair Hicks. Aberystwyth, Wales: Aberystwyth Arts Centre, 1987. unpaginated.

A parallel text in Welsh and English produced to accompany one of Paula Rego's first major British exhibitions which visited Barnsley, Cardiff, Brighton and Aberystwyth in 1987-88. Colour and monochrome illustrations illuminate Hicks' text which points out how Rego's paintings are characterized by their story-telling content. Also in 1988, Rego exhibited in London and forty-five colour reproductions of her works from the 1953-88 period are collected in *Paula Rego, Serpentine Gallery 15 October-20 November 1988* (London: The Serpentine Gallery, 1988. 64p.). They are accompanied by a revealing interview with John McEwen in which the artist discusses her fear of the outdoors.

639 Paula Rego.
John McEwen. London: Phaidon Press, 1997. 2nd ed. 288p. bibliog.

A large-format survey of the art of the London-based Portuguese artist Paula Rego, arranged into twelve chapters, and supplemented by an epilogue, interviews and two appendices. The appendices comprise essays by the artist Victor Willing (Rego's husband), written originally to accompany catalogues of exhibitions of her work. The volume is replete with colour reproductions of Rego's output. The first edition of this publication appeared in 1992.

The Arts. Decorative arts

Other artists

640   **Modern art in Portugal, 1910-1940: the artist contemporaries of Fernando Pessoa.**
John B. Serra, Fernando Guimarães, Fernando Cabral Martins, Paulo Henriques, Ana Isabel Ribeiro.   Kilchberg, Zurich, Switzerland: Édition Stemmle, 1998. 335p. bibliog.

The catalogue of an exhibition held in Frankfurt and Lisbon in 1997/98. Its prime stimulus was the 1997 Frankfurt International Book Fair, whose theme was 'Portugal in the 20th century'. Two-thirds of this volume comprises colour photographs of Portuguese artistic output from 1910 to 1940. The accompanying text describes the chaos ensuing after the 1910 Portuguese Revolution and the establishment of the *Estado Novo* of Salazar following the military take-over in 1926. There is also an account of the literary and cultural developments of this era, as well as biographical information on the artists represented in the book. The link with Pessoa suggested by the title is somewhat tenuous.

641   **Vieira da Silva, 1908-1992: the quest for an unknown space.**
Gisela Rosenthal.   Cologne, Germany: Taschen, 1998. 96p.

Maria Elena Vieira da Silva was a noted abstract painter and acquaintance of Matisse and Braque whose marriage to the Hungarian artist, Arpad Szenes, deprived her of her Portuguese citizenship. The volume recounts her life and developing talent from her early years in Lisbon through more than fifty years spent in exile, which included two spells in Paris and one in Rio de Janeiro. Many of her works are reproduced here in colour and monochrome amongst the book's 148 illustrations. A chronology of her life completes the volume.

Decorative arts

642   **Joalharia portuguesa. Portuguese jewellery.**
Rui Guedes, texts by Nuno Vasallos e Silva, translated by Richard Trewinnard.   Lisbon: Bertrand, 1995. 160p. bibliog.

A large-format book, full of colour photographs, which describes itself as 'a tour of Portuguese jewellery'. It embraces both ecclesiastical pieces and secular items, accompanied by a descriptive text.

643   **Namban lacquerware in Portugal: the Portuguese presence in Japan, 1543-1639.**
M. H. Mendes Pinto.   Lisbon: Edições Inapa, 1990. 127p.

Translated from *Lacas namban em Portugal: presença português no Japão*, this is a study of Namban lacquerware, which was decorated with gold and silver dust and encrusted with mother-of-pearl ornamentation. The text covers the Edo Period (1600-1868) and the Portuguese influence on lacquerware production. *Namban-jin* was the Japanese term for

The Arts. Ceramics

the 'uncivilised southerners', namely the Portuguese traders with whom they dealt. Excellent colour photographs show many examples of Namban chests, boxes and other containers. By the same author is *Namban screens* (Lisbon: Museu Nacional de Arte Antiga, 1986).

644 Design aus Portugal: eine Anthologie. Design from Portugal: an anthology.
Sociedade Portugal Frankfurt S.A. Stuttgart, Germany; London: Edition Axel Menges, 1998. 344p. bibliog.

Produced to commemorate the 1998 Frankfurt International Fair, whose theme was Portugal, this large book surveys a wide range of Portuguese artistic design. Amongst the items portrayed are cutlery, lighting units, domestic utensils and jewellery. Preceding a catalogue which comprises full-colour photographs of each artefact opposite brief descriptive details, a textual section reviews Portuguese design in which, as one writer states, 'functional austerity prevails'.

Ceramics

645 Chinese export porcelain from the Museum of Anastácio Gonçalves, Lisbon.
Maria Antónia Pinto de Matos. London: Philip Wilson; Lisbon: Instituto Português de Museus, 1997. 287p. bibliog.

Dr António Anastácio Gonçalves amassed one of the world's best Chinese porcelain collections at his home in the Avenidas Novas of Lisbon, its particular strength being its examples of Kraak ware. Three essays cover the porcelain trade, Chinese porcelain design and decoration, and the formation of Dr Gonçalves's collection. One hundred and fifty of the items are catalogued here, and all are finely illustrated by colour photographs.

646 Portuguese decorative tiles: azulejos.
Rioletta Sabo, Jorge Nuno Falcato, translated from the German by Russell Stockman, photographs by Nicolas Lemonnier. New York; London, Paris: Abbeville Press, 1998. 215p. bibliog.

A panorama of the Portuguese ceramic arts, richly illustrated by more than 200 colour photographs by Nicolas Lemmonier. The authors are, respectively, an art historian who has lived in Portugal for many years, and a travel guide. The origins of the *azulejo* in the traditions of the Chinese, Moors and Islamic peoples are explained, as are the techniques of production. Amongst the many buildings illustrated are the Royal Palace at Sintra, the Marquês da Fronteira's palace at Benfica, the S. Vicente de Fora church in Lisbon and various sites in the city of Setúbal.

The Arts. Plastic arts

647 **Decorative tiles of Luís Ferreira, 'Ferreira das Tabuletas', a Lisbon painter. Azulejaria de Luís Ferreira, 'Ferreira das Tabuletas', um pintor de Lisboa.**
Teresa Saporiti, translation by Margaret Kelting. Lisbon: Câmara Municipal de Lisboa, 1993. 232p. bibliog.

The work of the mid-19th-century ceramic artist, Luís Ferreira, is presented in parellel texts in English and Portuguese, in a profusely illustrated volume which uses full-colour photography throughout. Originally a sign-painter, Ferreira's designs frequently incorporated *naif* portrayals of animals, plants and figures but, as the book shows, he was also a keen imitator of classical scenes. His works include decoration at Lisbon's Palácio Trindade and Cervejaria Trindade (Trindade beerhall), the Palácio da Carreira at Santiago do Cacém, and various private residences in Lisbon and elsewhere. A brief biography completes the volume.

Plastic arts

648 **Escultura portuguesa. Portuguese sculpture.**
Sérgio Guimarães de Andrade, translated by Peter Ingham. Lisbon: CTT Correios, 1997. 271p. bibliog.

An attractive, all-colour volume with Portuguese and English texts throughout which, as it is published by the Portuguese Post Office's Collectors' Club, includes thirty commemorative stamps in a series depicting major examples of Portuguese sculpture. The works represented span the period from pre-Roman times to the present and exclude items held in private collections or which are otherwise of restricted accessibility. These works are presented in four unindexed sections covering, respectively, free-standing, tomb, architectural and outdoor sculptures.

649 **History of plastic arts.**
Maria Adelaide Miranda, Vítor Serrão, José Alberto Gomes Machado, Raquel Henriques da Silva, translated by Mário Pinheiranda. Lisbon: Comissariado para a Europália 91 Portugal/ Imprensa Nacional-Casa da Moeda, 1991. 203p. bibliog. (Synthesis of Portuguese Culture).

With seventy-six colour photographs of manifestations of the plastic arts, ranging from sculptures to ceramic tiles and paintings, this loosely-titled volume is actually a history of the Portuguese plastic arts, albeit in somewhat stilted English. Its four sections trace this vast subject from Visigothic and Roman times to 1990. A specific but magnificent example of the plastic arts is described and illustrated in *Portugal's silver service: a victory gift to the Duke of Wellington*, by Angela Delaforce and James Yorke, with a contribution from Jonathan Voak (London: Victoria & Albert Museum, 1992. 143p. bibliog.). This book depicts in five chapters of text and a multitude of both colour and monochrome illustrations, the sumptuous *Baixela da vitória* (Victory silver service) made in 1813-16 and given to the Duke of Wellington by the Portuguese nation in gratitude for

The Arts. Music

his pivotal role in ejecting the French from their country during the Peninsular War. Kept in Apsley House, the Duke's London residence, the silver service was designed by Domingos António de Sequeira, who is better-known as an accomplished painter.

Music

650 Opera in Portugal during the eighteenth century.
Manuel Carlos de Brito. Cambridge, England: Cambridge University Press, 1989. 254p. bibliog.
Developed from the author's 1985 thesis, this book has four parts, which unavoidably concentrate on the Portuguese royal house's role in the history of 18th-century opera. 'Opera during the reign of João V (1708-50)' and 'Court opera during the reign of José I (1750-77)' are the opening sections, before Brito addresses 'Court opera and music during the reign of Maria I (1777-92)'. Amongst those patronised by the royal court of João V of Portugal was Domenico Scarlatti. In contrast, the final part of the study is concerned with 'Commercial opera, 1760-93'. Eight contemporary illustrations of theatres and palaces are provided, together with a chronology of operas performed in Portugal during the 18th century.

651 Portugal e o mundo: o encontro de culturas na música. Portugal and the world: the encounter of cultures in music.
Salwa el-Shawan Castelo-Branco. Lisbon: Publicações Dom Quixote, 1997. 605p. bibliog.
This collection of twenty-three papers from the Sixth Colloquium of the International Council for Traditional Music is presented in both Portuguese and English, arranged into four parts. The first is 'Cross-cultural processes in music: Portugal and the world' and the second is 'Multiculturality and Portugueseness: aspects of Portuguese music history'. The final two parts cover 'Portugal in Asia' and 'Portugal, Africa and Brazil'. The authors are international experts in Portuguese music and brief biographies of them are provided.

652 The interpretation of 16th- and 17th-century Iberian keyboard music.
Macario Santiago Kastner, translated from the Spanish by Bernard Branchli. Stuyvesant, New York: Pendragon Books, 1987. 113p. bibliog. (Monographs in Musicology, no. 4).
Kastner points out that while most 16th- and 17th-century Iberian treatises were excellent as regards their treatment of principles and musical rules, they were weak when it came to interpretation. The eleven chapters of this survey address this problem and cover such topics as touch, fingering and articulation, slurs and syncopation, vibrato, rhythm and tempo, and repeats.

The Arts. Film and theatre

653 The new Grove dictionary of music and musicians.
Edited by Stanley Sadie. London: Macmillan, 1980. 20 vols. bibliog.
Volume 15 of this classic work of reference includes an entry on Portugal which, though brief (p. 139-48), provides a detailed overview of, firstly, so-called 'art music' by Robert Stevenson and, secondly, 'folk music' by Joanne B. and Ronald C. Purcell. Six photographs illustrate the article and a substantial bibliography is also provided. Volume 11 contains an entry on Lisbon (p. 24-26) which covers both its history and musical landmarks. In *History of Music* by Rui Vieira Nery, Paulo Ferreira de Castro, translated by Kenneth Frazer (Lisbon: Comissariado para a Európalia 91/ Imprensa Nacional-Casa da Moeda, 1991. 192p. bibliog. [Synthesis of Portuguese Culture]), Part 1 covers the mediaeval to baroque eras, whilst Part 2 addresses the modern era. Despite its title, it is a history of Portuguese rather than world music, and it boasts an extensive bibliography.

654 A history of the Portuguese fado.
Paul Vernon. Aldershot, England; Brookfield, Vermont; Singapore; Sydney: Ashgate, 1998. 114p. bibliog.
Fado has been the national popular music of Portugal since the latter part of the 19th century. Vernon provides a thorough review of the history and importance of the genre in Portugal, Brazil, Europe and America, paying particular attention to its dissemination by the mass media of television, radio, film and sound recordings. The book has nineteen illustrations and is also accompanied by a discography and a CD-ROM which contains twenty-four examples of the genre. Details are also provided of *fado* instruments and the social relevance of the music. In an otherwise admirable introduction to *fado* for English readers, the bibliography and the index are inconsistent with each other in their alphabetization of Portuguese names.

A poet's way with music.
See item no. 592.

The Lisbon traviata.
See item no. 616.

Film and theatre

655 Directory of Spanish and Portuguese film-makers and films.
Edited by Rafael de España. Trowbridge, England: Flick Books, 1994. 388p.
An alphabetical directory of Iberian film-makers of the period 1896 to 1994, which is necessarily selective. It includes directors active in Spain and Portugal rather than necessarily of Spanish or Portuguese nationality. Details of each director are provided which include lists of their films, both 'shorts' and 'features', with English as well as original titles. Artistic and commercial films are included and an index of more than 100

pages provides ready access by film title. A North American edition appeared in 1995 (New York: Greenwood Press, 388p.).

656 History of theatre.
Luíz Francisco Rebello, translated by Cândida Cadavez. Lisbon: Comissariado para a Europália 91-Portugal/ Imprensa Nacional-Casa da Moeda, 1991. 106p. bibliog. (Synthesis of Portuguese Culture).

Belying its general title, this book is entirely dedicated to the history of Portuguese theatre. Written by Portugal's leading theatrical commentator, it provides a chronological appraisal of its subject, illustrated by a number of photographs, mostly of play productions. It addresses all aspects of theatre, including marginal manifestations, such as children's theatre. An index of play titles would have been a useful addition. A useful survey of a period when censorship still restricted theatrical output is to be found in *Postwar Portuguese drama* by the Office of the Secretary of State for Information and Tourism (Lisbon: General Direction for Information, 1972. 31p. bibliog. [Portugal Today]). This small, illustrated volume is a useful record of activities of both individual authors and of student and other theatrical groups, such as the Cascais Experimental Theatre.

Dance and Costume

657 A window on folk dance, with special reference to the dances of the Iberian peninsula.
Lucile Armstrong, edited by Diki Gleeson. Huddersfield, England: Springfield Books Limited, 1985. 128p. bibliog.

Lucile Armstrong dedicated years to travelling and recording folk dances in Iberia. Here she records the origins and supposed meaning of Portuguese and Spanish dances, alongside notes on costume and musical instruments. In *10 dances from Portugal, collected in the country of origin* by Nigel and Margaret Allenby Jaffé (Skipton, England: Folk Dance Enterprises, 1988. unpaginated. [European Folk Dance Series]), the authors describe the steps and formation of the dances, with the aid of small diagrams. Unfortunately they provide no details of the region or era from which the dances emanate. By the same authors is the wonderfully idiosyncratic *My Portuguese workbook* (Skipton, England: Folk Dance Enterprises, 1988. 34p. maps. [European Folk Dance Series]). This is a fascinating hotch-potch of information on Portuguese folklore and folk dance. After a description of the country and its regions, Portuguese folk dancing is surveyed. Drawings of traditional costumes and an account of local customs and folktales follow, including a retelling of the legend of the Barcelos cock. The latter part of the book is even more diverse with recipes (including ones for Algarve almond mice and Portuguese rice pudding), together with directions for making items such as a mobile of the Barcelos cock, an embroidered handkerchief and a Portuguese bag.

658 History of dance.
José Sasportes, António Pinto Ribeiro, translated by Joan Ennes. Lisbon: Comissariado para a Európália 91 Portugal/ Imprensa Nacional-Casa da Moeda, 1991. 139p. bibliog. (Synthesis of Portuguese Culture).

The first part of this volume, by Sasportes, traces the history of Portuguese dance from the Middle Ages to the formation of a national Portuguese dance company in 1960. In part two, Ribeiro covers the 1965-90 period, including a history of twenty years of the

Dance and Costume

Gulbenkian Ballet (1965-85). An extensive tabular appendix lists all choreographic works danced in Portugal by Portuguese groups between 1940 and 1990.

659 Military dress of the Peninsular War.
Martin Windrow, with 100 colour paintings by Gerry Embleton. London: Windrow & Greene, 1997. 200p. maps. bibliog.

An attractive large-format landscape volume which covers the uniforms of both sets of forces involved in the Peninsular War conflict in the early 19th century. The fine colour paintings clearly show the attire but the accompanying text also serves to give an account of the War, arranged in chronological order of the various campaigns in Portugal and Spain. The modern era is covered by *Portugal élite forces insignia, 1951-present*, by Robert Bragg and Harry Pugh (Arlington, Virginia: C&D Enterprises, c.1995. 138p. bibliog. [Élite Insignia Guides, no. 5]). This is an illustrated guide to the insignia worn by the front-line specialist units of the Portuguese armed forces, including airborne troops and commandos. The volume is of use both to military historians and to modellers.

Customs and Fairytales

660 The hegemonic male: masculinity in a Portuguese town.
Miguel Vale de Almeida. Providence, Rhode Island; Oxford: Berghahn Books, 1996. 186p. bibliog.
The author, a Portuguese academic, went to live in Pardais in the Alentejo area of central, southern Portugal, to study the role of the male in this marble-producing area. He found that the model of the hegemonic male, socially dominant, monogamous and heterosexual, exercises a strong control over males and ritualizes behaviour to a degree which can impoverish men's lives.

661 In and out of enchantment: blood symbolism and gender in Portuguese fairytales.
Isabel Cardigos. Helsinki: Suomalainen Tiedeakatemia/ Academia Scientiarum Fennica, 1996. 270p. bibliog. (FF Communications, vol. CXV, no. 260).
This study is divided into two parts. The first addresses the theoretical and methodological aspects while the second assesses four examples of traditional European fairytales as found in the canon of Portuguese folklore. The four studies address the themes of 'The twins, or blood brothers', 'Faithful John', 'The snake helper' and 'The girl as helper in the hero's flight'. Above all, the author seeks to assess the feminine voice in the predominantly male fairytale discourse.

662 Tales and legends of Portugal.
Emily George. Lisbon: Published by the Author, 1983. 108p.
Emily George here reproduces seven Portuguese folktales which she chose as being characteristic of the national temperament, entertaining and relating to places in Portugal which visitors may know. Those selected are the legends of St Vincent's crows, the almond blossom of the Algarve, the stag of Nazaré, the Coimbra miracle, the dead queen of Alcobaça, the great architect of Batalha and the last bullfight in the Ribatejo. These are recounted in modern English in chronological order of the events they relate, dating from the 4th to the 18th century.

Customs and Fairytales

Nursery rhymes.
See item no. 632.

Food and Drink

663 The food of Portugal.
Jean Anderson. New York: Hearst Books, 1994. 304p. map. bibliog.

A new edition of a work first published in 1987 (London: Robert Hale) and illustrated by the North American author's own excellent colour photographs. It is based on her numerous visits to Portugal made over a thirty-three-year period, which encompassed experiencing the food and drink of all social strata and regions of the country. The first quarter of the book comprises general information concerning the country and its cuisine; the remainder of the volume, entitled 'The best of Portuguese cooking', consists of clearly laid-out recipes in the following categories: appetizers and condiments; soups; meats; poultry; fish and shellfish; vegetables; rice and salads; breads; and sweets.

664 Portuguese cookery.
Ursula Bourne. Harmondsworth, England: Penguin Books, 1973. 122p.

An unashamedly British perspective on Portuguese cuisine is provided here, with allowance made for the unavailability of some of the typically Portuguese ingredients of certain recipes. Unfortunately, the British origins of the books are also responsible for a number of errors in the use of Portuguese names and terminology. For North American cooks, *Uma casa portuguesa: Portuguese home cooking*, by Carla Azevedo (Toronto, Canada: Summerhill Press, 1990. 208p.) is an illustrated introduction to traditional Portuguese cuisine, written by a Canadian chef whose husband is Portuguese. The terminology and weights and measures employed in the recipes are North American rather than British.

Food and Drink

665 Practical cookery: Portuguese home cookery. A small manual of Portuguese home cooking.
Délia Brandão.   Estarreja, Portugal: Moderna Editorial Lavora, c.1998. 210p.

Like her British namesake, Delia Smith, the author of this attractive hardback guide to Portuguese cookery provides concise, no-nonsense recipe instructions. These are arranged into categories such as soups, fish and desserts, which are illustrated by colour photographs.

666 A guide to the Douro and to Port wine.
Manuel Carvalho, itineraries by Álvaro Costa, English version by Magdalena Gorrell Guimaraens.   Oporto, Portugal: Afrontamento, c. 1995. 234p. maps. bibliog.

An attractively colourful guide to the viticulture of the Douro region. The text comprises four unnumbered sections. The first, 'Getting acquainted with the Douro', describes the region; the next, 'Three centuries of Port wine', supplies historical detail. The final two chapters, entitled 'From the terraces to the glass' and 'Suggested itineraries', describe the wine-making process and supply suggestions of where to go, complete with hotel, restaurant and other practical details which are essential in these areas, as they often lie off the beaten track.

667 The Factory House at Oporto.
John Delaforce.   Bromley, England: Christopher Helm in association with Christie's Wine, 1990. 116p. bibliog.

Describing itself as a 'bicentenary edition', a reference to the age of the Factory House at Oporto, which was the commercial and social hub of the expatriate British community in that city, this informed account of its history is written by a member of one of the leading port wine shipping companies. Indeed, the Factory House was dominated by expatriate port shippers and its history is an integral part of the Portuguese wine trade. Illustrated by black-and-white photographs, this account reflects the rise and fall of the Oporto wine trade and the social role of the Factory House for the city's expatriate community.

668 Entrée to the Algarve.
Allan Edwards.   London: Quiller Press, 1994. 164p. map. (A Gatwick Eat and Sleep Guide).

Following some brief information on Portuguese food and related topics, such as cork, this volume offers a guide to the hotels and restaurants of the Algarve, presented as a travel guide through the various districts.

669 The cooking of Spain and Portugal.
Peter S. Feibleman, and the editors of Time-Life Books, photographed by Dmitri Kessel, Brian Seed.   The Netherlands: Time-Life International (Nederland) BV, 1973. 208p. + 110p. (Foods of the World).

Illustrated throughout by colour photographs, which show places as much as cuisine, this book has two chapters which address Portuguese cooking. The text is based on the

Food and Drink

author's own experiences in Portugal, which include an upper-class dinner party in Lisbon. The most notable feature of the work is its separate 110-page paperback booklet entitled 'Recipes, the cooking of Spain and Portugal' which repeats the sixty-six recipes included in the main hard-back volume and adds a further thirty-nine new ones. The avowed purpose of this supplementary volume is to facilitate use of the recipes in the kitchen itself.

670 Port wine quintas of the Douro.
Alex Liddell, photographs by Janet Price. London: Sotheby's Publications, 1992. 232p. maps. bibliog.

This is the first English-language study of the history, function and sociology of the port wine *quintas* of the Douro valley in northern Portugal. The *quinta* is the lodge which orchestrates the cultivation and production of the grapes in the upper valley before its transportation to Vila Nova de Gaia and Oporto for completion of the maturation process. In this beautifully illustrated book, which has numerous colour photographs, the *quintas* are presented in three geographical areas: the lower and upper Corgo valleys and the upper Douro valley. Four appendices include lists of each shipper's *quintas*, a glossary of Portuguese wine terminology and advice on visiting the area as well as statistical details.

671 Port to port.
Edited by Lisa Linder. London: LB, 1996. 191p.

A book whose central concept is based on the dual meaning of the word 'port'. It thus consists of essays by various authors on the use of port wine in the cuisine of various port cities of the world, including London, Venice, Antwerp and New York. Recipes are provided for each dish encountered and the volume also has a chapter on 'Literary port' which includes quotations about the drink from literature. There is also coverage of the wine's production in the Douro valley and its role in Portugal itself.

672 Gastronomy of Spain and Portugal.
Maite Manjón. London: Garamond, 1990. 320p. maps. bibliog.

The core of this book (p. 17-305) is entitled 'Illustrated dictionary of Spanish and Portuguese gastronomy', a title which underlines its structure. It comprises alphabetical entries for gastronomic terms relating to Iberia, although some curious terms merit entries, such as 'Francia' (the Spanish word for France) and 'Ford, Richard', the 19th-century British traveller. There are also, inevitably, quite a number of cross-references from Portuguese to equivalent terms in Spanish. Colour photographs show the countryside as well as some of the dishes described in the text; many line drawings further enhance the text.

673 The home book of Portuguese cookery.
Maite Manjón. London: Faber & Faber, 1974. 164p.

Divided into three sections, the third part is by the author's husband, Jan Read, and addresses 'Portuguese wines'. Part I, 'The recipes', and Part II, 'Marketing, cooking and eating out in Portugal', provide a brief general introduction to Portuguese cooking. Manjón seeks to give the visitor to Portugal practical information on buying food and sampling new dishes rather than solely concentrating on recipes for readers to try in their own homes.

Food and Drink

674 Portugal's wines and wine-makers: port, Madeira and regional wines.
Richard Mayson.   London: Ebury Press, 1992. 229p. maps. bibliog.

The author's aim here is 'to explain why Portuguese wines are different. The reasons are both good and bad'. The eighteen chapters provide clear explanations of the methods of cultivation and production before expanding in some detail on the table wines of the individual regions of the country. There are also chapters on port and Madeira wine, rosés and sparkling wines. The volume has a small number of drawings to illustrate cultivation techniques but contains no photographs.

675 The wines of Spain & Portugal.
Charles Metcalfe, Kathryn McWhirter.   London; New York: Salamander Books, 1988. 160p. maps. bibliog.

An attractive colourful guide to Iberian wines, whose Portuguese section (p. 110 *et seq.*) provides an introduction to the grape types and the products of the various regions of Portugal. Each section includes colour photographs of the region and of labels of typical products, together with maps. Recommendations of specific wines are made for each region.

676 Traditional Portuguese cooking.
Maria de Lourdes Modesto, photographs by H. Cabrito, A. Homem Cardoso.   Lisbon: Verbo, 1982. 333p.

A comprehensive guide to the cuisine of Portugal by one of that country's most famous cooks. It is a translation of her *Cozinha tradicional portuguesa* (1982) and its large hardback format renders it a little impractical for kitchen use. Nevertheless, it is packed with recipes and attractive colour illustrations which make it a useful source of culinary inspiration as well as an attractive guide to the regional as well as the national dishes of Portugal.

677 The food of Spain and Portugal: the complete Iberian cuisine.
Elizabeth Lambert Ortiz.   Oxford: Lennard Publishing, 1989. 290p. map. bibliog.

Unusually for books on Spanish and Portuguese cuisine there are not separate sections on each country in this book. Instead, after an historical introduction which stresses the cuisine-related aspects of the two countries' expansionist periods, there are eleven themed chapters on topics which include soups, fish, meat and rice dishes. A number of colour photographs record representations of food in art and line drawings further illustrate the text. The index includes Spanish and English as well as Portuguese terms for the dishes described.

678 The Century companion to the wines of Spain and Portugal.
Jan Read.   London: Century Publishing, 1983. 5 maps. bibliog.

A revised edition of Read's *Guide to the wines of Spain and Portugal* (London: Pitman, 1977. 126p. 4 maps) and distinct from his *The wines of Spain and Portugal* (London: Faber & Faber, 1973. 280p. 4 maps. bibliog.), for details of which see the *Lisbon* volume in the World Bibliographical Series, vol. 199, 1997, item no. 541. Five chapters of this 1983 title are devoted to Portugal, entitled 'The land and history', 'What the wines are',

Food and Drink

'Control and labelling', 'The regions' and 'Regional cooking'. Read's comments are based on numerous vineyard visits and he also provides advice to readers on how to organize their own itinerary.

679 The wines of Portugal.
Jan Read. London; Boston, Massachusetts: Faber & Faber, 1987. rev. ed. 190p. 3 maps. bibliog.

A new edition of a work first published in 1982 which takes into account new technology in Portuguese wine-making, as well as company mergers, reorganization and foundations since that date. This new edition also has many colour photographs to supplement those in monochrome. The ten chapters cover port and Madeira wine as well as the demarcated regions for table wine production. There are also chapters on rosé and sparkling wines as well as on Portuguese cork and the cuisine to accompany the wines.

680 Portuguese cooking: the authentic and robust cuisine of Portugal. Journal and cookbook.
Text and illustrations by Carol Robertson, photographs by David Robertson. Berkeley, California: North Atlantic Books, 1993. 166p.

This book is, in fact, part travelogue and part cookery book, illustrated by the author's drawings and her husband's photographs. The first part, 'Stories of Portugal', recounts the Robertsons' travels through the regions of Portugal, while the latter section of the book comprises recipes which they encountered en route, supplemented by information on Portuguese wines and on Goan cuisine.

681 The port companion.
Godfrey Spence. London: Apple, 1998. 224p. maps. bibliog.

A very attractively presented guide to port wine, with numerous colour photographs. Part I comprises the history of port wine and part II is a port 'directory'. In this latter section numerous port shippers are listed and their products described. Spence's tasting notes provide added information on specific vintages.

682 The taste of Portugal: traditional Portuguese cuisine.
Edite Vieira. London: Grub Street, 1995. 2nd ed. 244p. map.

An unillustrated but, nevertheless, solid introduction to Portuguese cooking. It has chapters on soup, bread, fish, meat, sauces, vegetable accompaniments, sweet things and drinks. The first edition was published in 1988 (London: Robert Hale, 243p. map) and differs only from this edition in that a most useful extra page and a quarter has been added to the later version. This addition tells the reader where to obtain Portuguese produce and food in London, the city in which the Portuguese author resides.

Food and Drink

683 Portuguese cooking.
Hilaire Walden. London: Apple Press, 1994. Reprinted, 1997. 127p. (A Quintet Book).

A large-format book, finely illustrated by colour photographs. Following an introduction, there are chapters on soups, starters, fish and shellfish, meat and poultry, vegetables and salads, breads and sauces, cakes and desserts.

684 Self-catering in Portugal: making the most of local food and drink.
Carol Wright. London; Sydney: Croom Helm, 1986. 132p. bibliog.

In addition to providing recipes for regional dishes of Portugal, grouped according to whether two people, four to six, or larger groups are being fed, this eminently practical guide also addresses shopping for groceries, the seasonal availability of Portuguese produce and how to cater for babies, children and those on special diets. Carol Wright also covers eating out in restaurants and gives helpful practical advice on what to bring with you from home. An English-Portuguese glossary of food and drink terms is also provided.

Frederick William Flower.
See item no. 19.

John James Forrester.
See item no. 261.

How to eat out in Portugal & Brazil.
See item no. 347.

Sport

685 A Bola: Jornal de Todos os Desportos. (The Ball: Newspaper of all the Sports.)
Lisbon: Sociedade Vicra Desportiva, 1945- . daily.

Published in Lisbon, this sporting newspaper enjoys a combined weekly circulation of 153,682 (1996) which makes it the leading publication of its kind in the country. Although football is its major subject, it also carries news and pictures of a wide range of Portuguese and international sports, including cycling, tennis, hockey and rugby. Unlike British popular sports coverage, that of *A Bola* is passionate yet does not stray into sporting xenophobia or exposés of individuals' private lives. Traditionally it has held an alleged bias towards the Lisbon football team, Benfica.

686 European football: a fans' handbook.
Peterjon Cresswell, Simon Evans, edited by Dan Goldstein.
London: The Rough Guides, 1998. 604p. + 64p. (Rough Guides).

The major football clubs of the Lisbon and Oporto areas are covered (p. 399-420) in this sporting addition to the Rough Guide series. A brief historical survey of Portuguese football and its achievements precedes descriptions of the individual First Division clubs of Lisbon and Oporto. The text also includes details of local hostelries, restaurants and locations of grounds. The style is down to earth and honest and concentrates on unpretentious establishments where the visiting football fan will feel at home. The volume is lacking in coverage of other regions of Portugal and is also deficient, surprisingly, in statistical data. A sixty-four-page coloured-paper insert comprises an update for the 1998/99 season.

687 European football yearbook, 98/99.
Mike Hammond.   Warley, England: Sports Projects, 1998. 1,120p. map.

After an opening section which describes the previous season's European international matches and the outcomes of the various European team cup competitions, this book has sections on each European country. The section on Portugal gives an account of the

Sport

previous season's First Division football campaign, with the results and scorers for each team and the final league table. Club addresses and lists of honours are also provided for each team, although the information on the three teams promoted in 1998 is very scant indeed. A colour section illustrates the kits worn by each of the teams in the Division, as well the clubs' official badges.

688   O Jogo. (The Game.)
   Oporto, Portugal: Jornal Investe Comunicação, c.1985- . daily.

This Oporto-based sports newspaper also has a Lisbon edition which is a rival to the dominance in the capital of *A Bola* and *Record* (qq.v.). A tabloid, it uses colour on its front and back pages in editions of, typically, forty pages. It has a high photographic content and whilst football is, not surprisingly, its main focus, it also gives significant coverage to other sports, including non-Portuguese events like Tour de France cycling, grand prix motor racing and international athletics.

689   Cricket in Portugal.
   d'Arcy Orders.   Lisbon: Published by the Author, [1990]. 74p.

The length of Britain's historical links with Portugal has meant that cricket has gained a toehold in the Iberian peninsula. After early contacts between Royal Navy cricketers and local expatriates, regular matches have been played for well over a century between teams from Oporto and Lisbon with teams made up largely, but not exclusively, of expatriate Britons. Orders provides detailed statistics of such matches as well as a thorough account of the history of the game in Portugal.

690   Record.
   Lisbon: Edisport, c.1950- . thrice weekly.

A tabloid sports newspaper enjoying a circulation of 136,274 (1998). With good quality colour pictures on its front and back pages, it competes with *A Bola* and *O Jogo* (qq.v.) in its coverage of a vast range of sports, of which football is predictably the most fully documented. Typical issues comprise around forty pages.

691   Golf's golden coast: Algarve, the complete course guide.
   John Russell, photographs by Nuno Campos.   Lagoa, Portugal:
   Vista Ibérica Publicações, 1994. 203p. maps (An Insider's Guide).

A full-colour guide for the overseas visitor to seventeen golf courses in the Algarve which are illustrated by numerous photographs, as well as diagrams of the courses themselves.

692   The Tagus Golf Society, founded 1982: the first ten years.
   Estoril, Portugal: Estoril Golf Club, c.1992. 11p.

An account of the first decade of the expatriate Tagus Golf Society whose members are predominantly British expatriates or of British stock, although other nationalities are also represented. The Club competes against similar bodies based in the Douro (northern Portugal) and Vilamoura (Algarve) areas of Portugal. The text is supplemented by a full list of the winners of the Club's various cups and competitions from 1982 to 1991 inclusive.

Sport

Bungs, bribes and bad language.
See item no. 306.

Recreation

693 Gardens of Portugal.
Text by Patrick Bowe, photographs by Nicolas Sapieha.   London: Tauris Parke Books, 1989. 223p. map. bibliog.

A general survey of Portuguese gardens with full colour photographic illustrations throughout. Thirty-seven gardens are portrayed and described, of which thirteen are in the Lisbon area, fourteen in central and northern Portugal, five in the south of the country and a further five on the islands of Madeira and the Azores. Amongst those covered are the Solar de Mateus and other country-house gardens in northern Portugal, whilst botanical gardens are also represented, with examples from Coimbra and Lisbon (Ajuda and Estufa Fria).

694 Portuguese gardens.
Helder Carita, António Homem Cardoso.   Woodbridge, England: Antique Collectors' Club, 1990. 314p. bibliog.

A more academic approach to Portuguese gardens is provided here than in Bowe's work *Gardens of Portugal* (see item no. 693). In a work beautifully illustrated by the colour photographs of Homem Cardoso, Carita traces the fascinating history of the Portuguese garden from Graeco-Roman times, through the Islamic period and developments from the 16th century to the late 19th century. In the ten chapters of the book, there are discussions *inter alia* of formal gardens, ornamental gardens, the garden as a walk and the 19th-century scenic garden. The book's origins as a translation of a Portuguese original, *Jardins de Portugal*, are betrayed by its copious quotation of sometimes lengthy extracts from Portuguese commentators which are not furnished with an English translation.

695 Gardens of Spain and Portugal.
Barbara Segall.   London: Mitchell Beazley, 1999. 144p. 5 maps. bibliog.

Arranged by the regions of Iberia, with accompanying road maps showing the location of the gardens, this guide gives a wealth of practical information as well as a description of

Recreation

the sites. The section on Portugal covers forty-one gardens, each with colour illustrations (which include both drawings and photographs). As well as descriptions of the gardens, practical information such as opening times is also provided.

Libraries and Archives

696 ACLAIIR Newsletter.
London: Advisory Council on Latin American and Iberian Information Resources, 1992- . annual.
ACLAIIR is an organization which comprises British and Irish librarians and information workers, in approximately fifty institutions, who share an interest in Iberian or Latin American studies. The *Newsletter*, typically twenty-four pages in length, includes news from libraries across the United Kingdom as well as serving as an interchange of information on book suppliers, electronic resources, web addresses and staff activities.

697 Ponto da situação da aplicação das novas tecnologias de informação às bibliotecas e o seu impacto na actividade das bibliotecas em Portugal. State of the art of the application of new information technologies in libraries and their impact on library functions in Portugal.
BAD, Associação Portuguesa de Bibliotecários, Arquivistas e Documentalistas for the Commission of the European Communities. Brussels, Luxembourg: Directorate-General Telecommunications, Information Industries and Innovations, 1988. 162p.
This report contains an excellent English summary reviewing the Portuguese library scene which is seen as lacking, at the time of writing, in areas such as an inter-library loan network and a national catalogue. The findings are based on a survey and many of the individual libraries' returns are reproduced here in facsimile with an English glossary. 556 libraries were covered, including the national library, 167 academic libraries, 103 public libraries and 285 special or other libraries. Large strides in library technology have been made since 1998 with the development of the *Porbase* electronic union catalogue of Portuguese library holdings, which is now available on the internet.

Libraries and Archives

698 Libraries and library services in Portugal.
Nell Buller. Halifax, Canada: Dalhousie University, School of Library and Information Studies, 1988. 121p. 2 maps. bibliog. (Occasional Papers Series, no. 46).

A useful survey of the Portuguese library system which covers all sectors of the field, from the national, through the academic and public to the special and foreign-language libraries in Portugal. The national and other archives are also described and a wealth of practical information is provided for the intending user of the facilities. A number of illustrations and reproductions of library guides are included, but the quality of their printing is not high. A list of the most important Portuguese libraries is to be found in the *World guide to libraries*, edited by Willemina van der Meer (Munich, Germany: K. G. Saur, 1999, 14th ed., vol. 1, p. 542-47. [Handbook of International Documentation and Information, vol. 8]). This directory includes addresses and brief details of holdings.

699 Iberian resources in the United Kingdom: a directory of libraries.
J. F. Laidlar. London: Advisory Council on Latin American and Iberian Information Resources, 1996. 175p.

A directory of more than seventy libraries in the United Kingdom which have significant collections of Iberian material or which have English-language collections relating to Portugal or Spain. As well as giving each library's address, opening hours and contact details, each entry also provides information on the collections and on the general services, such as photocopying and computing facilities, which are offered to outside users. Most of the libraries are academic but national, public and special libraries are also represented.

700 Library of Congress Hispanic and Portuguese collections: an illustrated guide.
Library of Congress. Washington, DC: Library of Congress, 1996. 84p. bibliog.

A guide to the extensive Hispanic and Portuguese collections of the world's largest library, which is copiously illustrated by colour photographs of material from the collections. After a 'General Overview', there are chapters on 'Literature and Philosophy', 'The Arts' and 'The Hispanic and Portuguese World', followed by a section providing practical information for researchers and a list of publications on the Hispanic and Portuguese collections. Amongst the collections mentioned are the wealth of Portuguese manuscript material purchased between 1927 and 1929, the Portuguese pamphlets collection covering the period 1610-1921, Portuguese colonial maps and material relating to Camões and to the historical phenomenon of *Sebastianismo*.

Discovery in the archives of Spain and Portugal.
See item no. 221.

British Council libraries in Portugal.
See item no. 750.

Museums

701 Calouste Gulbenkian Museum catalogue.
Maria Teresa Gomes Ferreira.   Lisbon: Calouste Gulbenkian Foundation, 1989. 2nd rev. and enlarged ed. 399p.
Calouste Gulbenkian, an Armenian who made a fortune from the oil industry, resided in Portugal for many years following his categorization by Britain as an alien during the Second World War. His legacy to Portugal was the funding of the magnificent Museu Calouste Gulbenkian in Lisbon of which this is a colour-illustrated hardback catalogue. The collections are particularly strong in Egyptology and Lalique glass ware, although fine art, furniture and ceramics are also well represented.

702 Focus on the Portuguese-speaking world.
Museum (Paris), no. 161, pt. 1 (1989), p. 1-61.
This collection of articles, edited by Fernanda de Camargo e Almeida-Moro, is divided into sections on 'Objects', 'Places', 'People' and a couple of contributions on ecomuseums and African museums under the interrogative heading 'And the future?'. 'Objects' includes contributions on Lisbon's coach, tiles and theatre museums, while 'Places' addresses museums in Macao, Brazil and Angola as well as the Queluz royal palace and the Conimbriga Roman remains in Portugal itself. Articles on carnival and samba are to be found in the 'People' section.

703 Visita ao Museu Militar. Visit to the Military Museum.
Museu Militar.   Lisbon: Museu Militar, 1992. 20p.
Although the joint title of this work is 'Visit to the Military Museum', the English text, which follows the Portuguese, is entitled 'The history of the Military Museum'. Accompanied by eleven colour photographs, the text provides a brief guided tour of the former army foundry and arsenal in Lisbon which today houses an extensive collection of arms and related material. The rooms themselves are of architectural interest and have important paintings,

Museums

mostly from the 18th and 19th century, adorning their walls. The museum was built after the 1755 earthquake to replace the arsenal destroyed by that cataclysm.

Publishing

704 Pedro Craesbeeck & Sons: 17th century publishers to Portugal and Brazil.
H. Bernstein. Amsterdam, The Netherlands: Adolf M. Hakkert, 1987. 229p. bibliog.
The printer, Pedro Craesbeeck, came to Lisbon, via Spain, from the Low Countries in around 1597. He and his family operated in the city until 1690 and this volume gives a full account of their activities, which is supplemented by a substantial catalogue of their published output (p. 171-229).

705 European Bookseller.
Special edition, no. 22 (October 1997), 84p.
This edition of the journal, *European Bookseller*, is devoted to the Frankfurt Book Fair at which Portugal was the 'theme nation'. It includes seventeen articles on various aspects of Portuguese publishing, including literary, linguistic, gastronomic and children's publications. Useful details such as publishers' and booksellers' addresses are provided and the volume incorporates many monochrome photographs and reproductions of book covers. Of particular usefulness to English-speaking readers are two articles on modern Portuguese African writing, an area on which information can be difficult to find.

Livros disponíveis.
See item no. 754.

Children's Publications

706 Portugal.
Neil Champion. Hove, England: Wayland, 1995. 48p. 5 maps. bibliog. (Modern Industrial World).

A colourful, large-format book aimed at the secondary pupil. Its chapters include coverage of Portuguese history, environmental issues, tourism, agriculture and industry. A number of boxes of statistical information, as well as colourful maps, reinforce the text.

707 We go to Portugal.
Sylvia L. Corbridge. London; Toronto; Wellington; Sydney: Harrap, 1963. 186p. map. (The 'We Go' Series).

Arranged in eleven chapters, this fictional work tells the story of an English girl, Joy, whose sister, Philippa, wins an essay competition prize which pays for a trip to Portugal for the girls and their brother, Max. They visit locations all over Portugal from the Oporto area to the Algarve and through their travels they relate the history and geography of the country for a young readership. The text is accompanied by a number of black-and-white photographs and line-drawings of tourist sights.

708 Peeps at many lands: Portugal.
Agnes M. Goodall. London: A. & C. Black, 1929. 88p. map.

Illustrated by eight colour plates and a map, this introduction to Portugal for young people covers topics which emphasize the folkloric aspects of the country, such as dances, pilgrimages and songs.

709 The voyage of Magellan.
Richard Humble, Richard Hook. London: Franklin Watts, 1988. 32p. maps. (Exploration through the Ages).

This is a version of Magellan's circumnavigation journey, specially written for children. Of similar ilk are Rebecca Stefoff's *Ferdinand Magellan and the discovery of the world*, and *Vasco da Gama and the Portuguese explorers* (both published in New York: Chelsea

House, 1990. 112p. [World Explorers]). A brief study of Prince Henry the Navigator is to be found in H. G. A. Hughes's *The Infante D. Henrique: the historical figure and the figure in history* (Afonwen, Wales: Gwasg Gwenffrwd, 1991. 24 leaves).

Child workers in Portugal.
See item no. 494.

Newspapers

Newspaper directories

710 Willings press guide, 1999. 125th annual issue.
Teddington, England: Hollis Directories, 1999. 2 vols.
Volume two of this authoritative press directory includes coverage of Portugal (p. 716-30) and provides a succinct list of the country's newspaper and news magazine production. Details for each title include publisher's address, frequency of publication, circulation, cover price and content, although the amount of detail varies from one entry to the next. However, some major titles are missing altogether, such as the *Comércio do Porto*.

Individual newspapers

711 APN, the Anglo-Portuguese News: the paper for the international community in Portugal.
Estoril, Portugal: APN Publicações Lda, 1937- . weekly.
With a print-run of 8,500, the *APN* describes itself as 'Portugal's leading newspaper in English'. Very unfairly dismissed by the *Time Out* guide to Lisbon (see item no. 69) as an 'amateurish weekly that looks like a parish handout', the *APN* has sought to expand its readership to those outside the expatriate British community who were for many years its sole constituency. Issues normally comprise twenty pages, with colour photographs usually confined to the front page. Coverage includes BBC World Service schedules as well as news from, and of particular interest to, the Anglo-American community in Portugal.

712 O Comércio do Porto. (The Commerce of Oporto.)
Lisográfica. Oporto, Portugal: Lisográfica, 1854- . daily.

The longest-established daily newspaper of Portugal's second city of Oporto. Despite converting to tabloid format, it had become somewhat staid and its circulation had dropped as low as 12,000 by 1999. In April 1999 it underwent a major reinvestment programme, an increase in its journalistic staff and a drop in cover price, aimed at increasing circulation to 80,000. A link has also been forged with Lisbon's dynamic *Correio da Manhã*, whereby that paper's Sunday supplement is annexed by the *Comércio*.

713 Correio da Manhã. (Morning Post.)
Lisbon: Presselivre, 1979- . daily.

A tabloid with a striking red and white logo which, combined with use of large headlines, lively prose and colour photography, has made this one of Portugal's largest circulation newspapers with around 100,000 readers. Weekday issues (with around eighty pages) have thematic supplements on topics such as sport and health. The Sunday edition (c.144p.) includes a colour magazine. The paper's audience is chiefly young and middle-aged upper-working-class people and its coverage is largely of national news.

714 Diário da República. (The Portuguese Republic's Daily Newspaper.)
Lisbon: Imprensa-Nacional Casa da Moeda, 1974- . daily, except Sunday.

An official newspaper, published in three 'series', which itemize new government legislation and decrees (series I), provide regulations for public appointments (series II), and offer details of official tendering procedures, of municipal posts and of company matters (series III). An excellent introduction, in English, to Portuguese government publications is to be found in *Official publications of western Europe*, edited by Eve Johansson (London; New York: Mansell, 1988. 2 vols). Volume 2 has a thorough essay by Robert Howes on Portuguese official publications (p. 149-70) which also includes coverage of the legislative process, Portuguese legal codes, official gazettes and statistical publications.

715 Diário de Coimbra. (Coimbra Daily News.)
Coimbra, Portugal: Diário de Coimbra, 1930- . daily.

One of the best of Portugal's regional daily newspapers, emanating from Portugal's historic university city of Coimbra, in the centre of the country and enjoying a circulation of 11,500 (1999). The paper has a strong Republican tradition and was also important in the aftermath of the 1974 Revolution when its Sunday issue, entitled *Domingo* (Sunday), was briefly the leading Sunday publication in Lisbon itself. Sister daily papers from central Portugal include the *Diário de Aveiro* (Aveiro Daily News) and the *Diário de Leiria* (Leiria Daily News). Another notable regional daily is the *Diário As Beiras* (The Beiras Daily News), which also emanates from Coimbra, but which seeks to cover the wider area of the former provinces of Beira Litoral, Beira Baixa and Beira Alta.

Newspapers. Individual newspapers

716 Diário de Notícias. (Daily News.)
Lisbon: Diário de Notícias, 1864- . daily.

Lisbon's oldest surviving daily newspaper, the *Diário de Notícias* survived the vicissitudes of the 1974 Revolution and maintains a respectable, and rising, circulation of 76,000 (1998). A tabloid with colour photographs and graphics, the weekday issues include a themed supplement. The *Diário de Notícias* is a stolid production, strong on both international and national news, as well as sport.

717 Expresso. (Express.)
Lisbon: Grupo Controljornal, 1973- . weekly.

A bulky, multi-part quality newspaper whose foundation just before the 1974 Revolution gave it an independent credibility missing from its longer-established and more conservative rivals. It appears every Saturday and together with its supplements, the number of parts can run into double figures totalling 300 pages or more. Its circulation is 149,838 (1998), a figure which marks a decline of more than ten per cent since 1996. Coverage is particularly strong on politics and the arts.

718 O Independente: semanário de informação geral. (The Independent: general information weekly.)
Lisbon: O Independente, 1977- . weekly.

Founded in the post-1974 Revolutionary period, this weekly newspaper appears every Friday. It enjoyed a particular vogue in the early 1990s, when it was at the forefront of opposition to the government, but its circulation has now declined to 71,987 (1998). Its readership is predominantly middle- and upper-class and the paper's strengths are its political, economic and financial coverage.

719 Jornal de Notícias. (The News.)
Oporto, Portugal: Empresa do Jornal Notícias, 1888- . daily.

With a circulation of 160,300 (1998), this recently revamped Oporto daily newspaper is now a colourful stablemate of Lisbon's *Diário de Notícias* and, with both an Oporto and a Lisbon edition, is more readily available nationally than was the case for much of its history. Its format is slightly larger than a normal tabloid and each weekday issue is typically made up of sixty pages; the Sunday issue has a colour magazine jointly produced with the *Diário de Notícias*.

720 O Público. (The Public.)
Lisbon: O Público, 1990- . weekly.

With a steady readership (76,468 in 1998), this relative newcomer to the Portuguese press is a serious-minded newspaper which concentrates on politics, economics and the arts rather than more popular themes. Apart from a Sunday colour magazine, the paper is somewhat sober in appearance. Weekday issues are typically of sixty pages, with daily themed supplements.

721 24 Horas. (24 Hours.)
Lisbon: Edipresse Prodiário S.A., 1998- . daily.

A bright and colourful daily tabloid launched in early summer 1998. A typical issue comprises forty-eight pages with sixteen of these being colour printed to a fairly high quality. It has already gained a circulation of 80,000 which makes it an important title in the Portuguese daily press. Despite its light appearance, it is not a sensationalist publication and, indeed, its good use of colour graphics is matched by serious handling of major stories, including international news.

722 The Weekly News: Portugal's weekend newspaper in English.
Loulé, Portugal: The News Group of Newspapers, 1983?- . weekly.

Formerly entitled the *Algarve News* and still published in that region, this English-language newspaper has attempted to widen its appeal both by a change of title and by its creation of a website, called *The News* (http://www.nexus.pt.com/news/news.htm), which has stolen a march on its chief rival the *APN Anglo-Portuguese News* (see item no. 711). The printed version appears every Friday and contains news from Portugal and abroad aimed at the expatriate and tourist market and with a more North-American bent than APN. A typical issue comprises twenty-four pages and is illustrated with colour photographs on its outside pages and monochrome elsewhere.

Periodicals

723 ACIS: Journal of the Association for Contemporary Iberian Studies.
London: South Bank University, 1987- . thrice-yearly.
This journal of the Association for Contemporary Iberian Studies has been renamed since 1995 as the *International Journal of Iberian Studies*. It addresses socio-economic and political developments in the Peninsula, with articles in English and the Iberian languages. Book reviews are included as well as coverage of the ACIS's annual conferences and debates on the direction of Iberian studies as taught in academic institutions in the United Kingdom.

724 The British Historical Society of Portugal Annual Report and Review.
Lisbon: The British Historical Society of Portugal, 1974- . annual.
In recent years this title has become an important source of articles on Portuguese history, having started out as a slim annual report and newsletter. Issues vary in size but are typically 150 pages and the contributors are nowadays a mix of locally-based authorities and British academics, including such names as H. V. Livermore and R. C. Willis. Since the 1996 issue, a subject index has been included which covers all volumes of the periodical issued since 1974.

725 Bulletin of Hispanic Studies.
Glasgow, Scotland: University of Glasgow Press, 1923- . quarterly.
A bizarre situation has existed since 1996 when the Liverpool-based *Bulletin of Hispanic Studies*, Britain's leading journal in the field of Hispanic literature and language, was relocated by its editor to Glasgow against the wishes of its publisher, the University of Liverpool. Since then two periodicals, with the same title and volume numbering have appeared from Glasgow and Liverpool, producing a bibliographer's nightmare for citations. A legal ruling awarded Glasgow the right to retain the title's ISSN (International Standard Serial Number). Each journal covers Portuguese as well as Spanish literature

and language and each annual volume comprises in excess of 500 pages, made up of quarterly issues. Until 1948 the journal's title was *Bulletin of Spanish Studies*.

726 Camões Center Quarterly.
New York: Camões Center for the Study of the Portuguese-Speaking World, 1989- . quarterly.

The Camões Center, founded in 1988, is based at the Institute of Latin American and Iberian Studies of Columbia University. The aims of the journal are to promote understanding of the Portuguese-speaking world, particularly in the United States, and to promote debate by giving space to diverse points of view. The quarterly issues are sometimes conflated into double issues.

727 Cultura. (Culture.)
London: The Portuguese Arts Trust, 1986- . irregular.

Formerly produced by Portugal 600, a body established to commemorate the 600th anniversary of the Anglo-Portuguese alliance, as manifested by the Treaty of Windsor of 1386. This informative annual magazine on Portuguese culture is expected to settle upon a frequency of one issue per year from the year 2000. Typical issues comprise twenty pages and carry photographs as well as informed articles on the Portuguese arts scene.

728 Hispania: a journal devoted to the teaching of Spanish and Portuguese.
Washington, DC: Georgetown University; Los Angeles, California: American Association of Teachers of Spanish and Portuguese, University of Southern California, Department of Spanish and Portuguese, 1918- . quarterly.

An authoritative and widely-read journal which contains scholarly articles on literature and linguistics as well as on historical and cultural matters pertaining to Portugal and Spain. Book reviews are also included as is news of pedagogical developments in the field of foreign languages.

729 Iberian Studies.
Keele, England: Centre for Iberian Studies, University of Keele, 1972- . biannual.

The emphasis of this journal is on socio-economics, history, politics and anthropology of Portugal and Spain in the modern era (from the 19th century onwards). Although notionally biannual, issues are sometimes irregular.

730 Journal of Iberian and Latin American Studies.
Bundoora, Australia: La Trobe University, 1995- . biannual.

A journal which publishes articles in English, Portuguese and Spanish on all aspects of the humanities and social sciences. In addition to these contributions, each issue includes book reviews, reports on research in progress, interviews and a debates section.

Periodicals

731 Luso-Brazilian Review.
Madison, Wisconsin: University of Wisconsin Press, 1964- . biannual.

Sponsored by the Latin America and Iberia Studies Program of the University of Wisconsin, each issue of this leading North American journal contains about 140 pages and is issued in summer and winter numbers. Typically its content consists of eight articles by academics, generally from the fields of literature or history. In addition, there is a large number of book reviews of recent publications in both the English and Portuguese languages.

732 Newsletter. Fundação Calouste Gulbenkian. (Calouste Gulbenkian Foundation Newsletter.)
Lisbon: Serviço de Comunicação da Fundação Calouste Gulbenkian, 1997- . ten issues per year.

A journal, produced in full-colour by the foremost independent Portuguese cultural body, the Calouste Gulbenkian Foundation. Gulbenkian, an Armenian whose fortune derived from oil, spent his last years in Portugal and bequeathed his magnificent art collections to the country. The *Newsletter* provides news of the many publishing and cultural activities of the Foundation, including those of its London office, which are recorded here in English.

733 Portuguese Literary and Cultural Studies.
North Dartmouth, Massachusetts: Center for Portuguese Studies and Culture, University of Massachusetts-Dartmouth, 1998- . biannual.

The intention of this journal is to publish material whose content transcends the traditional boundaries of academic disciplines. The first four issues are all collections of papers on a specific theme, namely 'Borders', the writers Lídia Jorge and Alberto Caeiro (i.e. Fernando Pessoa), and 'Brazil, 2000'.

734 Portuguese Review: Portugal's English language business magazine.
Cascais, Portugal: Revista de Propriedades Portuguesas, c.1990- . irregular.

An attractive, colourful, English-language magazine aimed at business-minded visitors to Lisbon, Oporto and the Algarve. Its circulation of 7,500 predominantly comprises free copies which are distributed through superior hotels in the above areas of Portugal. Occasional special issues are produced such as no. 25 on the Lisbon Expo '98 event.

735 Portuguese Studies.
London: W. S. Maney for the Modern Humanities Research Association, 1985- . annual.

In its relatively short existence, *Portuguese Studies* has established itself as a most authoritative medium for literary and historical studies. The journal is edited from the Department of Portuguese at King's College London, and one of its strengths is that its contributors are drawn from across the English- and Portuguese-speaking world. A bibliography of English-language publications relating to the Lusophone world appears in each issue. Its subject matter is equally diverse, addressing topics relating not only to European Portuguese matters but also to Brazilian and Lusophone African cultures. Volumes are typically of 240 pages.

736 Portuguese Studies Review.
Durham, New Hampshire: International Conference Group on Portugal, 1977- . biannual.

First published in 1977 as the *Portuguese Studies Newsletter*, this was the pioneering journal for Portuguese historical and political studies in the United States and its development owes much to its indefatigable founder, Professor Douglas L. Wheeler of the University of New Hampshire. Its early issues were duplicated typescript but continuous improvements in format culminated in its transformation into *Portuguese Studies Review* from 1991. It now has a professional appearance, a greater number of pages (c.200), a distinguished range of contributors and an equally impressive range of articles on the history, politics and literature of the Portuguese-speaking world. Each issue also contains bibliographical information on new publications and on forthcoming conferences.

737 Revista de Estudos Anglo-Portugueses. (Review of Anglo-Portuguese Studies.)
Lisbon: Instituto Nacional de Investigação Científica; Centro de Estudos Comparados de Línguas e Literaturas Modernas, 1990- . biennial.

Comprising approximately 150 pages per issue, this journal appears typically every two years. Its content consists of an opening section, usually on project developments at the Centro de Estudos Comparados, followed by a number of scholarly articles on Anglo-Portuguese topics. Studies on 18th- and 19th-century British travellers to Portugal are particularly prevalent. The third and final section of the journal comprises book reviews. The text of the journal is generally in Portuguese.

738 Society for Spanish and Portuguese Historical Studies Bulletin.
Nashville, Tennessee: Vanderbilt University, Society for Spanish and Portuguese Historical Studies, 1969- . thrice-yearly.

Formerly the *Society for Spanish and Portuguese Historical Studies Newsletter*, this journal addresses all aspects of Portuguese and Spanish history. In addition to scholarly articles, there are book reviews, bibliographies and news of individuals and other societies active in the same or related fields. Articles are accepted in the Iberian languages as well as in English.

739 Tesserae.
Cardiff: University of Wales, School of European Studies, 1994-96. biennial.

Tesserae, whose title is the Latin word for 'tiles', was originally a biennial journal dedicated to the language, literature and general culture of the Portuguese and Spanish-speaking worlds with articles in English as well as in the Iberian languages. After two issues (1994, 1996) it renamed itself *Journal of Iberian and Latin American Studies* (1997-), see item no. 736, albeit with the word *Tesserae* incorporated on its cover. Issues typically comprise 100 pages.

Periodicals

740 The Times Higher Educational Supplement. Portugal special.
Special edition, no. 944 (7 December 1990), p. 13-18.
This theme issue of the *THES* includes a number of lengthy articles on Portugal for an English readership. The topics covered include: the impact of the 1974 Portuguese Revolution; the relationship between Portuguese industry and university research; the higher education sector; Portugal's former colonies; and the publishing scene in Portugal. Occasional very useful supplements on Portugal also appear in *The Times*, such as on 26 July 1996, as well as in *The Times Literary Supplement*.

741 Vida hispánica: the Spanish and Portuguese Journal of the Association for Language Learning.
Rugby, England: Association for Language Learning, 1990- . biannual.
Previously published (from 1953) by the Association of Teachers of Spanish and Portuguese, this journal provides a forum for articles both on pedagogical matters and on linguistic and cultural topics. Both English and the languages of Iberia are employed by contributors and book reviews are also part of the journal's remit.

ACLAIIR Newsletter.
See item no. 696.

European Bookseller.
See item no. 705.

Encyclopaedias and General Directories

742 **The Encyclopaedia Britannica: a dictionary of arts, sciences, literature and general information.**
New York: The Encyclopaedia Britannica Co., 1910-11. 29 vols. maps. bibliog.

Articles on Portugal in the *Encyclopaedia Britannica* have varied from the discursive to the well-informed over the many editions of the last century, with the 11th edition of 1911 edition being particularly well-informed, though now dated. The 15th edition, *The new Encyclopaedia Britannica* (Chicago, Illinois: Encyclopaedia Britannica International, 1987), is split into a *Micropaedia* of short, dictionary-like entries in which 'Portugal' merits an entry in vol. 9 (p. 632-34). More expansive coverage of the country, its history, geography, history and culture is to be found in vol. 25 of the *Macropaedia: knowledge in depth* (p. 1,048-65, maps), where there is also a separate entry on 'Portuguese literature' (p. 1,065-68).

743 **Grande enciclopédia portuguesa e brasileira.** (Great Portuguese and Brazilian encyclopaedia.)
Lisbon; Rio de Janeiro, Brazil: Editorial Enciclopédia, c.1945-60. 40 vols.

This is the standard, traditional encyclopaedia of Portugal which has been updated by so-called 'appendix' volumes rather than by a policy of continuous revision of the original volumes. Entries on particular topics can thus be fragmented between the core volumes and the supplementary ones. Nevertheless, it remains a key source for historical information and has many illustrations, albeit not always of top quality. It also contains useful bibliographies within many of its entries and is helpful on the biographies of relatively minor figures in Portuguese culture and history.

Encyclopaedias and General Directories

744 Guia das fundações portuguesas. Portuguese foundations guide.
Custódia Lourenço Marques, translation by Richard Trewinnard.
Lisbon: Centro Português de Fundações, 1996. 3rd rev. ed. 375p.
map.
Founded in 1993, the CPF (Centro Português de Fundações – The Portuguese Foundations' Centre) grew from its three inaugural members to comprise some seventy bodies by 1996. This directory, however, has some 250 entries, each of which gives details in parallel Portuguese and English texts of non-State organizations which are active in fields such as culture, education and international cooperation. The information provided includes details of the founding of each institution, its purposes, Portuguese legal status, funds, expenditure, employees and publications. A wealth of statistical information and indexes of the foundations and their chairpersons complete the volume.

Historical dictionary of Portugal.
See item no. 183.

Dictionary of Portuguese-African civilization.
See item no. 230.

Who's who of the artists in Portugal.
See item no. 629.

Directory of Spanish and Portuguese film-makers and films.
See item no. 655.

Willings press guide.
See item no. 710.

Bibliographies and Catalogues

745 Bibliotheca lusitana; or, Catalogue of books and tracts relating to the history, literature and poetry of Portugal, forming part of the library of John Adamson.
John Adamson. Newcastle-upon-Tyne, England: T. and J. Hodgson, 1836. 115p.

After emigrating to Portugal in his youth, Adamson returned to England and set about developing his interest in Portuguese culture by building up arguably the best private library of material on the country to be held in Britain. The holdings are here presented in six fascicules, three of which cover poetry, drama and Camões. The other sections address history, religion and a variety of other topics, including the Portuguese language.

746 Portuguese language and Luso-Brazilian literature: an annotated guide to selected reference works.
Bobby J. Chamberlain. New York: The Modern Language Association of America, 1989. 95p. (Selected Bibliographies in Language and Literature, no. 6).

With 538 entries (albeit a substantial number of them are cross-references), this is an essential starting point for the student of Portuguese language and literature. The entries cover Brazil as well as Portugal and there is also some coverage of other Portuguese-speaking territories. As is to be expected, the English-language material in the bibliography is biased towards North American works.

Bibliographies and Catalogues

747 The Portuguese Revolution of 25 April 1974: annotated bibliography on the antecedents and the aftermath. A revolução portuguesa de 25 de Abril de 1974: bibliografia anotada sobre os antecedentes e evolução posterior.
Ronald H. Chilcote.   Coimbra, Portugal: Centro de Documentação 25 de Abril, 1987. 329p.

Parallel Portuguese and English texts are employed for the introductory and connective texts of this bibliography. Chilcote, an American professor, found only some sixty to seventy per cent of the works in this bibliography in the Portuguese National Library; most of the rest he culled from second-hand bookshops. Unfortunately he does not give library locations for any of the 1,116 monograph entries and 1,047 periodical articles which he lists. All of the entries are annotated in a generally neutral way. This is a monumental piece of work which will be of great value to students of the 1974 Portuguese Revolution.

748 Bibliographie des voyages en Espagne et en Portugal.
(Bibliography of travels in Spain and Portugal.)
Raymond Foulché-Delbosc.   Madrid: Julio Ollero, 1991. 349p.

A reprint of the classic bibliography of Portuguese travel literature by the celebrated bibliographer, R. Foulché-Delbosc (1864-1929). A brief preface, in Spanish, by Ramón Alba is the only addition to the original edition of 1896 (Paris: A. Ricard). The 858 entries are arranged chronologically from the beginning of printing to 1895. Each entry includes a summary list of the places visited or described by its author but the volume lacks an overall index of place-names.

749 Bibliografía ibérica del siglo XV: enumeración de todos los libros impresos en España y Portugal hasta el año de 1500, con notas críticas. (A bibliography of 15th-century Iberian publications: list of all of the books printed in Spain and Portugal up to the year 1500, with critical notes.)
Konrad Haebler.   Madrid: Julio Ollero, 1992. 2 vols.

This is a reprint of Haebler's classic bibliography, first published in 1903-17 (The Hague: Martinus Nijhoff; Leipzig, Germany: Karl W. Hiersemann, 2 vols). The same territory is covered in greater depth in *Bibliografia geral portuguesa, século XV* (General Portuguese bibliography, 15th century) (Lisbon: Academia das Ciências de Lisboa, 1941-44. 2 vols). For the following century, A. J. Anselmo's *Bibliografia das obras impressas em Portugal no século XVI* (Bibliography of the works printed in Portugal in the 16th century) (Lisbon: Biblioteca Nacional, 1926. Reprinted, 1977. 367p.) is the authority. Extensive coverage, particularly of the 18th and 19th centuries, is provided in the monumental *Dicionário bibliográfico português: estudos aplicáveis a Portugal e ao Brasil* (Portuguese bibliographical dictionary: studies applicable to Portugal and Brazil) (Lisbon: Imprensa Nacional, 1858-1958. Reprinted, 1972-73. 23 vols) by Inocêncio Francisco da Silva.

Bibliographies and Catalogues

750 British Council libraries in Portugal. Lisbon, Oporto, Coimbra. Special Anglo-Portuguese collection: books & periodicals.
Instituto Britânico em Portugal. Oporto, Portugal: Associação Luso-Britânica do Porto; Coimbra, Portugal: Casa da Inglaterra, 1958. 69p.

A catalogue of the holdings of the three British Council libraries in Portugal, of which the vast majority are from the Lisbon establishment. After a brief list of periodicals, the catalogue comprises four sections: English works (both about Portugal and printed in Portugal); English translations of Portuguese works; Portuguese works about Britain or printed in Britain; and Portuguese translations of English works. The catalogue serves as an excellent bibliography of Anglo-Portuguese culture and history.

751 Portuguese literature from its origins to 1990: a bibliography based on the collections of Indiana University.
Hugo Kunoff. Metuchen, New Jersey: Scarecrow Press, 1994. 497p.

Although essentially based on the holdings of one academic library, this is nevertheless a major contribution to the bibliography of Portuguese literature, although its coverage of colonial Portuguese literature is scant. The Library of Congress classification is used to arrange works coherently by period and genre. The bibliography of individual writers is split into three chronological sections and major serials in the field are also listed.

752 Lisbon.
John Laidlar. Oxford; Santa Barbara, California; Denver, Colorado: Clio Press, 1997. 252p. map. (World Bibliographical Series, vol. 199).

This is a companion to the present volume. An historical introduction and an overview of the administration of Lisbon are provided in addition to the body of the book which comprises 692 annotated entries on a wide range of topics including geography, history, flora and fauna, sport and religion. As is the policy of the World Bibliographical Series, the entries are all English-language works or works with English summaries or with a heavy pictorial content. However, an appendix lists a selection of major Portuguese-language books about Lisbon.

753 Bibliografia geográfica de Portugal. (Geographical bibliography of Portugal.)
Hermann Lautensach, adapted and enlarged by Mariano Feio.
Lisbon: Instituto para a Alta Cultura, Centro de Estudos Geográficos, 1948. 256p.

Lautensach's original bibliography, published in the *Geographisches Jahrbuch* (vol. 45 [1931]; vol. 59 [1946?]), covered the periods 1915-30 and 1930-43 respectively. Feio's adaptation brings the total of entries to 2,347 and coverage up to 1946. The work is arranged into thirty-two sections of which the last twelve are geographical divisions of Portugal. The preceding sections are thematic and cover topics such as maps, earthquakes and climate. A second volume by Ilídio do Amaral and Suzanne Daveau covers the period 1947-74 (Lisbon: Centro de Estudos Geográficos, 1982. 427p.), while further updating is to be found in the periodical *Finisterra*.

Bibliographies and Catalogues

754 **Livros disponíveis.** (Books in Print.)
Lisbon: Associação Portuguesa de Editores e Livreiros, 1985- .
annual.

This compilation of Portuguese books in print comprises a mixture of large cumulative volumes and slimmer ones of *Actualização e adenda* (Updating and addenda), the latter only including publications published or notified in the year in question. Entries are provided under titles, authors and in classified sequence using the Dewey classification system. For pre-20th-century publications there is Inocêncio da Silva's monumental *Dicionário bibliográfico português* (Portuguese bibliographical dictionary) (Lisbon, 1858-1958; Lisbon: Imprensa Nacional, 1972-73. 23 vols), whilst the *Boletim de bibliografia portuguesa* (Portuguese bibliographical bulletin), 1955-82, covers the more modern era. Useful for early translations is A. F. Allison's *English translations from the Spanish and Portuguese to the year 1700* (New York: Ungar, 1975).

755 **A new bibliography of the Lusophone literatures of Africa. Nova bibliografia das literaturas africanas de expressão portuguesa.**
Gerald Moser, Manuel Ferreira. London: Hans Zell, 1993. 2nd completely revised and expanded ed. 132p. (Bibliographical Research in African Literatures, no. 2).

Planned as a supplement to Moser's *Bibliografia das literaturas africanas de expressão portuguesa* (Bibliography of the Portuguese-African literatures) (Lisbon: Imprensa Nacional, Casa da Moeda, 1983. 407p.), in which the cut-off date was 1979, this is a more polished work, albeit lacking the illustrations of the former work. It brings coverage up to 1991 and also fills in gaps in pre-1979 coverage. It is divided into two sections: the first covers general bibliographies, while the second is sub-divided into five sections covering respectively Angola, Cape Verde, Guinea-Bissau, Mozambique and São Tomé e Príncipe. Each of the sub-divisions is further divided into sections on oral and creative literature, and literary histories and criticism. Almost 100 pages of biographical notes are included. The pioneering work in the field was Moser's *A tentative Portuguese-African bibliography* (University Park, Pennsylvania: Pennsylvania State University Libraries, 1970. 148p. + 2p. [Bibliographical Series, no. 3]), which covered folk literature, art and history as well as providing some very brief biographical details of authors.

756 **Bibliografia analítica das bibliografias portuguesas.** (Analytical bibliography of Portuguese bibliographies.)
Jorge Peixoto, introduction by Maria da Conceição Osório Gonçalves, Maria Teresa Pinto Mendes. Coimbra, Portugal: Biblioteca Geral da Universidade, 1987. 576p. (Catálogos e Bibliografias, no. 3).

A masterly compilation of some 2,542 entries comprising bibliographies arranged into subject groupings according to the Universal Decimal Classification (UDC). Unfortunately the index is by author only, so ready location of known works by title is difficult as is identification of subjects beyond the general headings provided in the 'Sumário' (summary).

Bibliographies and Catalogues

757 The Portuguese in Asia: an annotated bibliography of studies on Portuguese colonial history in Asia, 1498-c.1800.
Daya de Silva. Zug, Switzerland: IDC, 1987. 313p.

Accompanied by a set of microfiches which contains many of the items listed in this volume, this bibliography provides references to 2,773 items. The annotations for each entry vary from extensive descriptions of contents to the non-existent for some of the more obscure titles. The works are arranged into nine sections which cover: reference works; historiography; cartography; navigation; travel; Portugal's conquests, expansion and decline in Asia; religion; economics; and the impact of the Portuguese on Asian society.

758 A Gil Vicente bibliography, 1975-1995, with a supplement for 1940-1975.
C. C. Stathatos. Bethlehem, Pennsylvania: Lehigh University Press; London: Associated University Press, 1997. 187p.

A bibliography of Gil Vicente (c.1470-c.1536) who wrote in both Castilian Spanish and Portuguese and was the leading dramatist of his era in both Portugal and Spain. This volume is a sequel to the same compiler's *A Gil Vicente bibliography, 1940-1975* (London: Grand & Cutler, 1980. 132p. [Research Bibliographies and Checklists, XXX]). The 1975-95 volume has 634 annotated entries arranged into sections which comprise editions and adaptations of Vicente's works, translations and critical studies.

759 The Portuguese in Canada: a bibliography. Les Portugais au Canada: une bibliographie.
Carlos Teixeira, Gilles Lavigne. North York, Ontario, Canada: Institute for Social Research, 1992. 79p. maps.

With a textual introduction (to p. 28) in both English and French, this bibliography of over 1,000 items details the wave of Portuguese immigration which affected Canada after the Second World War. These newcomers, from mainland Portugal, the Azores, Madeira and the Portuguese colonies, were thus one of the later ethnic groups to arrive in Canada. Initially employed largely on the land and on the railroads, many have now moved to the cities of Toronto and Montréal. The bibliography is in eight sections covering: books; periodical articles; theses; newspaper articles; reports; papers; manuscripts; and forthcoming works.

760 The Portuguese in the United States: a bibliograppraphy [sic]. First supplement.
David J. Vieira, Geoffrey L. Gomes, Adalino Cabral. Durham, New Hampshire: International Conference Group on Portugal, c.1986. 126p.

This supplement to Leo Pap's bibliography (New York: Center for Migration Studies. 80p.) comprises items sequentially numbered from 801 to 2071, which are divided into two sections. The first covers Portuguese in the United States, the second, Portuguese in Portugal. The latter is chiefly background material on emigration from the homeland. The United States includes Hawaii and California as well as sections on broader regions of the country. There is also a section on fictional literature about immigrants.

Bibliographies and Catalogues

761 A list of the writings of Charles Ralph Boxer, published between 1926 and 1984, compiled for his eightieth birthday.
S. George West.   London: Támesis Books, 1984. 41p. (Colección Támesis, Serie A, Monografías, CX).

A bibliography of some 315 items arranged in date order and covering the period 1926-84. The items include books and articles. Boxer had been a Major and Japanese interpreter in the British Army, before he became Professor of Portuguese in the University of London. His prodigious output of material made him the leading authority outside Portugal on the country's maritime expansion, particularly in the East. Another equally important British lusophile scholar was Edgar Prestage (1869-1951) whose archive and publications are described in Richard Pound's 'Edgar Prestage's correspondence' in *Portuguese Studies* (vol. 3 [1987], p. 84-98) and in 'Edgar Prestage, Manchester's Portuguese pioneer' by J. F. Laidlar in *Bulletin of the John Rylands University Library of Manchester* (vol. 74, no. 1 [1992], p. 75-94).

Indexes

In the following pages indexes are provided by author, title and subject. As is normal practice, Portuguese compound surnames are filed under their last element, except where hyphenated. The few Spanish compound surnames included here are filed under their first element. Original spellings are used in titles but modern orthography is used for surnames and headings in the subject index. The indexes are all arranged in letter-by-letter order, not word-by-word.

Index of Authors

A

Aberystwyth Arts Centre 638
Academia das Ciências de Lisboa 749
Academia Internacional de Cultura Portuguesa 475
Achebe, Chinua 597
Ackerlind, Sheila Rogers 185, 271
Adam, E. 607
Adamson, John 745
Adeline, Duchess of Bedford 206
Advisory Council on Latin American and Iberian Information Resources 696, 699
Aeroportos e Navegação Aérea 474
Agência-Geral do Ultramar 220, 265, 292
Agra Europe 463
Alarcão, Jorge de 164
Alba, Ramón 748
Albuquerque, Afonso de 256
Alcoforado, Mariana 608-09
Alden, Dauril 352
Alexander, John 122
Algieri, Franco 407
Allen, Maria Fernanda 307, 330-31
Allison, A. F. 754
Almaça, Carlos 146
Almeida, Fialho de 601, 604
Almeida, Miguel Vale de 660
Almeida-Moro, Fernanda de Camargo 702
Almodovar, Antonio 421
Alonso, Claudia Pazos *see* Pazos Alonso, Claudia
Alonso, Pilar 10
Altabe, David 353
Alves, Afonso Manuel 24
Amaral, Ilídio do 753
Amaral, João Ferreira do 422
Ambrosio, Teresa 515
American Enterprise Institute for Public Policy Research 406
Anderson, Brian 53, 55
Anderson, Eileen 53, 55
Anderson, James M. 165, 293
Anderson, Jean 663
Andrade, António Alberto de 292
Andrade, Eugénio de 543
Andrade, Sérgio Guimarães de 648
Andresen, Sophia de Mello Breyner *see* Breyner, Sophia de Mello
Andrews, Norwood 548
Andrez, Jaime Serrão 452
Angel, Moema Parente 532
Angelillo, Antonio 495
Anglo-Portuguese Foundation 442
Anselmo, A. J. 749
Anti-Slavery International 494
Antique Collectors' Club 694
Antunes, António Lobo 544-46
Apoge, Atila 419

249

Araújo, Norberto de 31
Architecture + Urbanism 496
Armesto, António 497
Armstrong, Lucile 657
Arnold, Rosemarie 65
Ashwin, E. Allen 608
Aspler, Tony 610
Associação Amigos de Monserrate 153
Associação Portuguesa de Editores e Livreiros 754
Associação Portuguesa de Linguística 299
Association for Contemporary Iberian Studies 723
Association for Education in Journalism and Mass Communication 473
Association for Language Learning 741
Atkinson, Dorothy M. 596
Atkinson, William C. 180
Automobile Association 32, 343
Automóvel Clube de Portugal 33
Auvergne, Edmund B. d' 192
Avillez, Francisco X. M. 458, 465, 469
Axelson, Eric 116
Azevedo, Carla 664
Azevedo, Carlos de 354

B

BAD 697
Bacalhau, Mário 391
Baganha, Maria Ioannis Benis 274
Ball, Dorothy 590
Ball, M. G. 481
Ballard, Jane 101
Ballard, Sam 101

Balmuth, Miriam S. 166
Bandeira, António Rangel 395
Baptista, Maria de Lurdes 505
Barata, J. Martins 471
Barata, José Pedro Martins Roque 471
Barclay, David 355
Barker, Barry 625
Barnes, W. J. 1
Barnett, Lionel D. 356
Barnier, Bruno 77
Barreno, Maria Isabel 581
Barreto, Mascarenhas 257
Barrett, Pam 55
Barros, João de 118, 246
Barros, Jorge 23
Barry, Nicole Anne 70
Bartholomew 34
Batty, Robert 11
Baubeta, Patricia Anne Odber de 297, 530
Baxter, William 122
Baylis, D. J. 282
Beckett, Martin 482
Beckford, William 130, 263
Bedini, Silvio 186
Beirão, Caetano 173
Bell-Cross, Graham 116
Benington, J. M. 162
Benson, E. F. 258
Benson, Robin 503
Bentley, Jeffrey W. 459, 469
Berardo Foundation 151
Berardo, José 623
Berkeley, Alice D. 194, 624
Berlitz 344
Bermeo, Nancy Gina 460
Berndtson & Berndtson 35
Bernstein, H. 704
Berto, Al 582
Bertolazzi, Alberto 12

Bessa-Luís, Agustina 13
Bettella, Andrea 498
Bibliographisches Institut AG 339
Biblioteca Nacional de Lisboa 749
Bidwell, Mollie 561
Biers, Jane C. 167
Biers, William R. 167
Birmingham, David 174, 225
Black, Richard 461
Blackburn, Ruth 71
Blake, W. T. 135
Blamey, Marjorie 163
Blanco, José 556
Bleiberg, Germán 531
Boas, Ana Vilas 505
Bocarro, António 246
Bodian, Miriam 357
Bodley, Richard 208
Bolton, Mark 147
Bonaparte, L.-L. 294
Booth Steamship Company 57
Bosley, Keith 551
Botelho, Afonso 604
Bouchon, Geneviève 236
Boulton, Susie 58-60
Bouquet, Mary 386
Bourne, Ursula 664-65
Bowe, Patrick 693
Bowra, Maurice 547
Boxer, Charles Ralph 116, 218, 237, 759
Boyajian, James C. 440
Bradley, Fiona 633
Braga, Teófilo 604
Bragg, Robert 659
Branchli, Bernard 651
Brandão, Délia 665
Braund, Kathryn 148
Brettell, Caroline 275-76
Breyner, Sophia de Mello 583, 605
Brines, Callum 61

250

British Academy 168
British Broadcasting Corporation 320, 348
British Committee for Amnesty 416
British Council 190, 295, 750
British Historical Society of Portugal 176, 194, 282, 724
British Officer of the Hussars 203
British Overseas Trade Board 441
British Tourist Association 100
Brito, M. C. de 650
Broadbent, Geoffrey 499
Brøgger, Jan 462
Brookshaw, David 533
Brown, Clare 110
Brown, Reginald Albert 257, 501
Browning, Elizabeth Barrett 547, 611
Browning, Robert 611
Brummel, Chester E. V. 354
Bruneau, Thomas C. 391-92
Buchanan, Colin 358
Buescu, Helena Carvalhão 540
Buescu, Maria Leonor Carvalhão 532
Bull, Peter 308
Buller, Nell 698
Bureau Européen de Recherches 463
Burness, Don 597
Busk, M. M. 175
Bye, Basil 488
Byrne, John 593
Byrne, Nora M. T. 515

C

Cabral, Adelino 760
Cabral, Manuel Villaverde 625
Cabral, Martin 442
Cabrito, H. 676
Cadavez, Cândida 656
Caeiro, Baltazar de Matos 509
Caetano, José A. Palma 309
Calado, Jorge 17
Calouste Gulbenkian Foundation 117, 124, 133, 181, 188, 547, 551, 566, 589, 601-03, 606, 701, 732, 742
Câmara, J. Mattoso 296
Câmara Municipal de Évora 172
Câmara Municipal de Lisboa 505, 509
Camargo, Sidney 335
Camden, London Borough of 556
Caminhos de Ferro Portugueses 484
Camões Center for the Study of the Portuguese-Speaking World 412, 418
Camões, Luís Vaz de 547-48, 597
Camoin, Fabrice 103
Campbell, Roy 547, 558, 562
Campos, Nuno 691
Canço, Dina 390
Cann, John P. 226
Cardigo, Isabel 661
Cardim, Ismael 335-36
Cardoso, Artur Lopes 10
Cardoso, José Luís 421
Carita, Helder 694

Carlsen, Ivana Rangel 594-95
Carlson, Christine 149
Carlson, Kevin 149
Carnarvon, Earl of 122
Cartographia 36
Carvalho, Manuel 666
Carvalho, Maria de Lourdes Simões de 626
Carvalho, Maria Judite de 603
Carvalho, Mário de 584, 603
Castagnaro, R. Anthony 310
Castelo-Branco, Camilo 585, 596
Castelo-Branco, Salwa el-Shawan 651
Castro, Paulo Ferreira de 653
Catela, Maria Emília 516
Catling, Christopher 62, 85
Catz, Rebecca D. 128, 259
CEDEFOP 452, 515, 520
Center for Portuguese Studies, University of California 188, 585
Centre for Housing Research and Urban Studies 513
Centre for Iberian Studies, Keele 729
Centre for Portuguese Studies and Culture 733
Centre International de Gerontologie Sociale 385
Centro de Documentação 25 de Abril 747
Centro de Estudos Comparados de Línguas e Literaturas Modernas 737
Centro de Estudos de Economia Industrial 493

251

Centro de Estudos Históricos Ultramarinos 265
Centro de Estudos Ornithológicos 162
Centro Português de Fundações 744
Cerqueira, Henrique 63
Cesana, Laura 359
Chabal, Patrick 533
Chagas, Manuel Pinheiro 602
Chamberlain, Bobby J. 746
Champion, Neil 706
Chaney, Rick 277
Chantal, Suzanne 18
Charles, Ron 64
Chiaramonte, Giovanni 511
Chilcote, Ronald H. 393, 747
Chislett, William 436
Clausse, Guy 283
Clement, Richard W. 182
Clough, David 482
Coelho, Claudina Marques 332
Coelho, José Pimentel 465
Cogan, Henry 129
Cohen, Rip 598
Cohen, Thomas M. 360
Coimbra University Library 756
Cole, Ben 112
Cole, Sally 388
Collin, P. H. 333
Collins, Judith 633
Collis, Maurice 117
Colloquium on the Portuguese and the Pacific 188
Comissão Nacional para as Comemorações dos Descobrimentos Portugueses 118, 151, 514

Comissariado de Portugal para a Exposição Universal de Sevilha 14
Comissariado para a 'Europália 91' 7, 501, 525, 532, 649-50, 653, 656, 658
Commission on Inter-Church Aid 361
Confraria, João 423
Connell, Brian 198
Conover, Anna 561
Consortium on Revolutionary Europe 194
Constable, Olivia Rennie 187
Constâncio, Raul 153
Construction Industry Research and Information Association 457
Cook, Manuela 311-12, 319
Corbridge, Sylvia L. 707
Corkill, David 424-25
Cornman, Maura F. 167
Cornwell, Bernard 612
Correia, Luís Miguel 476-77
Correia-Afonso, João 120
Correios e Comunicações de Portugal 471
Correios e Telégrafos de Portugal 648
Côrte-Real, Manuel 176, 413
Cory, Dennis 465
Costa, Alexandre Alves 510
Costa, Álvaro 666
Costa, Elisa Maria Lopes da 284
Costa, Margaret Jull 550, 565, 567-69, 575
Costa, Maria Velho da 581

Costa, Sérgio Corrêa 260
Coulthard, Malcolm 297
Court, Alec 65
Couto, Diogo de 246
Cresswell, Peterjon 686
Crollen, Luc 408
Crusafont i Sabater, M. 439
Cumming, Alister 517
Cunha, Carlos 391
Cunha, Carlos A. 394
Cunha, V. de Bragança 205
Cunliffe, Barry 168
Cuyvers, Luc 123

D

Dacier, Liz 419
Dalgado, Sebastião Rodolfo 298
Dallmeyer, R. D. 51
Danby, Miles 500
Danvers, Frederick Charles 238
Daveau, Suzanne 30, 753
David, Ilda 123
Davies, Bethan 112
Davies, Vitoria 341
Davies, W. J. K. 483
Decker, Alexander 66
Decker, Gudrun 66
Delaforce, Angela 627, 649
Delaforce, John 261, 667
Demeude, Hugues 15
Department of Trade and Industry 441
De Quincey, Thomas 613
Detering, Klemens 2
Deus, João de 294
de Winton, Charles F. S. 518
Dias, Maria Caldeira 452
Dias, Marina Tavares 2, 16
Díaz-Andreu, Margarita 169

Dicks, Brian 28
Dickson, Peter 517
Dinis (King of Portugal, 1279-1325) 598
Direcção Geral das Florestas 150
Directorate General for Diffusion 417
Disley, Tony 157
Dixon, R. A. N. 67
Doell, Patricia 464
D'Orsey, Alexander J. 313, 346
Downs, Charles 379
Doyle, Mel 488
Doyle, Terry, 316
Duarte, Lia 92
Dubois, Marc 511
Duffy, James 227
Dun Bradstreet 443
Dunn, Joseph 314
Dunn, Paul 367
Dutra, Francis A. 188
Dykes, George 23

E

Earle, T. F. 118, 189, 256, 586
Early English Text Society 607
Economist Intelligence Unit 102, 427, 429-31, 455
Edições Melhoramentos 332
Edmondson, J. C. 170
Edward Totah Gallery 636, 638
Edwards, Allan 668
Embleton, Gary 659
English Tourist Board 100
Ennes, Joan 24, 658
Entwistle, W. J. 189
Erdik, Mustafa, 52
Esaguy, Eva Renata d' 31

España, Rafael de 655
Estate Publications 38
Estoril Golf Club 692
European Bookseller 705
European Communities 150, 389-90, 426, 428, 453, 493
European Investment Bank 438
European Trade Union Institute 489
Eurostat 428
Evans, David J. J. 68
Evans, Simon 686
Eves, Edward 287
Expo '98 6, 123

F

Fagundes, Francisco Cota 592
Falcato, Jorge Nuno 646
Faria, Isabel Hub 299
Feibleman, Peter S. 669
Feijó, Rui Graça 4, 380
Feio, Mariano 753
Fellows, Alice 86
Fernandes, Cláudia 347
Fernandes, José Manuel 501
Fernández de Figueroa, Martín 239
Fernández, Oscar 338
Ferrão, José Mendes 151
Ferreira, Alice Lamath 561
Ferreira, António 587
Ferreira, Cândida 491
Ferreira, Eduardo de Sousa 212, 283
Ferreira, Hugo Gil 214
Ferreira, Manuel 755
Ferreira, Maria Leonor Fernandes 437
Ferreira, Maria Teresa Gomes 701
Ferreira, Michael J. 302

Ferro, Manuela 465
Ferro, Maria Inês 501
Fiennes, Peter 69
Figueira, Francisco Correia 478
Figueiredo, António de 219
Figueiredo, Fidelino de 533
Filton, Mary 593
Finan, Timothy 458, 465, 469
Finlayson, Clive 152
Fisher, Barbara 12
Flanagan, Nell 566
Fleck, Brigitte 502-03
Fleming, Hilary 348-49
Fletcher, Paul 88
Floate, Sharon 284
Fonseca, Branquinho da 603
Fonseca, Manuel da 603
Food Research Institute 228
Fornazaro, Antonio 315
Fothergill, B. 263
Foulché-Delbosc, Raymond 748
Fowler, Barbara Hughes 599
Fox, Ralph 209
Fox, Roger 465, 469
Frain, Maritheresa 391
Frampton, Kenneth 510
França, Isabella de 119
Frank, Ben E. 362
Frazer, Kenneth 653
Freeland, Alan 316, 349, 401
Freitas, João Sande 153
Freitas, Lima de 547
Freitas, Maria João 299
Friends of Monserrate 153
Frier, David Gibson 585

253

G

Gago, José Mariano 525
Garay, René Pedro 578
Gaspar, João 429-30
Gastaut, Michelle 103
Gemmett, R. J. 263
George, Emily 662
Gerrard, M. 600
Gibbons, John 136
Gibbons, Stanley 472
Gibbs, Philip 206
Gidley, Charles 614
Gil, Albert 10
Gilbert, Emma Andersen 153
Gillespie, Faith 581
Gilman, Antonio 166
Glanz, Derek M. 70
Gleeson, Diki 657
Globetrotter 39
Glover, Michael 195
Godinho, Miguel 120
Goldman, Richard Franko 565
Goldstein, Dan 686
Gomes, Geoffrey L. 760
Gomes, Telmo 478
Gómez Alfaro, Antonio 284
Gómez Bedate, Pilar 543
Gonçalves, Madeleine 71
Gonçalves, Maria da Conceição Osório 756
Goodall, Agnes M. 708
Goodman, David C. 527
Gordon, David L. 471
Gordon, Helen Cameron, Lady Russell 137
Gostelow, Martin 72, 85
Graça, Wendy 478
Graham, Laurence S. 395
Grauert, E. F. 317
Greenlee, William Brookes 121
Greenwall, Harry J. 414
Greer, Germaine 637
Greer, Mick 478
Griffin, Jonathan 554-55
Griffin, Nigel H. 564
Grilo, Eduardo Marçal 520
Guedes, Rui 642
Guerreira, Irene 321
Guimaraens, Magdalena Gorrell 666
Guimarães, Fernando 640
Gunn, Geoffrey C. 240
Gurriarán, José Antonio 73

H

Hadjiyannis, Stylianos 393
Haebler, Konrad 749
Hakluyt Society 121
Hallwag 37-38, 40-41
Haltzel, Michael H. 403
Hamilton, Kimberly A. 410
Hamilton, Russell G. 533, 537
Hamm, Manfred 22
Hammond, John L. 490
Hammond, Mike 687
Hammond, R. J. 228
Hampshire, David 285
Hancock, Matthew 74, 308
Hardacre, P. H. 193
Hargrove, Ethel C. 3
Harland, Mike 334, 341
Harris, Martin 303
Harris, Peter 363
Harrison, Tom 396
Heale, Jay 9
Helder, Humberto 588
Hendry, Ann 623
Henry, P. 466
Heras Institute on Indian History and Culture 252
Herculano, Alexandre 596, 604
Herr, Richard 4, 215
Hertfordshire, University of 284
Hicks, Alistair 638
Hidalgo, Carlos Otero *see* Otero Hidalgo, Carlos
Higgins, Michael 518
Higgs, David 278, 381
Hill, Alison Friesinger 55
Hirsch, Elizabeth Feist 262
Hispanic Seminary of Medieval Studies 134, 589
Hobbs, A. Hoyt 104
Hogg, James 364
Holton, James S. 340
Honig, Edward 549
Hook, David 189
Hook, Richard 709
Hopkinson, Amanda 17
Horta, Maria Teresa 581
Horward, Donald O. 196
Houaiss, Antônio 335-36
Houilhan, James 592
Howard, Joanna 24
Howes, Robert 714
Hudson, Mark 431
Hudson, Sarah 83
Hughes, Ana de Sá 350
Hughes, H. G. A. 709
Hughes, T. M. 122
Huiskamp, Harrie 365
Hull University School of Management 437
Humble, Richard 709
Hunt, Michael 482
Hunter-Watts, Guy 105
Hwang, Christine N. 52
Hyamson, Albert M. 366
Hyland, Mike 350
Hyland, Paul 138, 535

I

Iberian Studies Group 215
Ihrie, Maureen 531
Ingham, Peter 648

Ingram, David 91
Institute for Comparative Research in Human Culture 462
Institute for International Education 516
Institute for Social Research, Ontario 759
Institute for Strategic and International Studies 411
Institute of Social and Economic Research (Newfoundland) 464
Institut for Sammelignende Kulturforskning (Norway) 462
Institut für Anglistik und Amerikanistik (Salzburg) 364
Institut für Europäische Politik 407
Instituto Britânico em Portugal 750
Instituto Camões 181, 551, 589, 601-03, 606
Instituto da Biblioteca Nacional e do Livro 11, 181, 551, 601, 603
Instituto de Investigação Científica Tropical 265, 269
Instituto Geológico e Mineiro de Portugal 42
Instituto Nacional de Investigação Científica 737
Instituto para a Alta Cultura 753
Instituto para Estudos Estratégicos e Internacionais 411
Instituto Português de Cartografia e Cadastro 43
Instituto Português de Museus 645
Instituto Português do Livro e das Bibliotecas 589
Instituto Português do Património Arquitectónico 501
Instituto Português do Património Cultural 130
International Association for the Evaluation of Educational Achievement 517
International Center for Gerontology 385
International Conference Group on Portugal 519, 736
International Conference in America on Iberian Archaeology, First 166
International Geological Correlation Program 51
International Meeting on Modern Portugal, Third 212
Interpropo 444

J

Jack, Malcolm 263
Jackson, K. David 123
Jackson, Pauline 107
Jaffe, Margaret Allenby 657
Jaffe, Nigel Allenby 657
Jalles, I. 453
Janitscheck, Hans 264
Japan Society of London 236
Jeffrey, Colin 366
Jenkins, C. 417
Jepson, Tim 75-76
Jesus, João 465
Jodidio, Philip 504

Johansson, Eve 714
John Hansard Gallery 625
John, of Empoli 269
Johnson, Charles 122
Johnson, Margaret 519
Johnston, David 577
Joliffe, Jill 106
Jorge, Manuela 465
Josling, Timothy 458, 469

K

Kaplan, Marion 5
Kastner, Macario Santiago 652
Kaufman, Helena 534
Kay, Emma 79
Kayman, Martin 213
Kayserling, Mayer 254
Keay, Simon 168-69
Kedslie, Moyra 437
Keefe, Eugene K. 29
Keenoy, Ray 575
Keeting, Margaret 647
Kennedy, Hugh 184
Kennedy, Olive 608
Kennedy, Richard 608
Kent, Sarah 630
Keskin, B. 455
Kessel, Dmitri 669
Kettenring, E. 519
Khorian, Michael 77
Kidder, Laura M. 78
Kimbrough, Emily 139
King, John 44, 99
Kirkman, J. S. 233
Klobucka, Anna 534
Köditz, Volker 520
Kompass Portugal 445
Kotowicz, Zbigniew 557
KPMG Peat Marwick 436
Krabielle, Katja 79
Kümmerly + Frei 45
Kunoff, Hugo 751

255

L

Laidlar, John F. 699, 752, 761
Lancastre, Maria José de 550
Lane, Helen R. 581
Langenscheidt 59
Langworthy, Mark 465, 469
Lappin, Anthony 557
Laski, Neville 368
La Trobe University 730
Lautensach, Hermann 30, 753
Lavigne, Gilles 759
Le Tellier, Sarah 58
Lea, M. Sheridan 165
Leal, Ernesto S. J. 201
Lees, Frederick 615
Lees-Milne, J. 263
Leite, Ana Mafalda 533
Lemonnier, Nicolas 646
Leonard, Albert 167
Levenson, Jay A. 627
Levitin, Alexis 543
Lewis, Graham F. 455
Lexus 350-51
Library of Congress 29, 700
Liddell, Alex 670
Light, Kenneth H. 197
Lima, Luís Leiria de 24
Linder, Lisa 671
Lindo, E. H. 369
Linguaphone Institute 315
Lipiner, Elias 370
Lira, Solange de Azambuja 300
Lisboa, Eugénio 551, 601-03
Lisboa, Irene 601
Lisboa, Maria Manuel 551
Lisbon Meeting on Child Language 299
Livermore, Harold 177, 180, 297, 724
Livingstone, Marco 623
Llewellyn, Cristina Mendes 319
Lloyd, H. Evans 234
Lobo, Vitálio 120
Loch, Sylvia 154
Lomax, Derek W. 286
Loomis, R. S. 189
Lopes, Fernão 187, 286
Lopes, Francisco Fernandes 265
Lopes, José da Silva 432
Lopes, Margarida Chagas 491
López, Fred A. 393
Loring, George Bailey 204
Lourenço, Eduardo 6, 403
Lowe, Elizabeth 546
Lowndes, Susan 124
Lucena, Diogo 422
Lupi, Luís C. 220
Luso-American Development Foundation 410
Lygum, Bjorn 438

M

Mabberly, D. J. 155
McCarthy, Mary 27
MacCarthy, T. 600
Macaulay, Rose 124, 140
Macauley, Neill 266
McCrank, Lawrence J. 221
Macdonald, N. P. 255
Macdonald, Scott B. 410
Macedo, Hélder 547, 554, 602, 622
Macedo, Suzette 557, 581
McElroy, Richard 107
McEwen, John 630, 639
McGuirk, Bernard 551
Machado, Diamantino 382
Machado, José Alberto Gomes 649
Machado, Júlio César 604
McIntyre, Barbara 320
McKenna, James G. 239
Macleod, Alex 392
McMutrie, Nary 156
McNally, Terrence 616
MacQueen, Norrie 229
McWhirter, Kathryn 675
Magalhães, Joaquim Romero 190
Magalhães, José Calvet de 411
Magone, José M. 397-98
Maguire, Gail 107
Malkiel, María Rosa Lida de 189
Manchester School of Management 491
Manjón, Maite 672-73
Manuel, Paul Christopher 400
Mar-Molinero, Clare 401
March, Charles W. 125
Maréchal, Jacques 111
Margarido, Graça 478
Marlborough Fine Art 631
Marques, Alfredo Pinheiro 126, 134
Marques, Custódia Lourenço 744
Marques, Domingos 279
Marques, Margarida 465
Marques, Mário Gomes 439
Marques, Paulo 640
Marshall, Michael W. 214
Marshall, Paul 107
Martin, Colin 116
Martin, Priscilla Clark 340
Martínez Soler, Dionisio 2
Martínez-García, E. 51
Martínez-Gil, Fernando 301

Martins, Fernando Cabral 640
Martins, Francisco 465
Martins, Graça 348
Martins, Guilherme d'Oliveira 7
Martyn, John R. C. 267, 270, 587, 591
Marujo, Manuela 279
Mathew, K. M. 241
Mathew, K. S. 242
Matos, A. Campos 561
Matos, José Sarmento de 26
Matos, Maria António Pinto de 645
Matos, Maria Filomena 517
Matthews, Henry 122
Mavor, William 178
Maxwell, Kenneth 216, 268, 402-03, 412, 418, 627
Mayor, Michael 71
Mayson, Richard 674
Meat and Livestock Commission 456
Medeiros, Manuela de 465
Meer, Willemina van der 698
Mello, António S. 442
Mello, Thomaz de 18
Melo, Alexandre 623
Melville, Herman 547
Mendes, Maria Teresa Pinto 756
Mendes-Víctor, L. 52
Merideth, Craig 171
Metcalfe, Charles 675
Metropolis International 80
Michel, de la Sainte Trinité 377
Michelin PLC 46, 81-83, 108

Miguéis, José Rodrigues 601
Military Museum and Memorials of Bussaco 201
Millar, Deyanne Farrell 148
Miller, Heidi 107
Ministério da Cultura 626, 629
Miranda, Maria Adelaide 649
Mocatta, Frederic David 571
Modern Language Association of America 746
Modesto, Maria de Lourdes 676
Mohammadi, K. 68
Moita, Ana Paula 505
Molder, Jorge 6
Monke, Eric 465, 469
Monke, Scott C. 418
Monteiro, Domingos 603
Monteiro, George 558
Moraes, Euzi Rodrigues 334
Morales Front, Alfonso 301
Morrell, Victoria 107
Moser, Gerald 755
Mota, Arlindo 628
Mota, Artur 520
Mourão-Ferreira, David 589, 602-03
Murphy, Paul 83, 85
Muscat, Cathy 79
Museu Bocage 146
Museu do Chiado 19
Museu e Laboratório Zoológico e Antropólogico (Lisbon) 146
Museu Militar 703

Museu Nacional de Arte Antiga 643
Museu Nacional de História Natural 146
Mykolenko, L. 466
Myscofski, Carole A. 372

N

Namora, Fernando 590
Napier, Sir William 198
Naro, Anthony J. 296
Nataf, Daniel 404
National Commission for the Commemoration of the Portuguese Discoveries *see* Comissão Nacional para as Comemorações dos Descobrimentos Portugueses
National Gallery, London 643
National Gallery, Washington, DC 626
National Museum of Women in the Arts 626
Negreiros, Almada 602
Neiermair, Peter 26
Nery, Rui Vieira 653
Neves, João Luís César das 433
Neves, Vítor 514
Newcombe, Norman 521
Newitt, Malyn 222-23
Newman, Penny 319
Nicolin, Pierluigi 510
Nitti, John J. 302, 309
Noivo, Edite 280
Noonan, Laurence A. 269
Nooteboom, Cees 617
Novais, Hilde M. 626
NTC 337
Nunes, J. J. 599
Nunes, Pedro 267
Núñez, Benjamin 230

O

Oakley, R. J. 286
O'Byrne, Simon 373
O'Callaghan, Jane 84
Oder, Craig E. 167
OECD *see* Organization for Economic Cooperation and Development
Office of the Secretary of State for Information & Tourism 656
Office of the Secretary of State for Tourism 7, 390
O'Hara, Trevor 532
Oldknow, Rev. Joseph 122
Oliveira, C. S. 52
Oliveira, Jura 338
Oliveira, Leonel de 467
Oliveira, Manuel de 467
Oliveira, Teresa 515
Oliver, Michael 200
O'Neill, Brian Juan 383
Opello, Walter C. 210, 212
Orders, d'Arcy 287, 689
Organisation for Economic Cooperation and Development 419, 434, 468, 522-23, 526
Ortiz, Elizabeth Lambert 677
Osborne, Esmenia Simões 320
Otero Hidalgo, Carlos 527
Ottolenghi, Daniel 438
Owen, Hilary 536
Ozbaran, Salih 243

P

Pacifici, Sergio 127
Packer, Jonathan 288
Paço d'Arcos, Joaquim 597, 603
Padró, Quim 497
Page, Kenneth W. 515
Page, Timothy J. 85
Paget, Julian 199
Pais, I. 52
Palmeirim, Jorge de 158
Paraschi, André J. 629
Parker, Jack Horace 579
Parker, John 127
Parker, June 113
Parkinson, Stephen 118, 303
Parreira, Rui 172
Partridge, Richard 200
Passos, José Manuel da Silva 2
Patrício, António 601
Patrocini, J. Tomás 524
Pattee, Richard 179
Paulo, João 21
Payne, Stanley G. 180
Pazos Alonso, Claudia 529
Pearson, M. N. 244-45
Pearson, Scott R. 469
Peixoto, Jorge 756
Peixotto, Ernest 141
Peres, Phyllis 537
Perez, Janet 533
Pérez Domínguez, María Cristina 390
Perista, Heloisa 491
Perkins, Juliet 321, 588
Perrin, Thierry 15
Perry, William 406
Pessoa, Fernando 549-557, 597, 601, 605
Pessoa, Marialice 327
Philips 47
Phillips, Edite Vieira *see* Vieira, Edite
Philological Society 294
Pieris, P. E. 246
Pina Cabral, João de 4, 384
Pinheiranda, Mário 649
Pinheiro, Patricia McGowan 564
Pinto, António Costa 217
Pinto, Celsa 446
Pinto, Fernão Mendes 128-29
Pinto, Jeanette 247
Pinto, M. H. Mendes 643
Pinto-Coelho, Maria João 506
Pires, Maria Laura Bettencourt 130
Pischai, Rainer 492
Pitcher, M. Anne 231
Placito, P. J. 155
Plaister, Elisabeth 626
Polt, John H. R. 4
Polunin, Oleg 159
Pomeroy, Jordana 626
Ponte, Carmo 321
Pontiero, Giovanni 297, 299, 570, 575-76
Port, Len 148
Portas, Nuño 510
Porter, Darwin 86
Porter, Jonathan 248
Portugal 600 727
Portuguese Arts Trust 727
Portuguese Philatelic Society 471
Portuguese UK Chamber of Commerce 447
Pound, Richard 761
Powers, James F. 191
Prados-Torreira, Lurdes 166
Prescott, David Alan 506
Prestage, Edgar 608
Price, Danforth 86
Price, Janet 670
Price Waterhouse 448
Pride, John C. 315
Pritchett, V. S. 563
PROCALFER 469
Pugh, Henry 659
Purcell, Joanne B. 653
Purcell, Ronald C. 653
Pye, Michael 618

Pye, Roger F. 160

Q

Quail Map Company 481
Quaresma, Maria de Lourdes Baptista 385
Quartenaire Portugal 385, 493
Queiroz, José Maria Eça de 562-64, 566, 569, 596, 601-02, 604
Quental, Antero de 596

R

Rabassa, Gregory 584
Raby, D. L. 211
Radasewsky, Werner 22
Raitt, Lia Correia 342
Rangel, Annegret 63
Rangel Carlsen, Ivana *see* Carlsen, Ivana Rangel
Raphael, David 347
Rasquilho, Rui 23
Ravenstein 36
Raymond, Th. de 466
RCC Pilotage Foundation 479
Read, Jan 678-79
Rebello, Luíz Francisco 656
Rebelo, Luís de Sousa 547, 622
Regelsberger, Elfriede 407
Régio, José 601
Rego, Paula 630-39
Reid, Colin 87
Reighard, John 296
Reinhard, Heidrun 88
Renouf, Norman P. T. 142, 485
Resende, André de 270, 591

Research Centre for International Strategy 423
Reynolds, S. D. 457
Ribeiro, Ana Isabel 640
Ribeiro, António Lopes 18
Ribeiro, António Pinto 658
Ribeiro, João 246
Ribeiro, Maria de Lurdes 505
Ribeiro, Orlando 30
Ricci, A. C. da Costa 346
Richini, Pierluigi 515
Rilke, Ina 617
Rimmer, Dave 69
Robertson, Carol 680
Robertson, David 680
Robertson, Ian 89, 181
Robinson, Christine 589
Robinson, Oz 479
Rocha Trust 147
Rodrigues, Maria João Madeira 375
Rogers, Francis Millet 4, 131, 271, 376, 475
Rose, Lawrence 161
Rosenblum, Robert 623
Rosengarten, Ruth 633
Rosenthal, E. 90
Rosenthal, Gisela 641
Ross, Stuart 109
Rossa, Walter 507
Rougemont, Rosemary de 289
Rowe, D. Trevor 486
Royal Geographical Society 3
Royal Historical Society 414
Royal Institution of British Architects 508
Rubira, Susan 363
Russell, Colin A. 527
Russell, John 691
Russell, Lady *see* Gordon, Helen Cameron

Russell, Peter E. 232
Russell-Wood, A. J. R. 8, 224
RV Reise 48-49

S

Sá e Silva, José 509
Sá-Carneiro, Mário de 567-68, 602
Sablosky, Juliet Antunes 391
Sabo, Rioletta 646
Sadie, Stanley 653
Sadler, Mike 479
Sadlier, Darlene J. 558-59
Sainte Trinité, Michel de la 377
Salema, Isabel 24
Sampaio, João 320
Sanisteban, Gómez de 131
Santos, Constantino José dos 533
Santos, João Camilo dos 188
Santos, José Paulo dos 510
Santos, Paulo 509
Sapieha, Nicolas 13, 693
Saporiti, Teresa 647
Saraiva, José Hermano 181
Saramago, José 569-76
Sasportes, José 658
Sauvage, Cynthia 110
Schäfler, Andrea 25
Schneider, Elena 70
Schneider, Gunther 22
Schneider, Marshall J. 539
Schümann, Beate 91
Schwartzman, Kathleen C. 207
Seed, Brian 669
Segall, Barbara 695
Sena, António 26
Sena, Jorge de 552, 593
Serpentine Gallery, London 638, 640

259

Serra, John B. 640
Serrão, Vítor 506, 649
Seymour-Smith, Martin 564
Shackley, Louise 236
Shaw, Caroline 533
Shaw, L. M. E. 449
Sheppard, S. 457
Shirodkar, P. P. 304
Sideri, S. 450
Siguan, Miquel 305
Silva, Alberto Araújo e 201
Silva, Ana Paula Ramos da 315
Silva, António Carlos 172
Silva, Inocêncio Francisco da 749
Silva, Joaquim Ramos 411
Silva, Jorge Tavares da 111
Silva, José Eduardo Cansado de Carvalho de Matos e 528
Silva, José Marmelo e 603
Silva, Manuel Luciano da 132
Silva, Manuela da 389
Silva, Maria do Carmo Gago da 20
Silva, Miguel Lago da 172
Silva, Nuno Vasallos e 642
Silva, Raquel Henriques da 649
Silva, Rebelo da 604
Sintra Museum of Modern Art 623
Siza, Álvaro 495, 501, 503, 505-06, 511
Siza, Maria Teresa 26
Slader, Bert 114
Slane, Kathleen Warner 167
Slavin, Neal 27
Smith, Angel 401
Smith, M. van Wyk 597
Smith, Roger C. 480

Smithes, M. F. 143
Smythies, B. E. 159
Soares, António 31
Soares, António Xavier 298
Soares, Mário 264, 403
Soares, Pedro 628
Sociedade Financeira Portuguesa 436
Sociedade Portugal Frankfurt S.A. 644
Sociedade Propaganda de Portugal 3
Society for the Diffusion of Useful Knowledge 175
Solsten, Eric 29
Sousa, Maria Manuela Stocker de 390
Sousa, Maria Reynolds de 390
South Bank University 723
Souza, George Bryan 249
Spence, Godfrey 681
Sta Maria, Bernard 281
Staines, Joe 58, 92
Stammers, Cintia 321
Stanway, Norma 111
Stathatos, C. C. 758
Stefoff, Rebecca 709
Steinberg, Marina 335
Steinherr, Alfred 438
Stern, Irwin 539
Stevens, Ann 563-64
Stevenson, Robert 653
Steves, Rick 93
Stockman, Russell 646
Stone, Christopher 319
Stone, Glyn 415
Stradling, R. A. 50
Strandes, Justus 233
Street, Eugène E. 144
Subrahmanyam, Sanjay 250-51, 272
Suomalainen Tiedeakatemia 661

Swetschinski, Daniel M. 378
Symington, Martin 58, 94
Symposium on Problems of Medieval Coinage 439
Syrett, Stephen 420

T

Taggie, Benjamin F. 182
Tamen, Miguel 540
Tams, G. 234
Tamulonis, Delfina Teixeira 321
Tangerman, Stefan 469
Tate Gallery, London 632
Tavares, Luís Valadares 524
Taylor, James L. 340
Taylor, L. C. 124, 181, 547
Teague, Michael 8, 133
Teixeira, Carlos 759
Tenison, E. M. 206
Tennyson, Alfred, Lord 122
Terlinden, Anne 560
Testa, Peter 510-12
Teves-Costa, P. 52
Thackeray, Susan 290
Thackeray, William Makepeace 122
Theoretical Archaeology Group 169
Thomas, Dorothy 322
Thomas, Hugh 291
Thomson, Graham 497
Thurow, Ethan 70
Timmins, Nick 95
Tisdall, Archie 96
Tisdall, Mary 96
Tomlin, Amanda 74
Tomlinson, David 152
Tomulonis, D. Teixiera 321
Torga, Miguel 594-95, 603

Tovar, Antonio 293
Tovias, Alfred 435
Traquina, Nelson 473
Treece, David 535
Trend, J. B. 541
Trewinnard, Richard 642
Trigueiros, Luíz 513
Tripp, Barbara 110
Tucker, Alan 97-98
Tucker, Brian E. 52
Tyson-Ward, Sue 323-25

U

United Nations Educational and Scientific Organization 702
United States Department of the Army 29
University of Kansas Museum of Natural History 158
Unwin, P. T. H. 470
Unwin, Tim *see* Unwin, P. T. H.

V

Vakil, Abdool Karim A. 401
Vambery, Arminius 129
Vasconcelos, Álvaro de 411
Vasiliu, Mircea 139
Vaz, Katherine 609
Velinkar, Joseph 252
Vernon, Paul 654
Vessels, Gary 626
Vicente, Gil 577-78
Vicente, Mário Gil Videira 515
Viegas, Leonilde 505
Vieira, David J. 760
Vieira, Edite 345, 682
Vieira, Nelson H. 542
Vieyra, Anthony 326
Vilas Boas, Ana *see* Boas, Ana Vilas
Villiers, J. 256
Vincent, Mary 50
Vincent, Nigel 303
Victoria and Albert Museum, London 649
Voak, Jonathan 649
Vowles, G. A. 162
Vowles, R. S. 162

W

Wachter, Gabriela 25
Waite, John 115
Walden, Hilaire 683
Wang, Wilfried 503
Ward, Helen B. 416
Warner, Marina 632
Warner, Robin 306
Way, Ruth 30
Webb, Robert 565
Webster, Neil 487
Weinreb, Matthew 500
Weissbort, Daniel 605
Welch, Sidney R. 235
Weller, Jac 202
West, S. George 761
Wheeler, Charles Gidley *see* Gidley, Charles
Wheeler, Douglas L. 183
Wheeler, Nik 77
White, Landeg 548
Whitlam, John 341-42
Wiarda, Howard J. 393, 406
Wiarda, Ieda Siqueira 406
Wibberly, Leonard 145
Wiggins, Colin 637
Wilkinson, Julia 44, 99
Williams, Alan 429-30
Williams, Edwin B. 327-28
Williams, Mary Wilhelmine 273
Williams, Suzanne 494
Willing, Victor 633, 636
Willis, Robert Clive 329, 621, 724
Wills, John E. 253
Wilson, Christopher Grey 163
Wilson, Robert 619
Wilson, Sarah 619
Windrow, Martin 659
Winius, George D. 134
Wise, Rosemary 155
Withyman (Martin) Associates 100
Wohl, Helmut 627
Wolf, Ronald Charles 438
Woodrow Wilson Center for Scholars 403
Workers' Educational Association 488
World Bank 458
Wormald, Philip 4876
Wright, Carol 684
Wyatt, James Larkin 330

X

Xavier Centre for Historical Research 446

Y

Yorke, James 649

Z

Zenith, Richard 21, 543-44, 551, 553, 561, 605-06
Zimler, Richard 13, 582, 620

Index of Titles

A

AA Baedeker Algarve 65
AA Baedeker Lisbon 65
AA Baedeker Portugal 65
AA Baedeker Spain & Portugal 32
AA Essential Portuguese phrase book 343
AA Essential Spain and Portugal 32
AA Explorer Portugal 75
AA glovebox atlas, Spain and Portugal 32
AA Thomas Cook travellers' Algarve and southern Portugal 58
ACIS: Journal of the Association for Contemporary Iberian Studies 723
ACLAIIR Newsletter 696
Across the rivers of Portugal 114
Act of the damned 543
Adventures of plants and the Portuguese discoveries 151
After the revolution 534
Age of Realism 562
Age of the baroque in Portugal 627
Agricultural policy in Europe 468
Agriculture and the regions 466
Alastair Sawday's special places to stay 105
Albuquerque, Caesar of the East 256

Algarve (Boulton) 59
Algarve (Brines) 61
Algarve (O'Callaghan) 84
Algarve and southern Portugal 54
Algarve, a travel guide 96
Algarve holiday map 34
Algarve plants and landscape 155
Algarve, southern lands 24
Algarve, with local tips 79
All the names 569
Álvaro Siza (Fleck) 503
Álvaro Siza (Jodidio) 511
Álvaro Siza (Testa) 512
Álvaro Siza: architecture writings 495
Álvaro Siza city sketches 503
Álvaro Siza, 1954-1988 496
Álvaro Siza, works & projects 510
Always astonished 549
O amor de perdição 596
Um amor feliz 589
Analysis of the hotel industry in Portugal 107
Anarchist banker and other Portuguese stories 549, 601, 603
Ancient languages of Spain and Portugal 293
Ancient languages of the Hispanic Peninsula 293
André de Resende's 'Poemata latina', Latin poems 591
Anglo-Portuguese Alliance 413

Anglo-Portuguese Alliance and the English merchants in Portugal, 1654-1810 449
Annals of the purple city 615
O ano da morte de Ricardo Reis 576
Anticlerical satire in medieval Portuguese literature 530
Antinous 552
Anuário estatístico de Portugal 387
APN, the Anglo-Portuguese News 711, 720
Archaeology of Iberia 169
Archaeometallurgical survey for ancient tin mines and smelting sites in Spain and Portugal 171
Architecture 501
Architectural practice in Europe: Portugal 508
Arcos de Lisboa 509
Arcos e arcadas de Lisboa 509
Arte de música 592
Arthurian legend in the literatures of the Spanish peninsula 189
Arthurian literature in Spain and Portugal 189
Arthurian literature in the Middle Ages 189
Ásia 118
Atlantic houses 497

263

Atlantic Spain and Portugal 479
Atlas of wintering birds in the western Algarve 147
Auto da barca do inferno 577
Auto dos danados 544
Aviz: uma história de Lisboa 106

B

Babel guide to the fiction of Portugal 575
Backwards out of the big world 138
Baltasar and Blimunda 570
Barron's travel-wise Portuguese 309
Bartholomew road atlas 34
Bartholomew's European travel map 34
Bats of Portugal 158
Battle of Buçaco 201
Battle studies in the Peninsula 200
BBC Talk Portuguese 319
Beckford of Fonthill 263
Beginner's Portuguese 323
Beginning of Portuguese mammalogy 146
Bem-vindos, a Portuguese language course 321
Berardo Collection 623
Berlitz pocket guide Algarve 83, 85
Berlitz pocket guide Lisbon 85
Berlitz pocket guide Portugal 85
Berlitz Portuguese phrase book 344
Berlitz travellers' guide to Portugal 97

Bibliografia das literaturas africanas de expressão portuguesa 755
Bibliografia das obras impressas em Portugal no século XVI 749
Bibliografia geográfica 753
Bibliografia geral portuguesa, século XV 749
Bibliografia ibérica del siglo XV 749
Bibliographie des voyages en Espagne et en Portugal 748
Bibliography of theses and dissertations in Portuguese topics completed in the United States and Canada 519
Bibliotheca Lusitana 745
Bica, the Portuguese Water Dog 148
O bilhete postal ilustrado e a história urbana da Grande Lisboa 20
Biographies from ancient kings to presidents 230
Biographies of Prince Edward and Friar Pedro 270
Birds of Iberia 152
Birdwatchers' guide to Portugal 157
Birdwatching guide to the Algarve 149
Blindness 571
Boat plays 577
O bobo 596
Bola 685, 688
Boletim de bibliografia portuguesa 754
Book of disquiet 550
Book of disquietude 550

Brazilian Portuguese 324
Breeding birds of the Algarve 162
Bride of two kings 192
British community handbook 287
British Council libraries in Portugal 750
British Historical Society of Portugal Annual Report 724
Brothers Corte-Real 265
Builders of the oceans 123
Building popular power 490
Bulletin of Hispanic Studies 725
Bulletin of Spanish Studies 725
Bulletin of the John Rylands University Library of Manchester 761
Bungs, bribes and bad language 306
Business Portuguese glossary 333
Bussaco Palace Hotel 111
Buying a home in Portugal 285
By the rivers of Babylon 593

C

Cacilheiros 476
Cais e navios de Lisboa 477
Calouste Gulbenkian Museum 701
Camilo Castelo Branco no centenário da morte 585
Camões Center Quarterly 726
Campaign against repression 416

Cantigas d'amigo dos trovadores portugueses 599
Career and legend of Vasco da Gama 272
Carnival stage 580
Carta de Portugal 43
Carta geológica de Portugal 42
Cartas de amor de Anna Conover e Mollie Bidwell 561
Cartographia Portugal Algarve 36
Cartographia Spain & Portugal 36
Cartuxas de Portugal 364
Uma casa portuguesa 664
Casas atlânticas, Atlantic houses 497
Case against Camões 548
Centenary Pessoa 551
Century companion to the wines of Spain and Portugal 678
Challenge of democratic consolidation 399
Changing architecture of Iberian Politics, 1974-1992 397
Chapel of St John the Baptist and its collections in São Roque Church, Lisbon 375
Characteristics of Portuguese literature 532
Child workers in Portugal 494
Chinese export porcelain 645
Christoph Columbus und der Anteil des Juden an den spanischen und portugiesischen Entdeckungen 254

Christopher Columbus and the participation of the Jews in the Spanish and Portuguese discoveries 254
Christopher Columbus and the Portuguese 259
Churches in Portugal 361
Churches of Portugal 354
Cidades indo-portugueses 507
5 poemas, poèmes, poems, poesie, Gedichte 543
Cities of Europe: Oporto and Lisbon 11
City and the mountains 562
City flash Lisbon 40
City pack Lisbon 76
City streets map 35
Civil war in Portugal and the siege of Oporto 203
Classification of educational systems 522
Closing the migratory cycle 283
Collected poems (Pessoa) 555
Collins field guide 164
Collins Gem Portuguese dictionary 334
Collins Gem Portuguese phrase finder 334
Collins Madeira holiday map 37
Collins pocket dictionary, Portuguese-English, English-Portuguese 341
Collins Portuguese dictionary 341
Collins Portuguese phrase book 345
Collins Spain and Portugal 37
Colloquial Portuguese (D'Orsey) 346

Colloquial Portuguese (Sampaio) 320
Colloquial Portuguese of Brazil 320
Comedia de Rubena 578
Comedia do viuvo 578
O Comércio do Porto 712
Complete Portuguese water dog 148
Computer-validated Portuguese-English transformational grammar 330
Concise history of Portugal 174
Conflict and change in Portugal 212
Consolation for the tribulations of Israel 374
Constitution of the Portuguese Republic 417
Contemporary Review 206
O conto da ilha desconhecida 575
Contos de montanha 595
Conversational Brazilian Portuguese 327
Cooking of Spain and Portugal 669
Copy of a letter of the King of Portugal sent to the King of Castile concerning the voyage and success of India 127
Cork 467
Corporate acquisitions and mergers in Portugal 438
Correio da Manhã 712-13
Costa do Estoril, blues and golds 24
Costa Verde 64
Counterinsurgency in Africa 226

Country profile Portugal 441
Country studies, Portugal 426
Cozinha tradicional portuguesa 676
Creation of the world 594
Criação do mundo 594
Cricket in Portugal 689
O crime do Padre Amaro 566
Crisis and change in rural Europe 461
Crisis of dictatorships 393
Cultura 727
Cultural atlas of Spain and Portugal 50
Cultures of the world, Portugal 9
Os cus de Judas 546

D

Damião de Góis 262
Dancing ostriches from Disney's 'Fantasia' 630
Daniel Webster and his contemporaries 125
Daytrips, Spain and Portugal 142
Death on the Douro 610
Decolonization of Portuguese Africa 229
Decorative tiles of Luís Ferreira 647
Dedalus book of Portuguese fantasy 602
Democratization and social settlements 404
Design aus Portugal 644
Deus passeando pela brisa da tarde 584
Development of accounting in Portugal and the establishment of the Aula do Commercio 437

Development of the Portuguese economy 424
Devotion to the immaculate heart of Mary 377
Diário da República 714
Diário das Beiras 715
Diário de Aveiro 715
Diário de Coimbra 715
Diário de Notícias 716, 719
Dias and his successors 116
Dicionário bibliográfico português 749, 754
Dicionário inglês-português 335
Dicionário prosódico 294
Dictionary of metaphoric idioms, English-Portuguese 335
Dictionary of Portuguese African civilization 230
Dictionary of the literatures of the Iberian Peninsula 531
Directory of Spanish and Portuguese film-makers and films 655
Discover Portugal 72
Discovering Portuguese 316
Discovery in the archives of Spain and Portugal 221
Distoguide Euromap 41
Dog woman 631
Doing business in Portugal 448
Dom Pedro 266
Dom Pedro, the magnanimous 273
Domingo 714
Duns Pep 7.500 443

E

Earliest Arthurian names in Spain and Portugal 189
Earthquake damage scenarios in Lisbon for disaster preparedness 52
Eating Portuguese style 668
Educational reform 516
Eight centuries of Portuguese monarchy 205
Elephant's memory 546
Eleven essays on Spain, Portugal and Brasil [sic] 541
Embarcações regionais da tradição portuguesa 478
Embassies and illusions 253
Employment of women 390
Encountering Macau 240
Encounters and transformations 166
Encyclopaedia Britannica 742
English art in Portugal 624
English contingent 1661-1668 193
English in Portugal 286
English poems 552
English translations from the Portuguese to the year 1700 754
Ensaio sobre a cegueira 571
Entrée to the Algarve 668
Epic & lyric 547
Epithalamium 552
Escultura portuguesa 648
Espagne, Portugal 108
España, Portugal 46
Essential course in modern Portuguese 329

Estrela Mountain Dog and its background 160
Estado das ciências em Portugal 525
Euro-City map Lisbon 48
Euro-Country maps 48
Euro-Holiday map Algarve 48
Euro-Holiday map Lisbon and its coastal region 48
Euro loco pocket book 487
European Bookseller 705
European Congress of Mammalogy 146
European destiny, Atlantic transformations 410
European football 686
European football yearbook 687
European loco pocket book 487
European Portugal 398
European railway atlas 481
Europe at school 521
Euro pocket atlas 39
Euro-Regional map, Portugal, Galicia 48
Eurostat statistical yearbook of the regions 428
O evangelho segundo Jesus Cristo 572
Every inch a king: a biography of Dom Pedro I 260
Exortação da guerra 577
Explanation of the birds 544
Explicação dos pássaros 544
Exploring rural Portugal 92
Export directory of Portugal 444
Expresso 717
Expulsion 1492 chronicles 374
Eyewitness travel guide 60

F

Fabled shore 140
Factory House at Oporto 667
Fado alexandrino 546
Fascism and resistance in Portugal 211
Fatima, a close encounter of the worst kind 355
Fatima, a story of hope 367
Fatima has the answer 373
Fátima in Lúcia's own words 377
Fátima, the great sign 377
Feminine in the poetry of Herberto Helder 588
Ferdinand Magellan 258
Ferdinand Magellan and the discovery of the world 709
Fernando Pessoa, a galaxy of poets 556
Fernando Pessoa & Co. 553
Fernando Pessoa: the bilingual Portuguese poet 560
Fernando Pessoa: voices of a nomadic soul 557
Fielding's paradors and pousadas 104
Finisterra 753
Fire of excellence 500
Fire of tongues 360
First Portuguese colonial empire 222
O físico prodigioso 593
501 Portuguese verbs 302
Flight into Portugal 208

Flowers of south west Europe 159
Focus on the Spanish and Portuguese-speaking world 702
Fodor's Portugal 78
Following story 617
Food of Portugal 663
Food of Spain and Portugal 677
Foreign economic relations of the E.C. 435
Frederick William Flower 19
From discovery to independence 230
From higher education to employment 523
Frommer's Europe 86
Frommer's Portugal 86

G

Gardens of Spain and Portugal 695
Gastronomy of Spain and Portugal 672
Gender, ethnicity and class in modern Portuguese-speaking culture 536
Genealogy of ecclesiastical jurisdictions 365
Geografia de Portugal 30
Geographisches Jahrbuch 753
Geography of Spain and Portugal 30
Get by in Portuguese: a beginner's course for holidaymakers and business people 319
Get by in Portuguese: the all-in-one language and travel guide 308

Getting to know the
    inferno 546
Gil Vicente 579
Gil Vicente and the
    development of the
    comedia 578
Gil Vicente bibliography
    758
Globetrotter travel guide 39
Globetrotter travel map
    Algarve 39, 84
God strolling in the cool of
    evening 584
Goldenbook Estoril coast
    and Sintra 63
Golf's golden coast 691
Gospel according to Jesus
    Christ 571-72
Grammar of the Portuguese
    language 314
Grand peregrination 117
Grande enciclopédia
    portuguesa e brasileira
    743
Great Powers and the
    Iberian Peninsula,
    1931-1941 415
Great shadow 567
Growing up English 282
Guia das fundições
    portuguesas 744
Guia horário oficial 484
Guide and plan of Lisbon 31
Guide to Portuguese
    railways 482
Guide to the Douro and
    Port wine 666
Guide to the Megalithic
    monuments 172
Guide to the wines of
    Spain and Portugal 678

H

Hebrews of the Portuguese
    nation 357

Hegemonic male 660
Hispania 519, 728
Historical dictionary of
    Portugal 183
History of dance 658
History of literature 532
History of music 653
History of photography 26
History of plastic arts 649
History of Portugal 177
History of Portugal and
    Spain 178
History of Portuguese
    economic thought 421
History of Spain and
    Portugal (Busk) 175
History of Spain and
    Portugal (Payne) 180
History of the Jews of
    Spain and Portugal from
    the earliest times 369
History of the Military
    Museum 703
History of the Portuguese
    fado 654
History of the Portuguese
    navigation in India,
    1497-1600 241
History of the Portuguese
    overseas expansion,
    1400-1670 223
History of the siege of
    Lisbon 571
History of theatre 656
Holiday Portuguese 348
Holiday tours in Spain,
    Portugal and Madeira 57
Home book of Portuguese
    cookery 673
Horse of white clouds 597
Hotéis, restaurantes,
    Portugal 108
Hotels of character and
    charm in Portugal 103
Housing in Portugal and
    Brazil 514

How to eat out in Portugal
    347
Hugo advanced
    Portuguese course 307
Hugo on the move:
    Portuguese 318
Hugo Portuguese
    dictionary 331
Hugo practical dictionary
    336
Hugo's practical
    dictionaries 336
Hugo's speak Portuguese
    today 307
Hugo taking Portuguese
    further 318

I

Iberia and Latin America
    406
Iberia and the
    Mediterranean 182
Iberia-Latin America
    connection 406
Iberian construction
    industry 457
Iberian identity 4
Iberian resources in the
    United Kingdom 699
Iberia Studies 729
Illustrious house of
    Ramires 563
Ilustre Casa de Ramires
    563
Imagem 474
Improvising empire 250
In and out of enchantment
    661
In Crete with the Minotaur
    593
O Independente 718
India and the West 252
Indian Economic and
    Social Review 250
Indo-Portuguese cities 507

Infante D. Henrique 709
Influência do vocabulário português nas línguas asiáticas 298
Inhabited heart 543
Inquérito ao emprego 491
Inquérito permanente ao emprego 491
Inquisitor's manual 546
Inscriptions 552
Inside ethnic families 280
Insider's guide Portugal 77
Insight compact Algarve 91
Insight compact Portugal 55
Insight fleximap Algarve 35
Insight fleximap Lisbon 35
Insight map Lisbon 35
Insight pocket Algarve 59
Insight pocket Lisbon 59, 66
Insight pocket Portugal 55
Instant Portuguese 322
Internationalism and the three Portugals 271
International Journal of Iberian Studies 723
International Tourism Quarterly 102
International tourism reports, Portugal 102
Interpretation of 16th- and 17th-century Iberian keyboard music 652
In the wake of the Portuguese navigators 133
Into the city: Álvaro Siza 511
Into the rising sun: Vasco da Gama and the sea route to the East 123
Intrepid itinerant 120

Introducing Portugal 7
Introducing Portuguese grammar 328
Introduction to Fernando Pessoa, literary Modernist 559
Introduction to fifty European novels 564
Introductory Portuguese grammar 328
Issues in Portuguese economic integration 423
Issues in the phonology and morphology of the major Iberian languages 301
Issues in urban earthquake risk 52

J

Jangada de Pedra 574
Japan Society of London, Transactions and Proceedings 237
Jardins de Portugal 694
Jewish vestiges in Portugal 359
Jews of Spain and Portugal and the Inquisition 371
Joalharia portuguesa 642
O jogo 688
John James Forrester 261
John of Empoli 269
Jornal de Notícias 719
José Matias 565
Journal of a visit to Madeira and Portugal 119
Journal of Iberian and Latin American Studies 730
Journal of the Society for Army Historical Research 193

K

Karen Brown's Portugal 110
Key to the Portuguese grammar 318
King Dinis and the Alfonsine heritage 185
Kompass 445

L

Lacas namban em Portugal 643
Landscapes of Algarve 53
Landscapes of Portugal: Algarve 53
Landscapes of Portugal: Costa Verde, Minho, Peneda-Gerês 53
Landscapes of Portugal: Sintra, Cascais, Estoril 53
Langenscheidt's pocket Portuguese dictionary 332
Langenscheidt universal Portuguese dictionary 332
Last Kabbalist in Lisbon 620
Laws and charities of the Spanish & Portuguese Jews 368
Legal situation of the Portuguese woman 390
Leisure map: Spain and Portugal 38
Let's go Spain, Portugal & Morocco 70
Letters from a Portuguese nun 608
Letters of a Portuguese nun 609
Liberal revolution, social change and economic development 380

Libraries and library services 698
Library of Congress Hispanic and Portuguese collections 700
El libro de los acuerdos 356
Linguaphone curso de português 315
Linguistic minorities of the European Economic Community 305
Lisboa ao cair da tarde 21
Lisboa desaparecida 16
Lisboa e o aqueduto 505
Lisboa e os seus arredores 10
Lisboa: Lisbon past and present 2
Lisboa, planta 46
Lisbon (Boulton) 59
Lisbon (Gonçalves) 71
Lisbon (Hamm) 22
Lisbon (Laidlar) 752
Lisbon: a guide to recent architecture 509
Lisbon Airport, 1942-1992 474
Lisbon and central Portugal 54
Lisbon and the aqueduct 505
Lisbon, an unforgettable city 73
Lisbon at day's end 21
Lisbon for less 80
Lisbon in your pocket 81
Lisbon, the mini-Rough Guide 74
Lisbon: the sparkling miracle on the western edge of Europe 25
Lisbon traviata 616
Lisbon world Expo 98 451

List of the writings of C. R. Boxer 761
Literary souvenir 613
Liturgies of the Spanish & Portuguese Reformed Episcopal Church 358
Live & work in Spain and Portugal 288
Living in Portugal 290
Living language common usage dictionary 338
Living language Portuguese dictionary 338
Livro de viagens 26
O livro do desassossego 550, 557
Livros disponíveis 754
Local development 420
Log book 583
Lucio's confession 568
Lucky in love 589
Os Lusíadas 294, 547
Lusiads 548
Luso-Brazilian Review 727
Lusophone Africa, Portugal and the United States 409
Lyric poet 565

M

Macau, the imaginary city 248
Madeira holiday map 34
Magellan's voyages 134
Magic of al-Gharb 87
Os Maias 564
Maias 564
Making of an enterprise 352
Making of Brazil 255
Making of Portuguese democracy 402
O Mandarim 565
Mandarin 565

Manual de pintura e caligrafia 573
Manual of calligraphy 573
Many races, one nation 292
Mapa das estradas 33
Marco Polo España Portugal 79
Mariana 609
Mário Soares 264
Masterpiece Library of Short Stories 604
Mean feat 115
Medieval Iberia 187
Melville's Camões 548
Memory of another river 543
Men who migrate, women who wait 275
Mensagem 554
Message 554
Metamorphosis 592
Migration of the Portuguese Royal Family from Portugal to Brazil in 1807/8 197
Military dress in the Peninsular War 659
Military interventions in Portuguese politics 395
Mirobriga 167
Modern art in Portugal, 1910-1940 640
Modern poetry in translation 605
Modern Portugal 217
Modern Spanish and Portuguese literature 539
Mountain doctor 590
Muse reborn 586
Music of Portugal 74
Muslim Spain and Portugal 184
My people, my country 281

My Portuguese workbook 657
Myth makers 563
My tour in Portugal 137

N

Namban lacquerware 643
Namban screens 643
Napoleon and Iberia 196
Narrow gauge railways of Portugal 483
Nationalism and the nation in the Iberian Peninsula 401
Natural history museum of the 18th century 146
Nazaré 18
Nazaré: women and men in a pre-bureaucratic Portuguese fishing village 462
New bibliography of the Lusophone literatures of Africa 755
New Encyclopaedia Britannica 742
New Grove dictionary of music and musicians 653
New history of Portugal 177
New history of Spain and Portugal 180
New information technology in education in Portugal 524
New lights on the Peninsular War 194
New method for learning the Portuguese language 317
New Portugal 215
New Portuguese letters 581
News 722

Newsletter of the Calouste Gulbenkian Foundation 732
1986-1995, Álvaro Siza 513
No garlic in the soup 145
North and central Portugal in the 1990s 429
Northern Portugal 54
North Portuguese agriculture in the European context 470
Novas cartas portuguesas 538, 581
Nove, nine Portuguese painters 625
Novos contos de montanha 595
NTC's compact Portuguese & English dictionary 337
Nursery rhymes 632

O

Occupational segregation in Portugal 491
OECD economic surveys 434
Official publications of western Europe 714
Off the beaten track in Portugal 95
Oldest ally 415
113 Galician-Portuguese troubador poems 606
On Portuguese simple sounds 294
On the contrary 27
Opera in Portugal 650
Ordinary Portuguese stamps 471
Origins of urbanization in Iberia 168
Ottoman response to European expansionism 243

Our Lady at Fatima 373
Our Lady of Fatima's peace plan from heaven 377
Our oldest ally 414
Overland journey to Lisbon at the close of 1846 122
Oxford colour Portuguese dictionary 342
Oxford Duden pictorial Portuguese-English dictionary 339
Oxford paperback Portuguese dictionary 342

P

Packaging in Europe, Spain & Portugal 455
Packaging in Spain and Portugal 455
Passport to Portugal 600
Património mundial 506
Paula Rego 633
Paula Rego, paintings 1982-83 636
Paula Rego, selected works, 1981-1986 638
Paula Rego, Serpentine Gallery 638
Paula Rego, tales from the National Gallery 637
Peasant of Portugal 613
Peculiarities of a fair-headed girl 565
Pedro Craesbeeck & Sons 704
Pedro Nunes, his lost algebra and other discoveries 267
Peeps at many lands 708
Peeps at Portugal 90
Pendle witches 634

Penguin guide to Portugal 98
Pequeno dicionário Michaelis 337
Peregrinações 117, 128
Personnes agées dans le monde 385
Peter Pan and other stories 635
Philips road map Spain and Portugal 47
Philosopher in Portugal 144
Planet talk 99
Playtime in Portugal 136
Pleasure by the busload 139
Poemas ingleses 552
Poemata latina 591
Poetic profession 510
Poet's way with music 592
Policies on labour relations and social dialogue in European countries 492
Political parties and democracy in Portugal 391
Political prisoners in Portugal 206
Politics in contemporary Portugal 392
Politics in the Portuguese empire 231
Pombal, paradox of the Enlightenment 268
Ponto da situação da aplicação das novas tecnologias de informação às bibliotecas 697
Pope's elephant 186
Port cities and intruders 244
Port companion 674
Port o' call 464

Port to port 671
Port wine quintas 670
Porto 22
Porto & north Portugal 28
Porto & northern Portugal 28
O Porto em vários sentidos 13
Portogallo fra Europa e Atlantico 12
Portrait of the regions, volume 3: Portugal 428
Portugal (Barrett) 55
Portugal (Bertolazzi) 12
Portugal (Carkovic)
Portugal (Champion) 706
Portugal (Decker) 66
Portugal (Demeude) 15
Portugal (Evans) 68
Portugal (Khorian) 77
Portugal (Reinhard) 88
Portugal (Robertson) 89
Portugal (Slavin) 27
Portugal (Unwin) 752
Portugal (Williamson) 99
Portugal: a companion history 181
Portugal: a country of forests 150
Portugal, a country profile 441
Portugal, a country study 29
Portugal: a Lonely Planet travel atlas 44
Portugal, an Atlantic paradox 411
Portugal, ancient country, young democracy 403
Portugal and Africa 227
Portugal and E.C. membership evaluated 432
Portugal and her overseas provinces 224

Portugal and its empire 219
Portugal and the Algarve 39
Portugal and the discovery of the Atlantic 126
Portugal and the Portuguese world 179
Portugal and the regions 466
Portugal and the sea (Rasquilho) 23
Portugal and the sea (Russell-Wood) 8
Portugal and the world 651
Portugal, a new era 436
Portugal, a short history 177
Portugal contemporâneo 14
Portugal elite forces insignia 658
Portugal e o mar 23
Portugal e o mundo 651
Portugal: from monarchy to pluralist democracy 210
Portugal, gateway to greatness 1
Portugal guide, your passport to great travel 62
Portugal: institutions and facts 7
Portugal in the 1980s 216
Portugal: investment and growth 436
Portugal, Madeira 46
Portugal, Madeira, the Azores 82
Portugal map 49
Portugal, 1998-99 427
Portugal now 209
Portugal: 1001 sights 165

Portugal: practical commercial law 417
Portugal railway map 481
Portugal's foreign community handbook 287
Portugal, Spain and the African Atlantic, 1343-1490 232
Portugal's pousada route 109
Portugal's Revolution, ten years on 214
Portugal's silver service 649
Portugal: status of women 390
Portugal's wines and winemakers 674
Portugal, the Algarve 68
Portugal: the Constitution and the consolidation of democracy, 1976-1989 418
Portugal, the pathfinder 134
Portugal: the price of opposition 416
Portugal, the U.S. and N.A.T.O. 408
Portugal to 1990 431
Portugal to 1993 431
Portugal, visitor traffic to the U.K. 100
Portugal, west Spain 49
Portugal, with Madeira and the Azores 48, 94
Portugal, with places of interest 45
Portugal: women in prison 416
Portugiesenzeit von Deutsch- und Englisch-Östafrika 233
O Português Cristóvão Colombo 257

Portuguese (Cook) 311
Portuguese (Parkinson) 303
Portuguese: a complete course for beginners 324
Portuguese Africa 227
Portuguese agriculture after accession 463
Portuguese agriculture in transition 469
Portuguese and the sultanate of Gujarat 242
Portuguese, Brazilian and African studies 621
Portuguese Columbus 257
Portuguese Communist Party's strategy for power 394
Portuguese cookery 664
Portuguese cooking 683
Portuguese cooking: the authentic and robust cuisine of Portugal 680
Portuguese decorative tiles: azulejos 646
Portuguese defense and foreign policy since democratization 412
Portuguese economy: a picture in figures 433
Portuguese economy since 1974 425
Portuguese economy towards 1992 422
Portuguese emigration to the United States 274
Portuguese empire in Asia 251
Portuguese-English dictionary 340
Portuguese financial system 438
Portuguese foundations guide 744
Portuguese gardens 694

Portuguese grammar, with the Portuguese words properly accented 326
Portuguese in Asia 757
Portuguese in Canada 759
Portuguese in India 245
Portuguese in the 16th century 190
Portuguese in the United States 760
Portuguese in three months 307, 318
Portuguese journey 135
Portuguese knights of the Order of the Garter 176
Portuguese language 296
Portuguese language and Luso-Brazilian literature 746
Portuguese life in town and country 144
Portuguese Literary and Cultural Studies 733
Portuguese literature from its origins to 1990 751
Portuguese meat and livestock industry 456
Portuguese merchants and missionaries in feudal Japan 237
Portuguese migration in global perspective 278
Portuguese military and the State 395
Portuguese palaeography 304
Portuguese period in East Africa 233
Portuguese photography since 1854 26
Portuguese phrase book (Freeland) 349
Portuguese phrase book (Lexus) 350
Portuguese pilgrims and Dighton Rock 132

273

Portuguese political prisoners, a British national protest 206
Portuguese primer 310
Portuguese Review 734
Portuguese revolution of 25 April, 1974 747
Portuguese rule and Spanish Crown in South Africa, 1581-1640 235
Portuguese seaborne empire 218, 224
Portuguese ships, 14th-19th century 478
Portuguese Studies 735, 761
Portuguese Studies Review 736
Portuguese: the land and its people 5
Portuguese trade in Asia under the Habsburgs 440
Portuguese-UK Chamber of Commerce yearbook 447
Portuguese verbs and essentials of grammar 325
Portuguese vocables in Asiatic languages 298
Portuguese vowels 294
Portuguese water dog 148
Portuguese way 56
Post-colonial literature of Lusophone Africa 531
Postwar Portuguese drama 656
Pousadas of Portugal 101
Practical cookery 665
Practical grammar of Portuguese and English 313
Practical guide to colloquial Portuguese 321

Pre-bureaucratic Europeans 462
Pre-Mesozoic geology of Iberia 51
Precision astrolabe 475
Presence of Pessoa 558
Problems of medieval coinage in the Iberian area 439
Proceedings of the international colloquium on the Portuguese and the Pacific 188
Production, marketing and consumption of animal products in Portugal 458
Professor Pfiglzz and his strange companion 603
Profiles of language education 517
Progressive Portugal 3
Provisional town postmarks of Portugal 471
Public enterprise in Portugal & Spain 453
O Público 720
Putting citizens first 419

Q

Queerspace 381
Queluz: the palace and the gardens 502
Quest for eastern Christians 376
Question of how 538
Quick & easy Portuguese 312

R

Reclaiming English kinship theory 386
Record 688, 690

Reflections 17
Regent of the sea: Cannamore's response to Portuguese expansion 236
Regional boats in the Portuguese tradition 478
Regional emigration 277
Relic 565
A relíquia 565
Reluctant cosmopolitans 378
Return of the caravels 546
Reviews of national science and technology policy 526
Revisionary history of Portuguese literature 540
Revista de Estudos Anglo-Portugueses 737
Revolution and counter-revolution 213
Revolutionary Left in Portugal 396
Revolutionary Portugal 205
Revolution at the grassroots 379
Revolution within the Revolution 460
Ribeiro's 'History of Ceilao' 246
Rick Steves' Spain & Portugal 93
Rise of scientific Europe, 1500-1800 527
River running by 614
Rivers of Babylon and other stories
Roads to today's Portugal 542
Romance languages 303
Roman Portugal 164

Rough Guide phrase book 351
Royal horses of Europe 154

S

Sacred and the profane 626
Sailing vessels in Portugal 478
Salazar's dictatorship and European fascism 405
Santa vida e religiosa conversação do Frei Pedro 270
Science in Portugal 525
Secret life of images 582
Selected poems 555
Selections of nineteenth-century Portuguese prose 596
Select views of some of the principal cities of Europe 11
Self-catering in Portugal 684
O selo base português 471
Sephardi heritage 356
Sephardim of England 366
Shades of Adamastor 597
Shadow's weight 543
Sharpe's enemy 612
Short history of Portugal 173
Signs of fire 593
Sinais de fogo 593
Sin of Father Amaro 566
Sketches and adventures in Madeira 125
Slave trade 291
Slavery in Portuguese India 247
Small death in Portugal 619

Social complexity and the development of towns in Iberia 168
Social inequality in a Portuguese hamlet 383
Social origins of democratic collapse 207
Society for Spanish and Portuguese Historical Studies Bulletin 730
Society for Spanish and Portuguese Historical Studies Newsletter 730
Society organised for war 191
Songs of a friend 599
Sonnets from the Portuguese, and other poems 611
Sons of Adam, daughters of Eve 384
Southern Portugal, Algarve in your pocket 81, 83
Southern Portugal in the 1990s 430
South of nowhere 546
Spain and Portugal 486
Spain and Portugal by rail 485
Spain and Portugal in your pocket 93
Spain, Portugal 1:800,000 49
Spaniard in the Portuguese Indies 239
Spanish and Portuguese Jewry before and after 1492 353
Spanish & Portuguese short stories 604
Stanley Gibbons stamp catalogue 472

State of the art of the application of new information technologies in libraries 697
Statistical yearbook of Portugal 387
Stone raft 574
Stranger's grave 613
Structural change and small-farm agriculture in north-west Portugal 465
Structure of Portuguese society 382
Studies in Portuguese literature and history 622
Studies in the Portuguese Discoveries I 118
Studies on the acquisition of Portuguese 299
Study on European forestry information 150
Subject in Brazilian Portuguese 300
Summary report on the services available for the unemployed 520
Survey of education in Portugal 518
Survey of English language teaching and learning in Portugal 295
Survival of empire 249
Synergy at work 407
Synthesis of Portuguese Culture 7, 501, 525, 532, 649, 653, 656, 658

T

Tabacaria 557
Tagus and the Tiber 122
Tagus Golf Society 692

Taking lives 618
Taking Portuguese further 318
Tale of the unknown island 575
Tales and legends of Portugal 662
Tales & more tales from the mountain 595
Tales from the mountain 595
Taste of Portugal 682
Teachers and trainers in vocational training 515
10 dances from Portugal, collected in the country of origin 657
Tentative Portuguese-African bibliography 755
Tesserae 739
Textiles and training 452
Theoretical issues and practical issues in Portuguese-English translations 297
Theses in Hispanic studies, approved for higher degrees 519
They went to Portugal 124
They went to Portugal, too 124
Things seen in Portugal 143
Third secret of Fatima 377
1386-1986 Portugal 442
35 sonnets 552
32 Cantigas d'amigo 598
This way Algarve 56
Three discovery plays 577
Through Spain and Portugal 141
Time for Portuguese 323
Time Out Lisbon 69
Times 740

Times Higher Educational Supplement 740
Times Literary Supplement 740
Tobacconist's 557
Today there is no misery 459
Todos os nomes 569
Tomás Taveira 498-99
Torrent of Portyngale 607
Toute la verité sur Fatima 377
Trade and finance in Portuguese India 446
Trade and power: informal colonialism in Anglo-Portuguese relations 450
Trade, exchange rates and agricultural pricing policy 458
Trade union movement in Portugal 489
Traditional Portuguese cookery 676
Tragedy of Inês de Castro 587
Tragedy of Portugal 206
Training of trainers in Portugal 515
Transactions and Proceedings of the Japan Society of London 237
Transculturation and resistance 537
Transition to democracy in Spain and Portugal 406
Transitions from dictatorship to democracy 393
Transportation and deportation 284
Travel guide to Jewish Europe 362
Travels in Portugal 122

Travels of Fernão Mendes Pinto 128
Travels of the Infante Dom Pedro of Portugal 131, 376
La Traviata 616
Treatise on the natural order of things 546
Trees of Monserrate 153
30 anos de engenharia civil 528
25th of April in the Portuguese public art 628
201 Portuguese verbs fully conjugated 302
Two industries in Roman Lusitania 170
Two Portuguese exiles in Castile 370

U

Uncertain outcome 400
Under the bright wings 363
Universal history, ancient and modern 178

V

Vanguard of Empire 480
Vasco da Gama and the Portuguese explorers 709
Vathek 130, 263
Veleiros de Portugal 478
Vestígios hebraicos em Portugal 359
Vida do infante D. Duarte 270
Vida Hispánica 741
Vieira da Silva 641
24 Horas 721
Visions of the self in the novels of Camilo Castelo Branco 585

Visita ao Museu Militar 703
Visit to the Military Museum 703
Visit to the Portuguese possessions in south-western Africa 234
Vocational education and training in Portugal 518
Vocational training in Portugal 520
Voices from an empire 533, 537
Het volgende verbaal 617
Voyage of Magellan 709
Voyage of Pedro Álvares Cabral 121
Voyages and adventures of Ferdinand Mendez Pinto, the Portuguese 129

W

Wage determination and sex segregation 491
Walking in Portugal 112
Walking in the Algarve 113
War in the Peninsula 198
We go to Portugal 707
We have already cried many tears 276
We, the future 6

Webster's English-Portuguese dictionary 336
Webster's Portuguese-English dictionary 336
Weekly News 722
Welcome to Portugal 67
Wellington in the Peninsula 202
Wellington's Peninsular victories 195
Wellington's Peninsular War battles and battlefield campaign 199
Western European broadcasting 473
When men walk dry 372
When millions saw Mary 377
Where to stay in Spain, Portugal and Andorra 58
Where to watch birds in Spain and Portugal 161
Who's who of the artists of Portugal 629
Wild flowers of the Algarve 156
William Beckford (Jack) 263
William Beckford (Lees-Milne) 263

William Beckford & Portugal 130
Willings press guide 710
Window on folk dance 657
Wines of Portugal 679
Wines of Spain and Portugal 675
Wines of Spain and Portugal 678
With hardened hands 279
Women in Portugal 390
Women, literature and culture in the Portuguese-speaking world 529
Women of the praia 388
Wondrous physician 593
Work of Álvaro Siza 504
Workers in Europe 488
World guide to libraries 698
World heritage 506
World on the move 224
Writings of Álvaro Siza 504

Y

Year in Portugal 204
Year of the death 571, 576
Your home in Portugal 289

Index of Subjects

A

Abbreviations 341
Aberystwyth 638
Abranavel *see* Abravanel, Isaac
Abrantes 138
Abravanel, Isaac 370, 372
Accommodation 74, 83, 101-11, 161, 312, 343
Accounting 436-37
Acronyms 334, 341
Aden 256
Administration 7, 419
Adverbs 256
Advertising 297, 321, 390, 444, 473
Afonso Henriques (King of Portugal, 1139-85) 177, 372
Afonso VI (King of Portugal, 1656-67) 192
Africa 8, 26, 116, 123, 133, 190, 211, 215, 220-21, 224-36, 255, 336, 402, 755
  culture 735
  East 233, 244, 251
  foreign relations 408-11
  immigrants to Portugal 291-92
  museums 702
  music 651
  religion 365
  Southern 235, 597
  see also Literature: Portuguese African
Aged people 385
Agriculture 274, 388, 428, 436, 456, 458-70, 491, 493, 706

Águas Livres aqueduct 505
Airborne troops 659
Airports 40, 474
Ajuda Botanical Gardens 693
Ajuda Palace 146
Albufeira 61
Albuquerque, Afonso de 236, 251, 256, 269
Alcácer-Kibir 372
Alcobaça 204, 494, 506, 662
Alcoholics' Anonymous 287
Alentejo 208, 282, 428, 660
  agriculture 458
  flora and fauna 152, 154
  food 668
  tourism 58, 84, 92, 95
Alfonso X (King of Leon and Castile, 1252-82) 185
Algarve 20, 24, 39-40, 290, 294, 428, 662, 707, 734
  almond mice 657
  economy 453
  expatriates 287
  flora and fauna 147, 149, 152, 155-56, 159, 162
  food and drink 668
  Moors 87
  religion 363
  shipping 479
  sport 691-92
  tourism 53, 59, 61-62, 63, 65, 67, 79, 81, 83-84, 88, 91-93, 95-96, 114

travel 135-36, 140
walking 113
Algeria 226
Aljube 206
Allies (Second World War) 414
Almada, Álvaro Vaz de 176
Almeida 196, 199
Almohads 184
Almond blossom 662
Almoravids 184
Alto Minho 95, 275, 383
Alvão, Serra do 461
Alvor 363
Amaral, Diogo Freitas do 392
Ameixial 193
Americas 255, 291, 711
Amirs 184
Amsterdam 357, 378, 381
Anglicans 358, 363
Anglo-Portuguese relations 193, 413-15, 449-50, 667, 737, 750, 755
Angola 225, 227, 234, 284, 409, 702
  arts 624
  literature 533, 535, 537, 546, 597, 600
  see also Literature: Portuguese African
Angra do Heroísmo 506
Animal products 457
Animals 647
Anthropology 386, 729
Anticlericalism 530, 566
Antwerp 671
Apocope 301
Apollinaire, Guillaume 131

279

Appetizers 663
Apsley House 649
Aquatints 155
Aqueducts 505
Arabia 117
Arabs 184
Archaeology 164-72
Architecture 23, 73, 354, 495-513, 624, 627, 648, 662
  Manueline 77, 500, 703
  oriental 500
Archives 211, 221, 249, 304, 306
Archways 509
Aristocracy 440
Arizona University 469
Armenia 732
Army, British 226, 761
Army, Portuguese 214, 226, 490, 546, 659, 703
Arnold, Matthew 313
Arrábida, Serra da 159
Arsenal, Lisbon 703
Art 261, 502, 542, 623-42, 677, 701
  20th century 3
  see also individual media by name
Arthur (King of Britain) 189
Articulation (musical) 651
Artillery 480
Artists 629
Arts 69, 442, 700, 717, 720
Asia 8, 26, 164, 188, 190, 222, 237, 247, 251, 410, 651, 757
  language 301
  religion 365
  trade 440, 446
  travels 118, 123, 128-29
Astronomy 339
Asturian-Leonese 305
Asturias 439

Athletics 688
Atlantic Ocean 8, 18, 24, 50, 126, 167, 274, 388, 475, 479
  politics 411-13
Augustus (Roman Emperor) 453
Aula do Commercio 437
Australasia 365
Autos da fé 362, 371
Aveiro 354, 429, 494, 715
  University 513
Aviation 474-75, 570
Avilés 439
Aviz, Hotel 106
Ayala y Cabrera, Josefa
  see Josefa, de Óbidos
Ayaz, Malik 242
Azores 8, 259, 271, 346, 428, 430, 506, 693, 759
  economics 428, 430
  flora and fauna 161
  geography 41, 48
  literature 542, 574
  politics 414-15
  travels 126, 132

B

Babies 684
Baedeker, Karl 89
Bags 657
Baixela da Vitória 649
Balsemão, Francisco Pinto 216, 392
Balzac, Honoré de 564
Banco Nacional Ultramarino 499
Banking 81, 289, 403, 436, 438, 491, 499
Baptista, Pedro 17
Barcelona 503, 513
Barcelos 494
Barcelos cock 657
Barnsley 637-38
Baroque 354

Barros, João de 118, 242
Bars 509
Basque 293
Bassein 507
Batalha 50, 208, 506, 662
Bath 263
Baths 167
Bats 158
Beaches 61
Beckford, William 130, 153, 263
Bedford (HMS) 197
Beer 453
Beiras 15, 92, 159, 276, 715
Beja 453, 500
Belém 31
Belfast 536
Benasterim 256
Benfica 646
Bengal 259
Berardo, José 623
Beresford, William Carr 198
Berlengas Islands 152
Berlin 503, 510
Bessa-Luís, Agustina 538
Bevis Marks synagogue, London 368
Bibliographies 745-61
Biblioteca Nacional de Lisboa 747
Bilingualism 517
Biography 256-73, 531, 629, 743
Biomedical sciences 525
Birds 147, 152, 157, 160-61, 339, 363, 543
  see also individual species by name
Birdwatching 147, 149, 161-62, 363
Blood 661
Boeing 707 475
Book collecting 263
Book reviews 737, 741

280

Book suppliers 295, 695
Bookkeepers 437
Bookshops 295
Bordeaux 357
Botanical gardens 693
Botany 146, 151, 155-56, 159
Botelho, Fernanda 538
Bottles 454
Bourgeoisie 404
Bouton, Noël, Comte de Chamilly 608-09
Boxer, C. R. 761
Braga 12, 20, 141, 494, 521
Braganza 164, 624
Braque 641
Brazil 26, 190, 197, 255, 260, 284, 291, 733
  immigrants 284
  literature 529, 535, 594-95, 749
  music 651-52
  religion 360, 371-72
  travels 121, 127, 133
  see also Brazilian Portuguese language
Brazilian Portuguese language 296, 300, 310-11, 315-26, 321, 327-32, 334, 336, 338, 340-42, 346
Bread 663, 683
Bribery 306
Bridges 13
Brighton 638
Bristol 19, 636
British (in Portugal) 282, 285, 287, 667, 737
British Broadcasting Corporation 711
British Council 749
Bronze Age 166, 168, 171
Brussels 582
Buçaco 141, 198-201, 500
Buçaco Palace Hotel 111

Budapest 182
Building 389, 457, 491, 514
Bullfighting 144, 154, 500, 662
Bureaucracy 231, 290
Burials 441
Burma 117
Buses 40, 142
Bus stations 509
Business 288, 404, 422, 438, 448, 451
  language 321, 333-34, 338, 341
Bussaco *see* Buçaco

C

Cabo da Roca 138
Cabral, Pedro Álvares 121
Cabral, Sacadura 475
Cabrilho, João Rodrigues 188
Cachão da Valeira 261
Cacilhas 476
Caeiro, Alberto *see* Pessoa, Fernando
Caetano, Marcello 214, 392, 411, 417
Cafés 69
Cakes 683
Calamond 607
Calicut, India 236
California 188, 760
Callas, Maria 616
Calouste Gulbenkian Foundation 188, 194, 732
  see also Gulbenkian, Calouste
Cambridge, University of 11
Caminhos de Ferro Portugueses 487
Camões, Luís Vaz de 294, 402, 547, 597, 700, 745

Canada 277-80, 401, 464, 664, 759
Canary Islands 41, 126, 572, 574
Cannamore 236
Cannes 273
Canning, Sir George 124, 198
Cantigas d'amigo 598-99, 605
Canto de S. Fins 383
Canton 253
Cape of Good Hope 116, 235
Cape Verde 221, 227, 409, 755
  literature 533, 537, 542, 597
Capitalism 393
Carcavelos 630
Cardboard 455
Cardiff 638
Carlos I (King of Portugal, 1889-1908) 205
Carnival 702
Cars 312, 343, 345, 441
Carthusians 364
Cascais 10, 24, 71, 614, 656
Casqueiro, Paulo 625
Cassiterite 171
Castanheira de Pêra 420
Castelo Branco 430, 453
Castelo Branco, Camilo 585
Castelo Rodrigo, Marquês de 502
Castile 286, 370
Castro, Inês de 587
Castros 168
Catalogues 697
Catamarans 476
Catherine, of Braganza 624
Catholic University of America 314

281

Cavaco e Silva, Aníbal 425
Caves 38, 165
Cellulose 453
Cement 453
Censorship 656
Censuses 404
Center for Strategic and International Studies 409
Centro Cultural de Belém 633
Centro de Arte Moderna 80
Ceramics 50, 63, 167, 316, 624, 627, 645-47, 701-02
Cervejaria Trindade 647
Ceylon 245
Cézanne, Paul 580
CGT-IN *see* Intersindical
Chalcolithic Age 169
Champs Elysées 562
Chaplains 178
Charles II (King of England, 1660-85) 193, 356
Charterhouses 364
Chaul 507
Chemistry 525
Chetham Library, Manchester 607
Children 494, 684
 language 301
 literature 706-10
China 117, 129, 220, 248, 252, 565, 645
Chinese 220, 248-49, 253, 645
Christianity 184, 376, 584
Chronicles 23, 236, 374, 530
Churches 31, 38, 179, 287, 354, 361, 382
Churchill, Winston Spencer 414

Circumnavigation 258
Ciudad Rodrigo 196
Civil engineering 528
Civil service 491
Class 381
Classicalism 647
Classics 597
Clements, Francesco 623
Clerics 122
Climate 30, 157, 753
Clothing 81, 444
Clubs 287
Coal 453
Cochin 507
Codfish 316
Coimbra 49, 141, 163, 201, 204, 206, 208, 453, 662, 693, 715
 University of 185, 513-14
Coinage 439
Cold War 402
Colleges 437
Colonies 179, 740, 759
Columbia University 726
Columbus, Christopher 134, 221, 224, 257, 259, 272
La Comédie humaine 564
Commandos 659
Commerce 352, 437, 440-51
Commission for Equality and Women's Rights 491
Commission for Equality at Work 491
Common Agricultural Policy 466, 469
Communications 7, 453
Communism 211, 412
Companies 441, 443-45, 447
Computers 330-31, 334, 524
Condiments 663

Conference on Nationalism and National Identity 402
Confession manuals 530
Congo 234
Conimbriga 702
Constitution 7, 292, 416-19, 491
Construction *see* Building
Contraception 390
Contracts 457
Conversos 357
Cookery 663-84
Cooperatives 383, 425
Copper Age 167
Corgo, Rio 670
Cork 282, 467, 679
Corporative State 414
Correia, Gaspar 240
Correia, Hélia 538
Correio da Manhã 712
Correios e Telégrafos de Portugal 648
Corruption 231
Corte-Real, Gaspar 132, 265
Corte-Real, João Vaz 132, 265
Corte-Real, Miguel 132, 265
Corte-Real, Vasco Anes 132, 265
Costa da Prata 67
Costa, Maria Velho da 529
Costa Verde 95
Cotton 231
Counter-Reformation 182
Counts of Portugal 178
Coutinho, Gago 475
Couto de S. Fins 384
Couto, Diogo do 242
Cova da Iria 367
Craesbeeck, Pedro 704
Cricket 689
Crime 308

Cromwell, Oliver 193, 356, 449
Crows 662
Cruises 57
CTT *see* Correios e Telégrafos de Portugal
Cuba 561
Cuisine *see* Food; Drink
Culture 5, 7, 9, 208, 529, 534, 536, 727-28, 732, 739, 742-44, 749
Cunha e Costa, Dr 206
Currency 78, 424
Curriculum 521, 524
Customs 660-62
Cutlery 644
Cycling 688

D

Dairy produce 458
Damão 241, 245, 507
Dance 532, 657-58, 708
Dão 95
David, Ilda 625
Death 384, 543
Decorative arts 642, 644
Decrees 714
Defence 27, 412
Degrees 523
Delgado, Humberto 211, 219, 264
Democracy 399
Demography 387, 389, 428
Dentists 346
Design 644
Desserts 663, 665, 683
Deus, João de 295
Devil 565, 593
Dialects 305, 307
Diário de Notícias 719
Dias, Bartolomeu 116, 597
Dictionaries 331-42
Diets 684
Dighton Rock 132

Dinis (King of Portugal, 1279-1325) 185, 597
Discoveries 8, 23, 116-18, 120-21, 123, 126-29, 132-34, 190, 221, 224, 232, 238, 254, 257-59, 265, 272, 376, 401, 480, 532, 577, 583, 757
Disney, Walt 630
Diu 241, 245, 507
Docks 451, 477, 479
Doctors 594
Doctrine 530
Dogs 148, 160, 287
Dolmens 172
Douro, River 13, 19, 28, 95, 261, 666, 670, 670-71, 692
Drake, Sir Francis 124
Drama 533, 534, 578, 656, 745
Dressage 154
Drink 458, 663-84
Driving 313, 441
Duarte (King of Portugal, 1433-38) 270, 286
Dumfries, Earl of 178
Dutch 243, 281
Dutch East India Company 440
Dutch Navy 440

E

Eanes, Ramalho 208, 392, 400
Earthquakes 52, 124, 268, 505, 703, 753
Eastern Europe *see* Europe
Eating 63
  see also Food
Ebro, Río 50
Ecclesiastical decoration 642
Ecology 155

Economy 7, 29, 210, 268, 387, 421-35, 441, 456, 493, 508, 718, 720, 757
Edinburgh 19
Edo period 643
Education 7, 295, 301, 390, 508, 515-24, 740
Edward III (King of England, 1327-77) 176
Egyptology 701
Elections 7, 391, 399
Electricity 290
Electronic resources 695
Elegies 586
Elephants 186
Eli, Kingdom of 236
Elizabeth II (Queen of England, 1952-) 106
Elvas 506
Embassies 287
Embroidery 657
Emigrants 212, 274-81, 389-90, 452, 759, 760
  agriculture 459, 461
  economic 422, 431
  language 316
  religion 356
Empire, Portuguese *see* Overseas territories
Employment 288, 389, 452, 515, 523
Employment law 508
Encyclopaedias 742-44
Engineering 528
England 189, 232, 366, 536
Engravings 11, 190
Entre Minho e Douro 92, 465
Environment 29, 387, 706
Epics 532
Epigrams 586
Epitaphs 304
Equal opportunities 389, 491
Erasmus, Desiderius 262, 270, 591

283

Espanca, Florbela 529
Estado Novo 16, 173, 179, 182, 208, 229, 381, 414, 640, 656
Estoril 24, 63, 71, 83, 137, 145
  railway 482
Estrela Mountain Dog 160
Estremadura 92
Estremoz 193, 362
Estufa Fria 693
Ethnography 459
Eurocommunism 402
Europe 270, 402
European Communities 33, 397, 403, 407, 410-12, 418-19, 424, 426, 428, 432, 435, 442, 453, 456-57, 493, 524
  agriculture 459, 461, 463, 465-67, 470
  language 305
  science and technology 527
European Exhibition of Art, Science and Culture 23
European Free Trade Association 423
European Parliament 398
European Union 423, 444
Evangelical Presbyterian Church 361
Évora 40, 95, 138, 267, 453
  architecture 500, 503, 506, 510
  education 521
  prehistory 164, 172
  religion 364
Examinations 295
Exchange rates 458
Exhibitions 451
Expatriates in Portugal 114, 130, 282, 285-88, 441, 692, 711, 722

Expo '98 6, 74, 451, 734
Exports 444

F

Factory House, Oporto 667
Fado 654
Fairytales *see* Folktales
Family 384
Fantasia 630
Fantasy 602
Faro 40, 49, 61, 83, 84, 453
Fascism 211, 405, 414, 490
Fashion 16, 346
Fátima 355, 367, 372-73, 376-77
Fauna 54, 73, 87, 146-49, 152, 154, 157-58, 160-61, 230, 752
Feedgrains 456
Feet 6
Feira Internacional de Lisboa 451
Feminism 538
Ferlinghetti, Lawrence 558
Fernando (King of Castile) 353
Fernando I (King of Portugal, 1367-83) 286
Ferreira, Antônio 586
Ferreira, Luís 647
Ferreira, Luísa 17
Ferries 40, 90, 476-77
Fertility 275
Fertilizer 453
Festivals 74, 381
Figueira da Foz 464, 593
Filipa, de Lencastre *see* Philippa, of Lancaster
Films 652, 655
Finance 7, 285, 422, 429, 436-39, 718
Financiers 527
Fires 150, 287

First World War 413
Fiscal policy 426
Fish 317, 478, 663, 665, 677, 683
Fishing 18, 148, 388, 462, 464
Fladgate shippers 261
Flora 54, 73, 87, 150-51, 155-56, 159, 163, 230, 693-95, 752
Florence 269
Florida State University 194
Flower, Frederick William 19
Flowers 156, 159
Folk dance 657
Folk festivals 7
Folk literature 755
Folklore 87, 657, 661, 708
Folktales 657, 661-62
Fontelas 383
Fonthill 263
Food 54, 64, 101, 343, 345, 362, 431, 453, 456, 458, 463, 663-84, 705
Football 14, 306, 686-88, 690
Footwear 444
Ford, Richard 672
Foreign and Commonwealth Office 228
Foreign exchange 429
Foreign languages 698
Foreign policy 212, 407-55
Forests 150
Forrester, John James 261
Fortifications 23
Foundations 744
Foundries 703
Fountains 505
France 159, 177, 196-97, 201, 208, 275, 459, 536, 562

284

Frankfurt International Book Fair 26, 640, 705
Frankfurt International Fair 644
French 207
French army 260, 608, 613
Fronteira, Marquês de 646
Frontiers 8, 733
Fruit 466
Fruit juice 455
Fuel 431
Funchal 119
Funds 744
Furniture 624, 701
Futurism 549

G

Galicia 479
Galician 305
Galician literature 531
Galician Portuguese 185, 598-99, 605-06
Galvão, Henrique 211
Gama, Vasco da 116, 123, 241, 272, 597, 709
Gardens 31, 146, 155, 502, 693-95
Garter, Order of the 176
Garum 453
Gastronomy *see* Food
Gays 381
Gender 384, 388-90, 491, 536, 660
Geography 11, 28-30, 72, 334, 436, 448, 508, 742, 752-53, 761
Geology 42, 51-52, 167-68
Gerês 152
German Evangelical Church, Lisbon 361
Germans 619
Germany 207, 512
Gerontology 384
Gersão, Teolinda 538

Gestural automatism 633
Gibraltar 142
Ginsberg, Allen 558
Giotto 582
Giovanni, d'Empoli *see* John, of Empoli
Glasgow, University of 725
Glass 454-55
Goa 239, 241, 245, 249, 256, 269, 304, 507, 680, 701
Godinho, Manuel 120
Góis, Damião de 262, 374
Gold 579
Golf 14, 691-92
Gonçalves, António Anastácio 645
Government 212, 494, 714, 718
Grammar 237, 298, 313, 345
Granada 184, 187
Grapes 675
Graves 293
Great Britain 249
Great Mother 588
Greece 393, 431, 527, 583
Greek 267
Greek gardens 694
Groceries 684
Gross Domestic Product 423, 444
Guarda 453
Guimarães 141, 494
Guinea-Bissau 409, 533, 597, 755
Gujarat 242
Gulbenkian Ballet 658
Gulbenkian, Calouste 106, 732
Gusmão, Padre Manuel 570
Gypsies 284

H

Hague, The 503, 511
Hamburg 357
Hamilton, Russell 533
Handkerchiefs 657
Harvard University 271
Havana 561
Hawaii 760
Health 7, 385
Health insurance 289
Hebrew University, Jerusalem 435
Helder, Herberto 588
Henrique (King of Portugal, 1578-80) 267
Henry, the Navigator 118, 131, 232, 286, 709
Heras Institute 251
Heroes 661
Higher education 522-23
Hindustan 507
Hispanic world 700
Hispano-Celtic 293
Historical Archives of Goa 304
Historic buildings 14
History 173-83, 705, 724, 736, 742-43
 bibliography 749, 752
 colonial history 218-55
 mediaeval period 185-91
 Muslim occupation 184
 17th/18th centuries 192-93
 19th century 194-204
 20th century
  to 1974 205-13
  from 1974 214-17
Holy Land 607
Homosexuality 381
Honduras 459
Hong Kong 240, 615
Horace 586
Horses 154, 346
Hospitals 287
Hostelries 687

285

Hotels 72, 77-78, 81, 83, 85, 90, 92, 101, 103-12, 135, 350, 485, 666, 668, 734
Housing 285, 288-90, 348, 497, 509, 511, 514
Hull 19
Humanism 262, 591
Humanities 730
Humpty Dumpty 632

I

Iberia 51, 672, 696
Iberian massif 151
Idanha-a-Velha 138
Igreja Lusitana 363
Illegitimacy 383
Immigrants 282-91, 667
Inchiquin, Earl of 193
Incunabula 749
India 117, 120, 127, 133, 222, 236, 238, 242, 243-45, 250, 252, 269, 446, 507
Indian Ocean 238, 241
Indo-China 226
Indonesia 117
Industry 7, 28, 231, 274, 387, 420, 428, 452, 527, 706, 740
Inflation 423, 426
Influenza 355
Information technology 524, 697
Inheritance 383
Inquisition 182, 262, 267, 360, 570, 577
Insignia (military) 659
Insignia (sport) 687
Institutions 7
Instituto Nacional de Estatística 491
Insurance 422, 443
Inter-Library Loans 697
International Communist League 396

International Conference Group on Portugal 183, 212
International Phonetic Alphabet 310, 314, 329, 334
Intersindical 488-89
Intonation 301
Invalids 122, 346
Investment 431, 438, 440
Ireland 515
Iron 453
Iron Age 167-68
Isabella (Queen of Castile) 353
Islam 376, 646
Istanbul 620
Italians 121
Italy 115, 207, 262, 515

J

Jamaica 263
Japan 117, 129, 237, 253, 387
Japanese 237, 282, 643, 761
Jesuits 268, 360, 374
Jesus, Lúcia de 377
Jewellery 642, 644
Jews 1, 176, 187, 254, 620
  religion 353, 356-57, 359, 362, 365-66, 368-71, 374, 378
João, de Lisboa 116
João I (King of Portugal, 1385-1433) 286
João II (King of Portugal, 1481-95) 370
João III (King of Portugal, 1521-57) 262
João IV (King of Portugal, 1640-56) 449
João V (King of Portugal, 1706-50) 570, 650
John, of Empoli 269

John, of Gaunt 232
John, Prester 372
John XXIII, Pope 377
Jorge, Lídia 538, 733
José I (King of Portugal, 1750-77) 268, 437, 650
Josefa, de Óbidos 626
Journalism 3

K

Keynes, Maynard 421
King's College London 346, 554, 622, 735
Kinship 386
Knights 176
Kosher food 362

L

Labour 292, 383, 422, 423, 430, 468, 488, 492-94
Labour movements 488-89
Labour relations 492
Lacquerware 643
Lagos 61, 164
Lalique 701
Lancashire 634
Land 383
Landscapes 14
Language 293-351, 438, 728, 745
Language schools 295
Lanheses 275
Lanzarote 572
Lapa, Alvara 625
Larmanjôt 483
Latifundia 458
Latin 267, 376
Latin America 435, 460, 574
Law 185, 288-89, 381, 385, 436, 441, 457, 508, 714, 744
Lawrence, D. H. 558
Leather 444

Leça 512
Legal codes 714
Leiria 141, 159, 430, 453
Leiria, Bishop of 367
Leisure 287
Lentition 301
Leo, X, Pope 186
Lesbians 381
Lexicon 296
Liberal Unionists 414
Liberalism 211, 380
Librarians 696-97
Libraries 31, 295, 376, 696-700, 745, 747, 749
Library of Congress 700
Liga Comunista Internacional 396
Lighting 644
Limoeiro 206
Linguistics 305, 525, 705, 724, 746
Lisbon 2, 10-12, 15-16, 18, 20, 187, 263, 269, 381, 409, 428, 430, 464, 704, 719, 734, 752
  airports 40, 474
  aqueduct 505
  architecture 494, 497-501, 503, 505, 509
  arts 623, 627, 630, 633, 641, 646
  castle 506
  docks 477
  earthquake of 1755 *see* Earthquakes
  flora and fauna 159, 163
  history 167, 177, 189, 204, 208, 226
  immigrants 282, 287
  literature 568, 589, 614, 619
  maps 31, 41, 45, 48, 50
  photographs 21, 24-25
  religion 362, 374
  São Carlos opera house 616
  sport 689, 693
  tourism 55, 60, 63, 65-67, 71, 73-74, 76, 80-81, 88, 90-91, 93-94, 104, 112, 114
  transport 476, 483, 485
  travels 119, 121-22, 125, 135-37, 141
  University 185
Lisbon districts
  Alfama 90
  Alto de S. João 31
  Amoreiras 497
  Avenida Fontes 106
  Avenidas Novas 645
  Baixa 40, 506
  Benfica 31
  Cais do Sodré 16
  Campo de Santana 31
  Campolide 31
  Campo Pequeno 31, 500
  Castelo de S. Jorge 506
  Chiado 503, 513
  Parque das Nações 451
  Portas de S Antão 16
  Praça Figueira 25
  Rossio 25, 40, 362, 500
  Rua das Janelas Verdes 617
  Rua do Ouro 16
  Santa Apolonia 485
Literary theory 536
Literature 3, 92, 381, 529-621, 671, 700, 705, 725, 731, 733, 735, 739, 742, 746, 751, 755
  Portuguese African 529, 531-32, 535, 537, 574, 705, 755
Liverpool, University of 725
Livestock 456, 458
Livingstone, Henry 227
Local government 420
Locomotives 487
London 356, 368, 381, 630, 633, 636-37, 671
London School of Economics 518
London, University 761
Lopes, Fernão 232, 286
Loulé 87
Low Countries 262, 704
Lusiads 547
Lusitania 453, 584
Lusitanian-Alcudian geological zone 51
Lusitanian Catholic Apostolical Evangelical Church 361
Lusitanian Church 358
Lusitanian Stud and Equitation Centre 154
Luso-American Development Fund 409
Lyricism 533

M

Macao 240, 249, 252, 444, 503, 528, 615, 702
Macau *see* Macao
Machinery 444
Madagascar 234
Madeira 41, 48, 157, 161, 259, 271, 346, 428, 430, 444, 693, 759
  tourism 57, 63
  travels 119, 125-26
Madeira wine 674
Madrid 503
Mafra 204, 570
Magdalene, Mary 572
Magellan, Ferdinand 134, 258, 709
Magellan, Straits of 258
Maia 512
Malabar 236
Malacca 256, 269, 281
Malaya 129
Malaysia 281

287

Maldive Islands 118
Mamale de Cananor 236
Mammals 146
Management 445
Manchester 600, 621, 637
Manchester, University of 621
Manini, Luigi 111
Manuale, de Cananor 235
Manuel I (King of Portugal, 1495-1521) 186, 258, 262, 272, 375, 577, 620
Manuel II (King of Portugal, 1908-10) 176
Manufacturing 491-93
Manuscripts 700, 759
Maps 10, 31-50, 65, 79, 116, 188, 190, 241, 481, 507, 700, 706, 757
Marble 660
Marchioni, Bartolommeo 291
Maria Francesca Luísa, of Savoy 192
Maria I (Queen of Portugal, 1777-1816) 260, 266
Marinetti, Filippo Tommaso 549
Marketing 441, 458
Marlborough (HMS) 197
Marranos 371, 378
Marriage 275, 383
Martins, J. P. de Oliveira 131
Marxist-Leninism 396
Masculinity 660
Mass media 338, 453, 652, 710
Masséna, Maréchal 196
Mathematics 267
Matisse, Henri 641
Matos, Norton de 264
Matosinhos 503, 510
Matriarchies 462
Meat 456, 458, 663, 677
Media *see* Mass media

Medicine 390
Mediterranean Sea 50, 140, 500
Megalithic Age 172
Melgaço 354
Melo, Manuel de 182
Memorials 201
Menus 323
Merchants 326, 440, 446
Mergers 429, 438
Messianism 372
Metal 171, 444, 455
Methodists 361
Methuen Treaties 450
Metropolitano de Lisboa 40, 74
Middle Ages 518
Middle East 435
Miguel, Dom (King of Portugal, 1828-34) 203, 260, 266
Milan 636
Militaria 224, 395, 701
Military insignia *see* Insignia (military)
Militias 191
Minerals 171
MINERVA 524
Minho 459
Mining 389, 453
Miracles 662
Miranda do Douro 305
Mirandês 305
Mirobriga 167
Mobility 523
Modellers 659
Mombassa 235
Monarchists 405
Monarchy, Great Britain 624
see also individual monarchs by name
Monarchy, Portugal 1, 5, 16, 50, 90, 174, 183, 194, 197, 210, 230, 440, 480, 591, 650

see also individual monarchs by name
Mondim de Basto 461
Monsanto 590
Monserrate 153
Montréal 290, 759
Monuments 31
Moors 177, 184, 191, 584, 646
Morais, Graça 625
Morocco 142
Morphology 296, 301
Moscow 381
Mother-of-pearl 643
Motoring *see* Cars
Motor racing 688
Mountains 67, 159
Moura, Eduardo Souto 513
Mozambique 219, 225, 227, 232, 235, 490, 755
literature 533, 535, 537, 597, 600
see also Literature: Portuguese African
Mudejar 500
Multiculturalism 651
Museu Militar, Lisbon 703
Museums 31, 73, 146, 483, 511, 701-03
Music 650-54
Musical instruments 657
Muslims 187
Mythology 583

N

Naharro, Torres 578
Namban lacquerware 643
Namora, Fernando 539
Napoléon, Emperor 197
National Gallery, London 637
National Gallery, Washington, DC 626
Nationalism 401, 628

288

National Library of Lisbon
see Biblioteca Nacional
de Lisboa
NATO 226, 408
Nature conservancy 150
Naval history 218, 232, 243, 440, 477, 480
Navigation 241, 267, 269, 475, 479-80, 757
Navigators 50, 126
see also individual navigators by name
Nazaré 18, 462, 662
Near East 131
Negro, David 370
Nehru, Pandit 243
Neolithic Age 169
Netherlands 249, 357, 378, 513, 617
New Christians 449
New Testament 572
New York 561, 634, 671
New Zealand 365
Newcastle-upon-Tyne, University of 529
Newfoundland 265, 464
Newspapers 211, 711-22, 759
Nightlife 63, 69
Nobel Prize 574
Nobility 122
Norway 607
Nunes, Pedro 267
Nursery rhymes 632
Nursery school 522

O

Oates, Joyce Carol 558
Óbidos 626
Óbidos, Josefa de *see* Josefa, de Óbidos
Oceans 451, 480
see also individual oceans by name
Oeiras 226

Official publications 714
Oil 426, 732
Ollendorf 313
Opera 616, 650
Oporto 164, 194, 198-99, 203, 388, 429, 464, 485, 624, 667, 688, 734
architecture 494, 498, 502-03, 506, 512
Campanhã station 485
children's publications 707
emigration 276
literature 583, 614
maps 45, 48,
newspapers 712, 719
photographs 11-13, 15, 19-20, 22, 28
sport 687, 689
tourism 63, 95, 112, 115
travels 135, 141, 144
wine 261
Oriental languages 298
Orthography 317, 340
Osório, Jerónimo 374
Ottoman Empire 243
Overseas territories 7-8, 26, 179, 220, 223, 225, 352, 415
Oxford University 231

P

Pacific Ocean 188
Packaging 454-55
Paço da Barca 384
Paço d'Arcos, J. 597
Painting 11, 50, 165, 580, 624, 649, 703
Palaces 500-01, 650
Palaeography 304
Pamphlets 700
Paper 381, 453, 455
Pardais 660
Paris 264, 381, 503, 562, 568, 641

Parque das Nações 452
Partido Comunista 211, 391, 394
Partido Revolucionário do Proletariado 396
Partido Revolucionário dos Trabalhadores 396
Partido Socialista Português 391
Pastoral care 521
Pedralva 459
Pedro, Dom (1392-1449) 131, 376
Pedro I (Emperor of Brazil, 1822-31) *see* Pedro IV (King of Portugal, 1826)
Pedro I (King of Portugal, 1357-67) 587
Pedro II (Emperor of Brazil, 1839-89) 273
Pedro II (King of Portugal, 1667-1706) 626
Pedro III (King of Portugal, 1777-86) 501
Pedro IV (King of Portugal, 1826) 203, 266, 273
Pedro (Prince of Portugal) 192
Pegasus Prize 584
Pego 138
Peninsular War 111, 175, 193, 198-200, 202-03, 413, 613, 618, 659
Pepetela 537
Perestrelo, Mesquita 116
Periodicals 723-41
Perón, Eva 106
Persian Gulf 129, 243, 426
Pessoa, Fernando 539, 559, 576, 597, 640, 733
Petrarch 586
Petroleum 453
Philippa, of Lancaster 176, 286

289

Philippines 258
Philology 295
Philosophy 6, 700
Phonology 296
Photographs 10-27
Phrasebooks 343-51
Pilgrim Fathers 132
Pilgrimages 114, 367, 708
Pina, Rui de 374
Pinheiro, Columbano Bordalo 3
Pinto, Fernão Mendes 117
Pirates 117
Pittsburgh 561
Plants 155
Plastic arts 648-49
Pliny, the Elder 167
Plymouth 637
Poetry 21, 185, 534, 541, 605, 745
Poland 262
Police 287, 593
Policy analysts 527
Political parties 391, 460
Political prisoners 206
Politics 7, 29, 380, 391-415, 508, 534
  newspapers 717-18, 720
  periodicals 729, 736
Pollution 428
Polytechnics 523
Pombal (town) 198, 204,
Pombal, Marquês de 146, 268, 437, 449, 627
Ponte de Barca 54
Pope 186
Popular movements 379
Population 7
Porbase 697
Porcelain 645
Port (wine) 19, 50, 261, 614, 666-67, 670, 674, 681
Portalegre 453
Porteiro, Frei Pedro 270
Portimão 19, 40, 61

Porto *see* Oporto
Ports (maritime) 671
Portucale 173
Portugal, Pedro 625
Portuguese Africa 292, 735
Portuguese Commission for Equality and Women's Rights 491
Portuguese Commission for Equality at Work 491
Portuguese Communist Party *see* Partido Comunista Português
Portuguese Embassy, London 413
Portuguese Foreign Ministry 228
Portuguese Methodist Church 361
Portuguese Nationalist Party 414
Portuguese Synagogue, London 356
Portuguese Vocational Training Institute 520
Portuguese Water Dog 148
Portuguese white fleet 464
Post 483
Post office *see* CTT
Postage stamps 471-72
Postcards 2, 20
Postmarks 471
Poulantzas, Nicos 393
Poultry 663
Pound, Ezra 547
Pousadas *see* Hotels
Pre-Mesozoic period 51
Presidents of Portugal 5, 90, 230
Press 710-22
Prestage, Edgar 256, 761
Príncipe 537
Printers 357
Printing 378, 704

Prisons 206, 416
Privatization 436
Proença, Pedro 625
Pronominal subject 300
Pronouns 302
Pronunciation 312, 314, 316-18, 323, 328, 331, 340-42, 345-46, 350
Property in Portugal 285, 288-90, 436
Prosody 302
Public appointments 714
Public Records Office 197
Public transport 41, 96, 474-87
Publishing 295, 704-05, 740, 749
Pyrenees 574

Q

Queiroz, José Maria Eça de 182
Queluz 10, 144, 502, 562, 627, 702
Quental, Antero de 3, 182
Quintas 666, 670
Quotations 671

R

Race relations 292
Radio 652
Rádio Televisão Portuguesa 473
Railways 40, 48, 93, 136, 142, 451, 481-87, 509, 759
Rebelo, Luis de Sousa 622
Recipes 657, 669, 673, 676, 684
Reconquest 187
Recreation 64, 693-95
Recycling 455
Red Sea 243
Refugees 208

Régio, José 539
Regionalism 4
Regions 425
Rego, Paula 625, 630-39
Reis, Pedro Cabrita 625
Religion 7, 252, 352-78, 382, 752, 757
  see also individual religions by name
Renaissance 262, 518
Republicans 205, 207
Research 525-27, 740
Resende, Garcia de 374
Restaurants 69, 334, 666, 668, 687
Retornados 283
Revolution (1910) 206, 282, 640
Revolution (1974) 7, 177, 210, 215, 226, 283, 379, 381-82, 417-19, 460, 490, 628, 718, 740, 747
  literature 533-34, 537-38, 573, 589, 619
  politics 391, 394-95, 397, 401-02, 404, 412
Rhinoceros 186
Rhythm 651
Ribatejo 92, 154, 662
Rice 663, 677
Richard II 442
Rio de Janeiro 197, 266, 300, 381, 475, 641
Rivers 28, 48
Rocha Christian Field Study Centre and Bird Observatory 363
Roliça 199-200, 202
Roman Catholics 358, 360, 365, 376-77, 405
Roman gardens 694
Roman numerals 306
Romans 163, 165, 167, 293, 453, 648-49, 702
Romanticism 609

Rome 607
Roque, São (church) 375
Rosengarten, Ruth 625
Royal Court 267, 579, 606
Royal Geographical Society, London 3
Royal Mint 579
Royal National Theatre, London 17
Royal Navy 197, 689
Royalty *see* Monarchy
RTP *see* Rádio Televisão Portuguesa
Rui, Manuel 537
Russia 220, 262, 367

S

Safa, Khwaja 242
Sailors 464, 478
Saint Andrew's Society 114
Salads 663
Salazar, António de Oliveira 27, 145, 173, 177, 179, 209, 211, 214, 219, 396-97, 405-06, 411, 417, 489, 543, 593, 640
Saldanha, Manoel de 253
Sales 445
Salvation Army in Portugal 361
Samba 702
San Francisco 381
Santarém 135, 138, 453, 506
Santiago de Compostela 114
Santiago do Cacém 167, 647
São Tomé e Príncipe 227, 409, 533, 537, 597, 755
Saramago, José 539, 600
Satire 530
Sauces 683

Scarlatti, Domenico 650
Scholars 527
Schomberg, Count 193
School buildings 521
Schools 52, 287, 292, 295, 327, 516, 518, 521
Science 525-28
Scots 114
Sculpture 582, 627, 648
Sea 8, 23, 334, 388, 451
Sebastianismo 700
Sebastião (King of Portugal, 1557-78) 372, 700
Second French Republic 207
Secondary schools 515
Second World War 208, 271, 413, 619, 695
Sephardim *see* Jews
Sequeira, Domingos António 649
Sermons 530
Serpentine Gallery, London 638
Seruca, Henrique 17
Servants 346
Setenave 488
Setúbal 48, 379, 453, 488, 646
Seville 14, 626
Sex discrimination 389
Sextants 475
Sexuality 381, 384
Shakespeare, William 297
Shellfish 662, 683
Sherman, Cindy 623
Shipping 218, 291, 476-80, 667, 681
Shipwrecks 117
Shopping 19, 63, 69, 71, 74, 77, 311, 334, 345, 673, 684
Silva, Maria Elena Vieira da 641

291

Sintra 10, 63, 125, 138, 144, 153, 204, 208, 483, 498, 506
Sintra Dogs' Home 287
Sintra Museum of Art 623
Sintra, Royal Palace 646
Siza, Álvaro 495-97, 503-04, 510-13
Slade School of Art 630, 632
Slang 308
Slaves 117, 234, 247, 255, 291
Smith, Woodhouse, Ltd 19
Soares, Mário 264, 400
Social anthropology 386, 494
Socialism 396
Social policy 7
Social science 525, 730
Society 177, 379
Society of Jesus *see* Jesuits
Solar de Mateus 693
Songs 708
Soups 663, 665, 677
Sousa, Alberto 3
Sousa, Felix de 291
South Africa 116, 278, 552-53, 560
South America 190, 258, 365
Southampton 119
Southend Wargamers' Club 200
Spain 174, 199-200, 224, 235, 255, 257-59, 288, 440, 455, 466, 479, 659
architecture 497
cooking 669
folk dancing 657
food 672
language 305, 480
literature 531, 724
politics 393, 398, 402-03, 407
printing 704

religion 365, 369
tourism 105, 117
travels 134-35, 141, 748
Spanish and Portuguese Jews' Congregation of London 368
Spanish and Portuguese Reformed Episcopal Church 358
Spanish & Portuguese Synagogue of London 356
Spanish Armada 124
Spanish Civil War 209, 593
Sport 63, 287, 685-92, 752, 762
St Andrews Society 114
St George's Chapel, Windsor 176
St John's (Newfoundland) 464
St Julian's School, Carcavelos 630
St Vincent, Cape 62, 140, 142
Stanford University 469
State enterprises 453
Stations 484-85
Statistics 7, 384-85, 387, 427-28, 433, 443, 448, 516, 670, 706, 714, 744
Street, H. 295
Students 527
Subsidies 458
Sudan 365
Swahili Coast 244
Swedish International Development Agency 516
Sweet, H. 294
Syllabuses 521
Symbolism 560
Synagogues 362, 368, 378
Syntax 326
Szenes, Arpad 641

T

Tagus 31, 40, 138, 428, 476-77
Tagus Golf Society 692
Taveira, Tomás 498-99
Tavira 354
Távora, Fernando 497, 513
Tax 429, 436, 508
Taxation 290, 505
Teachers 515, 741
Teaching 146, 295, 515, 741
Technical University, Lisbon 518
Technology 338, 469, 515, 526-27
Telecommunications 491
Telephones 41, 108, 422
Television 473, 652
Tennis 61
Textiles 231, 339, 388, 444, 452
Theatre 17, 31, 650
Theses 519, 759
Tiles 50
Timetables 483-84
Toilets 509
Tomar 138, 498, 506
Tomás, Américo 173
Tombs 648
Tordesillas, Treaty of 365
Torga, Miguel 539
Toronto 277, 759
Torres Vedras 194-96, 198-99, 202, 204, 483
Tour de France 688
Tourism 7, 53-115, 331, 344, 431, 474, 707, 722
Tourist Information Offices 41, 140
Tourist projects 505
Town plans 505
Trade 7, 218, 245, 234, 269, 378, 422-23, 440-51, 458, 468, 645

Trade directories 443-45
Trade unions 404, 488-89
Trademarks 445
Training 389, 452, 520
Trams 40, 90
Translations 142, 185, 297, 313, 535, 543-606, 749
Transport, public 321, 323, 345, 444, 453, 505
Transtejo 476
Trás-os-Montes 95, 461, 594-95
Travels 100, 116-34, 316, 624, 680, 737, 748
Treaties 365, 378, 413, 442, 727
Trees 153, 467
Trindade, Palácio 647
Troubadours 599, 605
Tutus 630
Tuy 135

U

UDC *see* Universal Decimal Classification
UFOs *see* Unidentified Flying Objects
UGT *see* União Geral de Trabalhadores
Unemployment 423, 428, 444
UNESCO 498
União Geral de Trabalhadores 489
Unidentified Flying Objects 355
Uniforms 659
United States 212, 274, 409, 519, 736, 761
Universal Decimal Classification 756
Universities 296, 518, 523, 740

see also individual universities by name
United States 132, 145, 204, 208, 226, 233, 274, 278, 329, 411
Utrecht, Treaty of 378

V

Vegetables 466, 663, 683
Venice 357, 503
Verbs 304-05
Viana do Castelo 380, 464
Vianna, R. G. 294
Vicente de Fora, São (church) 646
Vicente, Gil 540, 578-79
Vieira, Antônio 360
Vieira, Luandino 537
Vienne, University 398
Vietnam 226
Vila Chã 388
Vila Nova de Gaia 19, 670
Vila Real 382
Vila Real de Santo António 114, 140
Vilamoura 692
Vimeiro, 199-200, 422
Virgil 586
Virgin Mary 367, 373, 377
Viseu 163, 429, 453
Visigoths 354, 563, 649
Vocational training 515, 520
Volkswagen Foundation 458

W

Wages 389, 422
Wain, John 558
Walking 45, 90, 112-15
War, African 546
Warhol, Andy 623

Water 505
Water towers 511
Waterloo, Battle of 11
Weather 313
Weimar 207
Wellington, Duke of 194, 199, 201, 649
Willis, R. C. 621
Wills 289
Windsor, Treaty of 413, 442, 727
Wine '9, 261, 663, 666-67, o70-71, 673-75, 678-79
Wine-making 666, 679
Wine production 671
Women 275-76, 384, 388-90, 416, 462, 491
associations 390
in art 626
in literature 529, 534, 536, 538
Woollens 420
Workers' control 460
World Bibliographical Series 16, 752, 761
World War I *see* First World War
World War II *see* Second World War
World Wide Web 695
WWW *see* World Wide Web

X

Xabregas 31
Xitu, Uanhenga 537

Z

Zambesi 235
Zenith, Richard 599
Zoos 38, 186

293

Map of Portugal

This map shows the more important features.

ALSO FROM CLIO PRESS

INTERNATIONAL ORGANIZATIONS SERIES

Each volume in the International Organizations Series is either devoted to one specific organization, or to a number of different organizations operating in a particular region, or engaged in a specific field of activity. The scope of the series is wide ranging and includes intergovernmental organizations, international non-governmental organizations, and national bodies dealing with international issues. The series is aimed mainly at the English-speaker and each volume provides a selective, annotated, critical bibliography of the organization, or organizations, concerned. The bibliographies cover books, articles, pamphlets, directories, databases and theses and, wherever possible, attention is focused on material about the organizations rather than on the organizations' own publications. Notwithstanding this, the most important official publications, and guides to those publications, will be included. The views expressed in individual volumes, however, are not necessarily those of the publishers.

VOLUMES IN THE SERIES

1. *European Communities*, John Paxton
2. *Arab Regional Organizations*, Frank A. Clements
3. *Comecon: The Rise and Fall of an International Socialist Organization*, Jenny Brine
4. *International Monetary Fund*, Anne C. M. Salda
5. *The Commonwealth*, Patricia M. Larby and Harry Hannam
6. *The French Secret Services*, Martyn Cornick and Peter Morris
7. *Organization of African Unity*, Gordon Harris
8. *North Atlantic Treaty Organization*, Phil Williams
9. *World Bank*, Anne C. M. Salda
10. *United Nations System*, Jospeh P. Baratta
11. *Organization of American States*, David Sheinin
12. *The British Secret Services*, Philip H. J. Davies
13. *The Israeli Secret Services*, Frank A. Clements